Game Shows FAQ

Game Shows FAQ

All That's Left to Know About the Pioneers, the Scandals, the Hosts, and the Jackpots

Adam Nedeff

APPLAUSE
THEATRE & CINEMA BOOKS
An Imprint of Hal Leonard LLC

Published in 2018 by Applause Theatre & Cinema Books
An Imprint of Hal Leonard LLC
7777 West Bluemound Road–Milwaukee, WI 53213

Trade Book Division Editorial Offices
33 Plymouth St., Montclair, NJ 07042

The FAQ series was conceived by Robert Rodriguez and developed with Stuart Shea.

All images are from the author's collection unless otherwise noted.

Printed in the United States of America

Book design by Snow Creative

Library of Congress Cataloging-in-Publication Data

Names: Nedeff, Adam author.
Title: Game shows FAQ : all that's left to know about the pioneers, the scandals, the hosts, and the jackpots / Adam Nedeff.
Description: Milwaukee : Applause Theatre & Cinema Books, 2018. | Includes bibliographical references and index.
Identifiers: LCCN 2017061321 | ISBN 9781617136559 (pbk.)
Subjects: LCSH: Television game shows—United States. | Television quiz shows—United States.
Classification: LCC PN1992.8.Q5 N44 2018 | DDC 791.45/6—dc23
LC record available at https://lccn.loc.gov/2017061321

www.applausebooks.com

For Fred Wostbrock

Contents

Acknowledgments   ix
Introduction   xi

 1   The Pre-History: In The Beginning . . .   1
 2   The Uncle and the Professor: The First Big Things   4
 3   On the Tube: When TV Got Turned On   8
 4   The Brain Trust: Well, What Do You Know?   11
 5   Hit the Jackpot: Call, Collect   18
 6   TV Takes Over: DO Touch That Dial!   25
 7   A Human Puzzle: Who Do They Think You Are?   29
 8   When Goodson Met Todman: Some Guys Get All The Credit   38
 9   Funny Guys: Hitting the Joke-pot   44
10   The Stunt Men: Time to Win   52
11   Tear Jerkers: A Year's Supply of Tissues   61
12   Big Money, Big Lies: Do You Want to Know a Secret   66
13   A Pocketful of Ideas: Bob Stewart's Moment of Truth   83
14   Free Doughnuts and Bob Barker: Beulah Gets Buzzed   93
15   Back to Normal: It's Safe to Play Again   101
16   Con+¢entr+8ion: A Rebus is Puzzling   109
17   And This is My Partner: Hitch Your Wagon to a Star   114
18   The Lady or the Tiger: Deal Me In!   124
19   What's the Question: Who is . . . Art Fleming?   131
20   Popcorn for the Mind: A Barris of Riches   137
21   Square Biz: A Nine-Star Revue   145
22   Renaissance: Let's Do It Again   152
23   CBS Names Its Price: The Tiffany Network Comes Out to Play   160
24   Pyramid Climbing: Game Shows Get Their Money Back   169
25   Change of Fortune: Merv Griffin Goes for a Spin   178
26   The One-Hour Experiment: Daytime TV Takes Its Time   182
27   Talk Dirty to Me: Tell Me You Didn't Just Say That!   187
28   Nighttime Is the Right Time: Games You Play in the Dark   194
29   Bang the Gong Slowly: Talentless Show   203
30   The Redemption of Barry and Enright: Back in Business   214
31   Putting the Games Back on the Shelf: Let's Play Something Else   222
32   Out of Their Prime: "Feud" Holds Down the Fort   231
33   Spinning Wheel: The Boom Begins   234
34   Mr. Know-It-All: Nowhere-Near-Final Jeopardy!   243

35 Game Glut: They're Everywhere! They're Everywhere!   249
36 Changing Fortunes: For Every Flow, An Ebb   262
37 Drought: Where Have All the Game Shows Gone?   273
38 Youth Movement: Letting the Kids Out to Play   279
39 Cable Guys: Taking the Game Somewhere Else   289
40 The Comeback Kids: Everything Old is New Again   297
41 Is That Your Final Answer? Ask the Audience, and They Want More   301
42 Reality Biting: The Tribe Speaks   314
43 Shiny Floor Games: When Game Shows Became an Event   320
44 Social Superstars: When Game Shows Became an Event   328
45 The Summer of the Phoenix: Play it Again!   332
46 What's in the Future? Where Are We Going Now?   336

Bibliography   339
Index   347

Acknowledgments

T hank you to David Schwartz at GSN, who assisted with fact-checking and supplied photos. Paul Borelli and my father, Roger Nedeff, were also instrumental in gathering photos for this project. Victoria Avalon Ingram helped gain access to crucial research materials. Curt Alliaume, Chuck Donegan, Matt Ottinger, Stu Shostak, and Chelsea Thrasher also helped with research.

Thank you to all the extremely knowledgeable behind-the-scenes professionals who weighed in with their memories and insights into the business: Francine Bergman, Dick Block, Bob Boden, Howard Blumenthal, Dana Calderwood, Ron Greenberg, Shelley Herman, Jaime Klein, Wink Martindale, Mark Maxwell-Smith, Jim McKrell, Aaron Solomon, Sande Stewart, and Marc Summers.

Introduction

This book does not seek to be a complete history of game shows. Hundreds and hundreds of games have come and gone from radio and television in the past century and attempting to chronicle every one of them individually with any significant depth would have put the author significantly past his deadline and the price of the book past what sane people would declare reasonable.

Rather, this book delves into game shows by examining them in terms of what was trendy; the "stump the experts" games of the early forties, the big-money quiz shows of the fifties, the word games of the sixties, right up to the "shiny floor" extravaganzas of the new millennium. Along the way, the book examines noteworthy hosts and producers who left their marks on the genre, but again, not every one of them.

Let's put it this way. If you were teaching a course called "Game Shows 101," what follows is a valiant attempt at a textbook.

Game Shows FAQ

The Pre-History

In The Beginning . . .

S ure, playing games can be fun, and listening to the radio can be fun. But where did the idea come from to put those together?

I Hear a Bee

The grand prize offered by every game show has been exactly the same since 1923.

That's the year that we'll unofficially peg as the birth of game shows, at least until somebody can find evidence to the contrary. Commercial radio broadcasting was only three years old when a newspaper, the *Brooklyn Daily Eagle*, struck upon a new idea for selling papers. The *Eagle* had successfully held "current events bees" for area school children in the past six years.

The staff of the *Brooklyn Daily Eagle* couldn't help noticing a few things about the current events bees: First, they were held in one of the largest auditoriums in the city and routinely attracted standing-room-only crowds. Second, educational circles raved about the enlightening and rewarding nature of the quiz. Third, copycats were emerging; area churches started holding "Bible Bees," for example. After each Bee, the *Eagle* would print a special edition containing all of the questions and correct answers, and those special editions always sold better than on an average day.

Somebody on the staff—we don't know who—was observant enough of the audience's rapt attention during the Bees to think it might make good radio fodder. The staff devised a radio program with the extremely literal title *Brooklyn Eagle Quiz on Current Events* for station WNYC. Host H. V. Kaltenborn would simply recite questions to area high school students.

It appears that the program remained on the air for at least eighteen years; references to it could still be found in print as late as 1941. By that time, H. V. Kaltenborn was a respected newscaster and commentator (one writer called him "a professor at large in a global classroom"), and in a matter of years, he would even amass a few film credits. A seventeen-year run and a higher profile for the host? There's no available ratings data for *Brooklyn Eagle Quiz on Current Events*, but that sounds an awful lot like a hit.

But why? There was no cash prize, no car at stake. It was radio so there was certainly no flashy set, no graphics, no sexy models. And yet people tuned in. The show's main reward was a good feeling. A century later, nothing has changed.

People are still tuning into game shows. They're shouting the solution to an incomplete Hangman puzzle. They're shouting, "The second number in the price of the boat is an '8'!" or "Pick Door Number '3'!" They're smugly grinning at the person sitting next to them on the couch and saying, "What is Monticello?" They root for the contestants they like. They form a bond to the host. A big grand prize is nice, but the truth is, people like game shows because no other genre does a better job of making them feel like you're on the show, even when they're miles away from the studio.

Pop Quiz

Success breeds imitators. There's no way of knowing whether or not *Time* magazine circulation manager Roy E. Larsen was familiar with *Brooklyn Eagle Quiz on Current Events*, but we do know that one year after *Brooklyn Eagle Quiz* premiered, Larsen was proposing a radio quiz to sell magazines. He worked out a deal with New York station WJZ to secure free air time for *The Pop Question*. On each program, *Time* co-founder Briton Hadden read questions drawn from the most recent issue.

The Pop Question was even more barebones than *Brooklyn Eagle Quiz*. There weren't even contestants. Briton Hadden read the questions, and Roy E. Larsen would play a series of chimes, signifying a brief interval for listeners at home to ponder the correct answer, or argue about it with each other.

The Pop Question lasted three years, but it may have left an enduring legacy. Briton Hadden maintained that the iconic NBC chimes were inspired by the pauses on *The Pop Question*.

One of the pioneers of game shows, Jerry Belcher, who traveled the country, asking questions and doling out dollars on *Vox Pop*.

The Show That Traveled America

In November 1932, Jerry Belcher and Harry Grier from station KTRH in Houston, Texas, took to the streets and asked passersby what they thought about the upcoming presidential election. After November, Belcher and Grier certainly couldn't continue asking questions about the election, but the program had been so riveting that they kept taking the microphones out onto the streets to ask anything to anybody. They called their new concoction *Vox Pop*, inspired by the Latin phrase *vox populi*, or "voice of the people."

At some point, Belcher and Grier came up with the idea of grilling some passersby with trivia questions instead of asking for their opinions. The average person might have been a little shy about the unexpected quiz—nobody wants to look foolish, after all—so Belcher and Grier, and later Parks Johnson, took a fistful of money with them and gave a few bucks for correct answers. It was a nice incentive, and the combination of trivia and money for answers gave *Vox Pop* just cause to call itself the first true game show—there was a game and there was a prize. *Vox Pop* was never strictly a game show; the greater emphasis would always be the man-on-the-street interviews, which grew more elaborate as the years went on. Programs were done from hotel lobbies, world's fairs, movie premieres, six foreign countries, forty-one states plus Washington D.C., and the Alaska territory.

But even if you want to argue that it didn't "count," *Vox Pop* did strike upon the idea of offering a pot of gold at the end of their trivial rainbow. And it was the right idea at the right time. It was the Great Depression; the chance of getting some easy money for knowing a little something was enticing and fun.

The Uncle and the Professor

The First Big Things

Countless local radio stations seemed to have the same great idea: get some people into a studio or auditorium, ask them trivia questions, and broadcast the efforts. Surprisingly, it took a while for the major networks to get on board.

The Quiz Starts a Biz

Network radio had been surprisingly slow to jump onboard the Q&A bandwagon. The original quiz show, New York's *Brooklyn Daily Eagle Current Events Quiz* had spawned a batch of imitators, all local programs that came and went quietly. But in 1936, the radio quiz finally went nationwide, and it came out swinging; the first two national quiz shows were both hits.

On May 9, 1936, listeners in Washington, D.C., were introduced to a jocular but mysterious man identified only as Professor Quiz. On each program, Professor Quiz challenged contestants with questions that he had written himself. A large number of contestants stood on stage for a question bee, with the last five advancing to a "Battle of Wits" round where the Professor's questions now required multiple answers.

The program was a fast success and on September 18, 1936, *Professor Quiz* premiered on the CBS radio network, becoming the first national quiz show and spawning an avalanche of imitators. By the Professor's own count, about three hundred more quiz shows sprung up on local and national radio in the next four years.

My Name is Earl

Who was Professor Quiz? A very bright man who seemed to have no blind spots in his brain. He could effortlessly fire off extra facts after questions about history, art, music, literature, anything. The questions he penned managed to cover a broad range of knowledge with the brain busters that he whipped up week after week. Doing well as a contestant on *Professor Quiz* truly earned bragging rights.

But . . . who *was* Professor Quiz? Really? In the beginning, CBS went to great efforts to conceal the answer to that question. His name was kept secret from reporters who asked, and no publicity photos were made available. The people who sat in the audience and played the game were the only ones who got a glimpse of Professor Quiz, a tall, heavyset, bespectacled man with a moustache tracing his friendly smile.

He frequently made references to his wife, "Mrs. Quiz." *Professor Quiz* was a small operation, one that the Professor kept in the family. Mrs. Quiz was the show's contestant coordinator who answered all the mail applications from people who wanted to compete. A small staff sorted through mail from those who submitted questions for use in the game, only to sort out ones that were too similar to questions already used (scores of people wrote in to suggest, "What is the only bird that can fly backward?" and "What is the shortest verse in the Bible?"), or questions that seemed obtuse. Mrs. Quiz would sort through the remaining questions submitted until she had whittled it down to three hundred for her husband to consider for use that week.

Professor Quiz served as his own fact checker, personally responding to angry letters from listeners who disagreed with the accuracy of an answer given on the program. When a listener wrote in to say "tale" shouldn't have been accepted as an answer to a question about lubricants, Professor Quiz personally wrote back with definitions from three different dictionaries and a physics textbook. Occasionally, he admitted defeat; when he said very definitively that a pig's tail always curls to the left, dozens of farmers mailed him photographs of their pigs' derrieres. Professor Quiz conceded that the curl varied from pig to pig.

The identity of Professor Quiz remained a secret for a full year until *Radio Daily* outed him as Dr. Craig Earl. Once the secret was out, Dr. Earl was all too eager to discuss his past. As he explained, he was an orphan who overcame his hardscrabble youth to attend Tufts University, where he earned a degree in theology. He toured Europe as a magician and dancer before going to China to learn how to walk through fire. He also worked the vaudeville circuit with Harry Houdini ("a megalomaniac with an inferiority complex you could cut with a knife," remembered the professor) and did a juggling act with W. C. Fields ("He was a screwball"). After a stint as a tightrope walker, Dr. Earl practiced medicine and occasionally gave lectures in philosophy, and in what little spare time those efforts afforded him, he became a chess champion.

On his off-hours, he gathered more information. A speed-reader who could knock out an average book in ninety minutes, he committed himself to reading ten non-fiction books a week, and novels "just for fun." His hobbies included Victorian literature and Oriental philosophy.

My Name is Not Earl

Dr. Craig Earl's popularity was his own undoing; as the program grew more popular, he was seen by more and more people in the audience for his program and for numerous public appearances, at which he was invariably photographed.

In 1942, it was discovered that Dr. Craig Earl was actually Arthur Earl Baird; his ex-wife, who had been looking for him, had finally caught up.

Arthur E. Baird was not an orphan; his draft card in 1918 said that he lived with his parents. He did attend Tufts University for two years, but dropped out without earning any degree. In 1935, he vanished, leaving no indication to his wife of where he was going. That same year, he adopted the pseudonym "Craig Earl" and got a job at a newspaper, where he worked until selling that first radio station on *Professor Quiz*. Mrs. Baird took him to court, a judge ruled in her favor, and Arthur E. Baird was forced to pay $25,000 in restitution.

If you're thinking the bad publicity brought down Professor Quiz, you'd be wrong. By 1942, the show had been on the air for six years and that was plenty of time for the audience to get to know the Professor. He was genuinely well-read and witty, with vast swaths of knowledge to tug out from every corner of his brain. No, as it turned out, Arthur E. Baird was not a globe-hopping renaissance man. But whoever he was, he was a genius, and that seemed to be what truly mattered to the general public. Not only did Professor Quiz last another seven years, but nobody batted an eye when he continued using the name "Dr. Craig Earl" for the rest of his life.

Big Man on Campus

Professor Quiz grew so big that for six months out of the year, Craig Earl and "Mrs. Quiz" would tour the country, stopping in a city to visit schools, hospitals and orphanages, giving out Professor Quiz wristwatches as gifts wherever they went. All of these public appearances led up to the big main event in the area, Professor Quiz staging his program live in the local auditorium; 14,500 attended the show in Kansas City, with 5,000 turned away at the door.

Even Craig Earl acknowledged how silly it seemed that people would drive to a packed auditorium and cram themselves into a small seat to watch a program that they could have heard at home. So to give the touring show more reason for existing, Dr. Earl would play up his entrance at the beginning of the show to the hilt. He'd arrange for a rented Cadillac to drive him directly onto the stage; he'd step out of the car, decked out in a tuxedo with tails, tall top hat, and waxed moustache, then remove his white gloves and step up to the CBS microphone to start the show; it was an extravagant, extraneous bit of theatrics, but the locals always devoured it.

One from Column Bee

On September 26, 1936, eight days after the national premiere of *Professor Quiz*, the NBC Blue Network introduced *Uncle Jim's Question Bee*. (Because of the close proximity of the premiere dates, a large number of reference books say that *Uncle Jim's Question Bee* came first.) There was no surprise hiding behind that title; like *Professor Quiz* and the local quizzes preceding it, the show had a stage full of contestants who were eliminated one by one through their wrong answers.

The program's namesake was its original host, Jim McWilliams. Funnily enough, when McWilliams departed to host a new quiz show, *Ask-It Basket*, his first name remained in the title. New host Bill Slater took over, simply identifying himself as "Uncle Jim" for as long as he retained the gig. The program was a success, but a modest one compared to *Professor Quiz*. *Uncle Jim's Question Bee* expired in 1941.

We're Sorry You Didn't Win Anything . . .

"A lovely copy of the home game" is pretty standard for a game show that experiences even moderate success, but would you believe that the concept of a "home game" has been around since literally the beginning? *Professor Quiz* released two box games featuring wheels and dials that players used to select the questions they would be asked. Despite having a shorter run, *Uncle Jim's Question Bee* cranked out an impressive stack of adaptations: six home games and four books were published in the span of only five years.

Often Imitated

By December 1939, the glut of games was so hard to ignore that *Broadcasting Magazine* printed a list of quiz programs airing on the major networks by that point. NBC aired *Battle of the Sexes, Dr. I.Q, Town Hall, Information Please, Kay Kyser's Kollege of Musical Knowledge, Melody Marathon, Paul Wing's Spelling Bee, Pot O' Gold, Quicksilver, True or False, Uncle Walter's Dog House, We the Wives, What's My Name*, and *Youth vs. Age*. On CBS, you could hear *Ask-It Basket* and *Professor Quiz*. MBS offered *Name Three* and *Quixie-Doodle Contest*.

The same article seems a little perplexed as to what to call these programs. The word *quiz* appears in quotes as if it's a colloquial term and not really a proper identification, but it was so accurate and so appropriate (not to mention the word *quiz* itself is rather catchy) that it became the commonly accepted term for what was no longer a trend, but a genre that was just as present as the variety show or the comedy show. Quiz shows had arrived.

3

On the Tube

When TV Got Turned On

A flickering box named television gradually began appearing in American homes in the late 1930s and 1940s. Because it was such a cost-effective form of programming for what amounted to experimental broadcasts, game shows were among the first things viewers saw.

Turn On

If television as we know it has a birthday, it's July 1, 1941. It was certainly invented long before that, and television programs had certainly aired prior to that, experimental and primitive as they may have been. But in May 1941, the Federal Communications Commission declared that enough progress had been seen that television stations, effective July 1, could obtain commercial licenses, in essence turning the experimental medium into a fully functioning industry.

Three television stations went into business that day. NBC experimental station W2XBS became WNBT. CBS experimental station W2XAB became WCBW. Dumont station W2XVW was there too, keeping its cumbersome call letters because the smaller Dumont wasn't ready for commercial broadcasting yet; it remained experimental for the next three years.

On that historic first day, WNBT aired one hour of a test pattern, followed by the Dodgers/Phillies game at Ebbets Field. Lowell Thomas read the news, New York District Attorney Thomas E. Dewey hosted a fundraiser for United Service Organizations. After that: *Uncle Jim's Question Bee.*

Uncle Jim's Question Bee's first telecast was marred by a minor crisis behind the scenes: two scheduled guest stars both canceled and had to be replaced at the last minute, but once the program was actually on the air, it went off without a hitch. But the fact that *Uncle Jim's Question Bee* was the first game show is often forgotten. The credit often, and erroneously, goes to the program that directly followed it that night. One that history remembers much more clearly.

Truth is Stranger Than Fiction

Truth or Consequences had premiered on the NBC Radio Network the previous year, hosted by its twenty-nine-year-old creator, Ralph Edwards. Edwards was inspired by a couple of parlor games that he enjoyed as a youngster, "Fine or Superfine" and "Forfeits," both of which involved silly penalties for players who made mistakes.

Edwards would ask a question, often a trick question ("Does a hen sit or set when it lays eggs?" Actually, a hen stands) or a joke ("What starts with T, ends with T, and is filled with T?" Why, a teapot of course). "Beulah the Buzzer" would sound only a fraction of a second after the question was asked, and Edwards would giggle and tell the contestant "Since you didn't tell the truth, you must pay the consequences!" A woman had to simulate a fighter pilot's mission, sitting in a chair, with a broom acting as her navigation lever, as an actual military officer came onstage and gave her orders; the woman had to make all the sound effects with her mouth as she carried out the mission.

"Aren't we devils?!" Edwards would manically scream after explaining a consequence.

One of Edwards's favorite tricks was to sneak a surprise reunion into a game. For a consequence, two male contestants, Alfred and Leon, were sent into a room to get to know each other, and told that each of them had to deliver a speech about the other. Alfred rattled off a few facts about Leon that he had gathered in the past few minutes. Leon gave detailed accounts of Alfred's family and childhood, until Alfred realized that "Leon" was actually a cousin that he hadn't seen in thirty years.

Even on radio, there was no denying that listeners were missing out. A lady contestant was given a lamp and sent into the audience "to search for an honest man." Three women were hidden behind a screen and their husbands had to try to identify them only by looking at their ankles. A man acted as a human whack-a-

mole game while his wife hurled pies at him. A woman had to describe how to milk a cow without using her hands. Wouldn't this stuff be a lot more fun if you actually saw it?

A single special broadcast of *Truth or Consequences* aired on TV for that 1941 milestone day. For a consequence, a man had to crawl into an audience member's lap and cry like a baby. As he did so, a few of the show's staffers dashed out and wrapped the man in a diaper.

A critic reluctantly admitted that he enjoyed the show, but that he hoped it wasn't an omen: "All good clean radio fun, but it helped to begin television under commercial sponsorship on a pretty low level. . . . May destiny preserve this nation from the terrible example of smart-alekism which, with the aid of television if ever organized nationally, this kind of drunk-while-sober behavior represents."

Host Ralph Edwards (left) sets up a perilous predicament for a contestant on *Truth or Consequences*. Even though the radio version was a hit, Edwards was quick to recognize that these shenanigans would play better on the television screen.

Twist of Fates

If *Uncle Jim's Question Bee* and *Truth or Consequences* were just one-time-only specials for television's coming-out party, then you could reasonably argue that they don't really count. If your definition of "first TV game show" is the first one that aired at a regularly scheduled time, then the answer was a show that premiered the following night, July 2, 1941.

Gil Fates was a budding actor from Newark, New Jersey, who abruptly abandoned acting for a job at CBS when preparations got underway for commercial television. Part of the FCC's mandate for issuing a commercial television license was that a station had to air at least fifteen hours of programming per week. In the nascent stage of the medium, this was a daunting task, so Fates joined an informal brainstorming committee charged with conjuring up shows to fill fifteen hours. Fates suggested a quiz show, which went on the air with the straightforward title *CBS Television Quiz.*

Television didn't immediately shake off the dust of its experimental beginnings and go straight to well-polished commercial television. The contestants on *CBS Television Quiz* were mostly personal friends of Gil or director Worthington Miner. Random House publishing magnate Bennett Cerf dropped by frequently, as did composer Richard Rodgers and his wife.

The show didn't really have a set structure; Fates might ask trivia questions or have the players compete in stunts or races. For one, the players held bowls of peanuts between their knees and balanced bottles of milk on their heads; from that position, they tried to spoon peanuts into the milk bottles.

The program innovated the concept of the "lovely assistant." Fates was joined by Frances Buss, an aspiring actress who had taken a temp assignment working in the News department for CBS. She was a skilled pen-and-paper artist, so for early newscasts, she drew maps. But because she was strikingly pretty and comfortable in such unfamiliar surroundings, she was immediately whisked into a second task, scorekeeping on *CBS Television Quiz.* And what was the grand prize for the big winner?

According to Gil Fates: "A warm handshake."

CBS Television Quiz stayed on the air until May 25, 1942. Gil Fates left the country for a few years and became the commanding officer for a rescue cutter in the English Channel during the invasion of Normandy. Frances Buss stayed at CBS and became the network's first female full-time director.

4

The Brain Trust

Well, What Do You Know?

S ome of the most popular games on radio didn't pit contestant against contestant. Rather, it was a battle of Audience vs. Show.

Oh, *Please!*

"*Information Please!* A new type of question/answer contest in which you, the very much quizzed public, get to quiz the professors. Yes, the worm turns . . ."

And that was how, on May 17, 1938, NBC Radio fired the first shots at *Professor Quiz* on CBS with a new creation. *Information Please* (title inspired by the then-standard way of asking a telephone operator for what is now known as directory assistance) was the first truly interactive radio quiz. Sure, you could mail in questions to *Professor Quiz* for the chance to brag to your friends when ol' Professor Quiz himself said your name on the air, but on *Information Please*, audiences were pitted against authorities; a panel of experts on a variety of subjects tried to answer the trivia questions mailed in by listeners, with cash awarded for any listener who could stump the panel.

As show creator Dan Golenpaul explained to the *New York Times*, "I became weary of listening to the same type of quizzes and the same type of questions, and I thought it might be a good idea if the procedure was reversed; that is, have the public ask the questions for a change and have experts answer them."

Host Clifton Fadiman—a Phi Beta Kappa graduate of Columbia University who went onto become the chief editor at Simon and Schuster before joining the editorial staff at *The New Yorker*—was joined by a panel of intellectual heavyweights; lecturers, authors, professors, newspaper writers, and the like. If you think this sounds like an awfully stuffy program, that's just what they wanted you to think. The show used its rather uppity façade to maximum effect by loading each program with ad-libs and jokes, all delivered with the elocution and accents of upper-crust snobs who sounded like they didn't realize what was so funny.

Fadiman: The five-dollar penalty for an expert's failure to answer a question completely will be paid out from a kitty of one hundred dollars set up for each broadcast. And to make sure that the board works hard on each program, it's understood that what is left of the one-hundred-dollar kitty, if any after penalties are paid, go to the board for refreshments, such as a fine, cool glass of milk and a cookie.

Question: Why would it never be necessary for the man on the moon, if married to a chatterbox, to tell her to shut up?

Author Bernard Jaffe: There is no atmosphere on the moon. It requires air to transmit soundwaves. Therefore, she can talk from today until doomsday and nobody will hear her.

Fadiman: A real chatterbox on the moon could generate enough hot air to create her own atmosphere, wouldn't she?

The Original Trivial Pursuit

Information Please struck upon what made a quiz so interesting: the ability to dig down deep and find a nugget that really wasn't common knowledge. There are no bragging rights for knowing that George Washington was America's first president, but knowing who the third president was and what was unusual about his election? Well, that's something to smirk about. (Thomas Jefferson was the incumbent vice president and defeated his own president, John Adams, to take the office.) It's the same principle that's been put to work in the decades since in countless quiz shows, radio call-in contests, board games, and bar trivia nights. People don't just listen to quiz shows to be entertained; they're listening for a chance to feel good when they outsmart the supposed "experts."

And not very many people outsmarted them. In a November 1939 article in the *New York Times*, the paper reported that after eighteen months on the air, fewer than 150 wrong answers had been given in all the programs aired so far, which gave the panel greater than a 90 percent success rate.

Clifton Fadiman (far right, seated) asks the questions to the panelists on "the quiz show of the intellectual," *Information Please.* No sitcom stars or stand-up comics here. The panel tonight is, from left: *The New York World Telegram* radio editor Alton Cook, *New York Times* sports editor John Kiernan, author Alice Duer, and *New York Post* columnist F. P. Adams.

Illumination Please

Brain power was always prioritized over box-office power on *Information Please*. As Fadiman himself once explained, "We're not looking for celebrities, necessarily. They're a dime a dozen. We want people of accomplishment with minds that know how to play."

The know-it-alls on *Information Please* held their posts for year after year because they really did know it all: Franklin P. Adams ("F. P. A." to his friends), a prolific newspaper writer and satirist, acclaimed member of the Algonquin Roundtable—a group of writers who had lunch together every day at the Algonquin Hotel, and whose light remarks over the meal would frequently wind up being quoted in newspapers across the country the next day; John Kiernan, *New York Times* sportswriter and amateur botanist; and Oscar Levant, a sharply sarcastic pianist and actor. The fourth seat was always occupied by a special guest star, and even the guest panelists on *Information Please* carried some extra weight behind the eyes: playwrights George S. Kaufman and Moss Hart; journalists John Gunther and Quincy Howe; musicologist Sigmund Spaeth; critic Alton Cook; author Thomas Craven; screenwriter Ben Hecht; Yale literature professor William Lyon Phelps; Gov. Ellis Arnall of Georgia; actors Ruth Gordon, Orson Welles, and Basil Rathbone; and radio announcer Myron Wallace, later better known as Mike Wallace.

Who Knew? (Besides *Information Please*)

Information Please released a home game, of course (in book form, not in board game form), and in a rare achievement for a quiz, then or now, it was adapted for the silver screen. An *Information Please* short subject was filmed in 1940, featuring Clifton Fadiman, Franklin P. Adams, John Kiernan, Oscar Levant, and Republican Presidential nominee Wendell Wilkie. The strongest measure of its success is one that almost nobody today realizes. Even though *Information Please* went off the air in 1951, its legacy has been stunningly long-lived due to another promotional tie-in: *The Information Please Almanac* was first published in 1947 and continued publishing into the new millennium. It merged with *Time* magazine to form *The Time Almanac with Information Please*, continuing to print new editions until 2013. The website infoplease.com also traces its roots back to the classic radio quiz.

Kids' Stuff

The era of the know-it-all was young, and so too were the experts on radio's next big "stump the experts" offering. NBC introduced *Quiz Kids* on June 28, 1940, and the program stuck around for the next thirteen years.

As on *Information Please*, a panel of geniuses fielded questions mailed in by listeners, who could win a prize if they outsmarted the smart guys. The catch on *Quiz Kids* was that the smart guys were small fries. Children very strategically cast for radio—brains weren't enough, the kids also had to have outgoing personalities and senses of humor—and steered through a weekly quiz.

At least fifteen candidates auditioned to host *Quiz Kids* and got rejected; among them were news commentators, a newspaper editor, lecturers, professors, and radio announcers. The host chosen to oversee the panel of wunderkinds was, of all people, Joe Kelly, a third-grade dropout who was best known as the host of a hillbilly music program called *National Barn Dance*. The professors and newsmen may have seemed like better companions for juvenile genii, but all of them lacked the skill that Joe Kelly brought to the table: he was great with the kids, seeming more like a big buddy to them than an authority figure.

Early reviews brought forth nothing but raves. *Variety* and *Billboard* both glowed about the program. *Life* magazine marveled, "On the air barely a month, the five bright youngsters . . . have amazed their elders with their popularity, quickness on the uptake, their encyclopedia knowledge."

The premiere brought in more than twenty-six hundred fan letters. In time, that number would swell to about twenty thousand a week, with a loyal twenty million listeners tuning into NBC week after week, and not always to test themselves. Millions of children who weren't fans of the program were forced to listen to the show as an example. Even an only child could now be subjected to a parent's lament of "Why can't you be more like . . . ?" because Mom and Dad could now compare Junior's disappointing marks on a report card to seven-year-old Gerard's effortless explanation of apteryxes and antimacassars.

Roll Call

There were five children on each week's panel. The three kids who performed best would return the following week, while the other two went to the "back of the line," so to speak, while two other kids got their turn. Kids rarely *stayed* gone from the program, because they were all just too darn likeable to get dismissed. Besides, separating the kids into three winners and two losers was a bit misleading anyway. The kids as a whole had a 90 percent success rate; the "losers" in a given week never really performed poorly.

More than six hundred children appeared on *Quiz Kids* in its decade-plus on the air, but a handful became true celebrities. They were invited to the White House by Eleanor Roosevelt, they were guest stars on Jack Benny's radio program, they visited Hollywood and met W. C. Fields (the curmudgeonly comedian who supposedly hated children), all while collecting $100 for each *Quiz Kids* episode.

The program was created and produced by Louis G. Cowan, who later achieved fame, and then infamy, as creator of *The $64,000 Question*. When it was revealed that *Question* had been rigged, it cast a shadow on Cowan's previous work. It was acknowledged that in one sense, the show was "controlled"—the show's production staff was keenly aware of how knowledgeable the kids were, so they simply didn't use any listener-submitted questions that the kids didn't have a decent chance of answering. Contestant Joel Kupperman's mother remembered that the producers would occasionally ask what books the boy had read lately and if he had developed any new interests or hobbies; Mrs. Kupperman said she suspected that information was being used as a guideline for what questions Joel could handle. But the show was put together, the kids were truly bright, and they shone week after week before a national audience.

Quiz Adults

Ruthie Duskin was a regular on *Quiz Kids* for nine years, appearing on the program for the first time when she was seven and staying until she was sixteen. As an adult, she viewed being a Quiz Kid as a mixed blessing. Her winnings paid for college and the first year of her marriage. But at the same time, spending the bulk of her childhood in front of an audience gave her a lasting need for recognition—as an adult, her reaction to seeing her name in the byline of a newspaper article made her realize that she still had "a need for applause."

And there was one other drawback to being a Quiz Kid. As Ruth Duskin Feldman (her married adult name) explained to fellow writer Joseph G. Boyd, "Every child wants to fit in. But the gifted child is always singled out. In the 1940s, the world was more naïve. In our egalitarian society, the gifted child was stigmatized as arrogant, a brat, spoiled and stuck up. I did the show once a week and the rest of the time just tried to push it into the background."

Her experience compelled her to write a book, *Whatever Happened to the Quiz Kids?* She wasn't feeling nostalgic. She just wanted to know the fates of kids like her who spent their entire childhoods on a pedestal for being geniuses before being shoved into the adult world with everybody else.

Animal, Vegetable, or Mineral

Fred van Deventer was a know-it-all of some renown, the anchor of WOR's *Van Deventer and the News*, New York's top-rated radio newscast. On February 2, 1946,

A souvenir postcard mailed to listeners who sent in questions for the Quiz Kids to answer. Harve became an accomplished filmmaker, while Ruthie became an author.

he introduced a stump-the-experts game based on a rather familiar parlor game: *20 Questions*, turning it into a competition between audience and panel. Listeners mailed in subjects and the five-member panel asked yes-or-no questions to zero in on them.

Van Deventer appointed himself permanent panelist on the program, and didn't look particularly hard for other panelists. He was joined by his wife, Florence Rinard, and their son, who went by Bobby MacGuire. The program's producer, Herb Polosie, filled the fourth seat on the panel. A guest star (occasionally Nancy Van Deventer, daughter of Fred and Florence) was in seat number five. Sportscaster Bill Slater sat in the emcee's chair.

20 Questions never attained the levels of popularity that *Information Please* and *Quiz Kids* enjoyed in their prime, but made up for it with sheer volume of acclaim. Fred Van Deventer received three honorary doctorates stemming from the program, and Florence Rinard got one too. The U. S. Office of Education and Voice of America both lauded the program, and the panelists' question-asking and deducing skills were used as the basis for classes taught at three universities.

Still, it was a silly parlor game. How "good" could anybody be at *20 Questions*? The incoming mail brought in increasingly specific subjects and Bill Slater gleefully used them ("Bread" wouldn't make it onto the program but "The Bread Cast Upon the Waters in The Bible" was used). Time and time again, the Van Deventers and their friends solved the mysteries. During a public appearance in Pittsburgh, The Van Deventers complied with a reporter who challenged them to a personal session. Writer Edwin F. Brennan reported his own dismay in the *Pittsburgh Post-Gazette* when the Van Deventers guessed Pittsburgh Pirates left fielder Ralph Kiner in only ten questions; they needed a whole fourteen questions to guess "The Left Hind Leg of the Race Horse Citation."

20 Questions made the transition from radio to television in 1949, and between the two media, it stayed on the air for nine years. An estimated eight thousand subjects were used in those nine years. More than seven thousand were solved.

Ignorance is Bliss

Imitation is the sincerest form of flattery, but parody might be the sincerest form of oversaturation. When radio quiz shows first became truly ubiquitous, vaudeville comic Tom Howard concocted a weekly parody of the genre, gathering three fellow comics, uppity-sounding Harry McNaughton, razor-blade-gargling Lulu McConnell, and nasally George Shelton to sit on the panel.

For *It Pays to be Ignorant*, listeners were encouraged to send in the easiest questions they could think of. The magic of the show was listening to the panelists manage time and time again to screw it up.

Tom Howard: What great American actress is the Ethel Barrymore Theater named for? No help from the audience, please.

George Shelton: These questions are getting harder and harder.

Tom Howard: They certainly are.

Harry McNaughton: Mr. Howard, pardon me, did you say "great American actress"?

Tom Howard: That's right.

Lulu McConnell: Mr. Howard?

Tom Howard: Well?

Lulu McConnell: Would it be me?

Tom Howard: I said "great American actress." She is the first lady of the theater.

Lulu McConnell: I'm an actress!

Tom Howard: But you're no lady.

The questions would typically disintegrate into the panelists telling stories from their pasts ("I was a boxer once—Kid Accordion!") and swapping insults ("When you got hit, you folded up!") while straight man Howard, forever exasperated, kept trying to steer them back to the question that he had asked minutes before. *It Pays to Be Ignorant* enjoyed a nine-year run, getting canceled in 1951. Fittingly, *Information Please* met its demise that same year.

5

Hit the Jackpot

Call, Collect

In 1948, fifty-four radio shows awarded a then-astronomical total of $4,297,557. Here's how they did it.

The $64 Question

On April 21, 1940, CBS introduced a new kind of quiz called *Take It or Leave It*. After the swarm of question bees that audiences had come to expect from Q&A games, *Take It or Leave It* did something strikingly different with the radio quiz. Host Bob Hawk would draw names of audience members, one at a time, from a "MEN" fishbowl or a "WOMEN" fishbowl. The audience member was shown a blackboard with a variety of categories, picked one, and answered a series of questions. The monetary prize for answering the first question correctly was $1, doubling to $2 for the second question, and doubling again and again until the seventh question, dubbed "The $64 Question." The catch was that pursuing each question required forfeiting the prize money from the previous question, hence the quiz's title. It was a new concept in quiz programs: risk. To do well on this game, you had to have the heart of a gambler, willing to give up the sure thing to collect that modest, but very tempting, $64 payday waiting at the end of the rainbow.

Phil Baker took over the program on December 27, 1941, by which point America had entered World War II and a third fishbowl, "SERVICEMEN," was added to the game. Despite asking its players to take risks throughout, *Take It or Leave It* was actually a delightfully cheesy game. Clues for musical categories were squeezed out on a wheezy accordion. Phil Baker's invisible assistant, Beetle (even the audience in the studio couldn't see him) would taunt contestants who chose to risk their winnings with his sing-songy catchphrase, "You'll be sooooorrrrryyyy!" And because everybody wanted to see the servicemen do well, a running gag was that servicemen got blatantly easy questions, with Baker dropping "hints" throughout the game that totally gave away the correct answers.

Take It or Leave It proved so popular that in 1944, 20th Century-Fox released *Take It or Leave It*, a low-budget B-movie in which a contestant picked "Scenes from Motion Pictures of the Past" as his category, and every question led to an extended musical sequence from a previous 20th Century–Fox release.

Genial comedian Garry Moore (best known at the time for being Jimmy Durante's straight man) took over the show in 1947 and it became pure comedy at that point. Dozens of listeners wrote in over the years suggesting that the program at least raise the grand prize to $640, but the producers felt, quite correctly, that its low-stakes, funny Q&A game and its quick-witted host already had plenty of appeal without increasing the size of the checks.

Hush Up!

During World War II, Americans made impressive sacrifices: gasoline was rationed, scrap metal drives were held, and production of consumer goods was limited through the War Production Board. But after World War II, manufacturers were eager to spread the word that their products were available again. Radio quizzes and "giveaway shows" were a good way to do that. Prizes on the radio games were always token items: a dictionary, an encyclopedia, a small gift from the show's sponsor, a five-dollar bill . . .

Bob Hawk hosts *Take It or Leave It* on CBS Radio. The show's $64 question unexpectedly ushered in an era of massive jackpot giveaways on radio.

But higher-end items, like furniture, appliances, and cars were once again available in large supply, and an excited contestant being handed your company's high-end item in exchange for a winning answer, as the audience swooned with envy, was a perfect advertisement. Giveaway shows were more sumptuous than ever in their payoffs.

Ralph Edwards, host/creator of *Truth or Consequences*, noticed that prizes on the other shows were getting more lucrative. He devised a lavish giveaway on *Truth or Consequences*. He intended it to be a parody; it turned into a national sensation.

On December 29, 1945, *Truth or Consequences* listeners first heard the sotto voce of "Mr. Hush," a famous man. And that was all we knew about Mr. Hush; he'd recite a poem in his hard-to-decipher voice, offering a few clues to his true identity. Listeners were encouraged to write in if they wanted Ralph Edwards to call them on the phone with a chance to guess. Week by week, prizes were added to the jackpot, which finally swelled to about $13,500 worth of loot until a contestant correctly guessed that Mr. Hush was boxer Jack Dempsey (Edwards's original choice for Mr. Hush, Albert Einstein, said no).

Edwards decided to follow the stunt with "Mrs. Hush," adding a philanthropic touch to this contest. He had previously used *Truth or Consequences* to drive up money for the war efforts (for a time, audience members had to pay admission for the show, and were issued a war bond) and figured out a way to do a lot of good for another worthy cause. For a chance to guess Mrs. Hush's true identity, listeners first

The biggest secret on radio was the identity of Mr. Hush on *Truth or Consequences*. Only Ralph Edwards knew for sure.

had to make a donation to the March of Dimes.

Nobody expected the reaction to the Mrs. Hush contest; audience members were stumped, but captivated enough to keep sending in donations; prizes were added with every passing week as listener after listener failed to decipher the clues. After two months, a Mrs. McCormick in Lock Haven, Pennsylvania, finally guessed that Mrs. Hush was legendary actress Clara Bow. Mrs. McCormick's rewards for her correct guess: a 1947 convertible; an electric washer; a trip for two to New York City, including a suite at the Waldorf-Astoria; a silver fox fur coat; a trailer for a family of four; a diamond/ruby watch; a freezer unit fully stocked with frozen dinners; a gas range; a radio/phonograph console with 100 records; an Electrolux refrigerator; a billiard table; a furnace with a year's supply of fuel; a 144-piece china set; free maid service for a year; a complete house-painting job, interior and exterior, provided by Sherwin Williams; a typewriter; an airplane; a week's vacation in Sun Valley, Idaho; a diamond ring; a vacuum cleaner; and a complete wardrobe for every member of the immediate family. All told, about $18,000. Clara Bow herself was awarded a special trophy from the National Foundation of Infantile Paralysis for all that she did to get attention for the cause. The March of Dimes collected $400,000 worth of donations.

But the mystery of "The Walking Man" would leave Mrs. Hush speechless. The echoing footsteps of a mystery celebrity were first heard on January 3, 1948. With every passing week, donations poured in and prizes piled up: a washing machine, dryer, automatic ironer, a diamond/ruby watch, a Cadillac, a range, a 16mm projector and screen plus thirteen full-length movies, two weeks paid vacation in Sun Valley, vacuum cleaner, radio-phonograph-television console, diamond ring, refrigerator, Art-Craft Venetian for every room in the house, a Sherwin-Williams paint job, women's wardrobes for every season, a fifteen-foot freezer filled with Birdseye frozen dinners, an airplane, bathroom and kitchen tiles plus installation, a new living room, a new dining room, a trailer for four, typewriter, motorboat, Persian lamb coat, two years' worth of Lady Pepperell Sheets, $500 worth of electric appliances, electric blankets, men's suits, and a sewing machine.

Florence Hubbard of Chicago was the one who finally guessed that the Walking Man was comedian Jack Benny, who strolled out onstage to reveal that it really had been him the whole time. (Benny was so committed to the secret that he hadn't even told his wife about it, and it was revealed later that, for a time, leaving the house without telling her where he was going had put a bit of a strain on the marriage.) Hubbard came out of the contest with $25,000 in goodies. The American Heart Association collection $1.5 million.

Bank On It!

Prizes got bigger after World War II, and so did the amounts of cash. The first "big-money" quiz show on radio was *Break the Bank*, which premiered October 20, 1945 on Mutual and went through a revolving door of hosts in its first year before settling on jolly Georgian Bert Parks. Contestants were asked a series of trivia questions written by reference book author Joseph Nathan Kane. Answers started at $25 and grew to $500 for the seventh question, "the gateway to the

Nobody could accuse Bert Parks of phoning it in. His high-energy hosting style perfectly suited the exciting big-money quiz *Break the Bank*.

bank." Answering the next question correctly would break the bank. Two wrong answers ended the game and augmented the value of the bank by whatever amount of money the contestant had won up to that point. Breaking the bank paid $1,000 plus all the extra money that had accrued up to that point. Banks tended to get as high as $5,000 or $6,000, and occasionally swelled up to $9,000. Compared to the twenty-five dollars that *Quiz Kids* and *Professor Quiz* were offering at that point, this was quite a leap.

And the competition was feeling the heat. Between the "Hush" contests and the broken banks, poor Professor Quiz himself, Craig Earl, lamented to the press, "They give away too much for too little . . . I can't imagine anyone having fun answering a question where a house and a car are involved. You'd hate yourself for life if you missed the answer."

The plethora of prizes cluttering the airwaves inspired Dennis James, an early television figure with a few games of his own to his credit, to joke to *Radio Daily* that he was working on a new invention: a television with a built-in slot machine, so that audiences wouldn't have to listen to radio giveaways anymore.

Can't Stop, Won't Stop

But nobody cashed in on the encroaching big-jackpot craze like Mark Goodson, a successful announcer who found even greater success as a producer. He joined forces with comedy writer Bill Todman to create *Catch Me If You Can*, in which host

Bill Cullen guided contestants through trivia questions on a "ladder" that would lead them to a Golden Door; if a contestant could decipher the Secret Sentence at the Golden Door, a merchandise jackpot was awarded. In the wake of the success of the "Hush" contests on *Truth or Consequences* (which had set a few ratings records), Goodson and Todman changed *Catch Me If You Can* into *Hit the Jackpot*. Bill Cullen now called home listeners on the telephone, much as Ralph Edwards had been doing on *Truth or Consequences*, and offered them a chance to solve the Secret Sentence for cash and prizes totaling an astronomical $25,000.

With another business partner, Louis G. Cowan, Goodson formulated *Stop the Music*. A live orchestra onstage played a popular tune while a team of operators called randomly selected phone numbers across America. When a listener answered the telephone, announcer Kenny Williams would cry out "*Stop the music!*" and host Bert Parks would pick up his own phone onstage. When a listener correctly identified the song that had just been playing, they had a chance to guess the "Mystery Melody," for a jackpot that grew prize by prize and dollar by dollar until somebody guessed the correct song.

The program became a runaway hit on ABC Radio. The nation became so captivated that some newspapers began printing the staff's guesses for the Mystery Melody, so if a reader got the lucky phone call and gave a correct guess, the paper could get some of the credit.

Better Fred Than Dead

Airing in direct competition with *Stop the Music* was NBC Radio's *The Fred Allen Show*. Fred Allen, a sardonic, aging, former vaudeville star, had been a success on radio right up until 1948, when suddenly *Stop the Music* eroded his once-large audience. Fred Allen declared war. "[Giveaway shows] are ruining incentive for individual talent in radio," he told the Associated Press. "These giveaway programs are not just entertainment—just cheap lotteries."

Allen worked his competition woes into his program, announcing on one episode that The National Surety Corporation would bond every listener of *The Fred Allen Show* up to $5,000 for merchandise lost by listening to that program instead of *Stop the Music*. He even parodied *Stop the Music* one night with an episode in which he offered his own jackpot of prizes, including a saloon with bartender, four thousand yards of "practically new" dental floss, the gangplank of the Queen Mary, eight hundred pounds of putty for every member of the family, two floors of the Empire State Building, and twelve miles of railroad track.

At the same time Allen was airing the fake giveaway, a *Stop the Music* listener was correctly identifying "Turkey in the Treetop" for Bert Parks and being awarded $30,000 for it. Predictably, Allen's fake giveaway didn't capture the public the way the genuine article did.

Fred Allen took things further the following week, saying, "I read in some paper the other day that people on lots of those giveaway shows are called an hour or so before the program goes on the air to make sure they'll be home. So, if you're not called before the program starts, you can't be called during the program."

Mark Goodson emphatically denied that charge, even going so far as writing a letter to the *New York Times*, where he explained in detail how the phone calls for the program were made and addressing the suspicious way that people *always* answered their phone; no misdials, no phones that went unanswered. Goodson explained that multiple staffers placed telephone calls for each song, and the reason somebody always answered the phone was because completed calls were the only calls that aired on the program.

Also worth noting, at the same time that Fred Allen took his second consecutive swipe at the competition, *Stop the Music* crowned a Mystery Melody winner for the second consecutive week, awarding $15,000 to a Miami man who recognized "Ghost Dance." In total, *Stop the Music* would award $350,000 in cash and prizes during 1948. Fred Allen's program was canceled in 1949.

FCC Turns Games DOA

A little legal-ese to steer you through the next part of the story: The Federal Communications Commission prohibits broadcasting information or advertisements of "lotteries," with the exception of state-run lotteries, gambling conducted by a Native American tribe, or lotteries conducted for non-profit organizations. The FCC defines "lottery" as "any game, contest or promotion that combines the elements of prize, chance, and consideration."

All of a sudden, the FCC was turning a curious eye toward *Stop the Music*. There was a prize all right. And chance was involved; there was no qualification for *Stop the Music*, you could only hope that they happened to select your phone number that night. "Consideration," meaning payment for entering the contest, was where things started to get a little tricky. You didn't have to pay money to listen to *Stop the Music*. But you specifically had to listen to the show in order to win, and that turned into a semantics debut; did giving up thirty minutes of your time qualify as paying a consideration?

The FCC announced a proposed ruling that the recent wave of big jackpot giveaway shows constituted illegal lotteries and would be prohibited from radio and the newly emerging medium of television. ABC vowed to fight it. NBC said they wouldn't change their programming plans until a final ruling was in place. Mutual Radio spoke up in favor of the regulation. Frieda Hennock, at the time the only female in the FCC, wrote a dissenting opinion saying that giveaway programs didn't constitute an illegal lottery. The National Association of Broadcasters released a statement saying its members felt the FCC was overstepping its authority.

There were a few other objections; many radio programs involved some degree of giving time as a consideration. For "stump the experts" programs like *Information Please* and *Quiz Kids*, where listeners submitted questions in hopes of getting a prize for writing a question that proved too hard for the brainiacs, a listener did have to sit down, write a question, and drop it in the mailbox. That was a consideration too, but those programs had received critical acclaim for their educational merit and were generally regarded as quality programs. Even broadcasters who found the five-figure paydays for simple guessing games unbearable were now becoming quietly concerned that ALL games would be prohibited from the radio. And throughout the industry, people noticed that the FCC hadn't really taken action when big prize giveaways were few and far between. They were only stepping in when they became ubiquitous. And the notion that a genre should be wiped out because there were too many of that genre on the air seemed like a dangerous precedent.

Stop the Music continued undaunted, giving away twenty-seven more jackpots over the next two years, totaling $600,000. Every competing big jackpot show came and went quickly; in the span of two years, they were virtually all gone, leaving *Stop the Music* as the only show that actually had the FCC breathing down its neck.

The battle went all the way to the United States Supreme Court. Oddly, by the time the Supreme Court heard the case, *Stop the Music* was off the air. The show came to an end in 1952, and the Supreme Court case *FCC vs. American Broadcasting Co.* (Case no. 347 U.S. 284) began arguments on February 1, 1954.

In an 8–0 decision, the Supreme Court ruled that giveaway shows were not illegal lotteries, paving the way for games and quizzes to continue unencumbered. Almost as if taunting the FCC, ABC immediately revived *Stop the Music* on radio and on television, with Bert Parks handling the TV version, and Bill Cullen hosting on radio. Curiously, even though they now had the highest court in the land on their side, *Stop the Music* in its new incarnation was surprisingly conservative. Savings bonds worth $50 were awarded for correctly guessing the first qualifying tune, and solving the Mystery Melody paid a jackpot of $500 that went up only slightly when it went unclaimed. Audiences tuned in anyway, just because it was an intriguing game. It was a lesson that would come up over and over again in the succeeding decades; even if the payday is big, audiences won't care about a boring game. And even if the payday is modest, audiences will listen to a fun game.

6

TV Takes Over

DO Touch That Dial!

adio got pushed to the side, and television took over for good. Game shows adapted almost immediately to the new medium.

Cash In

Through a development called the coaxial cable, which allowed TV viewers in different cities to watch the same programs at the same time, network television as we know it began in 1946. Although NBC, CBS, and ABC would eventually get in the game, the first TV network with a regularly scheduled game show was the forgotten fourth network, DuMont, which ceased operations in 1956.

DuMont's game was *Cash and Carry* starring Dennis James. Airing on Thursday nights beginning June 20, 1946, *Cash and Carry* pitted contestants against each other in a game combining trivia and stunts. The set, resembling a grocery store (with Dennis wearing an apron and bowtie, looking more like a shopkeeper than a

In the beginning, Dennis James manned the store for Libby Foods. DuMont's *Cash and Carry* was the first regularly scheduled network game.

Photo courtesy of Micki James

master of ceremonies) was adorned with Libby's Foods grocery items; contestants would pick one, Dennis would reveal the money amount hidden on the bottom—as much as fifteen dollars!—and ask a question. The contestants would also have to perform a variety of odd tasks for additional money, like painting faces on top of bald men's heads, or riding a mechanical bull.

Network TV didn't quite hit the ground running. In 1946, barely 700,000 homes owned televisions, and owning a television didn't necessarily mean that you could pick up the signal for every channel in the area. Given those limitations, *Cash and Carry* had an understandable problem with one feature of the program; a weekly contest in which Dennis recited a poem describing an object hidden under a barrel. Viewers were encouraged to call the show and guess what was under the barrel. The same viewer—who later said that he never even got a busy signal—kept phoning in and winning the contest. Dennis finally brought him into the studio one night to take a bow in front of any audience that may have been tuning in.

Putting on a Charade

DuMont's next game, debuting on September 24, 1946, was hosted by a master of ceremonies with the unlikely name of Dr. Harvey Zorbaugh. Dr. Zorbaugh, a sociology professor at New York University, frequently held parties at his house and played charades with his guests. They almost never used the name "Charades." Someone in the room would say "Let's play the game!" When Dr. Zorbaugh convinced DuMont that it might be a fun game for television, he titled it *Play the Game*. To date, the only national game show to emanate from Schenectady, New York, *Play the Game* featured several guest stars acting out famous names and phrases. Viewers could call the studio and guess what was being performed and win cash for correct guesses. WNBT, the local NBC station in New York, did fundamentally the same game with Bill Cullen hosting, and switching between the titles *Act It Out*, *Say It with Acting*, and *Look Ma I'm Acting*.

Play the Game ran for only thirteen weeks on DuMont before resurfacing on ABC. DuMont, meanwhile, introduced another Charade quiz in 1947, with the uninspired title *Charade Quiz*.

"Independent Invention" is a phenomenon observed by anthropologists in which different cultures created new concepts, like agriculture and machinery, without being aware of each other. And as it turns out, this phenomenon applied to the earliest game shows. In 1939, a Los Angeles City College student named Mike Stokey rounded up some friends and played charades in a studio housed over a car dealer's garage. They called the program *The Game*. In 1947, at the same time that DuMont (which never expanded to the Pacific time zone) was airing *Play the Game*, Stokey introduced a game on local station KTTV called *Pantomime Quiz*. The show generated enough attention that WCBS in New York aired it the following summer, and by 1950, *Pantomime Quiz* was a full-fledged network show.

Pantomime Quiz pitted two teams of celebrity guests against each other, acting out fairly complicated puzzles, including quotations and poems (Sample answer: "The monkey married the baboon's sister/Smacked his lips and then he kissed her.") The appeal of the game wasn't just in the wacky puzzles. It was the chance to see stars letting their guards down; the game played out on a set resembling an apartment living room, with Mike looking very much like he had just invited his friends over for a party. That was how the games tended to look too. Stars would freely guffaw and tease each other for bad clues. Straight-laced dramatic stars would bound around the set, contorting their faces and flailing their arms desperately to convey the words one at a time.

And an impressive mix of stars dropped in to play the game week after week: Elaine Stritch, John Barrymore Jr., Jerry Lester, Dorothy Hart, Robert Alda, Tom Poston, Carol Burnett, Sebastian Cabot, Angela Lansbury, Vincent Price, Robert Stack, and Dick Van Dyke played the game and played it well. The key, according to Stokey himself, was that the stars couldn't be addicted to scripts.

"He has to be willing to let his hair down," Stokey explained in 1954, "and he has to be able to think fast. That's a rarer combination than you might think. Among the biggest disappointments, for example, were a couple of actors who had built their reputations in the field of pantomime. I expected them to be terrific on our program, but they just didn't have it. . . . The pantomime for which they'd become famous was material they'd been able to polish and perfect over a great many years. But creating pantomime on the spur of the moment just wasn't in their line."

Very often, stars would surprise him with their quick thinking and their uninhibited approach to the game. Preston Foster, an archetypical "tall dark and handsome" film actor, was handed the puzzle "Hand me a diaper, mother, I'm pinning one on tonight!" Most people would pantomime putting the diaper on a baby. Foster blindsided Stokey by pantomiming putting a diaper on himself, and the audience roared at the bizarre visual.

Pantomime Quiz would have a lengthy tenure on television, but it never stayed in one place for long. The major networks all used it to plug holes. When another series got canceled, a network would call up Mike Stokey to put *Pantomime Quiz* on the air for a few months while they looked for something else. CBS was also fond of using the program as a summer replacement when a hit show was taking a vacation. It even switched coasts, moving from Los Angeles to New York and back again during the 1950s. The show, eventually retitled *Stump the Stars*, would come and go from the airwaves until 1970.

First-Place Winner

Perhaps the most important game show of television's toddler stage was CBS's first network game, *Winner Take All*, in 1948. *Winner Take All* was a collaboration by a former soap opera announcer, Mark Goodson, and a former comedy writer, Bill Todman. Premiering on CBS radio in 1946, it was their first national series; more than fifty would follow.

The original radio version had been hosted by Bill Cullen, a CBS staff announcer who was asked to step in as host at the last minute. As a staff announcer, he had been making $55. Goodson and Todman were so impressed with how he handled *Winner Take All* that when the show began getting sponsors, they saw to it that he got nearly an elevenfold raise, $600 a week. Cullen would go on to host twenty-nine more game shows during the next forty years.

For television, Cullen, who was initially reluctant to go into television due to a prominent limp caused by childhood polio, was replaced by Bud Collyer, a handsome actor who had made his name as the voice of Superman on radio and in cartoons. Collyer would go on to host nine more game shows himself. Cullen and Collyer, though they rarely crossed paths professionally, were arguably the two most ubiquitous faces on TV game shows of the 1950s and 1960s.

On *Winner Take All*, two contestants would compete against each other in a series of trivia questions. They would press buttons in front of them to activate a noise, either a buzzer or a bell, for the right to answer. The first contestant to answer three questions correctly would receive a prize and remain on the show to meet a new opponent. Contained in this sample format were two major innovations: "buzzing in," which had never been done in a game before, and "returning champions," an idea suggested by Goodson, reasoning that there would be an added layer of suspense in seeing how long one player could hang on and keep playing. It would be the first of many innovations to come from the Goodson-Todman partnership.

7

A Human Puzzle

Who Do They Think You Are?

ost game shows begin with the host asking the contestant to "tell us about yourself." But the panel games of the early 1950s instead asked celebrities to figure out what the contestant wasn't telling.

Line, Please

In late 1949, *Stop the Music* co-executive producer Mark Goodson, and a *Music* staffer, Gil Fates (previously the host of *CBS Television Quiz*) collaborated with a producer named Bob Bach. Together, they whipped up a format for television similar to the "stump the experts" shows that had been so popular on radio, but with the unique twist that it wasn't any particular bit of knowledge that the panel was trying to provide. They were trying to guess a contestant's occupation. It was a new concept; Mark Goodson dubbed it a "human puzzle." No trivia or scholarly knowledge involved. The fact of the contestant's being was all that was required.

What's My Line? premiered on CBS-TV on February 2, 1950. A contestant would sign their name on a slate, then walk up and down the stage before the panel. Based on simple observation, each of the four panelists would give a "wild guess" as to the contestant's occupation. If all four failed (they almost always did, but once in a while, a miracle would happen), they would play a game akin to *20 Questions*. The panelists would ask yes-or-no questions to zero in on the occupation. A "no" paid the contestant five dollars. Ten "no" answers ended the game.

You can be forgiven for thinking this doesn't sound interesting. The game was driven by personalities. The host was South African newsman John Charles Daly, an erudite, stuffy stickler for semantics who would drive the panel batty with his nitpicky interpretations of their questions. He would dismantle inquiries word-by-word, like a prosecutor going in for the kill on an inept witness, visibly frustrating panelists who found themselves having to explain precisely what they meant by "Is the product that you manufacture found in the kitchen?" Daly would reason that it could be found in the kitchen as well as any other room of the home, and perhaps the real question is whether or not the product in question is more apt to be used in the kitchen.

When Daly won a Sylvania Television Award for Excellence as a Moderator or Master of Ceremonies, the judges' official statement read: "[He] performs the difficult task of being dignified without being pompous. His voice is thoroughly

The classiest game show of all time, *What's My Line?* On the panel are gossip columnist Dorothy Kilgallen, producer/talk show host David Susskind, actress Arlene Francis, and publisher Bennett Cerf. Joining them is moderator John Charles Daly.

agreeable, his speech is flawless, and what he has to say . . . is refreshingly literate and spontaneous."

The original regular panel: witty poet Louis Untermeyer; probing gossip columnist Dorothy Kilgallen, who could match Daly nitpick-for-nitpick; socially awkward comedy writer Hal Block; and risible actress Arlene Francis. Together, they would struggle with one occupation after another, with the game frequently going off-track because of John Daly's insistence that the questions be taken as literally as possible. The panel went up in smoke one night because Daly and the contestant agreed that, yes, the contestant dealt in education, and yes, he dealt directly with pupils. The contestant was a seal trainer.

The main event of each episode was the Mystery Guest. The panelists put on blindfolds and tried to solve the identity of a celebrity, who would throw them off-track by disguising their answers in a variety of ways.

What's My Line? would become a television institution. For seventeen years, the show was rock-firm in the Sunday night 10:30 p.m. timeslot on CBS and, for many Americans, it served as the nightcap after a weekend off from their cares and responsibilities.

And the Rest

While *What's My Line?* wasn't exactly an overnight success (Gil Fates said years later that he watched his kinescope of episode number 1 repeatedly, and couldn't figure out why CBS ever encouraged them to do a second one), it was clearly on the grow, and other networks and producers said "Me too!" and formulated their own "human puzzles."

NBC had *Answer Yes or No*, in which panelists tried to predict how a contestant would respond to a hypothetical situation. ABC introduced *QED*, in which the panelists predicted the outcome of mystery stories. DuMont tried *With This Ring*, in which married celebrity couples judged an engaged couple's responses to questions about their impending marriage. CBS itself tried to get more of a good thing by introducing *Who's Whose*, in which the panelists faced three men and three women and tried to figure out who was married to whom; the idea failed so badly that it was canceled before the show aired on the West Coast. The network even tried a rare daytime panel show, *I'll Buy That*, in which the panel tried to identify items that had been mailed in by home viewers.

ABC tried again with *Who's the Boss?*, in which a panel met employees and tried to guess what famous person they worked for. Some of the panel shows from the Golden Age of Radio saw the gold getting a little tarnished and migrated to television, but *Information Please*, *20 Questions*, *Quiz Kids*, and *It Pays to Be Ignorant* failed to make a significant mark on the new medium.

What's My Line? just had too many intangible advantages. Goodson-Todman found four perfect performers in Francis, publishing magnate Bennett Cerf, up-and-coming local talk show host Steve Allen, and Kilgallen. Daly gave the show an air of class unmatched on other shows. He and the panel represented the elegance and grace of the Manhattan upper class so well that the show's appearance switched from "Sunday best" to "formal wear" early on just to match the sensibilities of the stars. The show would frequently open with Daly and the panel discussing their glamorous lives. Bennett would mention the city where he had recently given a lecture for the rotary club. Dorothy would talk about the big story that she had just finished writing for the *New York Journal-American*. Arlene Francis would mention the tailor responsible for the lavish gown she was wearing that night. Steve Allen would discuss his new book. It might come off condescending if they weren't all so darn charming.

Dumont Viewers Get Down

In the parade of also-rans that followed, there were only two outstanding successes that came from outside of Goodson-Todman and CBS. DuMont introduced a panel game called *Down You Go*, which melded the "human puzzle" and "stump the experts" concept by way of the simple game of Hangman.

Venerable radio program *20 Questions* lasted for six years on television, an impressive run dwarfed by the decade-plus runs that Goodson-Todman panel games enjoyed. On the *20 Questions* panel were teenager Dick Harrison, producer Herb Polesie, series co-creators Fred Van Deventer and Florence Rinard, and guest panelist actor Aldo Ray.

Dr. Bergen Evans, an English professor at Northwestern University in Evanston, commuted to Chicago every week to host the game, joined frequently by panelists including Fran Allison (of *Kukla, Fran, and Ollie* fame), actress Toni Gilman, theater producer Robert Breen (*Porgy and Bess*), stage actress Carmelita Pope (Kim Hunter's understudy in the original Broadway production of *A Streetcar Named Desire*), and Boris Karloff. Dr. Evans would read clues to Hangman puzzles submitted by home viewers, with the viewer collecting money for each panelist who guessed a letter not in the puzzle.

Dr. Evans would sort through sixty thousand pieces of mail every week and personally select his favorites for each program. The panelists would call out letters until they solved the puzzle, or until each of them had called a letter not in the puzzle. Dr. Evans typically favored puzzles and clues that had wordplay ("Bad weather for rats" as a clue for RAINING CATS AND DOGS) although occasionally, he would choose a puzzle just because, for some other reason, it was appropriate. On one evening, the puzzle was a famous quotation from Calvin Coolidge: "I do not choose to run." One of the panelists on the show that night was the governor of Illinois, Adlai Stevenson.

"Do you choose to run?" Dr. Evans asked.

"He does not choose to answer," chimed in actress Francis Coughlin. The year was 1951, a year before Adlai Stevenson chose to run for president and was defeated by Dwight Eisenhower.

Down You Go was somewhat successful, although it was adversely affected by some turbulence. It bounced from DuMont to CBS to ABC to NBC. As network television swiftly drifted from the Second City, *Down You Go* would move from Chicago to New York; Dr. Bergen Evans would air-commute for the New York broadcasts, joined by new faces on the panel. Compared to *What's My Line?*, which stayed in the same time slot on the same network for seventeen years and looked nearly identical from week to week, *Down You Go* couldn't achieve that level of comfort that kept viewers tuning into *Line* so habitually.

A Costume Jewel

Of all the "human puzzle" panel games devised by other producers, arguably the biggest success was a cute entry from Wolf Productions called *Masquerade Party*, which took the Mystery Guest concept to another level. The panel didn't cover their faces with blindfolds. The premise was that the guests on *Masquerade Party* were the ones with their faces covered—in elaborate paint, make-up, latex, false beards, stage glasses, and anything else creating convincing disguises.

The panel on *Masquerade Party* tried to figure out who the celebrity guest was based on the disguises, which usually provided some sort of hint; Magda, Zsa Zsa, and Eva Gabor appeared on the program together, dressed as the Three Weird Sisters from Shakespeare's *Macbeth*. Gloria Swanson hinted at her silent movie past by dressing as a Keystone Cop (and then accidentally walked out of the theater still wearing the moustache). Detective novelist Mickey Spillane was given a scar across the cheek (and Spillane demanded extra blood on his face before he'd go onstage).

The costumes and disguises were designed by former paratrooper George Fiala and former detective Bill Herman, both of whom drifted into television by accident, but loved the job. They would design as many as twenty-seven molds for each mask they created, devoting about fifteen hours for each costume.

Masquerade Party amassed its share of memorable moments over the years. The September 26, 1954, episode was simulcast on all three major networks, with segments taking place in both New York City and Washington, D.C. One of the masqueraders who stumped the panel was Vice President Richard Nixon.

Other episodes had appearances that were memorable for the wrong reason. On August 4, 1958, actor/singer Johnnie Johnston was on the panel that night, and one of the masqueraders was his ex-wife, Katheryn Grayson, disguised as a harem queen. Johnston recognized her immediately ("Well, when you're married to someone for five years, you get to know their points pretty well," he explained after the fact). Grayson was so flustered at how quickly she had been found out that she became curt with the rest of the panel, then walked offstage in the wrong direction.

Masquerade Party had an unsteady eight-year run. Each network would have a turn airing it, usually as a stopgap; it typically reappeared every summer, and then disappeared when the fall lineup was unleashed. And while the panel remained somewhat stable—actress Ilka Chase, comic sexpot Dagmar, and poet Ogden Nash, (coiner of the phrase "Candy is dandy but liquor is quicker") all had long runs, hosts didn't stick around very long. Bud Collyer, Douglas Edwards, Peter Donald, Eddie Bracken, Robert Q. Lewis, and Bert Parks all got a turn before *Masquerade Party* finally left the airwaves for good in 1960.

Play It Again!

But the most successful rip-offs of *What's My Line?* would come from Mark Goodson and Bill Todman. Comedy writer Allan Sherman (later famous for the song "Hello Muddah, Hello Faddah!") surprised Goodson with a threat during a pitch meeting for a new panel show, warning him that he'd better start plagiarizing his own formats because "If you don't, some other producer will."

Goodson and Todman took the advice to heart and unleashed a steady stream of panel shows; so many that it became a joke in the industry that any time the two men saw a table and four chairs set up someplace, they would turn it into a television show.

For ABC, they concocted *The Name's the Same.* The panel faced a parade of contestants, all identified only as Mr. X or Miss X, and had to guess their names. All of the contestants had strange but easily recognizable names: a Kansas City salesman named Mickey Mouse; a fifteen-year-old Massachusetts boy named King Cole; Newburg, New York, native Goldie Locks; and Cincinnati's own Sherry Wine.

Given the nature of the program, the Goodson-Todman staff had stunningly good luck finding topical material. For Election Day 1952, they welcomed two children named Adlai Stevenson and Dwight Eisenhower. When Arthur Godfrey infamously fired singer Julius La Rosa on the air, the next episode featured a contestant named Julius La Rosa, who had been contacted by the staff only hours before show time.

In the long run, the premise proved to be somewhat confining (the show's format was eventually expanded to feature family members of celebrities, and the panel had to guess the famous relative), and unlike *What's My Line?*, with its extraordinarily harmonious regular panel, the panel for *The Name's the Same* was a revolving door of show business; no group seemed to mesh as well.

ABC also hosted another Goodson-Todman experiment called *What's Going On*, a too-ambitious project for the early, technologically limited days of television. The panel tried to guess what a celebrity guest was doing on location as remote cameras kept track of the action; the guest might be washing windows at the Empire State Building, throwing damaged money in a reserve bank's incinerator, or literally counting sheep at a stockyard. Unfortunately, the audience was counting sheep, too, and *What's Going On* disappeared in five weeks.

Over on CBS, Goodson and Todman introduced *It's News to Me.* John Daly hosted the show concurrently with his tenure at *What's My Line?* This one flipped the panel show concept around; it was now the panel furnishing the puzzle to the contestants. An actual object that figured prominently into a recent news story would be shown. One panelist would explain what the object was; sometimes it was a true explanation, sometimes it was a bluff, and a contestant could win or lose five dollars by correctly agreeing or disagreeing with the explanation.

The Goodson-Todman staff was exceedingly diligent in rounding up objects. Other producers would have done the economical thing by having a props department make facsimiles, but Goodson and Todman were adamant that whatever objects were shown had to be the true items. When King Baudoin of Belgium received his crown, he wore a set of royal medals, worn only by kings during their coronation. Three days later, those very medals were on John Daly's desk as a contestant tried to figure out what they were. In the midst of the Korean War, the panel demonstrated a tetrahedron, a weapon used for puncturing tires on enemy vehicles. The tetrahedron seen on the show had been used in battle earlier in the week, and then shipped across the country to the Goodson-Todman offices in New York. All that work for a game that played out in about ninety seconds.

Watching the kinescopes today reveals a few items that transcend "news" and now qualify as history. On the show's premiere, on May 11, 1951, John Daly showed the panel a baseball, and revealed that the New York Yankees' sensational new outfielder, Mickey Mantle, had hit this ball just a few days earlier for his first major league home run. Mantle himself walked out onstage to take a bow at the end of the game.

The show did occasionally stir up trouble with the newsworthy items they showed off. On one evening, they displayed a one-dollar bill that had been autographed by President Truman. A number of viewers called in expressing their concern, and *It's News to Me* released a statement acknowledging that, technically, yes, the President of the United States had committed a federal offense by defacing currency.

It's News to Me ran for about two years, disappearing on September 12, 1953. In the summer of 1954, it returned for eight weeks as a summer replacement for

Host Dennis James (center) is joined by the panel of *The Name's the Same*, one of many panel shows that languished in the large shadow cast by *What's My Line?* Joining James in this advertisement for sponsor Ralston-Purina are panelists Arnold Stang, Bess Myerson, Joan Alexander, and Gene Rayburn.
Photo courtesy of Micki James

Edward R. Murrow's *Person to Person*. During that summer run, *It's News to Me* was hosted, very appropriately, by Walter Cronkite.

Shh!

By far, the biggest success of Goodson-Todman's in-house ripoffs was one that Allan Sherman himself had proposed the first time he spoke to the bosses: *I've Got a Secret*. Rather than occupations or strange names, *I've Got a Secret* welcomed contestants who had odd facts to reveal about themselves: "I dived into an empty swimming pool"; "I've been struck by lightning eight times"; "I went on a date with Marilyn Monroe and she paid for dinner." And there was host Garry Moore's personal favorite: A ten-year-old boy had the secret "I collected forty bugs for a school project," and the boy's two-year-old brother added the secret: "I ate them all."

I've Got a Secret premiered in the summer of 1952 and initially looked quite a bit like *What's My Line?* It was quiet, it was smart, and the panelists asked probing questions. As time went by, it started looking less and less like a panel game and more and more like a variety show. Panelists Bill Cullen, Faye Emerson, Henry Morgan, and Jayne Meadows gradually stopped taking the game seriously, an attitude spearheaded by Morgan, who really didn't seem to be all that interested in the show. The laid-back attitude of the panel immediately made it stand out from shows like *20 Questions*, where the Van Deventers really played to win, and *What's My Line?*, where panelist Dorothy Kilgallen once went backstage and cried because she hadn't guessed an occupation in three weeks.

And then there were the secrets themselves. Secrets like "My name is Ivy Ivy and I have poison ivy" were perfectly amusing, but *I've Got a Secret* quickly decided that the real fun was in secrets that could be demonstrated. The show welcomed a six-year-old billiards master, a man who crammed six lit cigars into his mouth and whistled the song "Smoke Gets in Your Eyes," a man who could palm ten tennis balls simultaneously, a pickpocket who stole an audience member's wallet, and a man who pedaled a twenty-foot-tall unicycle. The show even welcomed a young drummer named Pete Best, whose secret was that two years earlier, he had left his job as a member of the Beatles.

Each week on *I've Got a Secret*, a celebrity guest appeared with a secret, usually one that the staff had conjured up for them. Howard Duff and Ida Lupino, equipped with a variety of props, broke obsolete laws while the panel questioned them. Buster Keaton judged the panel in a pie-eating contest, and Liberace gave them a crash course in the piano before playing tunes with them. Johnny Carson shot an arrow through the apple on Garry Moore's head. And some of the secrets were too grand for the studio to contain them. Paul Newman revealed that he had disguised himself as a hot dog vendor earlier in the day and sold Henry Morgan a frank.

I've Got a Secret managed to survive and thrive despite plenty of changes onstage and off. CBS forced the show to terminate a stagehand, Joe Papp (who later established The Public Theater and created Shakespeare in the Park) because he was accused of communist leanings. Producer Allan Sherman had done a bang-up job for the show he created over the years—when scheduled celebrity guest Paul Douglas refused to have a snowball fight with the panel, Sherman ditched him and rounded up a more cooperative star, Dane Clark, at the last minute. On another night, when a man who sculpted animals out of butter had his flight into New York canceled, Sherman miraculously managed to locate a different butter sculptor to make use of the four hundred pounds of butter onstage—but Sherman got himself fired after a segment involving Tony Curtis that Mark Goodson had found so boring that he took action. (Of note was that during the segment, Curtis revealed that he was about to become a father; of course, the baby would be a girl, named Jamie Lee Curtis.) Jayne Meadows and Faye Emerson would both depart the show, to be replaced by Betsy Palmer and Bess Myerson. Moore would eventually depart the show himself, to be replaced by Steve Allen.

But while show personnel came and went, the audience remained year after year. The secret of success, or, in this case, the success of *Secret*, was that it was run by people who weren't afraid to mix things up a little. Gil Fates, who worked as a producer on both *What's My Line?* and *I've Got a Secret*, lamented in his memoirs that *What's My Line?* seemed obsessed with consistency. "That's the way we've always done it" was the standard reply when anyone suggested doing something slightly different. Host John Daly would often tell Fates to "get yourself a new boy" if Fates suggested anything out-of-the-ordinary for a future segment. Fates termed it "hardening of the creative arteries."

Secret was just the opposite. Garry Moore proudly explained in 1960, "The success of *Secret* lies in its basic format, which allows us to do anything. It changes every week, with something new to see and talk about. We always have one guest with an unusual secret that he has with him. One week, there's a guest whose secret might be that he has a snake in his pocket; the next week a guest has with him a Gutenberg Bible."

Whereas viewers watched *What's My Line?* as a habit, they tuned into *I've Got a Secret* because they just had to see what was going to happen this week.

I've Got a Secret and *What's My Line?* both met their demise in 1967; it had been a fifteen-year run for *Secret* and a seventeen-year run for *Line*. It marked the end of an era; all of the imitators had expired years earlier. By the time the two Goodson-Todman stalwarts were canceled, they weren't just television institutions; they were seemingly relics of a bygone era. The game show had become something different by that point, and the concept of a "human puzzle" had turned into a missing piece.

8

When Goodson Met Todman

Some Guys Get All The Credit

Mark Goodson-Bill Todman Production!" This announcement, an audible thumbprint for three decades, was made at the end of thousands of episodes of classic game shows. But who were those guys?

The Beginning of an Empire

One was a Johns Hopkins School of Medicine student, one was a Phi Betta Kappa student with a degree in Economics. Both took sharp left turns into broadcasting. The Johns Hopkins School of Medicine student, Bill Todman, became an advertising copywriter. The economics major, Mark Goodson, became a soap opera announcer. But when they put their heads together, they unexpectedly became the most successful tandem in game show history.

In 1939, Goodson created and hosted a radio quiz for local station KFRC in San Francisco. He called it *Pop the Question*; contestants threw darts at a board covered with balloons. The color of the balloons they popped would determine the value of the next question. Goodson would later admit it was a silly premise in retrospect; it involved an athletic skill and colors, elements totally lost on a radio audience. Two years later, a fellow University of California graduate, Ralph Edwards, encouraged Goodson to move to New York.

Goodson and Todman met when they were working on a local New York quiz called *Battle of the Boroughs*, a contest between players from each of New York City's five boroughs. Goodson was announcer, and Todman was a writer. They found they had a couple things in common. They were both at crossroads and a career change; Goodson unexpectedly became stricken by mic fright and didn't want to be an announcer anymore, and Todman was looking to get out of copywriting and into freelance producing. The men also found that they had a fondness for games. They formed a production company, making the best of their respective skills; Goodson would develop games, and Todman would be the salesman and the man in charge of the money.

Together, they conjured up *Winner Take All*, an innovative game that invented "buzzing in" and the concept of the "returning champion." Goodson later attributed both ideas to his time on soap operas; he figured audiences were drawn to soap operas for the familiar characters and the constant conflicts they encountered. Contestants who continued playing as long as they continued winning became familiar characters, and by racing to hit their button before their opponent, they'd be in constant conflict.

In 1942, Goodson and Todman pooled together fifteen dollars to make an "audition program" (today it would be called a run-through) of *Winner Take All*; that's five dollars for the acetate they recorded it on, five dollars for the ham and eggs they fed their friends who acted as contestants, and five dollars to pay the engineer. Their first pitch to CBS went poorly. An executive listened to the audition program and wrote them a gruff note reading "We might as well dramatize a poker game."

They continued toiling at various gigs for the next four years until CBS Radio listened to the audition program again. This time, the network bit, and *Winner Take All* premiered on June 3, 1946. Mark Goodson and Bill Todman quickly became the network's go-to guys for new games, while *Winner Take All* host Bill Cullen became a go-to master of ceremonies. *Winner Take All* would cross over to television, and enjoy six years on the air.

What Should We Play Next?

Goodson and Todman continued developing new radio games quickly, like *Spin to Win*—D. J./M. C. Warren Hull would spin a record until a listener phoned in and identified it; the contestant could win a cash jackpot by identifying a second song, played backward—and *Rate Your Mate*, in which half of a married couple would try to predict if their spouse would know the answers to trivia questions.

They would transition into television by the end of the 1940s. Over the next thirty years, they would churn out *Beat the Clock, What's My Line?, It's News to Me, The Name's the Same, I've Got a Secret, Judge for Yourself, Two for the Money, What's Going On, Make the Connection, Choose Up Sides, The Price is Right, To Tell the Truth, Play Your Hunch, Say When!!, Number Please, Password, The Match Game, Missing Links, Get the Message, Call My Bluff, Snap Judgment, He Said She Said, Tattletales, Now You See It, Showoffs, Family Feud, Double Dare, The Better Sex, Card Sharks, Mindreaders,* and *Password Plus*. If you mistakenly credited them with a game show that they didn't produce, Goodson and Todman were hardly likely to correct you. Goodson pointed out that the average television viewer was under the mistaken impression that they were responsible for *every* game show, and he didn't see any advantage to be gained by correcting that misperception.

Haters Gonna Hate

Goodson and Todman were keenly aware that game shows weren't the most respected genre in broadcasting. Goodson referred to the prevailing attitude toward them as "upper brow contempt"; regular folks getting excited over winning a refrigerator while an emcee oozed congratulatory messages and the occasional joke was just so undignified. Goodson bluntly answered, "We're not in the uplift business, we're in TV to make money."

One big happy family, the Goodson-Todman empire, represented here by the cast of *The Name's the Same.* Standing with host Dennis James are Mark Goodson (left) and Bill Todman (right). Joining them are panelists Arnold Stang, Roger Price, Bess Myerson, Gene Rayburn, and Joan Alexander.

Photo courtesy of Micki James

Some barbs were playful teasing—there was a day when Bill Todman came into the studio, his arms filled with small appliances to be given away as prizes. He lost his balance and dropped the coffee pot, the toaster, etc., everywhere, and comedy writer Goodman Ace yelled "Hey Todman, you dropped your script!"

Some detraction came off almost as a compliment; Mark Goodson was particularly proud of a snide quip from a writer who said, "How can you explain how Mark Goodson and Bill Todman are able to make a fortune out of two tables and six chairs?" Two tables and six chairs were exactly the same set up for no less than six different shows that the two men developed for television, but one way or another, they would find a way to give the game being played on that furniture different characteristics and different atmosphere, justifying each one's existence.

Todman had a criticism that he rather enjoyed fending off. Game shows were so brainless that it was easy to come up with a new one, so creating a game show wasn't exactly a big achievement. As Todman said, "Our detractors keep telling us how amazingly easy it is to think of new gimmicks. Well then, how come networks or advertisers keep returning to *us*?"

The Factory

Networks and advertisers kept returning because audiences kept returning. The games Goodson and Todman cranked out were loved by the masses. How did

Goodson and Todman do it? Well, we can say definitely how they *didn't* do it. There was an urban legend in show business that the two men once deliberately locked themselves in an office and brainstormed for an entire weekend, until they had come up with thirty different ideas for game shows. They then spent their entire careers going through the ideas like a checklist, selling one after another.

Well, not exactly. There was more to Mark Goodson-Bill Todman Productions than Goodson and Todman. More accurately, the two men were foremen, overseeing a workshop of highly creative writers, producers, directors, and other staffers. Regardless of their job title, Goodson and Todman wanted and demanded their input, feedback, and even criticism. With a hit show worked and re-worked to perfection meaning potential contracts and fees in the millions, Goodson and Todman had no tolerance for yes-men or empty suits. Everybody was encouraged to contribute, and to refine.

Case in point: Goodson and Gil Fates, in 1949, whipped up a format called *Stop the Camera*. A camera would pan across the faces in the studio audience. Scattered throughout would be several celebrities; a home viewer would be called and encouraged to yell, "Stop the camera!" when the camera reached the famous face. In the testing stages the game didn't really work. One day, a staffer named Bob Bach walked in the office and mentioned to Gil Fates that while he was riding in the subway, he looked at another man on the train and began to wonder what he did for a living. Together, they developed a revised version of *Stop the Camera*. Ten ordinary people would be seated in front of the camera. A home viewer would be told that one of them was, for example, a bartender, and the home viewer would yell "Stop the camera!" when the camera was on the bartender . . . and then on the teacher . . . and then on the police officer . . . and so on. Stopping the camera on the correct face ten times in a row would award a big jackpot.

In Fates's words: "This worked better, but not better enough."

Around the office, they kept toying with what was now being called *Occupation Unknown*. The ten people were cut down to a single person. The home viewer was replaced by a panel. "Stopping the camera" was thrown away entirely, and the blind guessing was replaced by "20 Questions"–style rules. The format finally perfected, the Goodson-Todman staff devoted a full eight-hour workday to hammering out one final detail: Should it be called *What's Your Line?* or *What's My Line?* At the end of the day, the "My's" had it, and CBS wanted it.

Frank Wayne and Bob Howard were two other valued members of the Goodson-Todman staff. They created the zany stunts seen on *Beat the Clock* throughout the 1950s. In 1961, Frank Wayne came into the office to test a new idea. He gave everybody a piece of paper and a pen and told them, "Write a fact about elephants." The point of the exercise was to demonstrate that, given a seemingly wide-open question, everyone in the room wrote a very narrow range of answers; almost everybody wrote, "THEY HAVE TRUNKS" or "THEY ARE GRAY." Frank Wayne's experiment led to *The Match Game*. A decade later, the durable *Match Game* would inspire a Goodson-Todman spinoff where contestants tried to match, not each other, but the respondents in a national survey. *Family Feud* was born, but only after two years of refining and revising.

In 1980, a young staffer named Steve Ryan discovered an old game called "Hex" that made use of hexagonal game pieces. Using a jigsaw, Ryan built his own game board, brought it into the office, and demonstrated the idea he had. Before the end of the year, it was on the air, under the title *Blockbusters*.

But if all these people were the ones coming up with the game shows, what was Goodson doing? While he would rake in far more credit than he really deserved for creating the shows done under his banner—as far as any research can determine, the Goodson-Todman radio game shows were really the only ones plucked from his own brain—his staff adamantly maintained that Goodson deserves unlimited credit for his skill as an editor. He could zero in on flaws in faulty formats, and make alterations until it worked. He could take bad ideas and make them good, and he could take ideas that were already good and make them sensational.

It's in the Details

But working for Goodson-Todman required enormous amounts of patience. Goodson was a nitpicker, a trait that he demanded of virtually everybody else on the staff. An eight-hour workday devoted to the issue of "Your" or "My" was hardly an isolated incident. Meetings like that happened often. When *Password* was being developed in 1961, a number of staffers spent five hours trying to figure out how the host should hand off envelopes to the players for each round; should he reach out to them, or should he walk to them? Sound effects were relentlessly fretted over; was a bell in the proper key? Was the buzzer too harsh? If anybody complained, it fell on deaf ears. Goodson and Todman's bank accounts more than justified the amount of time they were spending on issues that struck others as inane.

This didn't exactly mean that everybody in the company was becoming extremely wealthy. Goodson "didn't believe in royalties," according to longtime producer Ira Skutch, so if an idea that you came up with ended up having a long run, or got sold to a network in a foreign country, you didn't see that revenue. If anybody asked for a raise, they were bound to hear a lecture from Bill Todman about how he had a box at home for pencils that he accidentally took from work in his pocket, and when the box got full, he would return all the pencils to the office to save money.

Attitudes about money could be quite contradictory. Staffers heard the "pencil" speech time and again, but it was whispered around the office that several of the most valuable employees were getting million-dollar bonuses at Christmastime. Staffers got raises if a show had a demonstrable change in viewership after a change that staffer suggested had been put into effect. And when it came to ethics and fair play on the air, Goodson had a mantra that "nothing is more expensive than bad publicity." If it seemed that something hadn't gone right during a game—a buzzer malfunctioned once or twice, or a host mispronounced a key word in a question—Goodson would not hesitate to cut a check for the loser of that game to atone for it.

Second in Command

In 2010, game show announcer and author Randy West explained, "Todman was a master salesman, adept at the art of the two-martini lunch that lubricated commerce in the TV and ad industry at the time. Goodson was always self-conscious about his not fitting in with that crowd, and Todman was his perfect front man . . . a WASP member of the country club set, with an impeccable society pedigree by virtue of his father's well-respected accounting firm."

Todman had a valuable function beyond pitching the shows—he also invested the company's money wisely. Unbeknown to most viewers, Mark Goodson and Bill Todman co-owned numerous local radio stations and newspapers, ensuring a steady cash flow for the company even during periods when the popularity of game shows ebbed.

But the Goodson-Todman staff was keenly aware that there was tension between the partners. Bob Stewart, a producer for the company in the late 1950s and early 1960s, observed that Todman "seemed to be along for the ride." He was almost never in creative meetings. Ira Skutch remembered in his memoirs that any time he tried to contribute an idea to a format in development, Goodson would harshly rebuke him by barraging him with several questions in a row; when Todman hesitated in answering one, Goodson would invariably say, "See that? You don't really understand what we're talking about!"

As Goodson-Todman game show host Gene Rayburn put it, Todman was seemingly "emasculated" by Goodson. He stayed in his office for the most part and made pitches—a job that, because of the company's reputation, became understandably easier as the years went by, to the point where you couldn't even call that a job for him. Eventually, Goodson hired another money man, Bud Austin, who assumed most of Todman's duties and, in most cases, increased the fees the company was receiving for its shows. In the 1960s, Giraud Chester became executive vice president of Mark Goodson-Bill Todman Productions. Todman moved to Florida, and when Goodson-Todman Productions expanded and set up office space in Hollywood, Todman didn't even have an office in the West Coast branch.

Bill Todman died in 1979, but his name stayed in the production company for another three years. When the company was renamed "Mark Goodson Productions" in 1982, Todman was acknowledged in a distinctive way. All of Goodson's announcers were instructed to say the name of the production company with a brief pause after Goodson's name. "This has been a Mark Goodson . . . Television Production." Every episode of every game show ended with a moment of silence for Bill Todman.

9

Funny Guys

Hitting the Joke-pot

 ure, a good game should be entertaining, but many of the early TV games were gut-busters. The game was secondary, and the shows were actually designed as vehicles for their funny hosts.

Say the Secret Word

Producer John Guedel was in the studio for a March 1947 radio show with a sensational pair of guest stars: Bob Hope and Groucho Marx. Bob was approaching the apex of his career, and Groucho was arguably on the way down. The Marx Brothers were done as an act, Groucho's movie career stalled, and four attempts at a regular radio series had all failed. But that night, Hope dropped his script on the floor. Groucho, up for a challenge, dropped his, and they ad-libbed an entirely new routine.

Guedel asked Groucho after the show if he felt capable of doing that all the time. Groucho insisted he could . . . but quickly recoiled when Guedel suggested hosting a quiz show. A big-time movie star, part of one of the most popular comedy teams in history, reduced to asking trivia questions? Guedel insisted it was the best use of his talents; the quiz itself didn't even matter. They just needed contestants onstage so Groucho would have people to talk to; the way Guedel saw it, no conversation could fail. If the contestants were dullards, Groucho could get laughs himself. If the contestants were lively and engaging, they could just get the laughs themselves.

You Bet Your Life premiered on CBS Radio on October 27, 1947. By the time it finally ended production fourteen years later, it would be Groucho's signature work in show business. Hosting a quiz show wasn't a step backward; it was a most perfect fit.

The actual game of *You Bet Your Life*, if it really mattered, was that two contestants pulled from the studio audience were staked $100 and then asked to wager part or all of their money on each of four questions. There was also a chance to win a $100 bonus by saying "the secret word," a word revealed only to the radio audience at the start of the program.

But the real magic of the show was the contestant interview. Groucho's conversations with the contestants occupied about 75 percent of the show's content, with Groucho firing off a mix of scripted lines and lightning quick ad-libs while getting to know the players.

Clergyman: Groucho, I want to thank you for all the enjoyment you have given the world.

Groucho: And I want to thank you for all the enjoyment that you've taken out of it.

The show was tailor-made to Groucho's strengths. It was never a live program; at Groucho's request, it was pre-recorded. Groucho adjusted his act for years onstage based on audience reactions; he didn't like the restrictions of broadcasting, where he'd have to stop the show at a certain time no matter what. So, Groucho was free to talk with the contestants as long as he wanted, and he'd only move on once he was sure he had wrung every drop of humor from the conversations. Most episodes actually ran around sixty to ninety minutes before editing, and then the tape was cut down to the best thirty minutes for broadcast.

In the following extract, Groucho is talking to a couple that wed after a series of chaperoned dates:

Groucho: Did you just go out with her, or were there other women, too?

Husband: No, I took her mother, too.

Groucho: What was her mother selling?

Husband: She was a perfect chaperone, so we took her along with us.

Groucho: You mean you went out on a date, you took the old lady along too?

Husband: Yes indeed!

Groucho: And what happened? . . . Silly question, right?

Husband: Well . . . now we have five children.

Groucho: Well, when you went out on these dates, what did the chaperone do? Curl up with a good book?

Husband: No, they did the same thing as we did.

Groucho: So you have *ten* children now?

Grouchovision

You Bet Your Life would eventually make its way to NBC Radio, where it would be one of the network's last big programs (it ran until 1956). That fall, NBC added a second *You Bet Your Life* episode each week, produced for television. Again, the television version was produced to Groucho's strength. With the dawn of videotape still a few years away, virtually all television was live, but Groucho insisted on having the show filmed and treated just like the radio show; he talked all he wanted and let the editing crew worry about the thirty-minute restriction.

Groucho could be in big trouble if he has to tell this contestant he's a loser. The six-hundred-pound wrestler Haystacks Calhoun is a contestant on *You Bet Your Life.*

You Bet Your Life was so popular that it launched a few contestants to fame. Pedro Gonzalez-Gonzalez, whose baffling last name delighted Groucho, wound up with a movie career. John Wayne was watching that night and enjoyed the show so much that he personally called in some favors. Pedro Gonzalez-Gonzalez would appear in twelve films, almost all of them with the Duke himself. A forty-one-year-old housewife named Phyllis Diller, trying to build a career as a stand-up comic, was a contestant in 1958 and despite a performance that she considered awful (in her own words, she talked too slow and she was too visibly nervous), the jokes that she slipped into the conversation won over Groucho and the audience, and she became a show business mainstay for five decades. William Blatty won a $10,000 jackpot during his appearance in 1960 and told Groucho that he would use the money to support himself while he took a year off from his job and wrote a novel; he wrote *The Exorcist.*

The Winners and the Hoosier

As Groucho's *You Bet Your Life* was charming audiences on radio and television, game show kings Mark Goodson and Bill Todman, probably feeling that they had a reputation to maintain, introduced their own version of *You Bet Your Life.*

Two for the Money debuted on NBC in 1952, the same network as *You Bet Your Life*, and stayed there for a season before drifting over to CBS. The host was Herb Shriner, a soft-spoken, awkward comedian who had originally risen to fame as a harmonica player. The show had a live band, led by accordionist Milton DeLugg, and Shriner would often open the show with a musical number, providing the mouth organ.

The game involved a pair of contestants pulled from the audience, who would, like on *You Bet Your Life*, engage in a lengthy chat with the host before the game got rolling.

Shriner: I imagine that driving a bus can be tough work sometimes.

Contestant: It's real murder.

Shriner: Bus company must have a good lawyer, then.

When it was finally time for the game, the contestants were asked three questions, each with multiple answers, and each played against a fifteen-second clock. For the first question, correct answers were worth five dollars apiece; for example, if seven correct answers were given, the payoff was $35. For the second question, that total would be the value of each correct answer. If, in our example, ten correct answers were given to that second question, the third would be played for $350 per correct answer.

Two for the Money tended to give away quite a bit more money than *You Bet Your Life*; it also tended to give away more money than Mark Goodson and Bill Todman would have liked. One of the hazards of the show was that the staff had trouble gauging the level of difficulty for certain questions; staffers would act as stand-in contestants for rehearsals, but occasionally, the real contestants drastically outshone the stand-ins.

One night, a couple was on their third question, with a stake of $350 per correct answer. The question was "Give as many words as possible ending in the letters TH." The staffers at rehearsal were only able to name a handful, finding it a tough question. When the clock started in the actual game, one contestant immediately blurted out "Thirteenth." Her partner answered "Fourteenth," and they kept going until the bell finally sounded and they had fired off fourteen answers, for $4,900. Another week, a question was "Name a football team competing in any of the upcoming Bowl games." As it happened, the contestant picker selected two college-age men from the audience to play; they rattled off twelve teams and won $3,600.

Though *Two for the Money* never had a legacy quite like the one that *You Bet Your Life* would enjoy, it performed respectably. CBS scheduled it after *The Jackie Gleason Show* on Saturdays, and the two programs performed so strongly that the competition on NBC, *Your Show of Shows*, ceased production a year later.

There was one key difference between *You Bet Your Life* and *Two for the Money* that probably doomed the latter program. Groucho Marx was fifty-seven years old when *You Bet Your Life* went on the air. He had already seen the greatest heights of show business and viewed *You Bet Your Life* as semi-retirement. The fact that the show lasted fourteen years was a bonus, as far as he was concerned. Herb Shriner was barely thirty-four years old and felt like the program was holding him back. In the fall of 1956, CBS pulled *Two for the Money* from its schedule and Shriner eagerly signed to do a variety show that would last only three episodes. *Two for the Money* would return the following spring with a new host, Sam Levenson, who was doubtlessly much happier to be there, but the program only lasted six more months.

Though *Two for the Money* expired after a total of only about five years, it too had its share of success stories. Dr. Mason Gross, the show's judge, would serve as president of Rutgers University for twelve years. Dr. Gross's substitute, who sat in the judge's chair during Gross's vacations, went on to greater things, too; his name was Walter Cronkite. Another newsman, Tom Brokaw, was just seventeen years old when he appeared on the show as a contestant; his partner was the then-governor of South Dakota, Joe Foss. Together, they won $1,200. Brokaw was supposed to fly home the next day, but Foss called Brokaw's parents and convinced them it might be a good idea to let the youngster stay a few extra days; Brokaw credited the experience with helping him set his goals for life. The final big success to come

The two hosts of *Two for the Money*, Sam Levenson and Herb Shriner.

out of *Two for the Money* was the man who briefly served as Sam Levenson's announcer: Ed McMahon.

Bill to Pay

Bill Cullen was a master of ceremonies by trade; he had never been a comedian and had a short (and by his own admission, dismal) tenure as a joke writer. But being a master of ceremonies brought out the best in him, particularly his sense of humor. So, when more producers began saying, "Me too!" and formulating their own comedy quiz shows, Bill Cullen got the nod to host three of the m.

The first, for NBC Radio, was *Walk a Mile*, so named in honor of its sponsor, Camel cigarettes ("I'd walk a mile for a Camel"). Bill proved to be game when it came to whipping off funny lines—"I wanted to write a book of terms used by golfers, but then I found out most of them are unprintable"—or chatting up a storm with contestants.

Despite the tremendous power that Camel wielded over the show, they recognized the appeal of the charming host and decided that they didn't have to dominate the program quite so much. Camel continued sponsoring the game, but cheerfully allowed it to be retitled *The Bill Cullen Show*. NBC appreciated Bill so much that they gave him a second comedy quiz, *Bank on the Stars*, on the television network, during the spring and summer of 1954.

Perhaps the greatest reward that Bill got from his time as host of *Walk a Mile* and *Bank on the Stars* was a seal of approval from the master himself. The one and only Groucho Marx referred to Bill as "the second-wittiest man on the air."

Paar Excellence

Bill Cullen was actually the second host of *Bank on the Stars*. The show originally debuted in the summer of 1953 with another host, Jack Paar. A gifted monologist, raconteur, and conversationalist, was well-suited to a comedy quiz, even if his sense of humor was a little more low-key than the typical host. Paar, who would go on to host *The Tonight Show* in 1957 and have an extremely rocky five-year tenure at that job, rather seemed to enjoy hosting a quiz show, and had some fun greeting the audience at the start of the show.

> **Jack:** Please don't give the correct answers. And I'll tell you why. We once had a sweet old lady, an old maid, I think, up on this stage. And she won a great, great deal of money. Later, I learned that she had a wire running down her leg to her sister in the audience who had an encyclopedia. So, I want to say, anybody who comes on stage tonight with anything dragging, we are cutting it off.

A Bunch of Dummies

Usually, you just need one host on a game show, but in 1956 CBS introduced a game show called *Do You Trust Your Wife?* and called on a quartet of emcees: Edgar Bergen, Charlie McCarthy, Mortimer Snerd, and Effie Klinker. Bergen was the ventriloquists and the rest were dummies, although their jokes could be pretty smart:

> **Contestant:** My wife and I have a television rental and repair business.
>
> **Charlie:** When did you decide not to go straight?
>
> **Edgar:** Is it a trend to have more than one television set in the house now?
>
> **Contestant:** Oh yes. I even had one customer who bought one for his bathroom.
>
> **Charlie:** Well, where does he go during the commercials, then?

The game was played by married couples. A husband heard a question and could choose to answer it himself, or he could trust his wife to supply the answer. A special feature of the program was the Trust Fund, a special question with multiple answers. Two couples competed against each other to give as many answers as possible; the couple that gave the most correct answers received $100 a week for one year, and could return again as long as they kept winning, in hopes of winning $100 a week for two years, three years, or more. One couple managed to win $100 a week for nineteen years.

Here's Johnny! (No, Really!)

Comedy quizzes had always been the domain of prime-time, but ABC, in dire need of strong shows for its daytime lineup (NBC and CBS both started their network schedules at 7:00 a.m.; ABC was in such rough shape that they didn't start until 3:00 in the afternoon) snapped up *Do You Trust Your Wife?* for a weekday afternoon slot. Edgar Bergen wasn't interested in doing five days a week, so the network hired a comic with a string of failed shows on his résumé; his name was Johnny Carson.

Johnny: There are good fencers and there are bad fencers. I suppose the difference is that a bad fencer is dead. . . . Do they still do much dueling in Europe?

Contestant: It's supposed to be outlawed . . . but they do a lot of it, especially in France.

Johnny: Why is that?

Contestant: It takes a lot of nerve.

Johnny: I suppose they do have a lot of DeGaulle.

A self-taught magician, Johnny Carson brought to his comedy quiz was his willingness to try anything once. Groucho occasionally danced, but that was as physical as the other comedy quiz hosts got. Johnny strongly favored contestants with unusual occupations, and he wanted to learn how to do what they did. The interviews on *Do You Trust Your Wife?* with Johnny Carson almost always culminated in a demonstration of some kind; Johnny dueled with the professional fencer. A professional pitchman taught Johnny how to use some of his kitchen gadgets. An auto racer showed him how to drive a midget car in laps (Johnny crashed into the set).

A few months into the run of the daytime *Do You Trust Your Wife?*, two changes were made to the show. The first was the title. The feeling was that the title was too confining for a show that needed to churn out five episodes a week; the contestants *had* to be married couples. So, the title was changed to *Who Do You Trust?* and the scope was expanded accordingly; *anybody* could be a contestant, so long as there were two of them.

Announcer Bill Nimmo departed from the program and Johnny Carson personally auditioned the replacements. After a conversation and a handshake that barely took one minute, he selected Ed McMahon. Carson saw something special in McMahon and made him more prominent in the program. He was more than an announcer; he was a sidekick. Carson even asked the program's wardrobe designer to coordinate their suits to emphasize the difference in size.

Johnny Carson and Ed McMahon began a thirty-year-plus professional relationship on the game show *Who Do You Trust?*

To say the least, *Who Do You Trust?* turned Carson into a hot property. He captured NBC's attention when he did a sparkling job filling in for Jack Paar one night on *The Tonight Show*, and Johnny got the gig full-time when Paar quit in 1962. Woody Woodbury took over *Who Do You Trust?*, but even that early in his career, Johnny Carson left some big shoes to fill. *Who Do You Trust?* went off the air in 1963 and formally ended the era of the comedy quiz show.

Life After *Life*

Groucho Marx, eager to sell *You Bet Your Life* into syndication, had ended the show in 1961 so he could do exactly that. He followed that with *Tell It to Groucho*, which

flopped on CBS and was gone in only a few months. But reruns of *You Bet Your Life*, sold into syndication under the title *The Best of Groucho*, became a television institution, even more so than the show had been when it was first-run. They became popular late-night programming for independent stations; they helped fill the schedule for early cable TV channels; they even found their way onto PBS in the 1990s. In fairness, the other comedy quiz shows were pretty darn good in their own right, but announcer George Fenneman wasn't kidding around about the way he introduced the host each week on *You Bet Your Life*. There really was "one and only" Groucho, and nobody could follow his act.

Groucho lives on in reruns. *You Bet Your Life* is a perennial favorite.

10

The Stunt Men

Time to Win

uestions and answers are plenty of fun, but pie throwing and pancake flipping races brought plenty of excitement to early TV game shows, too. Here's a look at the games where the fun got physical.

How the Clock Was Made

In 1948, Mark Goodson and Bill Todman developed *Time's A Wastin'* for CBS Radio. Host Bud Collyer would read a series of questions to a contestant as a clock ticked away, with a little bit of cash disappearing with every second. In 1949, the nighttime quiz disappeared, but fundamentally the same game appeared in the daytime with host Bill Cullen, now under the title *Beat the Clock*.

As Goodson and Todman moved into television, they were concerned about developing programs that actually made use of the new medium. They didn't want

The most popular stunt game of all time; Bud Collyer hosts *Beat the Clock*.

to put a show on TV just for the sake of having a show on TV, they wanted to make sure they were using the newly available visual element to its fullest. *What's My Line?*, for example, was a yes-or-no-questions guessing game that required the audience to see precisely nothing to follow the game. For the first few years of the show, *What's My Line?* would have the contestant start each game by doing a short walk up and down the stage and subject themselves to a peculiar "inspection" by the panel. Goodson-Todman actually got angry letters from viewers because of how condescending and dehumanizing it looked to subject the contestants to physical scrutiny, but the reason they did it that way, Goodson later admitted, was because it was the only idea anybody could think of for *What's My Line?* that couldn't be done on radio.

Beat the Clock had the same problem; you didn't really need to see it on TV. So,

Goodson and Todman reinvented it, jettisoning the questions and answers in favor of challenging physical tasks—the show called them "problems."

Beat the Clock premiered on CBS-TV on March 23, 1950, with Bud Collyer returning as host. A married couple would face a pair of problems, worth $100 and $200, and a "Jackpot Clock" in which the wife would see the words of a common expression scrambled on a board, and had to unscramble them for a prize. Among the problems:

- The husband and wife would sit on a couch cushion and scoot forward until they both reached a post on the other side of a stage.
- The husband wore a long wool cap that was tethered to a pole hanging from the ceiling; he had to run back and forth, picking up paper cups all over the stage, without the cap losing its slack and getting yanked off.
- A huge bowl of gelatin topped with whipped cream was brought out; the contestant had to fish out the ping-pong ball at the bottom of the ball with only the mouth.
- A telephone switchboard was rigged so that most of the switches were attached to pies. The wife had to remove switches, one at a time, until she found the one that wouldn't launch a pie into her husband's face.

Time Trials

Crafting the stunts, as silly as they were, was an example of the perfectionist attitude that permeated the Goodson-Todman offices. Most were created by Goodson-Todman staffers Frank Wayne and Bob Howard, though a young up-and-comer named Neil Simon contributed, too. A number of elements reappeared; tea cups and saucers appeared almost every week, as did cans of Reddi-Whip. The sky was the limit for whatever the staff could think of for stunts, with only one rule they had to follow; the stunts had to involve either common household objects or items that could be easily purchased. Goodson-Todman strongly encouraged home viewers to practice the stunts if they wanted to be contestants.

From there, a group of thirty stand-ins would perform the stunts; they were mostly actors between jobs in the New York area. Goodson-Todman would bring in half of them on a Thursday afternoon to test the new stunts they thought of during the week. The stand-ins would spend a full work day swinging a paper cup across the floor to scoop up a ping-pong ball, or stacking cups and saucers on top of a beach ball, just to see if this batch of new stunts was usable. If none of the stand-ins on Thursday were successful in a stunt, the staff would discard it. If it was successful, the other half of the stand-ins would be brought in on Saturday to perform the stunts one more time to see if there was anything further that the staff could do to make them easier—or in some cases, make them harder.

One stand-in proved particularly skillful, to the point that he lost his job. He solved every stunt the staff handed him, until the staff decided that he was an unreliable standard for figuring out what a contestant might do. The actor was disappointed about losing his gig, but he would eventually recover and find other work. His name was James Dean.

On each week's program, an alarm bell would sound at some point and the couple onstage was given a chance to solve the Bonus Stunt, a particularly difficult problem, for a cash jackpot that grew $100 per attempt until it was finally solved.

A pair of toupees hanging from strings were separated by only a few feet; to win the cash, a contestant had to put on a hollowed-out top hat, then stoop beneath the toupees and figure out a way to get both of them inside the top hat at the same time, without use of the hands. It took eight months and thirty-two episodes until somebody finally did it for $3,200.

When a Monday-through-Friday daytime version of *Beat the Clock* was introduced, a bonus stunt went 201 days without being solved; a pair of pegs was fixed onto a table and contestants had to roll rings across the table so that each peg had one ring around it. The winning couple took home a staggering $20,100. Occasionally, the show would receive angry letters from viewers about the "impossible" bonus stunts, for which the show had an interesting retort. During the "warm-up" in the studio that preceded each episode, Frank Wayne would come out onstage and flawlessly perform the bonus stunt himself. The point being that, again, these stunts could be practiced.

Clock Blockers

Beat the Clock was an easy target for critics who set their sights on game shows. Watching people get pies shoved in their faces or soaked from head-to-toe by a seltzer bottle just for a shot at some money? "Childish," "juvenile," "embarrassing," and just about every possible synonym came up in reviews.

The show appeared to throw critics a bone at one point; with no fanfare, whipped cream suddenly disappeared from *Beat the Clock* in 1957. Had the show "grown up"? Were they, at long last, above doing something so puerile?

Not quite. Whipped cream suddenly reappeared on *Beat the Clock* in the fall of 1960. Bud Collyer explained that it vanished for three years because the staff couldn't think of anything that they hadn't already done involving whipped cream. When a staffer finally walked in with fresh ideas, the whipped cream returned, as did the critics' barbs.

But those critics, and millions of viewers, would be a little surprised to learn that Mark Goodson fully agreed. He once said, "That show came back to haunt me many times. It was not my favorite."

Goodson and Todman both often flippantly said that they got into television mainly to make money, but Goodson craved respect from his peers and felt that he couldn't get it with a show like *Beat the Clock*. Nonetheless, television is a business of giving the audience what they wanted, and for years to come, they wanted more *Beat the Clock*.

Clock Faces

Beat the Clock left its mark on popular culture during its run. There was a *Beat the Clock*–themed episode of the iconic sitcom *The Honeymooners*, with guest star Bud

Collyer playing himself as Jackie Gleason as Ralph Kramden stumbled his way through the problems. The show also proved popular enough that some promotional tie-ins appeared on toy store shelves. Many game shows released board game adaptations over the years, and *Beat the Clock* was certainly no exception, releasing an elaborate board game with small balls, cups, sticks, a mechanical clock, and instructions for stunts. But perhaps more unusual was that *Beat the Clock* also released an official doll. Roxanne, the pretty blonde model who helped set up the props for each stunt, would conclude the messier, pie-and-seltzer problems by coming out onstage with a Sylvania "Blue Dot for Sure Shot" camera and snap a souvenir picture of the disheveled winners. She proved so popular that a Roxanne doll was sold in stores, each one toting a tiny camera that really flashed.

In the coming years, viewers got to know more faces than just Bud Collyer and Roxanne. Frank Wayne himself would step in front of the camera as guest host during Collyer's vacations. One night, Collyer gleefully announced that the lucky contestants onstage were going to get revenge on Frank Wayne and his writing partner, Bob Howard. A contestant would be blindfolded and told to spray Reddi-Whip at the two men; the audience howled as Wayne and Howard put on masks, covered their heads with boxes, and stood out of range of the target, avoiding every drop of Reddi-Whip.

The show's announcer, Bern Bennett, was the subject of an odd contest. Game show announcers are almost never seen on camera, and after seven years on the air, someone on the staff realized that Bern Bennett had never physically appeared on *Beat the Clock*. The show held a "Draw Bern Bennett" contest, finally revealing the announcer's face at the conclusion of the competition.

When *Beat the Clock* jumped to ABC in 1958, they got a new announcer, Dirk Fredericks. With stewardesses in the studio audience one day, Bud Collyer joked about fixing up Fredericks, a bachelor, with one of them. Nine months later, Collyer revisited the remark and gleefully announced that Dirk Fredericks had become engaged to Priscilla, a stewardess who had been sitting in the audience. *Beat the Clock* held a special "wedding shower" episode. Dirk and Priscilla were living props who figured into every problem that the contestants battled that day. And for every problem successfully solved, not only did the contestants win some money, but Dirk and Priscilla won wedding shower–style gifts, like cookware and bedsheets.

Moments of Truth

In 1950, as *Beat the Clock* was getting started, the "granddaddy of them all," *Truth or Consequences*, was celebrating ten years on radio with a spectacular publicity stunt. Host/creator Ralph Edwards issued a challenge to any American town to change its name to "Truth or Consequences." The town of Hot Springs, New Mexico, about 140 miles south of Albuquerque, held a special election, and in a landslide, the town changed its name to Truth or Consequences, New Mexico. As one resident put it, "There are thirteen Hot Springs in the United States, but there's only one Truth or Consequences." Edwards was so flattered that for the rest of his life, he made an annual visit to Truth or Consequences, New Mexico, to host some special productions of the namesake game.

But *Truth or Consequences* had more reasons to celebrate than just getting its own town. Edwards elected to give television a try in 1950. The video version was initially a bust, although its single season with Ralph Edwards as host held one unique distinction. In 1950, most television shows would air on the East Coast, and then a kinescope (a film made by putting the camera lens against a television picture tube) would be used for broadcast later on the West Coast. Philip Morris, which sponsored the TV *Truth or Consequences*, disliked the shoddy picture quality of kinescopes, so at their insistence, *Truth or Consequences* was filmed; it was the first TV game show to be recorded in that format. Philip Morris was so happy with how film looked that when they agreed to sponsor a new television show the following season, they insisted on using 35mm film. That show was *I Love Lucy*.

Truth or Consequences and television seemed to be a better fit than *Truth or Consequences* and radio. The look of disbelief on a contestant's face could now be captured when she realized that the entire population of her hometown had been brought to the studio with the help of some Greyhound buses. The ludicrous sight of servicemen in a race to see who could put on ladies' undergarments faster proved beyond imagination.

Opening night was jam-packed. Six middle-aged audience members were disguised as ballet dancers and sent to another studio to perform an unrehearsed ballet for an unsuspecting audience. A man was placed in an empty tank while his wife was shown a variety of new bonnets and told to pick one; unbeknown to her, as she tried to decide which one she wanted, her husband's tank slowly filled with water. A game of Musical Chairs was played with a single hot seat.

One of the most memorable moments on the TV version of *Truth or Consequences*, for better or for worse, was the broadcast of September 21, 1950. Edwards brought out two contestants onstage, an older woman named Mrs. Cunningham and a soldier. Edwards asked Mrs. Cunningham if she had ever seen a soldier before. Mrs. Cunningham explained that her son was actually stationed in Korea for the moment and that she was notified that he had recently been wounded. To start the game, Ralph Edwards told the soldier contestant to step behind a pup tent. From the other side emerged Mrs. Cunningham's son, discharged and happily reunited with his mother.

New York Times critic Jack Gould was horrified:

> Television reached a new low in taste last night. It came on the *Truth or Consequences* program, which inexcusably exploited a mother's understandable shock when she unexpectedly saw her son, a Korean combat casualty. . . . If television must stoop to this level for what it calls entertainment, then it deserves neither understanding nor sympathy. Video disgraced itself last night. The whole incident was a typical example of the warped sense of drama of Mr. Edwards, who by now is old enough to know better.

A few letters trickled into the *New York Times* from outraged viewers who similarly excoriated *Truth or Consequences* for the stunt, but even by 1950, Ralph

Edwards had determined that they were, by far, in the minority. The surprise reunions had been a staple of the radio version and audience feedback was so overwhelmingly positive that Edwards devised a program that successfully used the premise: *This is Your Life*. Debuting in 1948, a noteworthy figure would be lured to the studio under false pretenses and then taken by surprise when Ralph Edwards strolled onstage and proclaimed, "This is *your* life!" A parade of long-lost friends, relatives, and other acquaintances from that individual's past would stroll onstage for a reunion. It pioneered "reality programming" and, in 1952, it made the jump to television, where it would enjoy another nine-year run.

Truth or Consequences, on television, performed to mixed results. On the one hand, the three-camera-filming method that served sitcoms so well for decades to come just didn't work in the early experimental days of the technique; camera shots frequently had a herky-jerky look to them, and technical gaffes would require Edwards to film new scenes later that would be inserted into the show during the editing process. It wasn't very seamless; for one, the shots filmed later were clearly in an empty studio, and the lack of an audience was jarringly noticeable. The show languished in its time slot against a popular detective drama and expired after 1951. The good news was there was enough of a diamond in the rough that the show earned an Emmy for Best Audience Participation Show.

Inconsequential

Truth or Consequences only occasionally dabbled in the sentimental. At the heart of the program were the wacky and sometimes elaborate stunts that the show's staff concocted. When *Truth or Consequences* returned to television for the 1954–1955 season with host Jack Bailey (formerly the voice of Goofy), the show stayed just as wild as it had always been.

A nationwide search was held for Jack Bailey's "twin"—a person who looked exactly like him. The winner was George Benson, a man whose thin, slick-backed hair and mustache made him an optimal doppelgänger. He was flown out to Hollywood to collect a thousand-dollar grand prize. Jack Bailey then announced that his "great grandfather, John Ringling Bailey," had stored the money in a safe deposit box and left the key with a trustee. Benson was told to go home and wait for a key to arrive by mail. After Benson left the stage, Bailey encouraged everyone watching at home to mail him a key, supplying the contestant's home address in the process. As a result, Benson received fifty thousand keys. With all of these keys in his possession, he made a return visit to the studio and was given another chance to find the correct key. Benson opened a box, which contained an old phonograph record player. The record had the voice of John Ringling Bailey telling him to go to Des Moines, Iowa, where he was to contact a trustee named Higilby Thigilby. Thigilby gave him the precise location where a box containing the money was buried. By the time Benson arrived, half the population of Des Moines was already there, and the money had already been dug up. The show's producers told the man who had dug up the money that he could keep the thousand dollars, but that George Benson had to be given the box that it came in. The box contained a laundry ticket with "Boston, Massachusetts" scribbled on it, so Benson was flown there to figure out which laundry was the correct one. He visited 133 such establishments before finding the one that had the package. Returning to the studio once again, this time with the unopened package, Benson refused Bailey's offer to buy said package from him for $2,500. Benson was instructed to open the package then and there. He did so, revealing the contents to be one-half of a thousand-dollar bill, along with a note from John Ringling Bailey telling him to go home and wait for the other half of the thousand-dollar bill to arrive in the mail. After Benson's exit, Bailey once again revealed the contestant's home address to the viewing audience, this time asking everyone watching to send an empty envelope to said address. Benson had to wade through stacks of mail before *finally* getting the other half of that thousand-dollar bill.

Another contestant named Mrs. Walker was showered with prizes, including an electric coffee pot, a lamp, an end table, and a bookcase. She gradually realized that all of the prizes she was getting looked extremely familiar, and Bailey clued her in that the show had snuck her belongings out. Mrs. Walker was, in essence, winning her own house back.

Funny Business

People are Funny had been a radio institution for almost as long as *Truth or Consequences*. *People are Funny*, created by John Guedel (the same great thinker who talked Groucho Marx into hosting *You Bet Your Life*), went on the air in 1942 with host Art Baker. The following year, Baker was replaced by another Art, Art Linkletter. Unlike *Truth or Consequences*, which was predominantly interested in what kind of zany predicaments a person could be thrust into, the focus of *People Are Funny* was in the reactions of the people in those predicaments. The show was one madcap display of human nature after another.

Perhaps the perfect example of the *People Are Funny* mindset was in one of its most popular recurring games. An audience member was brought onstage, a phone number was selected at random, and the audience member was tasked with keeping the stranger on the phone as long as possible, without identifying themselves or explaining that they were on a game show. What could a person talk about with a total stranger? How patient would the average person be without knowing whom they were talking to?

Some of the experiments went wildly wrong. On a 1950 radio broadcast, a man was instructed to change into tattered clothing and paint on a black eye. He was to knock on the doors in a neighborhood and explain that a gang of hoodlums was after him. The experiment in this case would be, will the average person let a stranger in their home and risk trouble with a gang of hoodlums? To take the experiment a little further, the man's wife was instructed to follow him to any home that let him in and explain that they had just had a small argument and that there were no hoodlums. By the end of the half-hour, Linkletter was forced to announce to the listening audience that the man's whereabouts were unknown. One Good Samaritan had whisked him in so fast that the wife didn't even see where he went, and before the husband could explain that it was a gag, the police had shown up to question him; as it happened, a gang of actual hoodlums had been in the neighborhood the previous night, and an investigation was underway.

People Are Funny arrived on NBC television in 1954 with Art Linkletter still hosting the festivities. As with *Truth or Consequences*, the experiments of *People are Funny* just worked better when you could see them, such as a contestant trying to guess from pure observation which of three women onstage was a millionaire. A blindfolded five-year-old tried to figure out which man onstage was his father. A student from a memory-improvement course had to provide a detailed explanation of a pantomime performance that he had just watched. A woman was given ninety seconds to talk as much as she could about her husband—not enough time for her, or too much? And there were the contestants who were brought onstage for a yawning contest. The entire audience was encouraged to yawn, and the contestants stood to win prizes if they managed not to yawn. (And you probably yawned just reading this description, didn't you?)

Matchmaker, Matchmaker

People Are Funny was partial to using the show as a means of matchmaking. In May of 1957, the show held a Great American Marriage Round-Up. Single people were brought to the studio and encouraged to fill out a thirty-two-question personality quiz, with inquiries about race, religious beliefs, and even their personal preference for double beds or twin beds. Those questionnaires would be fed into a Univac computer, with the results being used to pair people up for dates.

A two-hundred-pound woman explained the type of man she was looking for: "I like 'em little, because they're easier to handle."

A man at the Round-Up explained, "I've been divorced four times, but I'm willing to come out of the chute for a fifth."

The Univac did its thing and for months, the show was devoted to the results of the dates created by the matchmaking machine. One woman had so much faith in the computer that she dumped her current boyfriend to go out with the man that the Univac recommended. A man wound up going on a date with twin sisters. Linkletter welcomed a hypnotist one night who tried to entrance a couple into tying the knot. The goal was unabashedly clear. Linkletter said that he was determined to get at least one couple married as a direct result of *People Are Funny*, to the point that he promised he would provide the ladder himself if a couple would just sneak off in the middle of the night and elope. Things didn't get that desperate, though. Bob Kardell and Shirley Saunders tied the knot in the summer of 1958.

Second Best

Dollar a Second started its life as *Cent Francs La Seconde* (100 Francs a Second), a French radio game. It came to the United States on the DuMont Network in 1953 and presented audiences with an interesting twist on *Beat the Clock*. Host Jan Murray welcomed a contestant, and the moment the contestant showed up, a clock started ticking up the winnings, with the contestant collecting a dollar for every second he or she remained onstage. Murray would start with a trivia game that kept going until a contestant gave a wrong answer. At that point, the contestant would have to pay a penalty. One contestant was blindfolded and spun in a chair until dizzy, and then had to step on the raw egg on the floor in front of him without seeing it. Failing to pay the penalty stopped the game immediately, and the contestant collected a dollar a second, plus a dollar for every correct answer given in the trivia game.

Threatening the contestant's winnings at all times was the dreaded Outside Event. This was an activity that the contestant had no control over. An audience member was given a pile of five hundred keys and had to locate the one that unlocked a chest. For another game, a model train made a lap around a scale model landscape, with a required number of complete laps selected from a stack of envelopes. If and when the Outside Event happened, the contestant lost all of their money.

When TV Got Real

Beat the Clock and *Dollar a Second* were certainly fun but could hardly be called influential. On the other hand, *Truth or Consequences* and *People Are Funny* tapped

into a vein that made some more prudish viewers uncomfortable. Contestants returned week after week for elaborate challenges, with attention devoted to the emotional impact that stunts had: the tears of a veteran seeing his wife or mother for the first time in over a year; the exasperation of a contestant being sent on what seemed to be a snipe hunt by Ralph Edwards; the notion that a stranger's romantic life could be used as fodder for entertainment. Although Art Linkletter said himself that he never envisioned people eating bugs for money decades later (on shows such as *Survivor*), he and Ralph Edwards were pioneers of reality television.

Jan Murray marvels at a contestant's washboard abs on *Dollar a Second*.

11

Tear Jerkers

A Year's Supply of Tissues

While shows like *Truth or Consequences* and *You Bet Your Life* cracked up viewers week after week with merry mirthmaking, other games had a very different approach to entertainment. Get out your tissues! Here come the Sob Shows!

An Audience with the Queen

A scant few years had passed since Professor Quiz had toured the nation, presenting his weekly program live from auditoriums across the country. But by 1947, one radio show was just too big for a mere auditorium. It would be making a stop in Dallas during its coast-to-coast tour, and to accommodate ticket requests, the program would emanate from the 45,000-seat Cotton Bowl. What was the big draw? A tough Q&A battle of wits? A thrilling and hilarious series of wacky stunts? A mind-boggling jackpot song to be identified?

Nope. The game's objective was to determine which contestant had the saddest life.

Queen for a Day began its life in New York on April 30, 1945, as *Queen for Today*, with host Ken Murray. After only a few months, the production moved to Hollywood, changed its title, and picked up a new host, former World's Fair barker Jack Bailey. The program grew so popular that, by 1951, a *Queen for a Day* movie was released, starring Jack Bailey as himself, and featuring Darren McGavin and Leonard Nimoy in minor roles. In 1956, the show would finally make the jump to television, with the radio version still hanging on for another year after that.

Each day, Bailey would welcome a group of women to the stage and conduct a detailed interview with them. On a typical episode:

- A woman raising four children all by herself while her husband was doing his second tour of duty overseas. She said she just wanted to be able to speak to him on the phone.
- A mother of seven needing hired help to take care of her family while she was in the hospital for two weeks to get major surgery; her husband couldn't help because of his job as a truck driver.
- A mother of two taking care of five additional children on behalf of a neighbor whose husband had left her.
- A woman needing an expensive dehumidifier to aid her asthmatic husband, who could no longer work due to his condition.

The audience, with their applause, would vote for the woman most deserving of becoming queen. In the example above, the audience voted for the woman who needed surgery. She won a Jacuzzi, a diamond watch, a washing machine, a Spiegel catalog gift certificate, a unicycle, a phonograph, a kitchen range, a painting of a clown, furnishings for a new den, a home-movie camera with film and projector, a year's supply of RC Cola, a kitten, a generous supply of Friskies cat food, a backyard swing set and slide, and seven bicycles for her seven children. None of this actually helped the queen with the problem she had described earlier about needing to find somebody to watch her children, and in fact, as the episode closes, the camera zooms in on her conspicuously perplexed face, but no matter. Someone in need got a haul of goodies.

Stories need not be tragic in order to win audience approval. One queen was a woman helping her husband fulfill a lifelong dream of owning a store. They had just secured the deed to one and she asked for, and received, a full stock of groceries to give them a head start. And some queens were just plain funny. Jack Bailey's favorite contestant was a woman who had been married for three weeks and said she needed a new bed because hers was totally worn out. Far more typical, though, was the woman who wished for tires and gasoline to help her get her adopted baby to San Francisco for medical treatment, and by the way, her unemployed husband had broken five ribs by falling off a ladder.

As producer Howard Blake unabashedly admitted, that's all he really set out to do. "It was exactly what the general public wanted. . . . We got what we were after. Five thousand queens got what they were after. And the TV audiences cried their eyes out."

The Club of Queens

Being Queen for a Day was mighty serious business for many women. On more than one occasion, the show found out after the fact that a winner had lied about the supposed hardships that brought her to the program, and *Queen for a Day* would even take back the prizes in such a scenario.

During a *Queen for a Day* tour stop in Monterey, California, an irate woman showed up, claiming that she owned the property where the show's technical crew was erecting their equipment. She loudly announced, "If there is going to be a Queen for a Day, it's going to be me!" and sat down on the show's throne, which had already been set up on the stage, refusing to budge unless she was promised the winner's prizes. Before the program went on the air, she settled for $300 and walked away.

But why should wives have all the fun? The show expanded its scope with occasional theme shows that looked further than usual for deserving winners. "King for a Day" honors went to an eighty-seven-year-old member of Chicago's Rotary Club; he was the club's fifth member when it was founded. On "Baby Day," a six-month-old with a foot condition that would require special shoes won enough shoes to accommodate her until age five, plus clothing, soap, talc, a year's supply of evaporated milk, a new crib, and a $2,000 scholarship. On Newsboys Day, the big winner was a boy who recently lost his mother and wanted an addition built onto his house so his brother could move in.

Rich in Spirit

Strike It Rich, touting itself as "the show with a heart," emerged on radio in 1947, and eventually made its way onto television with host Warren Hull. It was a simple quiz show; a contestant was given a series of categories and tried to supply a correct answer to each question for stakes that could reach $500.

What made *Strike It Rich* stand out from the rest of the Q&A shows was the contestants' desperate need as a prerequisite. A woman was on because her husband had been in a car accident and would never walk again, and she herself had to quit her job to tend to him. A widowed mother of five was on after her father was killed in a hit-and-run accident. A blind church choir needed a van for touring. Actor Richard Dern played on behalf of a wounded veteran who could no longer perform physical labor. A steady stream of needy parents appeared on the show; their children were either blind, deaf, disabled, and/or needed massive operations. Other parents had too-big families, with ten, eleven, twelve, thirteen, up to seventeen children.

And if a contestant came up short in the quiz, no problem. The ever-present Heart Line, a telephone, was onstage. Viewers were encouraged to call in and pledge money to the contestants just to lend them a hand. When a team of thirteen clowns appeared on the show to help a fellow circus performer who had been stricken blind, they won $500 on their own, but over $1,000 poured in on the Heart Line. And in one particularly embarrassing fiasco, a contestant collected $165 in Heart Line pledges plus a new apartment to live in, rent-free. It was subsequently discovered that he was an escaped prisoner.

Going on *Strike*

Strike It Rich outraged the state of New York. The welfare commissioner for the state publicly called the show "a national disgrace." When the program became popular, destitute families across the country flocked to New York in a scene straight out of *The Grapes of Wrath*, seeing the program as something of a last hope. When they didn't make it on the show, they'd hunker down in New York and apply for government aid. A family from Maryland with eleven children applied for welfare, and the state simply made special arrangements for transportation to return them to Maryland.

The state of New York eventually turned to threats, pointing out that just blatantly asking people for money was panhandling, and that if the show was going to continue the Heart Line feature on the show, host Warren Hull and the production staff would all be required to obtain special licenses in order to ask for funds legally. Producer Walt Framer amended the rules, setting requirements for those who could call the Heart Line and how they could go about it, and the amended rules were just enough for the state to back off.

Nonetheless, the backlash against *Strike It Rich* was hard to ignore. *Queen for a Day* had critics too, but by virtue of the fact that it aired in the daytime, it was generally considered "unimportant." *Strike It Rich* aired concurrently in daytime and nighttime, and critical backlash was near constant for four years until CBS finally caved to all the gripes by cancelling the nighttime version in 1955 just to silence the cacophonous outrage.

Sorry, Not Sorry

Walt Framer, the son of Russian immigrants, started in the broadcasting business as an advertising salesman for station WWSW in Pittsburgh, where one of the disc jockeys was a young up-and-comer named Bill Cullen. In high school, Framer's classmates had voted him "Most Likely *not* to Succeed," and Framer seemed to take the degradation as a challenge. He moved to New York to write for radio programs, and by the end of the 1940s, he had his own production company.

Another game show producer, Louis G. Cowan, categorized Sob Shows, particularly those produced by Walt Framer, as "Microscope on Misery" programs. Framer built an empire from other people's sob stories, and though critics tended to look down their collective noses at all game shows, even other game show producers despised Framer's shamelessly exploitative attitude about programming.

Framer was relentlessly remorseless, saying he was merely a businessman who was giving the public what they wanted. In 1953, he said, "I'm producing *Strike It Rich* for the benefit of Mr. America, the poor guy who works all day, comes home, eats his dinner, goes into the living room and puts on his slippers. This guy doesn't want *Studio One* or some artsy show. He's looking for *Lucy* or *Rich*. He has simple, elemental tastes. If I don't put on a real needy case, I get a dirty, nasty letter from Mr. America."

Framer apparently felt that he didn't take the concept of the Sob Show far enough. According to author Kent Anderson, Framer was, at one point, looking to put a series on the air called *Behind Closed Doors*, in which mentally ill contestants would have competed for a chance to win psychiatric care.

Put on a Happy Face

Queen for a Day and *Strike It Rich* may have been in poor taste, but they were exceptionally popular, and television is a business, so competing producers began assembling their own Sob Shows, this time going for tears of joy.

Wheel of Fortune, believe it or not, was the name of one of these shows; contestants were asked simple questions and then spun a wheel to determine their prize. The catch was that you had to be nominated to be a contestant on the show in the first place; all contestants were Good Samaritans, and before each game, the person who nominated them would briefly explain the good deeds done that entitled the contestant to a chance at winning some money.

It Could Be You!, produced by Ralph Edwards, made a game out of the surprise reunions that had already been enormously successful for him on *Truth or Consequences* and *This is Your Life*. Contestants would hear a series of clues to the identity of a person from their past and tried to identify the person with whom they were about to be reunited. The show took the concept of surprises to even further extremes. Host Bill Leyden would openly mention the show's staff of "spies" or "informants" gathering happy tidbits about people across the country and then arranging to surprise them with prizes during the live broadcast. No game, just the surprise and the prize. For example, Bill Leyden would announce the name of a married couple in Grand Rapids, Michigan, celebrating their twenty-fifth wedding anniversary.

"Go to your door right now! Our spies in Grand Rapids tell us it's your silver anniversary today!" And the couple would answer their door to be greeted by a camera crew bearing gifts.

The Greatest Man on Earth, from Walt Framer, creator of *Strike It Rich*, was a more lighthearted version of *Queen for a Day*. For *The Greatest Man on Earth*, five men were nominated for a variety of good deeds and positive traits. They would then compete in a series of wacky stunts and trivia quizzes, with the winner being declared Crown Prince.

And even Walt Framer attempted a kinder, gentler version of the Sob Show, creating a game called *The Big Payoff*, in which men wrote letters explaining why the women in their lives deserved to win prizes, and then the men themselves would compete as contestants to win those prizes.

Long Live the Queens

The Sob Shows would eventually go the way of stump-the-expert quizzes. *Strike It Rich* would disappear when demographic studies revealed the audience was too old, and *Queen for a Day* just didn't seem fit for a feminist world. Revivals were attempted in 1969 with Dick Curtis, and 1987 with Monty Hall, and a one-time-only special hosted by Mo'Nique in 2004, but applauding a woman for having it a little rough from day to day looked a little anachronistic, or, in a world of reality TV, not extreme enough.

Queen for a Day would be the show with the most enduring legacy. A *Queen for a Day* musical, starring Alan Thicke as Jack Bailey, opened in Toronto in 2012. And for fifty years, a Queen for a Day Club, comprised of past winners, gathered at luncheons in Las Vegas and Los Angeles, all sporting the crowns they won on their special days, and addressing all fellow members as "Your highness" or "your majesty." (Actually, not ALL of the members were former queens. One was on the show four times and never got voted queen. But since she had enough hardship in her life to merit four national television appearances, she was deemed worthy of membership.) The women had formed the group because they appreciated the good feeling of getting rewards during their time of need so much that they decided to pay it forward; the itinerary for the luncheons involved planning fundraisers and other events for worthy causes.

12

Big Money, Big Lies

Do You Want to Know a Secret

 lot of gold went up for grabs on 1950s quiz shows, but all that glitters . . .

I've Got a Bad Feeling About This

Louis G. Cowan, Mark Goodson's business partner for the sensational big-money radio show *Stop the Music*, had an idea for a new TV quiz. It was strongly based on *Take It or Leave It*, the quiz program with the famous $64 question. Cowan showed Goodson a proposal so simple that it only ran about a third of a page.

Goodson recounted the meeting in a 1985 lecture.

> Louis G. Cowan—who had been my partner on *Stop the Music*—proposed I join him in this new quiz. I agreed to examine the format, and was bothered by it. "There's a problem with this show. I don't believe you can make the game work unless you fix it." And he said, "What do you mean?"
>
> I said, "Look at your format. Your show is based on using civilian contestants playing for huge sums. You have a garbage man whose salary is $6,000 or $7,000 a year, and he will pick a subject of his choice, say opera. He answers a question and then must risk his money on the subsequent question. If he gets up to where he's got maybe $16,000, which is more than his salary for two years—and you ask him to gamble that on an unknown question in his field of opera—I don't believe contestants will take such a risk . . . unless you take them aside and say, "Don't worry, go ahead, you're protected."
>
> Cowan disagreed. "I don't think you're right," [he said]. They went ahead with *The $64,000 Question*.

Cowan secured a sponsor, Revlon cosmetics, and a network, CBS. For a host, he went to Garry Moore, who had hosted *Take It or Leave It*. Moore said no, predicting that for the amounts of money up for grabs, it was only a matter of time before some kind of "hanky-panky" would take place, and he didn't want his name attached to a scandal that he considered inevitable.

Cowan again resisted the arguments that he would have to rig the show. He, Revlon, and CBS went ahead with *The $64,000 Question*. The show premiered on June 7, 1955, and altered TV game shows forever.

"Where Knowledge is King, and the Reward is King-size"

The $64,000 Question found an emcee, actor Hal March. Designer Eddie Gilbert came up with a set boasting more traces of showmanship than any TV game seen to that point. Early TV games had sets designed for functionality; *The $64,000 Question* was designed to look like a *show*. The contestant entered from a staircase at center stage. A massive "computer" displayed categories and spat out a thick stack of question cards at the push of a button once a contestant announced what category he or she wanted to play (it was actually just a sorting machine with an elaborate façade built onto it, and regardless of what button Hal March pushed, it would distribute the same stack of cards). The questions started at $64 and doubled up to $128, $256, $512, and the next question worth $1,000, and then $2,000. If the contestant succeeded at $2,000, he or she went home and now only answered one question per week.

Once the stakes reached $4,000, questions were retrieved from a safe. A banker from Manufacturer's Hanover Trust, surrounded by armed guards, would hand the questions over to Hal March. To ensure that the contestant wouldn't hear anybody call out the answers, they would have to stand in a tiny soundproof booth, harshly lit with the camera giving the home audience an extreme close-up as the contestant agonized over the big-money puzzlers. A live orchestra in CBS Studio 52 played suspenseful music that reached a crescendo when the contestant's thinking time ran out.

Between the big money and the big presentation, the nation was captivated. The show rocketed to number 1 on television, averaging a stunning 47.5 rating every week; the queen of television, Lucille Ball, was just under a point and a half behind, at 46.1 every week. The appeal of the show, according to executive producer Steve Carlin, was its celebration of the working class. The show sought out average people who had extraordinary knowledge in unusual fields.

Up to the Challenge

True to the prognostications of Mark Goodson and Garry Moore, the hanky-panky began immediately. Charles Revson, the big boss at Revlon and, therefore, the big boss of *The $64,000 Question*, held regular meetings during which he discussed

The most famous booth in television history: The isolation booth on *The $64,000 Question*.

the previous show's ratings, the previous show's contestants, and the next show's contestants. According to director Joe Cates, Revson would make it emphatically clear how he wanted the games to play out. Revson initially didn't want any contestants to lose because he was afraid it would offend people; he wanted all contestants to either win the $64,000 or chicken out and take the money at a lower level. When Cates insisted that you needed losers for the winners to have credibility, Revson took it to heart; he began ruling over the contestants' fates with an iron fist. The 154 percent increase in Revlon's revenue since *The $64,000 Question* premiered caught the boss's attention, and he wanted to do what he thought was best to keep his top income generator interesting and popular.

Louis G. Cowan and Entertainment Productions, the company running the show, found themselves in demand. They hastily developed a new prime-time quiz for NBC, *The Big Surprise*, which launched on October 8, 1955. Originally hosted by Jack Barry, *The Big Surprise* assembled questions based on the contestant's own personal life, family, friends, hobbies, and similar subject matter, for payoffs that started at $1 and went up to $100,000. After five months, Jack Barry was abruptly fired and replaced by Mike Wallace, and the show switched to something more akin to *The $64,000 Question*, with experts selecting a preferred category and answering questions worth $100, up to $100,000. Ethel Park Richardson, a seventy-two-year-old who lived in a motor home and drove it all over America to attend concerts, won $100,000 with her knowledge of American folklore.

Entertainment Productions also unleashed *Giant Step*, an attempt to meld *The $64,000 Question* with a popular, but fading, concept of the past, *Quiz Kids*. On *Giant Step*, host Bert Parks welcomed child prodigies who were experts on subjects such as the American presidency and the United Nations for a chance to win a full college scholarship and an all-expenses-paid vacation to any location in the world after graduation. *Giant Step* would only last about seven months.

Meanwhile, one of the big problems that Entertainment Productions had with the increasing popularity of *The $64,000 Question* was that it created celebrities: Gino Prato, a shoemaker who won $32,000, landed an endorsement deal with an insole maker. Dr. Joyce Brothers, a trained psychologist who won the top prize with the subject of boxing, became an author and radio host. But because a $64,000 winner was finished on the show after six weeks, the show instantly lost any stars that it made. The staff responded to this problem by creating a spin-off, *The $64,000 Challenge*, in which contestants who had won $16,000 or more now competed against experts in the same subject for an additional $64,000. Sonny Fox, and later Ralph Storey, hosted the new series, also on CBS and also sponsored by Revlon, which controlled that show as tightly as *The $64,000 Question*.

Me Too!

It was only a matter of time before the competition felt the urge to get involved in the big-money quiz craze. Some approached it *very* reluctantly, most notably Mark Goodson, who complained that the shows substituted money for true entertainment value. The *What's My Line?* staff resisted a sponsor's request to boost the top prize from $50 all the way up to $1,000. On the other hand, Goodson-Todman produced a pilot called *Play for Keeps!*, an updated version of their earlier series *Winner Take All* in which cash prizes could climb to five figures. *Play for Keeps!* didn't sell, but it at least demonstrated that Goodson-Todman was receptive to the idea of a big-jackpot quiz. They did make one adjustment to an existing format. *Beat the Clock* introduced a Super Bonus stunt that started at $5,000 and grew by $1,000 per attempt until a couple solved it; fittingly, the jackpot was broken when it reached $64,000.

Groucho Marx was similarly skeptical of the new trend. In fact, he openly mocked it. The famous "secret word" on *You Bet Your Life* offered a $100 bonus for contestants who said it. One night, Groucho excitedly announced that *You Bet Your Life* was offering more money than ever before; the secret word was now worth $101.

Name That Tune, produced by Harry Salter, had previously given contestants a shot at $1,600 in the Golden Medley. In response to the big-money craze, the Golden Medley was revamped into the Golden Medley Marathon, a series of rounds that spanned five weeks and could pay off up to $25,000. One of the big winners was a Marine Corps pilot, Major John Glenn.

Break the Bank, which ten years earlier had been considered a big-money radio show with cash prizes that averaged about $7,000, transformed into *Break the $250,000 Bank*, a show which cribbed quite a bit from *The $64,000 Question*. It was yet another quiz in which experts selected a favorite category, a concept that was quickly wearing out its welcome. The major lesson of *Break the $250,000 Bank* was that it wasn't *just* money that people were interested in. The biggest winner of the series was a seventy-nine-year-old dentist who won $60,000 with his knowledge of religion; nobody else even came close to winning the quarter-million, and *Break the $250,000 Bank* went on a permanent break after only three months.

Game show host Dennis James came up with his own format, *High Finance*, in which contestants could sell off the prizes they won week by week in exchange for questions that were worth higher amounts of cash. The show offered up to $75,000 in cash, and for any contestant who survived the game for five weeks, the show would grant a wish. During the six-month run of *High Finance*, one woman became the owner of her own newspaper; another man got to move from New Jersey to Florida, where his very own miniature golf course was waiting for him. And former boxing champion Joe Louis was able to pay off some of the debt that he owed the IRS.

One of the more successful games to tag along in the wake of *The $64,000 Question* was *Treasure Hunt*, a game created by comedian Jan Murray, formerly host of the wacky stunt show *Dollar a Second*. Murray wanted to try an idea that hadn't been tried on game shows yet—a "grab bag." The stage had thirty treasure chests; the winner of a one-on-one trivia battle was offered a small cash prize guarantee, or the contents of one of the treasure chests. The prize could be a head of lettuce, tickets to a circus, a dream vacation, or a check for $10,000 or $25,000.

Dennis James shows off one of the more unusual prizes offered on a game show. A big winner on *High Finance* became the proud owner of a newspaper.

Photo courtesy of Micki James

Bet It All on *Twenty One*

The most successful competitor to the throne of *The $64,000 Question* would come from the minds of Jack Barry, the embittered former host of *The Big Surprise*, and his business partner Dan Enright. During the summer of 1956, they had added a game show to the NBC daytime lineup, *Tic Tac Dough*. Contestants added X's and O's to the board only by giving correct answers to questions, with every X and O adding money to an escalating pot. If the game ended in a tie, the money carried over, the symbols were cleared off the board, and the money just kept growing until somebody finally got three in a row.

But Barry and Enright's biggest success story was a show that was initially pitched to CBS and rejected. NBC, and sponsor Pharmaceuticals Inc., makers of Geritol, put the series on the air on September 12, 1956. The name of the game was *Twenty One*.

Barry hosted the show himself; two contestants, champion and challenger, stood in isolation booths. Barry would announce a category, and each contestant selected a point value from one to eleven; the more points, the harder the question, and neither contestant could hear the decisions or the answers given by the opponent; neither contestant knew the score. The object of the game was to come closer to twenty-one points than the opponent. A victory paid $500 per point separating the winner and loser; if games ended in a tie, the stakes would raise to $1,000 a point, then $1,500 a point, and so on until the battle was settled. If the challenger won the game, that individual's money was deducted from the champion's winnings.

The premiere of *Twenty One* was a dismal failure. The game was played legitimately on opening night, and the contestants gave seventeen incorrect answers. Pharmaceuticals, Inc. pointedly told Barry and Enright never to do a show that bad again, and the decision was made to start rigging the show.

The first big winner of the newly rigged *Twenty One* was an ex-G.I. named Herbert Stempel, who had amassed $69,500 when he was felled by handsome, charismatic Columbia professor Charles Van Doren after a series of ties, dropping his winnings down to $49,500. *Twenty One* would see its ratings skyrocket to the point that it did the unthinkable: it began beating *I Love Lucy* in its time slot; Lucille Ball and Desi Arnaz would even cease production on that series at the end of the 1956–1957 season. Van Doren graced the cover of *Time* during his ten-week stint on *Twenty One* before being defeated by Vivian Nearing, a lawyer and the wife of a contestant that Van Doren previously defeated. Van Doren left the show with $129,500, plus a three-year contract for NBC that led to Van Doren becoming *Today*'s cultural correspondent. Herb Stempel, on the other hand, would find himself swindled out of nearly all of his winnings by a shady investor and casually insulted by Jack Barry in a magazine article; Barry used the term "a freak with a sponge memory" at one point without specifically identifying a contestant, but Stempel was positive that Barry was talking about him.

It was somewhat fitting that *Twenty One* proved to be almost as successful as *The $64,000 Question* because they were almost yin and yang in presentation. In contrast to *Question*, *Twenty One* was in a tiny, cramped dimly lit studio, with near-constant tension permeating the entire show. No safe, no guards, no computer, no grand staircase. Just two contestants and a master of ceremonies in a studio so dark that Jack Barry almost seemed to be disappearing on the evenings that he wore black jackets.

Twenty One was so popular that Barry and Enright quickly found themselves becoming "the quiz show guys" for NBC. Barry and Enright begat *Dough-Re-Mi*,

a musical game show; a nighttime version of *Tic Tac Dough*; *Hi Lo*, in which a panel of experts estimated how many correct answers a contestant could give, and then a contestant could double or triple the money won so far by meeting the estimates; and *You're On Your Own*, in which a contestant was on a stage filled with research materials and had to figure out not only the correct answer, but how to find it. NBC was so happy with the results they were getting from Barry and Enright that the network bought the production company outright, and then paid the duo to continue producing shows they had already created.

Connecting the Dots

On January 6, 1958, CBS added a daytime quiz to its lineup. Jack Narz was master of ceremonies for *Dotto*, a game that added trivia to the childhood game of Connect the Dots. Contestants

An image that was first famous, then infamous: Charles Van Doren sweats it out while struggling, supposedly, with the answers on *Twenty One*.

separated by a partition would be given the same fifty-dot Dotto-Gram, a puzzle of a famous person's face. A contestant needed to supply correct answers to connect the dots, and the winner was the first one to solve the puzzle, with a payoff of $10 for every dot not yet connected. If both contestants solved the puzzle at the same point in the game, more games were played for $20 a dot, then $30, and so on until there was a clear winner.

Dotto quickly became the number-one show on daytime TV, averaging a 14.1 rating each morning on CBS. Each program featured a home viewer contest, and *Dotto* was deluged by three million contest entries per week. The show was one of the rare quizzes to receive critical acclaim. Even the *New York Times* offered a glowing review. The show's sponsor, Colgate, acted quickly on the success of *Dotto*, pushing for a nighttime version. Something unusual happened: NBC made a better offer for the nighttime show than CBS had, so as daytime *Dotto* continued on CBS, prime-time *Dotto* premiered on NBC on July 1, 1958.

In its short time on the air, *Dotto* even managed to create their own new star. Connie Hines, a pretty blonde who dominated the nighttime show for a few weeks, attracted so much attention that before she lost her final game, she already had a film contract; during the 1960s, she co-starred on the sitcom *Mister Ed.*

But on August 18, 1958, a startling announcement greeted CBS viewers tuning in expecting to see the daytime *Dotto*: "*Dotto* will no longer air on CBS. Please stay tuned for a new series."

Jack Narz certainly hadn't made any announcement on the previous episode, and for the highest-rated show on daytime TV, cancellation was obviously unthinkable. What happened?

What happened was before the live *Dotto* broadcast of May 20, 1958, returning champion Marie Winn was sitting backstage, busily reading something in a notebook. She told the other contestants that she was studying for a test. When she walked onstage, Edward Hilgemeier, the contestant standing by to play the next game, got a little curious, picked up the notebook, and found, to his dismay, the correct answers to the game in progress. He was able to follow along with the game as if reading from a script.

In the following months, a battle ensued between *Dotto* and Hilgemeier. The show's producers offered him $4,000 to keep quiet about the notebook (Hilgemeier had made copies of the pages and showed them to a lawyer that same day, so he had concrete evidence that the fix was in) and he didn't budge. The show went further, offering Hilgemeier a spot as a contestant on the nighttime version of *Dotto*, not-very-subtly implying that a fortune was waiting for him if he came on the show. Hilgemeier stood firm. In early August, CBS was notified by the FCC that Hilgemeier had made a complaint and shared what he now knew about the show.

Here was the strange thing: nothing illegal had happened. At the time, there were no laws against fixing quiz shows, mainly because it hadn't occurred to the FCC that anybody would do that. But now that the FCC knew, they certainly weren't pleased. The FCC had attempted to ban quiz shows only to be overruled by the Supreme Court in 1954. But now that they knew how unethically the big-money quiz shows were being conducted, the commission was suddenly considering regulating the shows.

The show that blew everyone's cover, *Dotto*.   *Photo courtesy of Zane Enterprises*

In mid-August, meetings were held with Hilgemeier's lawyer, plus representatives from CBS, Colgate, and Frank Cooper Productions, the packager that created *Dotto*. Frank Cooper confessed everything during the final meeting but made the following arguments: no money had been stolen from Colgate; mysteries and dramas fix their outcomes, too (true, but mysteries and dramas don't claim to be legitimate events); none of the rigging was unique to *Dotto*, that the entire staff had prior experience and was doing what they had already done on previous shows; and that he would stop rigging the show if asked.

CBS probably could have held him to his promise to stop rigging, but with the FCC now keeping a watchful eye over the Eye network, CBS reasoned that it had more to gain by cancelling the show outright, and that's exactly what they did. That day's game, which already aired, would be the final episode, and a Colgate representative went to Jack Narz's house to tell him not to come in on Monday. All parties did their best to keep all of this from escaping to the general public for as long as possible, but the abrupt disappearance of *Dotto* made it screamingly obvious that something was askew.

Columnist Janet Kern wrote,

> *Dotto*, from its first time out, had about it an air something short of Hoyle-like. It may have been clean as a whistle and straight as a die onstage, backstage, and everywhere else. But it didn't exactly inspire confidence in seasoned quiz-diagnosers' eyes. All of a sudden, Monday, when *Dotto* was slated to show up on TV sets tuned to CBS—no *Dotto*. Just as suddenly, NBC announced a series of filmed playlets substituting for its Tuesday night version of the same show. . . . No one concerned would say

officially *what* had happened nor would anyone *deny* any of the obvious sins suspected. Only one backstager shrugged a simple answer in private: "Someone got caught with the answers."

The $64,000 Question is "How Were They Doing It?"

The big-money quiz shows all had various ways of rigging their games, depending on their needs. There had been tremendous unrest among the staff of *The $64,000 Question* over Charles Revson's insistence that every game be rigged. As one staffer pointed out, no matter how much you insisted that the contestants had to keep things a secret, it was logical to presume that every contestant had a spouse, a best friend, parents, siblings, etc. Realistically, for every one contestant you fixed, you had to figure that four additional people were learning the big secret. With four contestants on every episode, that meant twenty people per week were finding out that *The $64,000 Question* was fixed. It was only a matter of time, in that case.

D.A. Joseph Stone was actually impressed by what he found in his investigations. A number of contestants denied that their games were rigged, and the more he learned, the more he realized that they might not necessarily be lying; in some cases, *The $64,000 Question* was doing their fixing so subtly that the contestants didn't even realize it was happening.

Captain Richard McCutcheon, a marine who was an expert on cooking, had figured out what was happening. When the show found a potential candidate to be a contestant, that person had to take a 200-question test just to confirm they actually were experts. Despite his unlikely background, McCutcheon genuinely was an expert on cooking. Every week, before the show, a producer met him backstage for a "warm-up session" in which he subjected McCutcheon to a battery of rapid-fire questions. If McCutcheon missed one, the producer would give him an answer. When McCutcheon was actually on the show, he realized, to his embarrassment, that he was being asked questions that he had heard in the warm-up sessions.

Gino Prato, a humble shoemaker who knew quite a bit about opera, is welcomed to *The $64,000 Question* by host Hal March.

The same thing happened to Gino Prato, a shoemaker who was an expert on opera.

His initial 200-question test indicated that he really only knew about Italian operas, so that was all they asked him. If Revson analyzed the ratings and mail and determined that Prato was an unpopular contestant, the show could have tripped up Prato by asking about a French opera. But since the ratings and mail indicated that America liked Gino Prato, he kept getting questions about Italian operas. This was actually the first crack in the quiz shows' façade. Viewers noticed that he was only getting questions about Italian operas and wrote in, asking why. The show responded that on Prato's first appearance, the show's graphic designer had made a mistake. The sign onstage was supposed to read ITALIAN OPERA, but the graphic erroneously said OPERA. This explanation seemed to satisfy most of the letter writers, but it was the first time that the method had been spotted.

Dr. Joyce Brothers's success was a comical tale. Charles Revson couldn't stand the prim-looking psychologist because she wasn't classically beautiful and eschewed the notion of glamour. Revson felt that she was detrimental to his cosmetics business and wanted her off the show. But she couldn't be tripped up; she knew which boxers were in which weight class; she knew dates; she knew arenas; she even knew the names of referees for specific fights. Revson watched with complete aggravation as Brothers kept winning and winning despite his wishes. The show couldn't find any information that Brothers didn't know.

Dr. Bergen Evans, the Northwestern University professor and former host of *Down You Go*, had been hired to write the questions for *The $64,000 Question*, but because he considered sports to be his personal weakness, he asked the show to outsource their sports questions to a freelancer. For Dr. Joyce Brothers's games, the show hired a sportswriter named Nat Fields. District Attorney Joseph Stone later discovered that Fields was a personal friend of the Brothers family.

For shows where contestants competed against each other, the rigging was more explicit. One of Herb Stempel's opponents on *Twenty One* told the D.A. that seconds before she walked onstage, a staffer ominously approached her and said, "Don't ask for any questions worth more than eight points, *or else*."

Herb Stempel maintained that *Twenty One* was so tightly controlled that it divided its contestants into three classifications: Lambs, Patsies, and Champions. Lambs were insignificant contestants whose sole function was to lose to the returning champion. Patsies were more interesting contestants who possessed some of the qualities that the show was looking for, but not quite all of them; a patsy would have a close, competitive game, and often one or more tiebreakers, before getting defeated. And Champions were exactly what they sounded like.

A *Tic Tac Dough* contestant, Elise Barron, explained that show's process to author Jeff Kisseloff. She was taken into a room filled with filing cabinets. Every drawer contained questions in a variety of categories. Elise was told to go through any drawer she wanted and read the information, to "trigger her memories" about certain subjects and help her feel more comfortable about answering questions. Once she was on the show, she saw that the categories on the *Tic Tac Dough* board were the categories from the drawer that she had rifled through. She won and came back the next day. The following day, she was specifically told which categories to pick and in which order. On the air, she got nervous, bungled the order, and won the game immediately instead of causing a tie. She was given no instructions at all before her third game, and her opponent in that next game mowed her down with ease.

Name That Tune was so blatant about its fixing that it was almost humorous. Producer Harry Salter would drive his staff crazy by inching his way onto the stage and whispering song titles to the contestants he wanted to win. *Name That Tune* also had a very unusual way of disposing with unlikable contestants. To name a tune, a contestant had to run across the stage and ring a bell hanging above them. When a contestant proved unlikable, the bell was raised so the contestant couldn't reach it! *Name That Tune* did have one slightly more subtle method for dispensing with contestants. The show assembled tunes for future games and divided them into "A" and "B" files. "A" songs were those in which the title was said in the first line of the song. "B" songs were the ones where the title was in the second line. When the average contestant heard a familiar melody, the gut instinct was to say the line that went with that melody, whether or not it was actually the title. So, if *Name That Tune* wanted a contestant to do well, the contestant got "A" songs; an unwanted contestant got "B" songs.

Dotto disguised its rigging as friendly conversation. A cab driver who appeared as a contestant told *Life* magazine that a staffer offered to ask him some "sample questions" to help him get warmed up for his game. During the warm-up session, the staffer gave him a pep talk, telling the cabbie that he looks smart enough to recognize the faces he sees on TV.

"You'd know a guy like Garry Moore, right?" the staffer asked.

The cabbie admitted that he had never really watched much of Garry Moore on TV. The staffer quickly told him that Garry Moore had a crewcut, and went on with the warm-up questions. Once the cabbie went onstage, he was surprised to hear that the actual questions in the game were the warm-up questions . . . and that the dots were connecting to form a head with a crew cut.

Another production staffer, speaking to *Life* magazine, described how his show rigged contestants without identifying the show he worked for. A staffer would approach a contestant before the game and strike up a friendly conversation. The staffer might ask, "Have you heard Sinatra's latest record?" They'd have a conversation about the record, and the staffer would casually mention that a guy as talented as Sinatra is probably going to have a long, successful career in the movies too. Once onstage, the contestant would be asked "Who won an Academy Award for his supporting role in *From Here to Eternity*?"

Staff members' friendliness might take on other forms. One contestant might hear a staffer rave about the fascinating book he had been reading, and the staffer would offer to loan out his copy of the book to the contestant, along with a detail like, "Chapter Four is *really* interesting!"

The Whistle Blowers

The incident at *Dotto* suddenly gave credence to Herb Stempel, a man who had previously been dismissed as a sore loser and a crackpot when he tried to clue in authorities and the press about what was happening at NBC's *Twenty One*.

Stempel was now in the New York District Attorney's office. D.A. Joseph Stone heard his allegations, and when Dan Enright showed up to rebuke whatever Stempel had told them, the investigation of the big-money quiz shows was officially underway. NBC issued a statement on August 29, 1958, formally denying all allegations; without specifically identifying Stempel, the network called the claims of rigging baseless. Stempel had already gone to Barry and Enright's offices a year earlier, presenting an affidavit that he had written about the way that *Twenty One* was rigged and threatening to go public with it unless he was paid $50,000. Enright arranged a meeting in which Stempel was secretly recorded admitting that what he was doing constituted blackmail. Enright then formally offered to help him pay for psychotherapy sessions, and by the end of the meeting, Enright successfully cajoled Stempel into signing a document stating that *Twenty One* was legitimate. Four days after NBC formally denied the allegations, Jack Barry and Dan Enright held a press conference in which they played the audio of Stempel's blackmail attempt and then displayed the document he had signed.

By 1958, there were signs that the quiz show boom was dying down anyway. Before any accusations had become public, ratings for all the big-money quiz shows were trickling down. The networks noticed but were hardly alarmed. A fad as hot as this had nowhere to go but down, and even if ratings were down, the big-money quiz shows were still popular enough to be called hits without hesitation.

But as summer turned into fall, ratings erosions turned into implosion. When Charles Van Doren was champion on *Twenty One* in early 1956, the Trendex ratings said 54.7 percent of television homes were tuning in. At the beginning of fall 1958, that number a dismal 10.3 percent. On October 16, 1958, *Twenty One* aired for the final time. On November 5, CBS aired the final *$64,000 Question*. The demise of *Question* was rather interesting because there hadn't been any specific accusations made about that show yet; it was merely a matter of collateral damage from the accusations being lobbed at the other shows.

The next whistleblower was Rev. Stoney Jackson, who won $16,000 on *The $64,000 Question* in the category of Great Love Stories. Jackson elected to quit with $16,000 when a staffer gently suggested that he should "move on." Having won $16,000 qualified Jackson to return for *The $64,000 Challenge*.

On *The $64,000 Challenge*, a producer named Shirley Bernstein had approached him backstage and casually asked, "Do you know who, other than Christopher Marlowe, wrote a song about Hero and Leander?" Without giving Jackson a chance to answer, she said, "It was Thomas Hood."

On the air, he answered "Thomas Hood." His opponent, asked the same question, guessed "William Shakespeare." Jackson won the game and an additional $4,000. Jackson was so suspicious that he called the loser the next day and asked why she said that. She said she had been told to study Shakespeare. Jackson had the option of continuing to play for up to $64,000, but the following week, he announced that he was taking his $4,000 and retired with a total of $20,000.

When Stoney Jackson went public with his accusations, Dr. Bergen Evans harshly wrote in *Life* magazine, "When he won, the reverend must not have thought his winnings were wicked. He didn't return them."

A few short weeks later, *The $64,000 Challenge* had a near-disaster with two opponents, Arthur Cohn Jr. and Wilton Springer. Unbeknown to the production staff at *The $64,000 Challenge*, Cohn and Springer struck up a genuine friendship outside of the show and were now talking frequently.

One night, before the Cohn vs. Springer match, Shirley Bernstein told Cohn that he seemed confident and relaxed and that he probably didn't need a warm-up session. Cohn agreed that he felt good about his chances in the upcoming game. A few minutes later, Springer told Cohn that Shirley Bernstein had grilled him with a series of questions about female character names in several plays. When Cohn and Springer went on the air that night, they were both dismayed to hear a series of questions about female character names. Neither of them said anything on the air—on all the quiz shows, contestants found the atmosphere of a big-time TV show so intimidating that many later admitted they didn't have the guts to sabotage the games—but Cohn walked out of the theater that night loudly announcing what happened to a passerby and threatening to sue the show. *The $64,000 Challenge* quietly disappeared on September 7, 1958.

For all of Herb Stempel's allegations about *Twenty One*, the contestant who blew up that show was a man named James Snodgrass. Snodgrass had been briefed before each of his games about what categories to choose, what the questions would be, what the correct answers were, and if he was to give a wrong answer, what his answer was to be. He was told to lose to his opponent after a series of ties, but that he'd walk away with $3,000 for cooperating. This amount was enough of a lure that Snodgrass cooperated, but he got a funny feeling that, someday, he might want to show people what he had done, so over the next several weeks, he got into a routine. He'd go to the Barry and Enright offices, receive instructions for how that week's *Twenty One* should play out, then go home and type up a letter detailing all of the information he had been given. He would then mail that letter to himself, sending it Registered Mail, and then once he received it, he put the letter in a drawer without ever opening it. When the D. A. came knocking, Snodgrass happily turned over all the letters in sealed envelopes. The D. A. found that the letters perfectly matched the way the games played out after the letters had been written, and it was now confirmed: *Twenty One* was fixed.

The press was now listening to Herbert Stempel. For a *Life* magazine article, a photographer snapped pictures of Stempel demonstrating various emotions the way that he had been coached by Dan Enright. Contestants either willingly stepped forward or found themselves thrust into the spotlight, sharply divided between spilling their guts and denying any and all chicanery.

Elfreda Van Nardoff, a $220,500 winner on *Twenty One*, maintained, "It's inconceivable they could have been fixed."

Ethel Richardson, a $100,000 winner on *The Big Surprise*, revealed that every one of her appearances on that program had been preceded by a lengthy conversation, and that "whatever I told them most about, the question would be about."

Teddy Nadler, the top quiz show winner of them all with $252,000 in winnings, insisted, "They never told me a damn thing!"

Truth and Consequences

NBC seized control of the Barry and Enright shows still on the air and fired the producers. *Dough Re Mi* (which was actually never implicated of game-rigging at all) remained on the air until 1960. *Tic Tac Dough* left prime-time but remained in daytime. Now played legitimately, a strange thing happened: *Tic Tac Dough* actually gave away more money than it had when it was rigged, racking up a budget deficit in the tens of thousands of dollars in a matter of weeks. The final game that Barry and Enright created for NBC, *Concentration*, went on the air just seven weeks before *Twenty One* was canceled; *Concentration* would remain on the air for more than fourteen years. Today, it's still the longest-running game in NBC history.

Grand jury hearings were conducted; Congress got involved too. Law enforcement's involvement was a little tricky in the early stages because nobody could determine if a law had been broken. There was a search for evidence that contestants had paid producers for the correct answers, because that would constitute bribery. The closest thing to such a scheme happened at *Treasure Hunt*, where associate producer Barney Martin promised prospective contestants that he would put them on the show in exchange for a percentage of their winnings. *Treasure Hunt* creator/host Jan Murray fired Martin immediately after learning of that con.

Charles Van Doren initially escaped scrutiny. Herb Stempel was adamant that Van Doren must have been in on it for the simple reason that he, Stempel, was. Logically, Stempel said, you can't rig the guy who's going to lose without also rigging the guy who's going to win, because if the "winner" blows the game, you're back to square one. Van Doren denied being a party to the rigging when he spoke to the grand jury, and denied it again in a private meeting with NBC executives. That seemed to be the end of it.

But then Van Doren did something odd, with D. A. Joseph Stone suspecting the professor got some extraordinarily bad advice from somebody at NBC. Van Doren sent out a telegram volunteering to testify before Congress, IF Congress felt Van Doren had anything to say. This struck Stone as a bizarre move; Van Doren seemed to be beyond suspicion and nobody was asking him to testify. Van Doren, by announcing that he was available to testify, appeared to be daring somebody to call his bluff. And that's exactly what Congress did.

The Congressional hearings on quiz shows, during October and November 1959, were a highly publicized, and in many ways, a sad affair. Herb Stempel eagerly watched kinescopes of his games and pointed out all the acting tips that he got; the way he bit his lip, the way he patted his brow when he began to sweat (pat your forehead, don't wipe it, he had been told), his awkward demeanor—Dan Enright had him fitted with suits that were too big, and Stempel was instructed to address the host as "Mr. Barry" to make him look like an awkward nerd. Child actress Patty Duke, who had been a contestant on *The $64,000 Challenge*, testified quite confidently that her games weren't rigged and everything was legitimate.

When a kindly but suspicious congressman on the committee very sweetly asked her, "Now Patty, was everything that you just told us the truth?" Duke burst into tears and confessed everything.

Damage control! Dan Enright and Jack Barry hold a press conference, playing an audio recording of an argument between Enright and contestant Herb Stempel that they maintained could prove that *Twenty One* had done no wrong. The effort was for naught. *Twenty One* was canceled, and for a time, the producers found themselves blackballed.

Fred Wostbrock Collection

Charles Van Doren, who briefly went into hiding when the Congressional hearings began, emerged to deliver a prepared statement on November 2, 1959. He read, in part,

> I would give almost anything I have to reverse the course of my life in the last three years. I cannot take back one word or action; the past does not change for anyone. But at least I can learn from the past. I have learned a lot in those three years, especially in the last three weeks. I've learned a lot about life. I've learned a lot about myself, and about the responsibilities any man has to his fellow men. I've learned a lot about good and evil. They are not always what they appear to be. I was involved, deeply involved, in a deception . . . I have deceived my friends, and I had millions of them.

Van Doren's statement was greeted with mixed results: a few commended him for being honest, one scolded him for expecting praise just because he had finally said something truthful. Van Doren was fired from NBC (with Dave Garroway weeping on the air as he made the announcement).

Following all the hearings, the final bit of fall-out was the enacting of new federal laws: U.S. Code Title 47, Chapter 5, Subchapter V, Section 509, which reads:

> *(a) It shall be unlawful for any person, with intent to deceive the listening or viewing public—[1] To supply to any contestant in a purportedly bona fide contest of intellectual knowledge or intellectual skill any special and secret assistance whereby the*

outcome of such contest will be in whole or in part prearranged or predetermined. [2] By means of persuasion, bribery, intimidation, or otherwise, to induce or cause any contestant in a purportedly bona fide contest of intellectual knowledge or intellectual skill to refrain in any manner from using or displaying his knowledge or skill in such contest, whereby the outcome thereof will be in whole or in part prearranged or predetermined. [3] To engage in any artifice or scheme for the purpose of prearranging or predetermining in whole or in part the outcome of a purportedly bona fide contest of intellectual knowledge, intellectual skill, or chance. [4] To produce or participate in the production for broadcasting of, to broadcast or participate in the broadcasting of, to offer to a licensee for broadcasting, or to sponsor, any radio program, knowing or having reasonable ground for believing that, in connection with a purportedly bona fide contest of intellectual knowledge, intellectual skill, or chance constituting any part of such program, any person has done or is going to do any act or thing referred to in paragraph (1), (2), or (3) of this subsection. [5] To conspire with any other person or persons to do any act or thing prohibited by paragraph (1), (2), (3), or (4) of this subsection, if one or more of such persons do any act to effect the object of such conspiracy.

(b) For the purposes of this section—[1] the term "contest" means any contest broadcast by a radio station in connection with which any money or any other thing of value is offered as a prize or prizes to be paid or presented by the program sponsor or by any other person or persons, as announced in the course of the broadcast. [2] The term "the listening or viewing public" means those members of the public who, with the aid of radio receiving sets, listen to or view programs broadcast by radio stations.

(c) Whoever violates subsection (a) of this section shall be fined not more than $10,000 or imprisoned not more than one year, or both.

Clean as a Whistle

The only TV game show production company to survive the quiz show scandals totally unscathed was Goodson-Todman. Goodson, in particular, was fiercely committed to running ethical games long before any whiff of discussion toward rigging had ever come up, and that attitude permeated his entire staff. Frequent Goodson-Todman panelist Betty White later said that rules and ethics were considered "sacrosanct" in the company.

There were a couple of reasons for this. The first was that Goodson-Todman seldom dabbled in big paydays for their game shows. *I've Got a Secret* offered a top prize of $80, which led Garry Moore to joke after the scandal, "Apparently, [the government] figured as that only $80 was given away on our show, we were too cheap to be crooked. They were right."

The only Goodson-Todman show that ran the risk of being perceived as fixed was *The Price is Right*, which gave away lavish prizes into the tens of thousands of dollars week after week, including luxury cars, boats, and even a private island on one show. Goodson was so committed to running an ethical company that he secretly hired a detective to have his own company spied on, and a thorough investigation determined that *The Price is Right* was indeed all right.

Funnily, in the fall-out from the quiz show scandals, Goodson-Todman was subjected to inquiry, but for a totally unrelated reason. In the wake of the Payola scandals prevalent in radio at the time, television shows found their clearance logs (detailed sheets tracking any copyrighted music used on each program) being scrutinized carefully. A sampling of Goodson-Todman's clearance logs found that 90 percent of the music featured on *The Price is Right* and *Beat the Clock* was owned by Music Publishers Holding Corporation, a division of Warner Bros. Despite the unusually strong leaning toward a specific music publisher, an investigation of Goodson-Todman determined no wrongdoing.

Who's in Charge Here?

During the 1950s, networks had a penchant for buying out certain shows from producers if they proved to be particularly successful. CBS bought *What's My Line?* and *I've Got a Secret* from Goodson-Todman, for example, while paying them a fee to continue producing the show on the network's behalf. A few months before the government began investigating quiz shows, a ruling had explicitly stated that networks could only own a specific number of their shows; going beyond that number would constitute restraint of trade and a possible monopoly.

The problem, the networks quickly found, was that they suddenly became afraid of their own shows. They were reluctant to give input to producers on the grounds that if they did so, they'd be claiming ownership of the show and therefore running the risk of creating a monopoly. After the quiz show scandals, the network practice of outright buying a successful show died down considerably, as networks wanted to maintain that ability to look over a producer's shoulder, without having to worry about the government looking over theirs.

13

A Pocketful of Ideas

Bob Stewart's Moment of Truth

Goodson-Todman Productions just wasn't interested in the big-money craze. They were more interested in strong formats. Some of the strongest were developed by a producer who joined the company in 1956. His professional name was Bob Stewart.

A Kid from Brooklyn

In the early 20th century, Brooklyn became a popular destination for Russian immigrants just arrived in the United States. And so, it was for a Russian couple, the Steinbergs, who settled into the area to start their family. They already had a son and a daughter when, on August 27, 1920, they welcomed a son, Isidore.

Despite being in the fourth-largest city in America, the Steinbergs lived a small-town existence. There were no cars on the street, so Isidore played punchball on the concrete with the other kids, and the block had enough businesses that everything anybody needed was on that one stretch of road; there was no reason to go anywhere else. Isidore came of age during the Great Depression, and his family learned to make every penny count. His father, a tailor, made all of Isidore's clothing, but none of the shirts had tails, as a way of saving material. Isidore was also taught the importance of sleeping with his wallet under his pillow.

Isidore's favorite form of recreation was playing games—not just the baseball and basketball teams at school, but at home. He played checkers, his father taught the family how to play penny poker, and as a teenager, he became fond of a Saturday night radio show called *Scramby Amby*, in which the emcee would announce a series of scrambled letters and contestants had to form a word with them.

Seeing the Future

Isidore lived near Corona Park, site of the 1939 World's Fair, where he got a good look at a new device called a television set; for many New Yorkers, the 1939 World's Fair would be remembered for decades after as their first exposure to the contraption. Isidore was mesmerized by a ball game that was being played several miles away, but being presented to him up close on a seven-inch screen.

By 1943, Isidore was married as well as serving in the Air Force. He remained stateside throughout the war, playing on his unit's football team and occasionally dabbling in communications; he was fascinated by teletype machines, an otherwise-ordinary typewriter that would duplicate whatever had been typed at a separate location. His life took a sharp turn when a commanding officer complained that not enough was being done for troop morale and abruptly put Isidore in charge of writing a four-page newspaper.

Once Isidore was discharged, he made use of the G.I. Bill to take a writing course at a city college. He took to the written word so naturally that for the first time in his life, he gave thought to a career other than factory work. On New Year's Eve 1946, he became a writer for radio station WNEW. He was tasked with writing commercials, as well as jokes for Gene Rayburn, who hosted two of the station's shows. Around this time, Isidore, who had an infuriating encounter a short time earlier with an anti-Semitic factory owner who refused to hire him, began going by the name Bob Stewart.

The Game's the Thing

Bob Stewart began writing for a wider variety of programs, including a dramatic series called *Play It Straight*, in which popular radio comedians would perform completely humorless roles. And he dabbled in game shows with *You Can Lose Your Shirt*, in which the panel tried to answer questions submitted by listeners, and a panelist forfeited a personal item of clothing for each wrong answer. He moved on to writing scripts for soap operas and detective dramas, too.

But a strange thing kept happening: one way or another, he kept drifting back to games. He wrote funny lines for *Songs for Sale*, in which aspiring songwriters would perform their songs, and a panel of musical experts would judge them. He moved on to producing a stunt game for kids, *The Sky's the Limit*, on the local NBC station in New York.

Stewart had a chance encounter one day with Monty Hall, a then-unemployed master of ceremonies. Hall had acquired some contact information for the lawyer who represented game show impresario Mark Goodson, and Stewart and Hall made a pact: Hall would give Stewart the contact information. If Stewart could come up with a game show under Goodson's employ, he would hire Monty Hall to become host.

Through Goodson's lawyer, Bob Stewart secured a job interview. Goodson emerged from his office and jokingly asked, "Does anybody out here have any ideas?"

Stewart jumped on the line. "I've got a whole pocketful of them, and I'm your next appointment."

Stewart got the job, although Goodson nixed his request to hire Monty Hall for any shows that he pitched. Now all Bob Stewart had to do was get some shows on the air.

Truth Be Told

The first idea Stewart threw at Goodson was a format that he named *Cross Examination*. Three contestants would claim to be the same person. A celebrity panel would cross-examine them and cast votes on who was telling the truth. Goodson disliked the idea instantly, saying that three ordinary people couldn't convince a panel of four celebrities—all of whom would almost certainly have some acting experience and training—without giving themselves away somehow. Stewart had so much faith in the idea that he promptly told Goodson to call up four celebrities, and Stewart would organize a demonstration for the staff at Gene Rayburn's house.

Stewart brought in a personal friend and two impostors. He gave some information to the Goodson-Todman staff about his friend and, to prove the strength of the concept, he didn't limit it to the four guests. He invited everybody in the room to cross-examine the three contestants for a grueling twenty-minute session. Once everybody had asked every question they could possibly think of, Stewart told the staff, "If you're positive that you know who the real person is—and by that I mean you'd be willing to bet money on this—raise your hand."

Nobody raised their hands. Goodson-Todman promptly went to work pitching the series to the networks, and CBS bought it. Finding a host proved tricky; Mike Wallace hosted the pilot, but dropped out by the time the show was ready to go to series, saying that he wanted to focus strictly on journalism. Walter Cronkite happily accepted the offer, but CBS News vetoed the plan. Actor Ralph Bellamy was deemed a worthy candidate because he had played several detective roles, but he was unavailable, though he would join the panel many times. Bud Collyer, who was already hosting *Beat the Clock* for Goodson-Todman on CBS, was asked to host the show at virtually the last minute.

The show's title was shaken up once again, this time just before its premiere. Called "Nothing But the Truth"—it was even listed that way in *TV Guide*—it was

Bob Stewart's pride and joy, *To Tell the Truth*, one of two games he developed during his first year at Goodson-Todman Productions. The host was Bud Collyer.

retitled *To Tell the Truth* due to a copyright issue involving a book. The series premiered on December 18, 1956, and stuck around for the next twelve years.

Please Stand Up!

Each game of *To Tell the Truth* began with the show's announcer—often Bern Bennett or Johnny Olson—asking the contestants, "Number one, what is your name, please?" Contestant number one would say, "My name is . . ."—and would say the name of the individual being highlighted. The same process would occur with contestants numbers two and three. Bud Collyer would then read a sworn affidavit explaining who the noteworthy person among the three was. The panelists would take turns asking questions of the contestants; the impostors could lie as much as they wanted, but the subject of the affidavit had to answer the questions honestly. The panelists would cast individual ballots numbered one to three, depending upon which contestant they believed was telling the truth. The contestants split $250 for every panelist who voted wrong.

Part of the show's appeal was its ability to put faces to some famous names for viewers; the central characters for many games were people who had become well-known without becoming celebrities. Over many years, the show would welcome cosmetics magnate Mary Kay Ash, *The Exorcist* author William Peter Blatty, H&R Block co-founder Richard Block, Alice's Restaurant owner Alice Brock, Bugs Bunny creator Bob Clampett, ice skater Peggy Fleming, disc jockey Alan Freed, *MAD* publisher William M. Gaines, pollster George Gallup, Dr. Seuss (Theodore Geisel), Motown founder Berry Gordy, *Dick Tracy* artist Chester Gould, and electronic music pioneer Robert Moog, among hundreds of others.

The Truth is a Funny Thing

Bob Stewart tried to run a tight ship at *To Tell the Truth*; contestants were brought in early for a detailed practice session where they became well-acquainted with the central character, and told how to give answers in a convincing fashion, but things often could, and did, go wrong.

On a night when the central character's name was Mickey Sullivan, an impostor confidently introduced himself by saying, "My name is Mickey Spillane!," then visibly cringed and started to walk off-stage. When the contestants all claimed to be a professional bowler, panelist Kitty Carlisle accidentally stopped the game cold by asking one of them, "How much do men's balls weigh?"

On the other hand, the contestants could stop Kitty Carlisle cold. She once asked a supposed zoologist, "How do gorillas breed?" The contestant answered, "Through the nose."

The game typically ended with Bud Collyer asking the contestants, "Will the real (_____) please stand up?" Periodically, though, the show would try to mix things up by finding different ways to reveal the real one; it was a miracle that *To Tell the Truth* kept doing that because it almost never went right. For contestants who tended to birds, Bud Collyer once took a bird out of its cage and set it loose, with the idea being that it would land on its caretaker's shoulder. The bird flew right past the contestants and perched itself on the shoulder of a stagehand. The central character one night was a quick-draw target shooter. All three contestants had guns in holsters. At the end of the game, Bud Collyer asked all three contestants to take their guns out of the holsters and fire a shot. Problem: One of the impostors managed to fire his gun first.

A Pricey Proposal

The other game show that Bob Stewart suggested to Mark Goodson was a premise called *Auction-Aire* (which, oddly, had actually been the title of a short-lived series in 1949). Stewart had been going to a local department store on his lunch breaks and watched an auctioneer selling off the store's wares. The auctioneer would announce the true retail price of every item after the close of bidding, and the bidders assembled always had an interesting reaction, in Stewart's eyes. If the final bid was anything below the true retail price—even, say, just five cents below—the bidders would give the winner a congratulatory round of applause. If the final bid was over the actual retail price, even if it was only a penny over, the buyer was treated like he had lost.

And maybe that WAS a game, Stewart thought. He told Mark Goodson he wanted to make a game show where people guessed the prices of the prizes being offered. Goodson disliked the idea until he called a few people into his office and asked, "How much did I pay for that lamp?" and to his amazement, arguments broke out. Fun arguments.

CBS and NBC both expressed interest in the show. Goodson-Todman took NBC's offer, but a pilot went so poorly—equipment broke down and host Bill Cullen was accidentally thrust into a wall because of a technical problem—that NBC made Goodson-Todman an offer to break the deal and never debut the show. Bill Todman nearly accepted that offer, but Bob Stewart objected so strongly that Mark Goodson overruled his business partner and forced NBC to hold up their end of the deal. The game, which Goodson re-titled *The Price is Right*, debuted on NBC's daytime schedule on November 26, 1956.

Originally, the show was to be hosted by an up-and-coming comic named Dick Van Dyke. Van Dyke remembered in his memoirs that there were two big problems working

Bob Stewart and his best friend/emcee, Bill Cullen, prepare for a segment on *The Price is Right*.   *Fred Wostbrock Collection*

against him: for one, he got the impression that the bosses, Mr. Goodson and Mr. Todman, didn't care for him very much. For another, he thought it was the worst idea for a game show he had ever heard.

Over a series of several days, Van Dyke came into the Goodson-Todman offices and hosted practice games. Every day, he went home to his wife and groused, "This is the dumbest idea. People are just trying to guess how much things cost. That's a show? It's never going to go."

Van Dyke bowed out, and the job went to Bill Cullen.

The Right Show at the Right Time

The daytime *Price is Right* instantly became the number-one program on daytime television, and by the following fall, it had a spot on the NBC prime-time schedule. In 1958, when the big-money quiz shows collapsed in scandal, Goodson-Todman wasn't implicated at all. The audience loved the allure of big payoffs but turned away en masse from the programs when they were exposed. *The Price is Right*, which had extravagant prizes up for bid—it offered Ferris wheels, a mile of hot dogs, elephants, Picasso paintings, houses, motor homes, and even a stereo system that converted into a bed—and did so completely on the level, gave viewers their fix with an exciting game. And unlike the hard quizzes that pushed gray matter to its very limits with near-impossible queries, *The Price is Right* was a big-time prize giveaway that *anybody* could play. Contestants placed bids, the one who was closest to the actual retail price without going over won the prize. That was it.

Author Kent Anderson later wrote, "*The Price is Right*, hosted by Bill Cullen . . . proved to be a healthy antidote to the surfeit of dollars on the television screen. Probably more than any other show on television, *The Price is Right* was calculated to do what all commercial television programming is designed to do: to encourage the American consumption ethos. No other quiz sparked greater interest in the process of buying and consuming. *The Price is Right* offered merchandise, the ultimate use of money to most viewers."

This was a lesson that Bob Stewart stumbled upon early in the series. The Picasso painting got an "oooooooh" from the audience, but the barbecue grills and dishwashers always got an "OOOOOOOH!" Viewers watched the show for a vicarious thrill, but that vicarious thrill came from items that were actually *needed* in a home. Winning a prize isn't exciting; winning a prize that you can use is the exciting part.

As Mark Goodson aptly summarized the lesson, "Money on television has become just a lot of numbers, but an icebox is still an icebox."

And that was all it took to reach number 8 in the Nielsen ratings. *The Price is Right* was a national phenomenon. Each week, home viewers were offered The Showcase, a package of prizes that could be won by the viewer who mailed in the best bid. A million postcards a week came in for the daytime Showcases. When the show expanded to prime-time, that number grew to staggering 19 million postcards per Showcase.

The Price is Right, created by Bob Stewart, was television's hottest game in daytime and nighttime. Bill Cullen's game of bidding, buying, and bargaining ranked as high as number 8 overall in the Nielsen ratings for the prime-time version.

Giving Notice

The problem was that as Bob Stewart's creations grew popular, he found the rewards for his efforts somewhat lacking. He was offered a negligible share of profits for the programs he created, but still felt that he was somewhat underpaid, considering exactly *how* popular his shows were. To his disdain, Goodson was obsessed with taking credit for all shows done under his banner. Stewart once asked that Goodson trust him to run *The Price is Right* by himself, and Goodson trusted him and obeyed those wishes; Stewart once went a full eight months without seeing Goodson, running *The Price is Right* without any input from the big boss. Goodson, in turn, insisted on accepting the awards that the show accumulated and taking credit for the show's development in interviews.

Things came to a head in a 1964 meeting when Stewart pitched a new idea that he had for a game. Goodson hated the idea, but Stewart asked permission to pitch the show to networks himself. Goodson said he would grant permission but that, if asked, he would tell network executives that he hated the concept. Stewart gave his notice. Mark Goodson, in a last-ditch effort to keep his star employee onboard, offered him an ownership stake in the company, but again, it came down to a matter of credit. Stewart asked if Goodson would rename the production company to include his name. Goodson said no. Bob Stewart walked.

Goodson-Todman staffer Mike Gargiulo later said, "It's really a shame Goodson and Stewart couldn't find a way to co-exist. If those two could have got along, the company would have grown to the size of Warner Bros."

Eye on the Prize

Bob Stewart Productions came into existence in 1964, but because network executives were afraid of Goodson-Todman's attorneys, it took over a year for Stewart to get a show on the air. In January 1966, Bob Stewart's first independent game, *Eye Guess*, went on the air. Bill Cullen, fresh off *The Price is Right*, which had been canceled the previous September, hosted *Eye Guess* in exchange for a cut of the profits.

Eye Guess was a memory game; contestants were shown a board with eight answers and given eight seconds to study it. The answers were covered up, Bill Cullen asked questions, and the contestants had to remember which space on the board was hiding the answer.

The show lasted for almost four years, even though Stewart himself admitted that the show was a dog. He told a reporter, "*Eye Guess* is a second-rate idea for a show. No, not second-rate. It is third rate. Bill Cullen holds up the show. If it weren't for him, it would be nothing."

In a 1998 interview, Bob Stewart was asked to describe the creative process that led to the creation of *Eye Guess*. By his own admission, there was nothing creative about it. "Sometimes, when you're looking for an idea for a game show, it doesn't come from anywhere except staring at a piece of paper or a typewriter and trying to get something—a couple of things to sound interesting in your mind. 'What would happen if . . . ' 'Would people enjoy doing this?' More importantly, 'Would people enjoy watching this process?' *Eye Guess* certainly wasn't an original idea."

By Stewart's own admission, he didn't really have high standards in his first few years on his own. CBS executive Fred Silverman once called and asked if he had any ideas for a prime-time series. Stewart bluffed and said, "Yes." When Silverman told him to be in his office in one hour, Stewart grabbed a magazine and some

Bill Cullen helps Bob Stewart go into business for himself. *Eye Guess* was Stewart's first creation as an independent producer.

Fred Wostbrock Collection

scissors, cut up the photos in the magazine, and then told Silverman that his idea was a game where contestants had to identify photos of celebrities from fragments of photos. *The Face is Familiar* made it onto CBS's schedule in the summer of 1966. Stewart got a prime-time series only one hour after he got the idea.

You've Got Charm, *Personality*

Stewart's personal favorite creation was a game that premiered the following summer, *Personality*, hosted by Larry Blyden. Three celebrity guests played on behalf of home viewers. Two of the celebrities would hear a question that had been asked of the third in a pre-taped interview and try to guess how that celebrity answered. A correct prediction was worth $25 for the home viewer, with the top score of the day earning a dream vacation as a bonus.

Stewart liked the show so much because of the hands-on approach he took to it. In the developmental stages, Stewart brainstormed about two thousand questions that he figured a celebrity could give an interesting answer to, and over the next two years, he updated it constantly. To save money, he conducted the interviews himself, and he had a remarkable knack for getting even the most private celebrities to open up to him. Stewart managed to keep some of them talking for as long as four hours per session, and more than once, a celebrity quipped that it felt like a therapy session.

"They gave away a good deal of their own personality while they were sitting there," Stewart reflected. "We'd come out to California; on any given day, I would take a little camera crew, we'd film them, I'd ask personal questions, we'd have coffee and cake. It was wonderful."

Stewart found that celebrities who lived in New York weren't as receptive to having a camera crew in their home—most New York celebrities lived in upscale apartments that weren't hospitable to the amounts of technical equipment that had to be set up for filming—so often, he'd have the celebrities come into his own office for filming. Not wanting the home audience to catch on to the fact that so many interviews were being done in a single location, Stewart bought a dozen paintings. Before each interview conducted in his office, he would hang up a different painting, so it always looked like a different location on the air.

All By Myself

Stewart maintained that the secret to his success was that he did things a bit differently from the big guys. "The Goodson-Todman operation was very big, very unwieldy. And there were many times when Mark Goodson would call twelve guys into a conference room. 'Let's think of an idea!' Now to my knowledge, nobody has ever had an idea with eleven other guys in the room. It also becomes a place where you have contention, you have show-offs . . . this idea of putting a group in a room was totally unusable. . . . My company, for the most part, was a one-man company in regards to putting the show together. I had no ego satisfaction in having somebody

I never met give me an idea for a show, putting it together for them, and getting it on the air. If there wasn't ego satisfaction, I wouldn't do it."

In the decades to come, Stewart built up a strong stock of successful, entertaining games, but one game of Stewart's would overshadow all of his other productions, casting a large, triangular silhouette. *Turn to Chapter 26 for the next part of Bob Stewart's story.*

14

Free Doughnuts and Bob Barker

Beulah Gets Buzzed

A s big-money quiz shows devoured prime-time schedules, one of the most cheerful, silly shows of the golden age of radio made its return to television, and along with it came a newcomer who would stick around for just a little while.

On the Reservation

Byron Barker was a migrant electrical worker installing high lines throughout the state of Washington. He and his wife, Tilly, were living in a tent city along with the other electrical workers and their families when they realized that Tilly was about to give birth, so she was sent to live in the nearby town of Darrington until she welcomed a son, Robert William Barker, on December 12, 1923.

Barker grew up in Mission, South Dakota, population 200 and eight miles away from the next town, on the Rosebud Indian Reservation, where he spent summers playing in the creek and winters ice skating at the river dam. He had a fondness for dogs; whenever his mother couldn't find him, she would climb onto the roof and look for dogs; whenever she saw a large pack of them, she knew she had found her son.

As a kid, broadcasting was never on Barker's mind. He was an athlete; he joined the baseball, basketball, and track teams throughout school. His real dream in life was to pitch for the St. Louis Cardinals, but hampered by what he called "a complete lack of talent," he focused on his studies and searched for some other trade to ply. He had been the public-address announcer for some football games in high school, and a teacher gently suggested that the young man should pursue radio. Barker politely declined, graduated from high school, and attended Drury College on a basketball scholarship.

In the Air, On the Air

After two years, Barker left college and became a Navy aviator; he earned his wings in 1944, married his high school sweetheart Dorothy Jo in 1945, and waited for his orders. But instead, World War II suddenly ended and Barker was out of the Navy.

In search of a job, Barker heard about a local radio station manager, G. Pearson Ward, at KTTS in Springfield, Missouri, who was obsessed with airplanes as a hobby, and Barker thought back to the suggestion he had received years earlier that radio might be a good outlet for him. Barker wore his Navy uniform to his job interview and spoke off the cuff about airplanes until he was hired. He wrote the news and did a local sports update for five minutes each day.

It was a mischievous prank that led to Barker's termination. A competing radio station, KWTO, would have its announcers say, "This is KWTO: Keep Watching the Ozarks!" Barker, referencing a co-worker who was known to be a heavy drinker, went on the air one night and said, "This is KTTS: Keep Ted Tucker Sober!"

The job hadn't been a total loss: Barker had an opportunity to host what was known at that time as an audience-participation show. It was a genre that he was mesmerized by. He was a big fan of *Breakfast in Hollywood*, in which host Tom Brennan would just go from table to table and chat with people who were having breakfast, and he was rather fond of Ralph Edwards's work as master of ceremonies for *Truth or Consequences*. When Ted Tucker was a no-show one day, G. Pearson Ward forced Barker to fill in for him on an audience-participation show.

"That's what you should be doing!" Dorothy Jo told him when he got home from work that day. "You did that better than anything else you've ever done!"

California, Here We Come!

Barker and Dorothy Jo packed up for Palm Beach, Florida, and station WWPG, where he hosted interview programs and played Santa Claus for Christmas promotions at a nearby store. The interview programs Barker didn't have much use for, but he was crazy about playing Santa Claus. He would have lengthy conversations with each child, and with an audience gathered around, he would prompt funny lines from the kids. He was amazed to receive fan mail from adults who watched him play Santa Claus, and again, Barker got a sign that unprepared conversations with strangers were the job for which he was best suited.

Buoyed by Dorothy Jo, who really believed that her husband had a strong future doing audience-participation programs, Barker decided to move to Hollywood in August 1950, with no job, no contacts, and no agent, and decided he'd be better off finding a job behind the scenes. His master plan was to get a job as a commercial salesman, seek out sponsors for an audience-participation show, and then suggest himself as host when the subject came up. He applied for a sales job at KFMV on Sunset Boulevard. The interviewing manager hired him on the spot and blindsided him with his plans for the rest of the day: "I'm trying to sell a supermarket on an audience-participation show. If you can help me convince them to sponsor it, you can be the host."

Barker sold everybody on a local radio show that he immodestly named *The Bob Barker Show*. Bob wove games into the format, but the main part of the program was Barker talking to audience members and demonstrating the sponsor's appliances. The program was a hit with audiences and, more importantly, with the sponsors; appliance manufacturers regularly experienced a sales boost for whatever products were featured on the latest episode of *The Bob Barker Show,* and Westinghouse eventually signed Bob to host his first TV show, a local talent program called *Your Big Moment.* Southern California Edison, the electric company that oversaw most of Southern California, commissioned him to do shows throughout the state, usually two a day in packed auditoriums. He also hosted *Talent in High,* a talent show for teenagers.

Barker's Break

Meanwhile, Ralph Edwards, the perpetually cheerful host of *Truth or Consequences* for many years on radio, had become a full-blown entertainment mogul, developing *Place the Face* and *It Could Be You!* for prime-time airwaves, as he continued hosting *This Is Your Life.* In late 1956, Edwards had successfully negotiated with NBC to launch a five-day-a-week daytime version of *Truth or Consequences.*

Edwards quickly realized that he couldn't host the new version. He had a full-fledged business to run, and he couldn't tend to it responsibly if he was doing rehearsals and a live broadcast during the daytime five days a week. He needed somebody to host it for him. Edwards auditioned dozens of candidates in Los Angeles and New York. NBC had already sent out the press release and the date was in stone; Edwards needed a new host before December 31, 1956. By mid-December, Edwards *still* hadn't found the right person for the job.

Ralph Edwards was driving his daughters to an ice-skating lesson one December afternoon and he happened to turn his radio dial to *The Bob Barker Show.* Edwards got to a telephone as soon as he could and reached out to Barker for a meeting. On December 21, Ralph notified him that he was the new host of *Truth or Consequences,* starting in ten days. Barker took over the show on December 31, 1956.

"Remember this name, you're going to be hearing a lot of him," Ralph Edwards assured viewers at the opening of the premiere broadcast. "Bob Barker!"

Barker, looking understandably nervous on day one, said to Edwards, "Following you and Jack Bailey, I feel like I'm hitting after Babe Ruth and Lou Gehrig."

Edwards cheerfully replied, "Well, we gotta bring the DiMaggios and the Mantles along."

Truth or Consequences emanated live each morning from the NBC studios on Sunset and Vine (it's a bank now) until the program relocated to the El Capitan Theatre. The show started at 8:00 a.m. to accommodate the 11:00 a.m. time slot on the East Coast. As an incentive for showing up that early, free food was promised for audience members. The marquee on the El Capitan Theatre read: "TRUTH OR CONSEQUENCES—FREE DOUGHNUTS AND BOB BARKER."

Once he became more established in the role, Bob got top billing. A few months after *Truth or Consequences* with Bob Barker was on the air, Art Linkletter came to the theater and watched the show from backstage.

Sensing the same promise that Ralph Edwards had seen, Linkletter told Barker, "You're gonna be around for a while."

Barker's secret to success: He knew his role. He said about his job as host, "The main thing is to hold things together and let the other people get the attention. It's really a variation of the straight man's role."

Marc Summers has a rare perspective on Bob Barker. As a child, Summers watched Barker on *Truth or Consequences*. Barely out of college, he became a writer for the program. It gave him a deeper understanding of Barker's skills as a host.

Summers explains, "When I was a kid, Bob Barker stood out to me. Here's a guy who looks great, he talks great, and it's clear that he's in charge of the show. Bob Barker loved listening to Jack Benny on the radio. Benny would never take command of a scene. Benny would let other people be the star. He'd put the focus on everyone else in the scene. And what happened was, over so many years, Jack Benny made so many people look good that his approach came full-circle and he began getting credit for how good he was, and people began thinking of Jack Benny as the greatest comedian. Bob Barker did the same thing. He would let other people be the star. He would set people up so that they'd say funny things. He would let them get the laugh. *Truth or Consequences* was so much fun to watch because Bob gave so much of the spotlight to the contestant. And the same thing ended up happening to Bob. He put the focus on other people so often that people began realizing how great he was at this job."

Barker's Follies

Barker made the program his own, on the air and off. Unlike most television program hosts, he conducted his own warm-up, and it was a lengthy one too. He talked to as many audience members as his time allowed, making mental notes of which people seemed like the ideal contestant for each individual consequence on that day's show. Among Barker's mental notes: Middle-aged women were the best contestants. Young women were self-conscious and more focused on their own looks, but middle-aged women just didn't care and they were up for anything.

Live television created plenty of hazards for Barker to navigate, and day after day, he handled them beautifully. There was the day of a torrential rainstorm when Barker had to do a full thirty minutes of audience participation with only two audience members. On another day, there was a woman in the audience who had moved to America from Italy thirty years earlier. Unbeknownst to her, her sister from Italy had been flown in to surprise her. The sister walked onstage, and the woman fainted from the shock, not regaining consciousness for the rest of the program. Barker and the staff agreed that it should be addressed the next day so viewers would know that the woman recovered just fine. They brought her onstage, she assured everyone that she was okay, and then they brought her sister back out. The woman, apparently not expecting to see her sister a second time, fainted again.

A regular feature of the show was "Barker's Follies." Barker would pick contestants from the audience and spontaneously gave them a song, a dance, or a dramatic role to perform, regardless of if they had the talent or the desire to perform. It was something of an anti-talent show. He would also pick people from the audience and "cast them" for celebrity interviews. He would tell two people from the audience, "You're going to be Cary Grant and Judy Garland," and then Barker would interview the contestants, who would respond to all of his nosey questions as if they were Cary Grant and Judy Garland.

Bob Barker continued the grand *Truth or Consequences* tradition of getting people to do the most ridiculous things and draw them out over multiple shows. For one episode, they gave a contestant a rowboat and had him paddle across the country to New York. They told him that he could get there by going to the Los Angeles River and then making turns at the right times into connecting tributaries, but when the man refused, they surprised him by revealing that the rowboat was mounted on top of a car. With a driver inside making the actual trip, the contestant had to stay seated in the rowboat and row continuously until reaching New York City. For a week, a couple was "marooned" on a traffic island in the middle of Hollywood Boulevard.

Truth Goes Down in History

Truth or Consequences, which had innovated three-camera filming in 1950, back when Ralph Edwards was hosting the show in prime-time,

Bob Barker's broad grin was a familiar sight day after day as the hilarity ensued on *Truth or Consequences*.

made history again by becoming the first TV show regularly recorded on videotape. This would allow every time zone in the country to see a high-quality version of the program every time it aired, and more importantly, it meant that the show no longer had to be done at 8:00 a.m. for the benefit of the East Coast, and everyone on the staff could sleep a little bit more. They also saved money by not having to buy doughnuts for all those audience members.

NBC, wanting a color version of *Truth or Consequences*, insisted that the show relocate from the El Capitan Theatre to the NBC studio complex in Burbank, which was fully equipped for color programming. Barker would later maintain that this hurt the program. NBC Burbank was, at that time, in the middle of a field. Tourists and passersby didn't drift inside the way they always had at the busier Hollywood Boulevard theater, and it took some of the fun out of the show. *Truth or Consequences* left NBC in 1965.

But Ralph Edwards had the amazing capacity to look at this show, twenty-five years after he first put it on the air, and believe that there was still life in it. In 1966, he offered local stations a new syndicated version of *Truth or Consequences* for five-day-a-week scheduling. They started the 1966 season with only six stations, but by 1967, they were all over the country once more.

Big Barker is Watching

During the syndicated run of *Truth or Consequences*, the show became particularly fond of hidden-camera stunts. Very often, they'd play a prank on an unsuspecting person on the street, and once Bob Barker addressed them from a hidden public-address system and revealed that they were on camera, the victims would receive a prize for being a good sport.

But these hidden-camera stunts didn't always go perfectly. There was a day when a "construction worker" was hoisting a piano on a large rope. The construction worker's rope was actually separate from the rope holding the piano, but everything was rigged up so it looked like a single rope. The construction worker called over a bystander and asked if he could just hold the rope for a moment because he had to step away. The man held the rope for a moment when the piano came free from the rope, hit the concrete, and shattered into toothpicks. The man turned tail and ran from the scene so fast that he didn't hear Bob Barker's voice trying to give him a prize.

Barker's favorite was the day when a *Truth or Consequences* writer, Milt Larsen, was taking care of a "gorilla" (actually a costumed actor) sleeping in a cage. He asked a large ex-football player if he could watch the gorilla for a few minutes; the gorilla was asleep, so how much trouble could it be? Sure enough, the gorilla woke up and erupted from his cage, chasing the man inside Grauman's Chinese Theatre. The burly football player switched from cocky to terrified so quickly that Barker couldn't even let him off the hook: he was laughing too hard to talk. The audio crew, on the other hand, was making notes for the editing crew because the man had done nothing but swear since the cage door swung open. Barker finally regained his composure and let the man know a hidden camera was watching. He eagerly announced that the man was getting a beautiful new billiard table, and the football player dejectedly asked, "What the hell am I supposed to do with that?"

History Again

Truth or Consequences ended production in 1974, but because the show's taping schedule was so efficient, and because syndicated programs were delivered by mail instead of by satellite at that time, new episodes continued airing until 1976. At that time, Bob Barker entered the Guinness Book of World Records as "TV's Most Durable Personality" for hosting the same TV show for eighteen years, a span that seemed impossible to fathom at that time. Of course, by 1976, Barker was a few years into a gig that would dwarf even that eighteen-year run.

By that point, Ralph Edwards had cheerfully referred to *Truth or Consequences* for years as "the granddaddy of audience-participation shows."

Mark Maxwell-Smith joined the writing staff in 1970. "By the time I came onboard, it had been thirty years since the show premiered, and with that much time on the air, there was a constant sense of turmoil because politics were all over the place. There was tension between the writing staff and Bob Barker because the writers had been with the show since it was on the radio, so they knew Bob back when he was 'the new guy.' And after fourteen years, he was 'the king' and the dynamic of that relationship was altered. And everyone felt a sense of power and seniority, so there was a lot of "I say this!' and 'Don't listen to him! Listen to me!' to deal with."

But there were more issues than just navigating the political waters. The syndicated run, operating on a much lower budget than any prior incarnation, was much more restricted. Whereas the zany *Truth or Consequences* of old shone with star-studded surprises and stunts, and occasionally sending contestants to airplanes and boats to travel for their stunts, the syndicated *Truth or Consequences* was confined to the studio, with little more than Bob Barker to carry whatever the writing staff could dream up. It's a testament to Barker's ability that the daily *Truth or Consequences* sustained itself without so many of the earlier, weekly version's luxuries. The reason so many writers had hung on since the good old days was because so few younger writers understood how to write for *Truth or Consequences*. Gag writers who got their feet wet in sitcoms and sketch comedy would wither at *Truth or Consequences* because they were so accustomed to writing a set-up and a punchline. On *Truth or Consequences*, you had to write a set-up that was so strong it had to lead to a funny conclusion no matter what—and the conclusion was nothing you could control; it was entirely in the hands of the contestants.

Mark Maxwell-Smith adds, "I forget who coined it, but there's a saying in television that there are only about twelve plots for sitcoms. *Truth or Consequences* was the same way. We taped six episodes at a time, each episode had three acts, so that's eighteen ideas you had, and only about twelve gags to sustain them. A lot of the show was dressing up what had already been done. For the first few weeks I was there, every time I pitched an idea, one of the other writers in the room would mutter '1949' or something like that. Sometimes my ideas were used, sometimes they weren't, but either way, every idea I pitched was followed by a writer muttering '1953.' They finally explained that they were reminding each other of the year that they first tried the idea I was suggesting. That show debuted in 1940; by 1970, they had done absolutely everything. I remember coming into the office one day really excited because I had a great new idea that had never been tried before, and when I pitched it, a writer said, 'Oh, yeah, we call that bit Mouse-in-a-Box; we do that in the live touring *Truth or Consequences* show because it plays so well.

"So, after all those years, you didn't really get a new idea on *Truth or Consequences*. All you could hope to do was pitch a used idea and add the phrase 'Except this time' we'll have a relay race, except this time, they're passing a lobster back and forth."

"Here's an example of an 'Except this time . . . ' We did a game once called Blonde, Brunette, or Redhead. We pulled a married man out of the audience and we introduce him to three beautiful models, and we tell him he has to rate which one kisses best, but he'll be blindfolded. We sent him offstage to get prepared by a staffer who blindfolded him, but while he's offstage, we bring his wife down and we switch her with one of the models, and we tell the wife that we'll award a prize if her husband picks her. So, the joke was that when it was his wife's turn to give a kiss, she absolutely gave her husband a tonsillectomy, and he didn't realize it was her. It played so well that we did it again a few weeks later, except this time, while the husband was offstage we told him what we were doing and offered him a prize if he would sabotage the bit and pick one of the other kissers."

By 1976, not only was it the granddaddy, it was the sole survivor. Audience-participation shows had been a staple of radio for years. Every local station in the country had some program where an emcee welcomed people from town and played small games with them, or just talked to them. They had all disappeared when TV took over. Audience-participation shows were a part of early TV to some extent, but they came and went. Year after year, *Truth or Consequences* held on. But even when it went off the air for good in 1977, its legacy survived. If you check a map of New Mexico, you can still find Truth or Consequences.

15

Back to Normal

It's Safe to Play Again

fter the Congressional hearings, game shows got back to normal. Surprisingly, the genre not only survived, it would thrive. These are the games that helped weather the storm.

Making Changes

Although the term "game show" is freely used to refer to shows dating all the way back to the 1920s, the term didn't become common until 1959. Prior to that, a variety of terms were used—audience-participation shows, giveaway shows, quiz shows—but when the big-money shows became popular, "quiz shows" became the preferred all-encompassing term. Once the scandals hit, networks and producers who still wanted to put the genre on the air needed to distance themselves from the ugliness. "Quiz show" went by the wayside, and the term "game show" became the popular classification.

This didn't make everyone completely happy. Mark Goodson in particular disliked the term "game show" because of how imprecise it was. Take two shows like, for example, *The Price is Right* and *To Tell the Truth*. Those shows had nothing in common, and lumping them together, in Goodson's eyes, did a disservice to the merits of both. Nonetheless, the term stuck and endures to this day. As different as shows like *The Price is Right* and *To Tell the Truth* are, they are both games, and they are both shows. Different as they may be, "game show" just works.

One of the early changes made to game shows in the post-scandal years was that the screening of contestants became more sophisticated, and one type of contestant in particular was carefully weeded out. In the years following the scandals, game shows would be played for very low stakes, just a couple hundred bucks here and there. And the people in charge of picking contestants went about their job with the knowledge that avarice would not be tolerated.

Producer Merrill Heatter told a reporter during the post-scandal days, "You have to give the impression of wanting to play for the fun of the game, rather than for the prizes involved."

Art Alisi, who worked at the time as Heatter's "headhunter," going out to search for good potential contestants, said in an interview, "We look for an outgoing personality, someone who's bubble and effervescent. We don't care, as we did in the old days, about interesting professions or needy financial circumstances. All we're concerned with is finding people who convey the image of having a great time playing the game."

Heatter's business partner, Bob Quigley, was certain that the days of big money were gone forever. "It will never go back to those days. Once a lot of money is at stake, a contestant gets tense, it becomes a matter of life or death and, well, it's just too possible that someone will try to fix it so that winning is assured."

Bowl Game

Exactly one intellectually challenging quiz show emerged in the year following the quiz show scandals; not only did it survive the jaded attitude that the public had toward harder quizzes, but it became an institution, and transcended mere television and became a part of the "real world" outside studios. It was *G. E. College Bowl*.

Don Reid was a college basketball player who once brainstormed a nebulous idea for a quiz show that would be a "mental basketball game." He never really fleshed out the idea beyond a title: *College Bowl*.

A producer named Grant Tinker showed the idea to a friend, NBC radio personality Allen Ludden. Ludden, an advocate for high education standards and an advocate for portraying younger people in a more positive light in mass media, had a stunningly enthusiastic reaction to the vague proposal. Tinker watched as Allen Ludden pulled out a yellow writing tablet and scribbled down complete rules, plus some logistical details for how to present the program. *College Quiz Bowl* (NBC insisted on adding the word "quiz" so people wouldn't think it was a sports program) debuted on NBC's fading radio network on October 10, 1953. Allen Ludden served as host.

Ludden hosted the program from a studio in New York while two teams of college students, sat in auditoriums on their own campuses, with a "referee" (a local NBC affiliate announcer) joining each team. Ludden's studio and the two schools were hooked up with a complex arrangement of telephone wires and microphones. Ludden would ask a toss-up question and the players rang in to answer. The team that gave the correct answer had a chance at an unopposed bonus question for more points. The team with the most point at the end of two eight-minute halves received $500 worth of scholarship funds for their school and returned the following week to meet new opponents.

On January 4, 1959, Allen Ludden and the show arrived on CBS television, with a sponsor, General Electric, and accordingly, a new title: *G. E. College Bowl*. The game was fundamentally the same, except for a change in payoffs. First prize for the winning school was $1,500, and $500 for the runners-up (Allen Ludden detested the word "loser").

CBS made it clear they'd be keeping a close eye on the program, but there were three small indicators to the audience that that they were watching a legitimate quiz: 1) By the standards of the now-fizzled big-money quiz shows, $1,500 was a paltry payoff; 2) The money wasn't even going to the players; it went straight to the school; 3) A rule that *any* team had to leave the show after winning five games.

There didn't seem to be much point in rigging a game that capped its potential winnings at $7,500.

And so, the public, which had so quickly turned off their dials when *The $64,000 Question* suddenly had the stench of scandal about it, now enthusiastically tuned in on Sunday afternoon to marvel at how genuinely brilliant these players obviously were:

> **Question:** What would a person be referring to if he said, "I'm holding the baby because it may be a sleeper and I might get a melon"?

> **Answer:** Playing the stock market; "holding the baby" means to keep a stock in hopes of making a larger profit later; "sleeper" is a stock that does not immediately appear to have much value; "melon" is a large dividend.

G. E. College Bowl was viewed with a level of prestige afforded to few game shows; schools across the country diligently recruited their best and brightest for a trip to New York to compete on the television version (Yale and Harvard both sat out, fearful of the harm that a loss would do to their reputations). *College Bowl* would follow the lead of college football with an annual Army-Navy game, which always drew big ratings. Parents and teachers across the country lavished the show with praise, mailing in numerous accounts of students who became more committed to their schoolwork after getting hooked on *G. E. College Bowl*. In 1963, it received

"The varsity sport of the mind," *G.E. College Bowl.*   *Fred Wostbrock Collection*

the final Prime-time Emmy Award for a game show. During the same decade, it was given a prestigious George Foster Peabody Award.

The Peabody Committee's statement:

> Through contests between two teams of students, *G. E. College Bowl* helps to focus the nation's attention on the intellectual abilities and achievements of our college students. The competitions emphasize quick recall of specific facts, and therein lies its appeal, which is illuminating, educational, entertaining, and exciting. The program provides weekly scholarship grants to colleges and universities. Allen Ludden, as the moderator, deserves a special mention for his excellent work. *G. E. College Bowl* is given the Peabody Award for television youth programs for 1960.

Wild *Hunch*

Goodson-Todman steered clear of hard quizzes when they were en vogue. On June 30, 1958, right at the tail end of the big-money-quiz craze, Goodson-Todman introduced *Play Your Hunch*, a preposterously simple guessing game that turned its host into a star.

Play Your Hunch was *To Tell the Truth* boiled down to its core. Host Merv Griffin would show two married couples three of something, and give them a simple problem to solve. For example, a live band would play a tune. Three band members would stand up, wearing labels reading X, Y, or Z. The couples were asked to pick the one that wasn't really playing. A correct guess won $50; three correct guesses won the game. A bonus round for a car was eventually added; the couple drew straws, and avoiding the short straw won a car.

For one noteworthy game, the contestants faced three men who were all songwriters, but they had to pick out which one was the one who wrote "Hound Dog." Jerry Leiber was Mr. X; after the game, Griffin revealed that Mr. Y and Mr. Z were Burt Bacharach and Norman Gimbel. Other games included appearances by Bob Hope, Boris Karloff, Jonathan Winters, and even The Three Stooges.

Separating *Play Your Hunch* from *To Tell the Truth* is that it used more than people. The contestants could be shown three dogs and asked which one was the father of the other two; for another game, the contestants saw three wheelbarrows with their loads concealed by blankets, and had to guess which wheelbarrow was the heaviest. They were even shown clips from new movies and asked to predict the next line of dialogue when a clip abruptly stopped.

A handful of future stars popped up in the problems contestants had to solve. One day, the contestants met a man who said he had a twin brother; out walked three people, X, Y, and Z, and the couples had to figure out which was the twin. One of the impostors was a young unknown actor named Robert Redford, who later remembered that the audience booed because they felt he didn't look enough like the twin to really fool anybody. Future *Nightline* host Ted Koppel appeared in another game as part of a problem, and then became flustered thirty years later when Merv Griffin brought it up during a *Nightline* appearance.

Simply Mervelous

Merv Griffin was a bigger winner than any *Play Your Hunch* couple. Griffin showed an early spark for producing games, showing up at staff production meetings—which hosts almost never attended at any game show—often with a notepad full of his own ideas for problems that contestants had to solve. *Play Your Hunch* producer Ira Skutch remembered that Griffin's ideas were always at least worth considering and almost always ended up being used; he had a mind for what made the show work.

Merv Griffin wants you to choose X, Y, Z, PDQ. It's *Play Your Hunch*.

Play Your Hunch began making more use of all the skills Griffin had to offer. Children were used for problems more frequently after the show found that the cordial host was exceptionally good at interviewing them. Musical games became more common when they realized that Griffin, who started in show business as a big band singer, could carry a tune.

And Griffin had a certain charm for making the most out of a mistake. There was a day when he walked onstage in shirtsleeves with no jacket and opened the show by announcing that he had locked himself out of his dressing room. On another day, the contestants had to figure out which of three crackers was strong enough to support a small weight. Merv—and everybody else—were a little stunned to find that all three crumbled and collapsed. Merv's reaction to this was to bring Ira Skutch onstage and have him give a detailed explanation of why the show had just presented an unsolvable problem. (The matzo in the middle worked just fine in rehearsal.)

NBC took note of how much Griffin had to offer and asked Goodson-Todman to release him from his *Play Your Hunch* contract so he could host a daytime talk show for the network. A new guy named Johnny Cason had just taken over for *The Tonight Show* and nobody was sure if Johnny would work out. NBC made Griffin their plan B, and he set about a talk show-hosting career that would span three decades, even though that Johnny guy worked out just fine.

Village People

One of the hallmarks of the big-money quizzes had been the deadly serious tone they all had, with suspenseful music, isolation booths, sweating contestants, hard questions, humorless emcees.

And then, on July 1, 1960, CBS introduced a new game, *Video Village*, which made a firm 180-degree turn away from all of that. The music was bright and cheery. The set was a sprawling design that looked like a tiny town, with shops, bridges, benches, and even a fun-size "bus" that gave the contestants a ride at the end of each game. Host Jack Narz (billed as "The Mayor of Video Village") was having a blast, the contestants were just there to have fun, and all advance publicity of the program hyped the "modest" budget for prizes. *Video Village* was cheap and proud of it. They didn't need $64,000 to draw viewers; the game was the thing.

Video Village was the creation of Merrill Heatter and Bob Quigley; Video Village itself was a massive board game. The contestants themselves served as the game pieces, moving from space to space after a die had been rolled by town crier (announcer) Kenny Williams. Assisting them was "Associate Mayor" (lovely assistant) Joanne Copeland, later wife number 2 of Johnny Carson. The head of CBS daytime programming, Larry White, said, "You might call the show Parcheesi with people."

Video Village consisted of three "roads," Money Street, Bridge Street, and Magic Mile. Scattered throughout the streets of *Video Village* were spaces like Do It Yourself (completing a simple stunt), Town Council (guessing the result of an audience survey), Go to Jail (you can only leave by correctly predicting the next die roll), and cash prizes of $5, $10, or $15—CBS told you it was modest, didn't they?

Magic Mile was home to an array of storefronts, like the Appliance Shop, the Silversmith, the Bank. When a contestant landed next to one of them, it was worth a key that would give them a prize if they were the first to reach the finish line and win the game.

Jack Narz departed (resigned from office?) after only two months, replaced by Mayor Red Rowe and then Mayor Monty Hall. The fanciful nature of the show lent itself perfectly to children, so a Saturday morning version, *Video Village Jr.*, was added to the CBS schedule.

Video Village went off the air in only two years, but, in a strange way, it endures today. In the film business, "Video Village" is now jargon for an area for the actors and crew to review the footage as it is being filmed.

What's the *Camouflage* Hiding?

While the blackballing of quiz show producers was unfortunate, it did create opportunities for newcomers. Host Don Morrow, who had never been the star of anything prior to the premiere of *Camouflage*, later said that "producer Gil Cates and his associate Ronnie Greenberg had only recently turned in their NBC page uniforms. But we had one saving grace. All of us were learning together. We didn't have any preconceived notions about video, or the professionalism of the 'old pro.' We had a good time just being ourselves."

Don Morrow hosted the game, which, like *Concentration* and *Dotto*, was inspired by a children's activity—"hidden picture" drawings. The contestants saw a cartoon drawing and were told of a specific object that was concealed within the artwork. Morrow would ask a series of trivia questions, and the first to give a correct answer got a chance to see the drawing with some of the camouflage removed. It was a bit of game show magic accomplished with the help of a service called Cel-O-Matic. A staff artist would create an elaborate drawing of, say, a beach scene with a rabbit concealed in the lines that formed the drawing. The Cel-O-Matic staff would create a stack of images based on that drawing. A few lines would be removed from the original drawing, which was then turned into a cel, and that would be the layer of camouflage removed after the first correct answer. They'd remove a few more lines, turn that into a cel, and that's what you'd see after the next correct answer. "Removing the camouflage" simply amounted to all the cels being stacked, and one cel being removed from the top of the stack after every answer. The winner of the game was the first contestant who could successfully trace the hidden drawing with a schoolmarm-style pointing stick.

Networks were so wary of trivia questions that *Camouflage* was conspicuously "rig-proof." The questions were printed on tiny scrolls that were rolled and bound by rubber bands, all piled in a drum in front of Don Morrow. Morrow would stick his arm in the drum, wave it around, and pluck out one scroll, making a show of the fact that he had no control over which questions were asked or in what order. For good measure, the questions—so easy that nobody would ever accuse them of being worth $64,000—were all true/false. Nobody suspected *Camouflage* of chicanery because there just didn't seem to be a way to do it.

Mr. Standards and Mr. Practices

The biggest change to TV game show operations was the implementation of a department called Standards and Practices; they were initially ex-FBI agents, and at all the networks, they set up rules for how all TV game shows had to operate. A Standards and Practices representative was present at every taping to ensure that the rules were tightly enforced.

In many cases, these were rules that didn't really need to be set in stone; they were things contestants were already doing. It was now strictly enforced that contestants and hosts couldn't talk to each other before the games (even when quiz shows were fixed, this wasn't really a problem). Contestants couldn't know anybody who worked on the program. It was now explicitly stated that members of the show's staff couldn't keep any prizes that went unclaimed by contestants. To prevent this, shows themselves could no longer coordinate the prizes to be given away; network departments or third-party agencies now acquired the prizes, with the show awarding them in exchange for giving the company a plug.

Contestants themselves now had to fill out a mountain of paperwork, promising that they hadn't cheated and pledging to report it immediately if they sensed anything suspect took place during their game, while the show was on the hook to make atonements immediately, to everybody's satisfaction, if something unfair had happened (a "wrong answer" to a trivia question was found, after some fact-checking, to be correct, and the contestant who lost the game would be brought back).

From show to show, individual regulations were designed and enforced. If the show involved a deck of cards, for example, the Standards and Practices representative had to count the deck and make sure that all fifty-two cards were there, and that the shuffle and cut had been satisfactorily random.

Some shows were asked to go to ridiculous lengths to prevent cheating. Norm Blumenthal later wrote of the absurd regulations that NBC Standards and Practices expected him to go to for ensuring a fair game of *Concentration*. The thirty pieces of the rebus puzzle were to be placed in a box with every side taped shut. That box would be placed inside a heavy-duty Kraft envelope, taped shut. Wax was to be poured over the tape, with Norm Blumenthal using a customized ring to make an imprint of his initials in the wax after it hardened, and then placed in a suitcase with five locks—two regular and three combination locks. Blumenthal argued against that level of security with some hard-to-dispute logic. If any contestant managed to open the five locks, break the wax seal, peel off the tape, see the puzzle, and put everything back together, that contestant deserved to win.

The more valuable the prizes, the more elaborate the measures were against rigging. In the late 1960s, ABC introduced *Dream House*, a game that offered married couples a chance to win, as you could probably guess, a house. The show deliberately invited too many couples to come to each taping, using a series of coin tosses backstage to determine which one would be sent to the stage to play the next game. The show's writing staff prepared multiple stacks of questions per game, sealing each stack in an envelope, and the standards and practices representative selected one envelope at random before the game started. That practice continued for years afterward; in the 1980s, NBC's *Sale of the Century*, which taped five episodes in a single session, would prepare eight sets of questions. A Standards and Practices representative would draw five at random, and then decide which one would be used for Monday, for Tuesday, etc.

And then there were games like *Play Your Hunch*, which was so simple and so luck-based that host Merv Griffin later remembered seeing a Standards and Practices representative in the studio and not being able to figure out what he was doing there.

But what they're doing, to this day, is making sure that what you see is what you get. After all these years, the Standards and Practices representative is still present at every game show, making sure every contestant has a fair shake and making sure every game is exactly what it seems.

16

Con+¢entr+8ion

A Rebus is Puzzling

Concentrate on Success

The most enduring post-scandal show was actually the last hurrah from the company most thoroughly implicated in the scandals. *Concentration* was introduced on NBC by Jack Barry and Dan Enright Productions on August 25, 1958, only about six weeks before their prime-time quiz *Twenty One* went up in smoke. NBC, which owned Barry and Enright Productions, seized control of the show and fired the men in charge.

Based on the children's card game, *Concentration* pitted two contestants against each other in a game of memory. A puzzle board of thirty numbered boxes was hiding fifteen pairs; some prizes, some instructions like "Take One Gift" from your opponent or "Forfeit One Gift," and a pair of WILD cards that matched anything. Contestants took turn calling out numbers two at a time to make matches. Every match claimed a prize and revealed two pieces of the hidden rebus. Why a rebus? In development, the staff determined that just matching prizes didn't build to a logical climax, so they decided something should be hidden behind the prize cards. Hangman-style word puzzles and photos of famous people were considered, but other game shows had already done that. The staff finally decided on rebuses, strictly because it was the one idea no other game show had tried yet.

Concentration didn't invent the rebus by a longshot. They appeared in *Poor Richard's Almanac* by Benjamin Franklin. Blumenthal had drawn rebuses for a children's magazine before *Concentration* was even a spark in the brains at Barry and Enright. But rebuses became so closely associated with *Concentration* that many viewers probably erroneously drew the conclusion that the concept was created for the show. In common vernacular, rebuses were even sometimes referred to as "Concentration puzzles."

The puzzle board, constructed by Messmore and Damon, a firm that designed and built many of the mechanical floats for Macy's Thanksgiving Parade, was an impressive feat. A stagehand with a push-button console could flip over the numbers that were called and reveal pieces of the puzzle as needed. In its finished form, it never really worked "like magic" the way most stuff on TV game shows appeared to work. In the weeks leading up to the series debut, Messmore and Damon and the *Concentration* staff were stymied by the problem that the board couldn't be silenced. Every turn of a numbered box let out a *ka-chunk*, and no modification

Hugh Downs in front of the *Concentration* game board. What pictures and prizes might it be concealing today?

could muffle it. In the coming years though, *Concentration* gradually found that viewers liked it that way. Producer Norm Blumenthal recalled in his memoirs that fans always mentioned the sound whenever they talked about the show. The *Concentration* game board was a machine, and the fact that it sounded like a machine just added to its charm. Sure, a box got stuck in mid-turn and had to be manually fixed every now and then, and yes, there was that time that a taping had to be stopped because of a fire, but the amazing ka-chunking game board was a calling card. There was nothing else on TV like it.

A *Concentration* home game was released too. Like the TV show, it was fondly remembered for its imaginative mechanism. No, there was no massive push-button-operated electric game board. The *Concentration* home game printed more than sixty rebus puzzles on a lengthy roll of paper (made with the help of a Milton Bradley business contact who manufactured novelty bathroom tissue), and players could change the rebus puzzles with the aid of the "Roll-o-matic," a knob-operated console. In its first year in production, the *Concentration* home game sold one million units. It took Scrabble three years to sell that many; Monopoly took twenty-five years. But *Concentration* was a monumental success for Milton Bradley. Every year, a new edition with new rebus puzzles went into print; the *Concentration* home game stayed in production all the way until 1982.

Trying to Concentrate

Watching an episode of *Concentration* today is a jarring experience. Of all game shows that have ever been on television, there's never been one with fewer frills. The live soundtrack came from Milton Kaye on organ and celeste, and Moe Goldenberg on percussion. The host was Hugh Downs, better known as a newsman. He spoke in a low tone and didn't really get excited. That attitude passed along to the contestants too. They'd quietly ask "Number 21, please?" and that was about as much as you heard from them. The audience offered some courtesy applause for a successful match and the solving of the puzzle, but that was it. No oooohs, no aaaaahs, no gasps or screams.

Concentration producer Norm Blumenthal was an art school graduate and assistant art director for *Esquire* magazine who had joined Barry and Enright Productions for their groundbreaking children's show, *Winky Dink and You.* The company retained him as an art director after that show was canceled. Blumenthal was originally charged with designing the rebuses, but when Barry and Enright fell apart and NBC seized control of *Concentration*, Blumenthal more or less ran the entire production. Despite his artistic background, Blumenthal resisted flash and frills so much that *Concentration* holds the distinction of being the last NBC TV show to switch from black and white to color. Blumenthal had battled the change for so long because he was fearful that color would make the rebuses too easy to solve.

Blumenthal explained in 2011, "If a drawing of a round object was in white or another monotone, it could be anything—but if only a small portion of it was red, as in APPLE—the player might know [the answer] was 'H+APPLE+E Ever After.'"

Only after getting assurance from NBC that he could keep the puzzles black and white did Blumenthal finally concede to color. Color *Concentration* began on November 7, 1966, and NBC was finally able to start advertising itself as "the full color network." Grateful for the compromise he was able to strike, Blumenthal tried to make the puzzles at least a little eye-catching by making all of the symbols, letters, and numbers pink and putting them against a maroon background.

Far from the Norm

Rather than depend on a staff of puzzle designers and writers, it was Norm Blumenthal himself who sat down with sheets of grid paper and meticulously designed every rebus puzzle, sketching out letters to make them as unrecognizable as possible until they were fully revealed (partially exposed D's looked like L's at first glance; W's looked like V's). Blumenthal also kept a close eye on the way contestants played the game and adjusted his puzzles as he gained more experience. With a free choice of any of thirty numbers, contestants, for some reason, gravitated toward the same handful of numbers for their first few picks in every game. Blumenthal would put the most helpful symbols behind numbers that players were prone to pick late in the game, and even the prizes were arranged in a way that would help build things to an exciting climax. The numbers commonly picked earlier in the game would reveal a prize of "1,000 Gallons of Gasoline." Hugh Downs would excitedly hint that there might be another prize on the board that would make the gasoline, and when contestants finally drifted toward the less common numbers, there was a shiny new car waiting.

Concentration would occasionally liven things up with bonuses, like The Envelope and Its Unknown Contents, or the Cash Wheel, but those bonuses were always limited-time specials that came and went. Blumenthal resisted long-term gimmicks, believing that the *Concentration* audience was tuning in to see those rebuses, and he strenuously avoided anything that took time away from numbers and prizes.

In 2011, Norm Blumenthal explained why he presented such a straightforward show:

> My primary rule was never stray from our unique format. We were not a quiz show, a stunt show . . . or talent search. Most of all, I was persistently at odds with the network, who wanted more stress and valuable game playing time devoted to "live" and glitzy prizes. I fought and won by refusing to include most of their ideas. Here's one stupid one that never got on the air. They wanted me to open my show with thirteen can-can dancers, bending over backward and one by one, flipping up their skirts, thereby spelling out all the letters in the title, CONCENTRATION, on their rear ends. Our ratings remained high because we kept our format from becoming a sad imitation of our competition. I never tried adding gimmicks like a ridiculous million-dollar giveaway that could never be awarded.

And here's how hands-on Blumenthal was. When Milton Bradley began manufacturing *Concentration* home games, Blumenthal went to the trouble of providing original rebuses. Many game show home game adaptations would use actual material from games. Game show reruns were non-existent at the time, and it was a small, small chunk of the audience that tuned in day in and day out. So, most home games simply collected questions and answers.

Blumenthal typically designed three or four rebus puzzles for each episode of *Concentration*; however, the vast majority of episodes only had two. On the rare occasion that a third puzzle could be played, Blumenthal quickly recognized that there wouldn't be very much time left in the half-hour to play it, so those third and fourth puzzles were intentionally more simplistic. Recognizing that children would want to play the *Concentration* home game with their parents, Blumenthal supplied Milton Bradley with a batch of unused third and fourth puzzles for the home game, putting players young and old on equal footing.

Here's Looking at Hugh

For the low-frills presentation that Norm Blumenthal preferred, there was perhaps no more perfect host than the man who originally landed the job, Hugh Downs. Downs was born and raised in Akron, Ohio, where he attended a little red country schoolhouse, heated by a large stove as his teacher read the class passages from the Bible and Zane Gray's western novels. The idyllic outer layer just barely concealed trouble brewing among the class. Downs would later recall that one classmate, who brought a pistol to school one day, went to prison for a bank robbery; another devoutly religious Sunday school regular was later nabbed for a string of burglaries.

Quiet, studious Hugh made the most of his education, heading for Bluffton College, a Mennonite school, where he sang in the choir. A performance by the choir on NBC radio convinced him to walk to a nearby radio station on a lark to give what he recalled as a very bad audition . . . but just good enough to land the job.

Hugh's father, hearing the boy's news when he got home, said, "You continue to look for a real job, but if you don't find one you can go with the radio station."

In 1958, Hugh Downs smiled and told interviewer Earl Wilson, "I never found a real job."

Downs was already the low-key announcer/sidekick to controversial, high-strung Jack Paar on *The Tonight Show*—among Downs's career highlights was abruptly taking over as host for one night when Paar stormed off the set, incensed that NBC censored one of his jokes. On weekends, Downs served as one of the many "communicators" on NBC Radio's legendary series *Monitor*; Downs was part-reporter, part-talk show host, part-disc jockey for four hours each weekend, displaying a versatility that served him well when more opportunities presented themselves. In 1958, he beat out Gene Rayburn to become the host of *Concentration*, a job he'd keep for the next ten years.

Hugh Downs the game show host was friendly and personable, but not prone to exaggeration, or shouting, or high drama. He simply got out of the way and called the game like a play-by-play announcer. "Number 17 is a tea set . . . Number 6 is a sofa. Not a match. The board goes back."

In 1962, Downs became co-anchor of NBC's *Today* but continued hosting *Concentration* for six more years, occasionally napping on a cot in his dressing room to keep his energy up between the two programs. His loyalty to *Concentration* irked NBC brass quite a bit; network bosses were happy that the game show was a hit, but somewhat concerned that it could be a threat to Downs's journalistic integrity as he delved into major stories for *Today*. Downs himself was aware of the image he needed to maintain. When a soup manufacturer sponsored *Concentration*, Downs refused to taste their soup for an in-show commercial announcement; he would only look at the bowl and smile; going further, Downs felt, would be too much for a newsman.

Downs departed from *Concentration* in 1968, briefly triggering a swirl of drama. Norm Blumenthal wanted announcer Bob Clayton to be promoted to host. NBC wanted, and got, Johnny Carson's sidekick Ed McMahon as new host. But McMahon's bombastic boozehound shtick on *The Tonight Show* seemed to alienate him from daytime audiences, and ratings slid. Bob Clayton took over as host and continued the series in Hugh Downs's unassuming style. *Concentration*, television's least noisy game show, kept bringing viewers in high volume to NBC for a few more years.

17

And This is My Partner

Hitch Your Wagon to a Star

 Goodson-Todman ace producer struck upon a new way to incorporate celebrities into his game, and unlocks some new concepts for game shows in the 1960s.

Pass It On

One of the most popular game shows of all time was conceived in a laundromat. Nat Ligerman, a laundromat owner who desperately wanted a career in television, suggested to Monty Hall in 1956 that word-association tests might make an interesting TV game. Hall was intrigued, and a short time later, he gave producer Bob Stewart the contact information for Goodson-Todman. The two men made a deal—something Monty Hall would later become an expert at—wherein if Stewart was hired by Goodson-Todman and created the format for a game show that got on the air, Hall would be hired to host it.

As it turned out, Stewart was never really in a position to live up to his end of the deal, but when Hall fleshed out Nat Ligerman's idea about a word-association game show, Bob Stewart pledged to pass it along to his bosses. In the next few months, a frustrating series of meetings would ensue, at which Goodson would suggest changes to Stewart, Stewart would relay the changes to Hall, Hall would make the changes and submit the revised idea to Stewart, Stewart would relay the revisions to Goodson, and so on. Hall became frustrated with the process—particularly because, for some reason, Goodson wouldn't meet him face-to-face about the idea—and eventually gave up.

Bob Stewart, however, wasn't quite ready to give up. He devised a premise in which two contestants competed against each other; one would see a prepared hint and hear a clue given by the opponent, and try to guess a word from the hint and the clue. The problem, Stewart quickly realized, was that there was no way to prevent contestants from giving bad clues, and really, if the premise of the game was for two opponents to give clues to each other, giving bad clues was the optimum strategy, and what fun would there be in watching that?

Stewart had an aha moment, eliminating the written hint, increasing the number of players to four, and having them play as teams of two. Now, the goal of the game would be to help your partner. This idea worked better, but still not quite to Stewart's own liking. He felt that with four players onstage, and with the camera probably focusing on two of them at a time, it would be hard for a viewer to focus. Stewart's solution: bring in celebrity guests to play on each team. The two-contestant teams would now consist of a single player and a famous partner.

This would be a monumental shift in game shows. Celebrities and game shows had gone hand-in-hand for years, but it was always a competition between celebrities and contestants. On panel shows like *What's My Line?* and *I've Got a Secret*, the contestant had some mystery about them, and the celebrities were trying to keep them from winning money by solving that mystery. Having celebrities work side-by-side with contestants was a wildly different approach.

The Goodson-Todman staff played some practice games. To say that everybody liked the idea wasn't enough. This was something special. Goodson-Todman treated their new format with great care. They intentionally designed a low-frills, minimalist set, sensing that the game would appeal to people who weren't game show fans. Host casting was crucial. Humorist Henry Morgan and hammy Gene Rayburn were rejected, because Bob Stewart reasoned that the game itself was so strong that they needed a host who would stay out of the way. *G. E. College Bowl* host Allen Ludden, who brought an intellectual flair to everything he did, got the job. Goodson held a staff meeting that went on for hours, in which the staff hotly debated how the host should extend his arms while distributing the words to the players. When the set was built, Goodson hired a group of five actors to sit on the set, so that the director and cameramen could shoot them from a variety of angles and make sure the game looked right.

Word Up!

Password with Allen Ludden debuted on CBS on October 2, 1961. Two celebrity-contestant teams competed against each other. One member of each team would see the password and, using only one-word clues (no hyphens allowed, and co-editor Dr. Reason A. Goodwin of the World Book Encyclopedia was present for every game, buzzer in hand, to zap players who gave illegal clues), tried to convey the password to the partner. Passwords started at ten points and diminished one point per clue until it was guessed. Twenty-five points won the game and a chance at the Lightning Round. The winning team played fundamentally the same game, but now played it for speed against a sixty-second clock, with up to five passwords and a $50 award for each password guessed.

The Lightning Round was another special element of *Password*. It wasn't the first bonus round ever seen on a game show (*Name That Tune* had the Golden Medley round in the 1950s, with contestants trying to name seven tunes in thirty seconds.) But it was the bonus round that standardized the concept. Several producers noticed over the years that within months of *Password*'s premiere, TV executives just expected you to have a bonus round in your proposal for a new game.

Password was comfortably seated as the most popular game show of the 1960s. Over the next five years, ABC and NBC would plug in a total of fourteen different shows in the 2:00 EST time slot, but none of them could touch *Password*. A CBS prime-time *Password* became a fixture, too.

Many celebrities were actually afraid of playing *Password*—the game was such a mental exercise that the "beautiful people" voiced a fear of being exposed by playing the game. But the allure of winning the game, being seen as one of the smarties in show business, was irresistible to others. As the show continued attracting massive audiences, the A-list came to play *Password*: Jimmy Stewart, Ginger Rogers, Mel Torme, Douglas Fairbanks Jr., Olivia de Havilland, Robert Goulet, Ann Bancroft, Rita Moreno, Raymond Burr, Joan Crawford, Shelley Winters, Lena Horne, Sammy Davis Jr., Chuck Connors (who was so addicted that he offered to pay his own airfare to be a guest), and Lucille Ball came to the game time and again to match wits with one another.

Who were the best of the best, though? Peter Lawford was considered the strongest male player, holding the record for the fastest Lightning Round, which he and a partner completed in only twelve seconds. Among women, there were three stand-outs: *Bewitched* star Elizabeth Montgomery, whom Allen Ludden referred to as "Queen of *Password*" several times; Carol Burnett, who used her acting skills to fullest effect on every game (as Allen Ludden explained in one interview, "She can communicate a word of meaning with just one word. When she says 'Me-e-e-ssy,' it's the messiest mess"); and the one and only Betty White, adored by viewers, adored by contestants lucky enough to play with her and win, adored by the show's staff—director Mike Gargiulo once said that it almost never mattered who the other player was when Betty was on the show, that person would just be "the other celebrity"—and adored most of all by host Allen Ludden, who married her on June 14, 1963. The ceremony took place in Las Vegas, after which the couple promptly returned to New York to play *Password*, with Betty competing

Allen Ludden welcomes June Lockhart and Ray Bolger to *Password*.
Fred Wostbrock Collection

against Jack Paar. For that game of *Password*, the passwords included "sorry," "romance," and "henpecked."

One of *Password*'s most devoted fans was a disc jockey by the name of Wink Martindale. As he fondly recalled:

> I was on the air on KFWB every day, and as soon as my shift ended, I rushed home to watch *Password*. I was addicted to that show. First of all, the game itself was just wonderful. It was fun to play along with, it was fun to shout at the TV when you thought of a better clue than the person on the screen was giving. It was simple, too—you'll always see a correlation between simplicity and success with game shows. It was easy to follow and fun to play along with. And watching the stars play that game gave it some added allure. The stars are always on such a pedestal, but now, here's a game where they're on equal footing with everybody else, and it's neat to see how well a star plays compared to how you or anybody else plays. It's fun to think of yourself as being comparable to a famous person, in some sense.

Password released a durable home game, first issued in 1962 by Milton Bradley, with new editions being released all the way through 1987. Jimmy and Gloria Stewart brought their *Password* home game to every social gathering; Lucille Ball kept hers in her dressing room, and would pass the time during rehearsals for her TV show by gathering cast and crew to play with her. And they had plenty of company. *Password* was the second-best-selling game in America during the 1960s, second only to Monopoly.

A Winning Match

Goodson-Todman always maintained a policy of "ripping off" their own shows whenever they struck upon a successful new format. It was a good way of keeping competitors at bay by saturating the market themselves. In 1962, Goodson-Todman producer Frank Wayne came up with the company's next celebrity/contestant team game. He came into the office one morning and told everybody "Write a fact about elephants" and they compared answers afterward, seeing who in the room had written the same answers.

From that idea sprang *The Match Game*. Premiering on NBC on New Year's Eve 1962, *The Match Game* would pit two teams of three—a celebrity guest and two contestants—against each other. Host Gene Rayburn, who got the nod for this show a year after being rejected for *Password*, would read a simple question like "Name a branch of the military" or a fill-in-the-blank statement like "Cigarette (blank)" and the six contestants would write answers individually, attempting to write the same answers as their partners. The idea was so similar to the one that Monty Hall had originally proposed to Goodson-Todman a few years earlier that he nearly sued, but at the time he was hosting *Video Village* for CBS, the same network that aired *Password*, and a CBS executive gently talked him out of filing a lawsuit against a company that was producing another show on their network.

Although Mark Goodson hoped *The Match Game* would acquire a reputation for being a low-key, cerebral game like *Password*, host Gene Rayburn reshaped it into a comedy show. Rayburn found the show so boring that he would freely joke around, or drag people from offstage to do shtick. Goodson wrote multiple memos complaining that Rayburn was getting too many laughs and detracting from the game, but Rayburn fired back that there wasn't enough of a game to detract from. In 1965, the show was canceled by NBC but got a reprieve when question writer Dick DeBartolo—who also wrote for *MAD* magazine—began writing questions in a more salacious vein, like "Mary likes to pour gravy on John's (blank)."

The questions were a perfect fit for the comedic approach that Rayburn already took toward hosting, and that settled it: *The Match Game* was meant to be a comedy show, and that was precisely how it was presented. Ratings went up and NBC kept the show on the air. It stayed for another four years.

Like *Password*, *The Match Game* attracted a stunning array of celebrity guests over the years. Talent booker Rae Pinchon and writer Dick DeBartolo had a rather unscientific approach to scheduling guests for the show—they called celebrities that they personally wanted to meet. And amazingly, many of them said yes; among them, Rod Serling, Sal Mineo, Lauren Bacall, Dorothy Lamour, Mickey Mantle, Roger Maris, Ethel Merman, Gloria Swanson, David Susskind, Hal Holbrook, Dustin Hoffman, James Brown, David Frost, and Burt Reynolds.

Lauren Bacall once said that she would always do the show because she adored Gene Rayburn. Other stars invited had a rather helpful epiphany about the program. Dick DeBartolo once comforted a nervous Ethel Merman before her first appearance on the show by laying out the rules of the game and bringing it to her attention that "this is the game on television that doesn't deal in right or wrong answers." Celebrities were more receptive to appearing on *The Match Game*, DeBartolo opined, because the very nature of the game meant it was impossible to be "wrong."

Contestants filled in the blanks for Gene Rayburn on NBC's *The Match Game*.

That's the Word That You Don't Say!

Although Monty Hall had been compelled not to file suit against Goodson-Todman, they themselves had no compunction about going to court when they felt they had been ripped off.

Three months after the NBC debut of *The Match Game*, the network introduced a new word-association game from Ralph Andrews–Bill Yagemann

Productions, *You Don't Say!* The show had aired locally on Los Angeles station KTLA in 1962, with host Jack Barry. Because he was considered undesirable to NBC due to the quiz show scandals, *You Don't Say!* had weekly guest hosts in the months leading up to its national debut, in search of a new master of ceremonies. The job went to Tom Kennedy, a popular commercial announcer formerly known as the host of *Big Game* and *Dr. I.Q.*, two shows hastily shoved into production as the big-money quiz shows collapsed.

You Don't Say! was, like *Password*, a contest between two celebrity/contestant teams. Instead of words, *You Don't Say!* dealt in names—names of people, characters, places—with an unusual style of clue-giving. The players tried to convey the names by giving clues to words that sounded like fragments of the famous name.

For example, if the name was "Tom Kennedy," a player might give the clue "A factory where soup or some other food is packed into tin containers is called a . . ." The clue sentence had to be structured so that the thing being described was the final word of the sentence, but that's the word that you don't say! From there, the person receiving clues had to figure out that the partner had been describing "Cannery," and then guess that "Cannery" sounds like "Kennedy" and that the famous name was "Tom Kennedy."

The method of clue-giving was unorthodox enough that the show had a massive "cheat sheet" on the set, just out of view of the cameras, reminding all players of what constituted a legal clue on the program. But even with those precautions, on at least one occasion, the show dealt with a celebrity guest who absolutely could not grasp the game.

Tom Kennedy said in 1987:

> I really don't want to use his name. He was one our best screen actors. Played many roles and always gave an outstanding performance. Anyway, he shows up to tape the show. . . . This particular subject name was John Wayne. Our celebrity player proceeded to whistle the theme from *The High and The Mighty*. I of course tried not to embarrass him but I had to stop the game and stop the tape from rolling. I told him he wasn't allowed to give clues like that. He looked at me, with a very serious expression on his face, and said, "But he was in that movie." I again explained the concept of the game to him and we then again started the taping. It wasn't thirty seconds into the taping and he again blurted out an answer that was completely against the rules. I again stopped the tape. I felt so sorry for him. Here he was this giant of an actor but he simply didn't understand the game. He finally just looked off stage at our producer and said he just didn't get it and he felt it would be better to just call it a night. We of course agreed and he left and we simply replaced him with another celebrity. But that was funny—this great actor whistling the theme from *The High and The Mighty* and then saying, "But he was in that movie."

Goodson-Todman kept a watchful eye on *You Don't Say!* and didn't like what they were seeing at all. It was a word-association game between two celebrity/contestant teams, after all. It was too much like *Password* for their tastes, and

Beverly Garland and Lee Marvin joining Tom Kennedy for a game show? *You Don't Say!*   *Fred Wostbrock Collection*

Goodson-Todman took Andrews-Yagemann to court. To Goodson-Todman's dismay, the court, for the most part, was on Andrews-Yagemann's side, ruling that *You Don't Say!* was different enough. However, the judge did side with Goodson-Todman on one oddly specific point: he agreed that the basic design of the set was too similar to *Password*, and *You Don't Say!* had to modify its set so that Tom Kennedy stood next to the players, instead of between them.

To Goodson-Todman's further irritation, it seemed like they were truly the only ones bothered by the knockoff game. Not only did Betty White freely play the game, but when Allen Ludden was courting her, he stood backstage for several tapings. And Allen Ludden would eventually appear on camera as a guest player.

The Object of the Game

ABC got into the word-association game business on December 30, 1963, with *The Object Is* from producer Wilbur Stark. Dick Clark was making his game show hosting debut on the game, which seemed designed specifically to avoid a lawsuit from Goodson-Todman. The game involved six players in total, three celebrities and three contestants, who competed individually. They sat in a line. Dick Clark would reveal a famous name to the first person in line. That player would name an object associated with that famous person (for example, if the answer was "Dick Clark," you might give a clue like "record player" or "microphone"). If a player failed to guess the answer, that individual was shown the answer and then tried to convey it to the next player in line, and so on. Score was kept only for the civilian contestants in line, who earned points by guessing the answer from a star's clue or conveying the answer to a star. In the bonus round, Clark would announce a category, like "nursery rhyme characters," and a contestant had thirty seconds to name as many as possible for five dollars apiece.

The Message is Clear

But when *The Object Is* flopped and went off the air in only thirteen weeks, ABC was not dissuaded from pursuing word-association games. They turned to the experts for a replacement—Goodson-Todman developed a game that seemed to weld *Password* and *The Match Game*, and called it *Get the Message*.

Like *The Match Game*, it was played between two teams of three—this time, a single contestant and two celebrities—and, like *Password*, the object of the game was to communicate a secret word, or words. The messages on *Get the Message* could be anything, a popular saying, a song title, a famous person's name. Two members of a team would individually write a one-word clue, the goal being to try to write a helpful clue that was different from the helpful clue that your partner had written, to give the third member of the team as much help as possible.

The host of the show was to be Betty White. Goodson-Todman had no qualms about the fact that they were ripping off their own properties, and given how well known Betty White was for her game show appearances, and particularly how well associated she was with *Password*, they figured she was the right woman for the job. ABC insisted that a man host the show—the feeling at the time was that game shows needed male masters of ceremonies because that role needed an air of authority, something women lacked.

The job initially went to Frank Buxton, who left the show to go to work on the children's series *Discovery*. He was replaced by Robert Q. Lewis. Eight years later, Buxton would be a writer on *The Odd Couple* and pen perhaps the most famous episode of the sitcom's run—the one in which Felix and Oscar are teammates on *Password*, with special guest stars Allen Ludden and Betty White.

Say What?

What's This Song? wasn't a word-association game, but it capitalized on the other key component of *Password*: celebrity partners. *What's the Name of This Song?*, as it was originally titled, had actually enjoyed a long run on the Mutual Network in the 1930s and 1940s before moving to television in the 1950s, airing locally on Los Angeles television for ten years. In 1963, producers Stu Phelps, Jack Reeves, and Jesse Martin bought the rights to the format for a thirteen-week run on Los Angeles station KTLA. The producers were lucky enough to find a host who could sing: Wink Martindale, whom the producers discovered hosting another game on KTLA, *Zoom* (contestants watched the camera zoom out from a close-up shot and rang in to identify the object they were seeing).

NBC liked what they saw on the local show and took it national, asking for two

Wink . . . er, Win Martindale, the host of *What's This Song?*   *Photo courtesy of Zane Enterprises*

changes: the title had to be shortened to *What's This Song?*, and the host had to shorten his name, too. "Wink," NBC reasoned, was "too juvenile" a name for a master of ceremonies. On October 26, 1964, NBC introduced the nation to debuting host Win Martindale.

Two celebrity/contestant teams would compete against each other. One team would hear a song and had to identify the name of the song for twenty points, and then sing the first four lines of the song for an additional twenty. The opposing team could challenge and earn twenty points themselves if they correctly guessed that the lines given were wrong.

Surprisingly, most of the celebrity guests on the show were not professional singers. Stu Phelps later told author Wesley Hyatt, "We'd get people who purposely couldn't sing but were great raconteurs. People would laugh, and the contestants would help them."

The show lasted just under a year on NBC before being sacrificed in favor of a soap opera. The program returned in 1968 in first-run syndication as *Win with the Stars*, with Allen Ludden hosting and a regular contest that viewers at home could participate in by picking up entry forms at the local grocery stores that sponsored the program.

No Bluffing

Call My Bluff was Goodson-Todman's next celebrity/contestant word game. This time, the teams played something similar to the parlor game "Dictionary," giving three possible definitions to an obscure word so the opposing team could try to figure out which definition was correct. In the bonus round, a guest came onstage, and the losing team listened to the winning team give details about an accomplishment in the guest's life. The losing team could earn the right to stay for the next game by guessing which opponent was giving them truthful information. If the winners fooled them, though, they won a cash jackpot that started at $200 and grew $200 per game until it was cracked. Those stakes were a mere drop in the bucket compared to the $8,425 that host Bill Leyden spent on airfare commuting from Los Angeles to New York for each taping of the show's six-month run.

Final Judgment

Other production companies and other word games came and went—*Chain Letter* with Jan Murray, from Stefan Hatos–Monty Hall Productions, and *Fractured Phrases* with Art James, from Joelson-Baer Productions, both disappeared in thirteen weeks apiece. But Goodson-Todman seemed to have the magic touch with the concept, even when their own employees admitted that one such entry was "anemic."

The "anemic" word game from Goodson-Todman was *Snap Judgment*, hosted by Ed McMahon. It was extremely close in form to *Password*—the key difference was that all four players saw the words they'd be giving clues for before the show began, wrote down the clues they intended to give, and could only give the clues they had prepared once they were onstage.

The concept worked—to a point. *Snap Judgment* premiered on April 11, 1967; on September 15, 1967, *Password* was canceled. Over a year later, on December 23, 1968, the rules of *Snap Judgment* were changed. The game was now played identically to *Password*. The modified *Snap Judgment* came to an end thirteen weeks later, on March 28, 1969. The celebrity/contestant word-association boom had died down.

18

The Lady or the Tiger

Deal Me In!

Away from the word games and the celebrity partners, the 1960s brought one of the most enduring games of all time, a simple series of "this or that?" dilemmas that captivated the country.

A Short Story

In 1882, author Frank R. Stockton penned a short story titled, *The Lady, or The Tiger?* A cruel king brought a man accused of a crime into an arena with two doors; one is hiding a beautiful woman, the other hiding a hungry tiger. The accused must select one door, and luck will determine the verdict; if he picks the beautiful lady, he is acquitted and married, but if he picks the tiger, he is ruled guilty and eaten.

The story left an impression on a bright young Winnipeg boy named Monte Halparin. Born on August 25, 1921, Monte was an exceedingly smart kid—he entered fourth grade two years early—who devoured whatever entertainment he could get near. He read voraciously, listened to the radio, and covered sports for the school newspaper. At age fourteen, he graduated from high school and went to work for his father's butcher shop until a philanthropist offered to pay his full college tuition, so long as he maintained straight A's. Monte held up his end of the deal and earned his degree at the University of Manitoba.

Monte was a member of the drama club when he was recruited to do some acting on a radio drama. By the time Monte graduated, he had a regular six-hour disc jockey shift; the station manager was so dazzled that after Monte had been there for nine months, he handed Monte a map of Toronto with dots marking the locations of local radio stations.

"Go," said the station manager.

Monte moved to Toronto and instantly found a job at station CHUM, where the station manager, Jack Part, asked him to modify his name to Monty Hall. Hall hosted a variety of programs for the station and for station CFRB. Jack Part shared a memory from childhood of traveling from town to town in upstate New York, doing what were called "medicine shows." A salesman would pull up his wagon and sell patent medicine to the townsfolk, but before making his pitch, he would play a small game with the crowd where he would ask for specific objects—"Does anyone have a rubber band in their pocket?"—and give small trinkets to anyone who could produce one. Part thought that could be done on radio, and called the game *The Auctioneer*. He hired Monty to host.

Monty wanted to form his own production company, but the radio and nascent television industries in Canada were such tough roads to navigate, and for such paltry money, that Monty decided to try American broadcasting. After a frustrating six months in New York, Monty took an odd approach to job-hunting. He began writing a weekly newsletter, "The Memo from Monty," consisting of funny things that had happened to him, jokes he had heard, and places he had visited, all while hunting for a job; it was an early form of a blog, being sent out to anybody with the power to hire him. After several months, Monty gave up writing "The Memo from Monty." And then a concerned NBC executive, Steve Krantz, called him, upset that he hadn't received his issue of "The Memo from Monty" that week.

By the end of that day, Monty had a new job, filling in for Gene Rayburn on a local New York game show, *The Sky's the Limit*, while Rayburn recuperated from a broken leg. That led to briefly guest-hosting *Twenty One* for Jack Barry—Monty maintained that the production company used him as "a patsy" and that he wasn't clued in that the show was fixed—plus a stint hosting an improvisational comedy show called *Keep Talking*, an old-movie anthology called *Cowboy Theater*, a boring daytime game called *Bingo at Home*, and a weekend stint as a "communicator" on NBC Radio's legendary series *Monitor*. From there, he replaced Jack Narz as mayor of *Video Village* (a job he took with less than twenty-four hours' notice) and produced a game of his own creation, *Your First Impression* for NBC.

Let's Make a Partnership

Hall quickly became exasperated with the daily phone calls from NBC executives trying to tinker with his show, as well as all the other details involved in running a production company; he quickly decided it wasn't a one-man job, so he hired Stefan Hatos, the producer who had been in charge of the game show that *Your First Impression* replaced. Hatos, a former concert oboist who moved into radio and television, was, as Monty recalled, a "real nuts and bolts guy," who had a feel for all the mechanisms that kept a television production running smoothly; within days of his arrival, for example, the staff of *Your First Impression* had made the switch from handwritten notes on the backs of envelopes to typewritten scripts for each day's game. Monty was so grateful for the contributions that his new partner was making that he renamed the production company Stefan Hatos–Monty Hall Productions.

During a lunch meeting one day, Monty brought up *The Auctioneer*, not realizing that Hatos had done a show with a similar premise on a local station in America. Monty also brought up *The Lady or the Tiger?* and made the off-the-wall suggestion that this short story about a barbaric monarch and his warped sense of justice might actually make an interesting game show. They kicked the idea around, making all kinds of suggestions for additions, like buying and selling prizes, trading and swapping goods.

On the walk back to the office, Hatos froze in the middle of a crosswalk and blurted out "How about this for a title: *Let's Make a Deal!*"

Both men sensed a problem with their format; as much as they tried to spice it up, the premise was so preposterously simple that they couldn't get a sense, sight-unseen, of if it was anything that your average TV viewer would want to watch. Hatos and Hall came up with a barebones form of the game using envelopes and a rubber chicken. They went to a variety of clubs and offered themselves as "free entertainment" for the guests, workshopping the game and gauging the audience reaction to figure out what worked and what didn't. The audience reaction was beyond anything Hatos and Hall imagined. Monty would open an envelope and reveal a card that simply read, "REFRIGERATOR," and the spectators would erupt, even knowing that they weren't watching a real game or being awarded real prizes.

Hatos and Hall's conclusion: The idea worked. And it worked because no matter how basic the premise was, viewers just had to know *what* was in the envelope.

CBS said no outright. NBC at least allowed them to produce run-throughs. Again, the audience loved it; the contestants loved it; even the executives seemed happy with how it went. But then those same executives just as abruptly said, "No."

"What was wrong with it?" Hatos and Hall asked.

"What do you do the *second* day?" the executives asked.

Monty argued, "More of the same! That's what a game show is, it's variations on the same concept every day."

Hatos and Hall kept doing more demonstrations, mystified that each new presentation was followed by, "What do you do the second day?" Somehow the fact that they had now seen multiple presentations escaped the NBC brass. On May 25, 1963, Hatos and Hall finally produced a full-scale pilot, with a set consisting of three big doors. NBC still wasn't all that crazy about the format, but after six months, the network was getting desperate for a hit show to plug into a lagging time slot, so they reluctantly put *Let's Make a Deal* on the air on December 30, 1963.

On the first day of taping, December 16, Hall, a heavy smoker, stepped in the hallway and pulled out a pack of cigarettes. He started to light up, but then bluntly issued a challenge to himself. With the show's thirteen-week contract in mind, he announced to a member of his staff, Nat Ligerman, "Nat, I won't smoke another cigarette for as long as this show is in production!"

Monty Hall never smoked again.

The Deal Makers

Each day, thirty-two people from the studio audience are brought down to a special reserved section called The Trading Floor, where Hall picked some of them throughout the show to make deals.

A typical episode of *Let's Make a Deal*: Monty Hall spots a bald man and offers him $200 for a comb, and his wife $100 for an earring. A contestant is offered $250 or a huge box; she chooses the huge box and gets a washer/dryer combo. Another woman is offered $300 or a curtain; she chooses the curtain and gets living room furniture plus a stereo. Monty offers a third woman her choice of the washer/dryer or the furniture . . . or a popcorn billboard. She chooses the furniture and the billboard swings away to reveal she rejected a broken-down wagon and a cheap champagne bottle. A married couple is shown five small gifts and tries to guess the prices; if their guesses are close enough, they win a car. A man is given two envelopes and is told to keep one for himself and give one to another contestant; he keeps one for himself, and then just as quickly forfeits it for a curtain, which is hiding a new wardrobe and a color TV. The other contestant gives up her envelope for a big box and gets a selection of new appliances. And at the end, Monty offers two contestants from the past half-hour to try for The Big Deal of the Day. They have to forfeit the prizes they've already won, and in exchange they can pick one of the doors, attempting to "trade up." One of the doors is hiding that day's Big Deal, which can be worth thousands and thousands of dollars in prizes and cash.

"What *do* you do for the second day?" you ask if you're one of those concerned executives.

Monty picks three contestants to play "Follow the Leader." Each of them is given an either/or decision to make involving a known prize or an unknown prize, with the twist that the other two contestants are automatically committed to whatever decision that contestant makes. Next, Monty gives three contestants a wad of money; only the outer bill is visible in each wad, and the contestant has to decide between their wad of money or what's in a box. A married couple is given five small gifts and has to put them in a line from least expensive to most expensive; doing so wins a car. And then it's time for the Big Deal of the Day. It was more of the same, all right. But every day, as Monty promised, it was something different.

NBC was happy to concede they were wrong. Other detractors were converted, too. Competitor Mark Goodson, who initially dismissed the premise as "flipping a coin for thirty minutes" (and admittedly, that's not totally off the mark), came around and admitted that, in reality, Hatos and Hall had come up with a brilliant way of mixing up the show and making it interesting.

Part of the magic was the Zonks, the booby prizes hiding behind the curtains and the boxes. Contestants who played the wrong hunch at the wrong time would trade away $500 or a color television set and wind up with an oversized stuffed animal, dilapidated furniture, announcer Jay Stewart struggling with a stubborn mule or camel that wouldn't walk all the way on stage, or a Zonkmobile, a battered old car that was more dilapidated with each return appearance.

In Disguise

Precious few bits of photo and video from *Let's Make a Deal*'s early days exist, and the audience is conspicuously plain-looking. The men are in suits. The ladies are in their Sunday dresses. What happened?

Here's what happened. A woman showed up at the studio one day with a sign slung around her neck on a string, reading, "Roses are red, violets are blue, I came here to deal with you!"

The sign got Monty's attention, so he picked her for a deal. Within days, everybody was showing up at the studio with signs hanging around their necks.

Monty Hall deals out the dough to a contestant on the world's biggest daily costume party, *Let's Make a Deal.*

That went on for a few months, when suddenly another woman showed up wearing a bizarre-looking hat. The hat was so distracting that Monty couldn't help picking her. And then everybody showed up wearing bizarre hats.

And then more time went by. Suddenly, the studio was filled with ghosts, vampires, Frankenstein monsters, football players, farmers, kings, queens, clowns, cowboys, nurses, and any other costume the audience could scare up. It was initially so bizarre that Stefan Hatos considered issuing an edict forbidding people from wearing costumes to the studio, but he changed his mind when a staffer pointed out that no other show on television was doing it; those creative audience members gave the show an identity that nobody could have expected. When a viewer turned on the TV and saw *Let's Make a Deal*, there was no confusing it for any other show.

In Disgust

Critics didn't love *Let's Make a Deal*. There was nothing earth-shattering about that. There appears to be some fine print in every newspaper and magazine columnist's contract that specifies that they're required to dislike game shows, always and forever.

But Monty Hall, over the years, was truly taken aback by how venomous the criticism of *Let's Make a Deal* could be. Although he tried to take the high road and say the criticism didn't bother him, after so many years of slings and arrows, Monty admitted that the sheer hatred that his show inspired truly disturbed him, and he was very openly defensive about it.

Chief among their complaints was the way that the show glorified greed. The contestants would beg Monty to pick them, scream when he did, moan ecstatically when handed a stack of hundred-dollar bills, and then embrace Monty and plant a huge kiss on him when they wound up with a new dining room and a cruise at the end of their deal. Isn't that *greedy?*

Monty was sensitive to the charges of greed. He grew up poor, which he blamed partially on his father's penchant for gambling, always confident that the next hand of poker or the next horse race would be the one where he finally won big.

He argued to one reporter, "First of all, it's an entertainment form. Secondly, it's not a greed show. . . . If it were a greed show, they'd say, 'Run down the aisle, collect everything you can and put it in your basket, and grab and grab and grab and grab and grab until time runs out.' But in [*Let's Make a Deal*], every time you make a move, you're giving something up. It's no longer greed; it's taking a risk. There's a whole different psychology."

Even viewers who *dared* to watch *Let's Make a Deal* were the target of disdain. Columnist Rob Word wrote, "It isn't likely that Monty Hall has a large personal appeal, nor are the prizes particularly spectacular. The appeal of the show may be, at least in part, the humiliation which the viewers see, enjoy, and identify with. There is no need to feel jealous of these contestants. They have no special ability, and unlike the viewer, they have no dignity."

A grown adult with his own newspaper column couldn't grasp the concept that people enjoy a vicarious thrill from playing the game at home and seeing how well they could do. No, a viewer of *Let's Make a Deal* must like it due to a deep abiding hatred of people . . . It made sense to Mr. Word, at least.

Hall was also taken by surprise by the lack of respect that he got from the entertainment industry. "[They] didn't want to know anything about me. They didn't want to go below the surface . . . I suffered."

When Hall went to NBC in 1968 and asked for a regular prime-time slot (it had been used as a summer replacement the previous year), an executive dismissively told him, "We don't put those kind of shows on in prime-time."

Monty snapped back, "You know, if your wife doesn't treat you well, you might drift to the hussy across the street. I want to let you know that the hussy across the street is starting to look real good!"

On December 27, 1968, *Let's Make a Deal* aired its last episode on NBC. Three days later, *Let's Make a Deal* premiered on ABC.

Deal Me Out

Monty Hall voluntarily shut down production of *Let's Make a Deal* in 1977 after taping a final season of his much-prized prime-time version at the Las Vegas Hilton. Hall explored his options for the next few years and was surprised by what he discovered: stage acting required too much travel for his tastes, and film acting—particularly a day when he had to shoot a single scene thirty-five times—bored him. He lost interest in hosting talk shows when he realized how saturated the television market was with them.

Deal Me Back In

And so, Monty dedicated himself to *Let's Make a Deal*. In 1980, he launched a new version of the show in Canada, which came to an abrupt end when the distribution company that handled the show for syndication went bankrupt.

The All-New Let's Make a Deal popped up in America in 1984 and survived for two seasons and eventually became an institution through frequent reruns on various cable channels. NBC picked up an ill-fated revival in 1990.

A drastically different version appeared on Fox in 1996. Retitled *Big Deal*, Mark DeCarlo hosted the program, with swing group Big Bad Voodoo Daddy providing live music. This show now incorporated physical stunts, like launching teddy bears with a slingshot, or attaching a contestant to a giant crane, raising and lowering them to grab prizes in a human version of an arcade claw game. This version came and went in only six weeks.

In 2003, the show returned to NBC prime-time as a summer replacement show with host Billy Bush, nephew of President George H. W. Bush and cousin of President George W. Bush, serving as host. Monty Hall, who still technically owned the show but had minimal control, openly complained that he disliked this version, which disappeared after its summer run.

On the Wayne

Game show fans got some very unexpected news in 2009. It had been fifteen years since a game show other than *The Price is Right* had aired on network daytime television, but CBS felt the time was right to bring the genre back. *Let's Make a Deal* was the show, and actor/comic Wayne Brady was the new host.

The new show was tailored heavy to Brady's strengths. Sketch comedy was now woven into many of the deals; on a given deal, contestants might have to make deals with a comic book superhero called Wayneman, or a film noir detective parody where the clues led to prizes, or announcer Jonathan Mangum reading entries in the host's diary. Pianist Cat Gray supplied live music in the studio, with Wayne, a talented singer and spoofer, doing parodies of hit songs for some games.

It's been more than fifty years since Stefan Hatos and Monty Hall sat down at lunch and kicked around the deal of letting a contestant choose one door or the other. With every incarnation, with every episode, the concept was refined and reinvented. In so many ways, the show bears no resemblance to the first episode way back in 1963, but at its core, it's still the rubber chicken and the envelope that Monty Hall took from luncheon to luncheon. *Let's Make a Deal* successfully accomplished a second episode, and about six thousand more after that.

What's the Question

Who is . . . Art Fleming?

 nly a few years after the scandals, the quiz show of record debuted on NBC. This is the story of America's favorite answer-and-question game.

A Man Named Merv

As mentioned in an earlier chapter, Merv Griffin knew quite a bit about game shows. In 1958, he was offered a chance to host *Play Your Hunch*, a new daytime show from the undisputed game show kingpins, Mark Goodson and Bill Todman. A simple thirty-minute rehearsal each day followed by a live broadcast was more in tune with Griffin's tastes and he cheerfully accepted the job. More opportunities followed. He replaced the vacationing Bill Cullen for a few weeks in the summer on *The Price is Right* and briefly hosted a prime-time comedy quiz on ABC, *Keep Talking!* It was easy to see why game shows suited Griffin so well. He was a people person who devoured the opportunity to talk to the contestants and special guests. And his whole life, he had been a fanatic for games himself. An avid cruciverbalist who had surprisingly fond memories of childhood car trips, during which he and his sister played Hangman in the backseat, Griffin saw game shows as potentially a long-term career for himself.

By 1961, Griffin had impressed NBC so much that the network offered him an afternoon talk show. Although fate seemed to be handing him a new career path, Merv Griffin always retained a soft spot in his heart for game shows and never fully abandoned the genre.

Mrs. Griffin Has the Answer

Griffin would indulge his creativity and nascent entrepreneurial streak by developing a game show format for NBC. *Word for Word*, which premiered in 1963, saw Griffin at the helm as contestants were given lengthy words and attempted to form as many shorter words as possible from the same letters. Word games like *Password* were "in" at that point, so it was certainly the right game at the right time, but Griffin looked at the television landscape and noticed another type of game was missing.

Even though the hard quizzes of the 1950s had been fixed, Griffin had been as transfixed by them as the rest of the country. During a plane trip with his wife

Julann, Griffin talked about how much he liked hard quiz shows, but the scandals of the late 1950s had made it nearly impossible for the networks to consider one.

Julann, sounding as if she was kidding, suggested, "So why not just give them the answers to start with?"

Merv, taking it as a joke, didn't really say anything until Julann abruptly said, "79 Wistful Vista."

Merv responded, "What is Fibber McGee and Molly's address?"

When their plane landed in New York, Griffin went straight to his office and drew up an idea called *What's the Question?*

"I Didn't Get One Right"

Griffin assembled a modest format. Ten categories, each containing ten answers with different cash awards, would be displayed on a game board. The contestants would pick categories and dollar values, and ring in to supply the question. NBC was interested enough that they allowed Griffin to stage a demonstration in a small section of Radio City Music Hall. Before the demonstration even started, there was some indication that the game needed rethinking. The game board didn't fully fit on the stage, and a large portion of it hung over the edge, into the first few rows of audience seats. Other than that, the game went well, but not great. An NBC executive was quick to point out how difficult it would be for a camera to shoot the large game board, so Griffin split the game up into two rounds with six categories apiece, and scaled back from ten questions per category to five.

Another executive told Griffin, "I like what I see, but the game needs more jeopardies."

Griffin became fixated on that term. The executive continued talking, but Griffin later admitted, "I didn't hear another word he said."

Griffin repeated the word to himself over and over again, marveling at what a distinctive sound it had. He loved it so much that he abandoned his original title, and *What's the Question?* became *Jeopardy!*

Griffin staged another demonstration, and, taking the executives' advice to heart, he added more jeopardy to the game, and not just to the title. In Griffin's revision, an incorrect question now deducted the value of an answer from the player's score, even if it took the player below zero. The game was scaled down from a hundred answers to sixty-one, divided over three rounds: Jeopardy, Double Jeopardy, and a single category with a single answer called Final Jeopardy; the rewards and the risks increased as the game progressed. Griffin's second demonstration added Daily Doubles, clues that allowed contestants to wager all or part of their winnings so far on a single clue. (NBC bristled at the term Daily Double, fearing that conservative viewers would be offended by the reference to horse racing, but Griffin won that battle.) Head of NBC Mort Werner watched the demonstration game from start to finish, and then in exasperation, threw his arms in the air at the end and said, "I didn't get *one* right!"

That would have been a death sentence if another NBC executive, Grant Tinker, hadn't been in the room. Tinker had helped develop *G. E. College Bowl*, the only hard quiz on the air following the scandals. *College Bowl* had enjoyed

A scholar, a gentleman, and a pretty darn good host for *Jeopardy!*, the great Art Fleming.   *Photo courtesy of Zane Enterprises*

consistently strong ratings over the years, and Tinker knew first-hand that difficulty wasn't a death sentence.

"Buy it," Tinker told Werner.

Werner reluctantly put it on the air, warning Tinker that he'd be held responsible if the show failed. For a host, Merv Griffin hired Art Fleming, an actor that he had spotted in a TWA commercial. *Jeopardy!* premiered on March 30, 1964.

What's So Funny About That?

While *Jeopardy!* was lucky enough to find an audience right away, it didn't hit the ground running. One of the things that had appealed to NBC and to Griffin as the idea took shape was the potential for humor. Steve Allen and Johnny Carson had both done recurring comedy bits—"The Question Man" and "Carnac the Magnificent"—that involved a man being given an answer and trying to divine a question, so NBC was expecting a comedy quiz. Griffin planned on delivering a straightforward hard quiz, but thought there would be a good opening for humor with a rule that said the contestants not only had to supply the correct question, but that the question had to be grammatically correct. As an example, Griffin remembered years later this exchange that happened between himself and a contestant for one of his demonstration games.

"What is Abraham Lincoln?"

"Can you rephrase that?"

"Where is Abraham Lincoln?"

"Again, please."

"How is Abraham Lincoln?"

Once the series went to air, though, those delays interfered with a fast-paced and elegantly simple game, so the grammar rule was cast aside.

Another problem was that Griffin's contestant coordinator, aware that Griffin wanted a hard quiz show, went to Greenwich Village and recruited intellectuals for contestants—and they *looked* like intellectuals. They were dullards with brooding expressions who wore black capes into the studios. Another contestant coordinator was able to round up more crowd-pleasing players who also happened to be really smart.

Jeopardy! aired on NBC weekdays at noon, which meant it grabbed a sizable audience among college students who watched between classes, and working folks who tuned in during lunch breaks. It was effective counterprogramming by NBC; it competed against soap operas on CBS and, more often than not, sitcom reruns on ABC. The *Jeopardy!* audience was one that wasn't seeking out soap operas or sitcoms in the daytime.

Though NBC was obviously happy with the success of their hit show, *Jeopardy!* mystified the network somewhat. Researchers assembled numerous focus groups that indicated that a hard quiz was too much of a turn-off for daytime television viewers and continually suggested to Griffin that he scale back the level of difficulty. "Seventh grade" was usually the guideline that NBC suggested. Griffin—who was all too willing to admit that even *he* found his own creation too difficult—ignored the feedback time and again, not even bothering to tell his staff that the network had called him into the office. Week after week, *Jeopardy!* survived. Month after month, *Jeopardy!* survived. Year after year, *Jeopardy!* survived.

Dick Block, of the University of Southern California School of Cinematic Arts, offers his theory:

> There was a tremendous change happening in American education in the 1960s, in that college was now considered mandatory. College was thought of as optional; you went straight to work after high school, or your parents said, "Maybe you'll go to college." After World War II and the introduction of the G. I. Bill, that all changed. The generation of students in the 1960s was the first to think of college as mandatory. And at the time, there was a joke inside the TV business that *Jeopardy!* was popular because it validated your college education. Yeah, it's a joke, but there was more than a bit of truth to that. College students were watching this show while they ate lunch and they were seeing, in effect, other people being rewarded for having a higher education.

A Quiz with a Brain . . . and a Heart

So why did *Jeopardy!* flourish? For one thing, the emphasis was more on the glory than the prize. The cash awards on the original *Jeopardy!* were a bargain basement $10–$50 for the Jeopardy round and $20–$100 for Double Jeopardy. A big winner seldom came away with more than $1,000 for the day.

Despite offering cash prizes that were modest, and a rule that said winners had to leave after five days (a safeguard against accusations of rigging), *Jeopardy!* managed to crown plenty of big winners, many of whom went on to greater fame, and in some cases, notoriety. In 1965, a newlywed naval aviator named John McCain was a one-day champion. Seventeen years later, he became a U. S. Congressman; in 1987, he moved over to the Senate. The 1968 *Jeopardy!* Tournament of Champions was won by Hunter "Red" Gibson, who amassed more than $5,700 plus a trip to the West Indies for his efforts. Gibson's son went on to become a well-known film star. Yes, Mel. The following year, the big winner was Jay Wolpert. Wolpert would go on to produce many game shows himself before turning his efforts to screenwriting. Among his efforts: *The Count of Monte Cristo* and *Pirates of the Caribbean: The Curse of the Black Pearl*.

The thrill of *Jeopardy!* was in the glory, both for the contestants and the audience. To do well, you *had* to know something, and what better forum to show what you know than national television? Contestants smiled confidently as they fired off tough answers. The audience gasped with admiration when players made a big wager on a Daily Double. Meanwhile, home viewers could smirk with satisfaction when they knew something that tripped up the players. All over the country, housewives and their kids made it a point to remember Final Jeopardy so they could stump Dad when he came home from work.

And even if you were stumped, you could at least say you learned something that day. In 1978, author Maxine Fabe recounted a day when the category was Famous Quotations. The answer: "What Jim Jeffries's manager said to him before the Bob Fitzsimmons fight."

According to Fabe, the audience audibly booed the clue. Jeffries vs. Fitzsimmons was not a particularly noteworthy boxing match, and how could anybody know what a manager said to his man beforehand?

And then came the response: "What is 'The bigger they come, the harder they fall'?" The audience reacted with an audible "Ahh . . . "

After a decade where experts were crammed into stuffy isolation booths on dimly lit stages, *Jeopardy!* put a friendly face on the hard quiz. The set was delightfully chintzy, even by the standards of the mid-1960s. The contestants sat at three tiny desks in front of a pressboard backdrop, each contestant with a visible paper cup of water next to their buzzers. The rest of the studio was filled with a homey arrangement of curtains, woodgrain, and even a plant tucked away in one corner. The game board was a wood grid holding thirty slabs of cardboard, each with a dollar amount carefully stenciled on it. An unseen stagehand would yank them out one by one, with an audible *THWACK* that unintentionally made itself part of the aural atmosphere of the show. Behind the dollar amounts were thirty more slabs with the printed answers, often with scattered apostrophes and periods abbreviating the too-wordy contributions from the writers.

And adding to the homey feel was master of ceremonies Art Fleming. Fleming, despite a six-four linebacker's frame and a voice that could replace a full brass section, was as antonymous to "imposing" as Mr. Chips. Every statement he said came with utmost grace and politeness. Audience applause was received with a grateful "Thank you, my friends!," and commercials were preceded by "Please watch . . . thank you." Correct answers were rewarded with a booming "*Well done!*" Contestants who fared poorly were encouraged with "Get out of that minus!"

Fleming's friendly, worldly persona was an honest one. The grandson of an opera conductor and the son of an Austrian dance team, Fleming was a navy

A special game of *Jeopardy!* played by the game show hosts of NBC: Bill Cullen (*Three on a Match*), Peter Marshall (*The Hollywood Squares*) and Art James (*The Who, What or Where Game*). Recognize the fellow in the baseball uniform? That's Joe Garagiola.

Photo courtesy of Zanè Enterprises

veteran who captained the football team at Colgate University before finishing his education at Cornell. He had starred on three dramatic series and collected numerous film credits. He was a wine connoisseur, an avid collector of antiques, a gourmet cook, a furniture builder, and obsessive reader. When he wasn't doing any of that, he was a deacon at a Manhattan church and managed a telephone crisis center. And when Dwight Eisenhower's grandson David married Richard Nixon's daughter Julie, Art Fleming was an usher.

Fleming's popularity as host of *Jeopardy!* brought with it some awesome responsibility—he was frequently recognized in restaurants by couples who wanted him to settle arguments about obscure facts because, surely, Art Fleming knew the correct answer.

No Question About It

Jeopardy! was an institution for NBC, but more importantly than that, it breathed new life into an ailing concept. The proof was out there that you could have a smart game and that you didn't have to lie about it. And most importantly, viewers would tune in. The doors were open for more Q&A, and viewers were willing to give the genre a second chance after being deceived in the previous decade.

The funny thing was, unlike many hit television shows, *Jeopardy!* didn't particularly spawn very many imitators. There were plenty of game shows in the succeeding years that would use questions and answers, but none could be mistaken for *Jeopardy!* In a medium where success breeds imitators, *Jeopardy!* did the hard (and honest) Q&A game so well that knockoffs were few and far between. Thus, *Jeopardy!*'s success in the 1960s made it THE quiz show of renown. It was a reputation that would stick for quite a while.

20

Popcorn for the Mind

A Barris of Riches

C huck Barris was a game show magnate, which was odd considering that by his own admission, he didn't like game shows. The games Chuck Barris created were some of the strangest concepts ever unleashed on the American viewing public, and he couldn't have been prouder.

Philadelphia Freedom

Charles Hirsch Barris was born and raised in Philadelphia, Pennsylvania, on June 3, 1929. The nephew of singer/songwriter Harry Barris, Chuck was raised by parents who didn't particularly seem engaged in his life, and he was left to explore for himself. He wrote for the school newspaper, took up the guitar, and graduated from Drexel Institute of Technology.

He went straight to New York City and got a job as a page at NBC; he submitted a phony résumé with several NBC executives listed as references, and he was hired without anybody calling the bluff. He went to ABC to serve as a Standards and Practices representative overseeing *American Bandstand*. The job gave him so little to do—despite adult misgivings about rock and roll, *American Bandstand* hardly pushed the envelope with regards to content—that Chuck penned songs to pass the time. He sold one, "Palisades Park," to *American Bandstand* guest star Freddy Cannon. The move actually landed Barris in hot water with his bosses; in the years following the Payola scandals, in which certain songs were played in heavier rotation on the radio in exchange for cash or other favors, the network thought it was inappropriate for an employee to collaborate with a singer.

Despite the trouble he got himself into, he was promoted to ABC vice president in charge of daytime programming, with a specific charge to pick new game shows to put on the air. Barris so disliked the pitches

Chuck Barris . . . he didn't quite have the look of a show business mogul, but he'd leave his mark on television with some of the most unusual game shows ever devised.

he was hearing that he took a gamble and left his spot at the network to form a production company and develop his own ideas for game shows. He rented an "office"—it was really more of a closet—in the Beverly Hills Writers and Artists Building for twenty-five dollars a month. Size didn't matter: Barris chose the office because it had a prestigious address that could grab a potential show buyer's attention when they checked the mail.

An Up-to-Date Concept

Barris immediately returned to ABC to pitch his first idea. It was based on a twinge of inspiration he felt while he was still working at the network.

He later explained, "I was looking at [a show called] *Where the Action Is,* which was aimed at the audience between eighteen and thirty-five, and it occurred to me that there might be something interesting in having a teenager talking to a few guys and picking one for a date. It would be a sort of Russian roulette—particularly if out of the bunch she happened to pick somebody famous. It would be just as interesting to see her reaction if she skipped him for somebody else."

Barris created a game in which single women would ask a series of questions to three men whom she couldn't see. The bachelor that she felt best answered the questions would win a date with her. *The Dating Game* starring Jim Lange (a long-time disc jockey in San Francisco who would commute to Los Angeles to host the show) premiered on December 20, 1965. Chuck Barris went out of his way to make it a different game show than anything else seen on daytime; for the first few months of the series, the show even had a live rock band and dancers. It wasn't just a new game. It was a young game.

A decade earlier, the dating scene, as presented on television, was idle chatter in a malt shop. The dating scene as depicted on *The Dating Game,* however, proved that the era of the birth-control pill had arrived. Much of the time, the questions were fairly familiar flirtations—"Where would we go on a first date?" or "If you cooked dinner for me, what would you make?"—but *The Dating Game* questions, all prepared for the bachelorette by Chuck Barris' staff, were eye-poppers.

- I play a little trombone . . . If you were my trombone and I blew you, what would you sound like?
- I like Dustin Hoffman, Al Pacino, and jockeys. I guess you could say I like small men . . . what's really small about you?
- If you lived in a gay neighborhood, how would you react if someone broke into your apartment and did your hair?

And while the questions could raise a few eyebrows, sometimes the answers positively made your hair stand on end.

Bachelorette: My worst subject is spelling. How do you spell "relief"?

Bachelor: F-a-r-t.

***

Bachelorette: What's your favorite thing to do to torture your parents?

Bachelor: I told them I wasn't Jewish when they knew I was . . . Actually, my mother was Welch, and my father was Hungarian, which makes me Wel-Hung.

***

Bachelorette: I'm a dress designer. My fitting model is out and my deadline is drawing near. Would you be willing to get into my dress?

Bachelor: Baby, I'd be willing to get into your dress, your pants, and anything else you'd want!

***

Bachelorette: If you were a detergent, what would your slogan be?

Bachelor: "The harder you rub me, the cleaner I come."

Shelley Herman was a fan of the show, and in her late teens, a contestant. As she recalled: "In its time, what more did you need for good TV? You had this set full of good-looking people saying such outrageous things. It didn't look like any of the other stodgy game shows on television. Not that there's anything wrong with the stodgy shows, per se, many of them are quite good. But *The Dating Game* just spoke to me the way other game shows didn't when I was a teen."

Getting in on the Act

The Dating Game used up contestants at a pace that worried Chuck Barris: it aired five days a week; each day had two games, each with a bachelorette (and, occasionally, a bachelor) asking the questions, plus three more contestants to answer them. That worked out to forty contestants per week. And Chuck Barris gleaned early on that the show only worked if you had contestants quick-witted enough to keep up with the salacious questions being fired at them. Finding that many good *Dating Game* contestants every week was a tall order.

As an enticement to get trained actors to appear as contestants on the show, Barris agreed to pay "scale" (the minimum compensation required for a professional performer on television; several hundred dollars at the time) to any members of AFTRA, the radio and television performers' union, who appeared as contestants, whether they won or lost. Barris would even encourage contestants that he felt were particularly engaging to return to the show multiple times under aliases. This wasn't completely ethical, but it wasn't rigging the game; since part of the show's central premise was that the bachelorette made her choice without learning any of the contestants' names, it didn't really matter what name they gave to Jim Lange and the home audience.

As a result, *The Dating Game* became, in hindsight, a treasure trove of before-they-were-star sightings, as countless performers on their way up the ladder appeared on the show, more interested in getting the rent paid that month guaranteed than getting a date. Among the future stars who played *The Dating Game*: Mark Harmon, Andy Kaufman (in character as "Foreign Man"), Don Johnson,

"Kiss!" Jim Lange, the contestants, and the signature close of each episode of *The Dating Game*.   *Photo courtesy of Zane Enterprises*

Steve Martin, Paul Reubens (in character as "Pee Wee Herman"), John Ritter, Bob Saget, and Robert Wuhl.

Each day also featured a special guest star in search of a date: Arnold Schwarzenegger said he was looking for a woman with similar measurements; Don Rickles hurled insults at three men vying for a date with his daughter; Dick Clark played on behalf of an *American Bandstand* dancer; fourteen-year-old Michael Jackson was looking for his first date; legendary stripper Gypsy Rose Lee warned her man that "I don't kiss on the first date!" Ron Howard, Farrah Fawcett, Suzanne Somers, Richard Dawson, and even Burt Reynolds showed up in search of love.

Here Come the Newlyweds

The Dating Game was a hit for ABC, a network that, in 1966, needed hits. So, when a pair of television producers, E. Roger Muir (best known as creator and executive producer of the pioneering kiddie show *Howdy Doody*) and Robert "Nick" Nicholson presented ABC executives with a premise so simple that it was literally written on a napkin, ABC executives handed the idea directly to Chuck Barris and paid Nicholson and Muir royalties for the idea.

The idea: newlywed husbands and wives are asked the same questions and try to match answers. That's it.

Los Angeles disc jockey and concert promoter Bob Eubanks (two years earlier, he had taken out a second mortgage on his house to pay for The Beatles' famous Hollywood Bowl concert) reluctantly auditioned for the show, even though he thought it was the worst concept he had ever heard. In auditions conducted with actual newlywed couples, he had so much fun stirring up arguments that he changed his mind.

ABC executives and a few other VIPs were brought in for a demonstration game; if ABC executives liked the demonstration enough, Barris would be given a fee to produce a pilot episode; if the pilot episode looked promising, it would go on the ABC schedule. The demonstration was blessed with two bits of good luck: actor Dom DeLuise, just a few months before his big break, was one of the contestants, and Eubanks recalled that the DeLuises got huge laughs every time it was their turn to answer. (Dom's wife, Carol, was also an actor.)

The next bit of good luck came when the wives were asked if they had any nicknames for their husbands. One wife answered "Numbnuts." The game stopped cold for several minutes because the ABC executives in the pseudo-audience couldn't stop laughing. The demonstration went so well that the network skipped the pilot and bought the show immediately. *The Newlywed Game* premiered on July 11, 1966, a day when, coincidentally, CBS and NBC were pre-empting their daytime lineups for a Vietnam War update from Secretary of State Robert S. McNamara. The result: millions of TV dials were switched to ABC because it was the only channel not airing a press conference, and a massive audience saw the premiere of *The Newlywed Game*.

The Newlywed Game was excoriated by some critics but adored by millions more television viewers for its naughty and uproarious questions and answers. Couples would overshare to a degree not yet heard on television to that point—one bride admitted that when she first met her now-husband, it only took a week for her to "give in," and another gasped in horror when she revealed that a story about taking a shower had taken place before they got married.

The show affected broadcast history in a way that not many knew. Eccentric billionaire Howard Hughes had put in a bid to buy the American Broadcasting Company, but changed his mind when he took a gander at some of their more successful daytime programs. Hughes sent a note to his chief of staff, which read: *Cancel my bid on ABC. I would never buy anything that played crap like* The Newlywed Game.

Although Howard Hughes wasn't impressed, millions of viewers were captivated by the naughty little game. Jaime Klein, a Chuck Barris Productions staffer, says, "What happened so often on that show was husbands and wives would forget they were on TV playing a game. There would be a question, their answers wouldn't match. And they would argue. They'd argue even though Bob Eubanks was staring at them, and even though there was an audience in the studio, and even though there were cameras right in front of them, and this couple would just air all of their grievances and let each other have it. They weren't 'people on TV' anymore. They were a real couple and you were seeing the inner nature of a real marriage. That is spellbinding to watch."

What Was Chuck Thinking?

The success of the nighttime *Dating Game* and *Newlywed Game* surprised many, but Chuck Barris himself maintained that they were successful because they fulfilled a purpose on a prime-time schedule. He told reporter Charles Witbeck,

"The programs act as breathers in the midst of all the film products. They also all have heart."

One of the noticeable quirks of Barris's games is that you really couldn't play along with them (unless you happened to be a personal friend of one of those newlywed couples). That, and they were so preposterously uncomplicated that they barely qualified as games. And that was fine with Chuck Barris. He wasn't in it for a good game. He was in it for a good contestant.

"I supposed I do these shows because I don't find any fun in intellectual games," he told writer Cynthia Lowry in 1967. "To me, the interest is entirely in the revelation of the personalities . . . . What we're looking for is people, as opposed to playing with words and clues. My idea is to pick some lively people, put them into a format and get them talking. You never know what is going to come out, but whatever it is, it's spontaneous."

Barris's empire grew with speed. As the premiere of *The Dating Game* approached at the end of 1965, there were six employees on the payroll. By Christmas 1966, Chuck Barris Productions had grown to a staff of sixty. Barris, by necessity, expanded his office space, although he still habitually referred to his own office as "the closet."

Barris, at age thirty-seven, was by far the elder statesman of the company; the median age of a Chuck Barris Productions employee in 1967 was twenty-four. Many employees were attracted to the less-than-formal way that business was conducted. There was no dress code; if a new employee showed up in a suit on their first day, procedure was to destroy his necktie with a pair of scissors and then send them home to change into something more casual. Barris encouraged employees to bring musical instruments to the office, and jam sessions were a near-daily occurrence. But perhaps the defining characteristic of Chuck Barris Productions was the ceremony for announcing that a new series had been sold. Barris would gather all of his employees in a circle, stand in the middle, and pour beer over his own head as he made the declaration.

Shelley Herman was a contestant on *The Dating Game* several times before striking up a friendship with some Barris staffers and making her way to the office. "It was crazy at that office," she recalls. "Now when you talk about the 1960s and say people acted crazy, everyone assumes you mean smoking dope. Nobody was smoking dope. They just acted crazy in general. After hours people partied a little bit and they may have smoked on their own time, but acting crazy in the office meant playing foosball, it meant Chuck putting on different hats just to make everybody laugh, running up to his employees and hugging them. He'd get out his guitar and gather everybody into the office for music time.

"It sounds like goofing off. Maybe it was goofing off. But everybody got their jobs done. Everybody got their questions written for *The Newlywed Game*, and did the screenings for *Dating Game* contestants, and got all the prizes coordinated. Everybody had a job and worked very hard at it. And I think the secret there was the amount of fun that you had working for Chuck. If your boss encourages jam sessions, and parties, and foosball games, you fall in love with that job so much that you dread the idea of working anywhere else. So, in a way, everybody worked as hard as they could so they could keep goofing off. Good employee motivation there."

Wink Martindale, who spent only a few months on the Barris payroll, remembers, "I hosted two shows for Chuck and neither one lasted very long, but it left a lasting impression. He had a really fun staff at Fountain and Vine. In my entire career, I never saw a company that had more fun knocking out TV shows than Chuck's staff. It was such a great environment."

As much success as they were having with game shows, Chuck Barris Productions wasn't thinking of itself as a game show production company. At least the boss wasn't. In a 1968 interview, he laid out his true career plans: "Actually, the real purpose of our group is to produce motion pictures, and more than that. We have used the game shows as a base so that we can get into other things, and I constantly live in fear of being called a 'game show producer.'"

Barris bought the rights to several novels, including *Or I'll Dress You in Mourning* and *Walk Egypt*, with the intention of turning both into feature films, but that idea never panned out.

Not Quite a Midas Touch

Not everything Barris did was pure magic. While *The Dating Game* and *The Newlywed Game* were established hits both in the daytime and in prime-time for ABC, a number of shows from Chuck Barris Productions were odd experiments that came and went quickly, if they came at all.

ABC was reticent about putting some of Barris's more dangerous ideas on the air. They rejected a format called *The Divorcee*, and a game show idea called *The Three of Us* in which, as Barris proposed to the network, a business executive would be put onstage with his wife and his secretary. The wife and secretary would compete to see which one knew the executive better.

Barris did get a few more game show formats on the air in 1967, and all three of them were flops:

There was *Dream Girl of '67*, a daily beauty pageant. Four women competed each day, the four winners returned on Friday, and each week's winner returned at the end of the year. There were two notable problems with the show: number 1, it went through four hosts in a single year. Dick Stewart was there for the first six months. Bob Barker stepped in as interim host until Wink Martindale took over. Martindale was pulled from the show by Chuck Barris so he could host a different show—more on that later—and Paul Petersen finished out the series. Problem number 2, as newspaper columnist Charles Witbeck pointed out, was that daytime TV was an odd forum for a beauty pageant. This was the 1960s; men were at work, so daytime TV targeted housewives, and did the average housewife want to sit down every day and watch young pretty women compete to see who was prettiest?

Next came *The Family Game*. Premiering June 19, 1967, *The Family Game* holds the distinction of being the last new network television series to air in black and white; after *The Family Game*, every network TV series debuted in color. The game was played similarly to *The Newlywed Game*, but now played by parents and their young children. The host was Bob Barker, who clashed quite frequently with Chuck Barris's staff for a variety of reasons. According to Bob Eubanks, Barker once objected to a question that included the term "belly button" and locked himself in his dressing room until a new question was written. Barris tried going into his dressing room and smoothing things over. Instead, Barris emerged from the dressing room, eyes narrowed, and muttered to a staffer, "Belly button is out."

The show ended only six months later. Unsurprisingly, Bob Barker never worked for Chuck Barris again.

The last 1967 oddity debuted on December 4. Wink Martindale hosted the new show that bore the unforgettable title *How's Your Mother-in-Law?* Three mothers-in-law, nominated by their families to appear on the program, were paired up with three stand-up comedians. The comedians would address a "jury" of ten unwed audience members, pleading the case for each mother-in-law that she was the best of the three, often with jokes that made use of embarrassing personal stories that the families had supplied before the show. The jury voted for the "best" mother-in-law, who received $100.

Barris churned out one more minor success for ABC, a variety show called *Operation: Entertainment*, so titled because each week's show emanated from a different military base for an audience made up entirely of servicemen, four of whom would be invited onstage to flirt and cavort with the *Operation: Entertainment* Girls, the show's sole regulars; among them was model/actress Sivi Aberg, Miss Sweden of 1964. Barris assembled a stunning roster of performers for the endeavor, including comedy team Marty Allen and Steve Rossi, Louis Armstrong, Anita Bryant, Ray Charles, Roy Clark, Jimmy Dean, Patti Page, the Mills Brothers, Richard Pryor, Martha Raye, and Don Rickles.

To close out the decade, Barris expanded his empire into first-run syndication. He produced *The Game Game*—in which a contestant and three celebrity guests took a psychological test, and the contestant won money for each celebrity who got a lower score—and *The Parent Game*, in which three married couples tried to match answers with a child care and psychology expert.

Jim McKrell, a Texan who had just arrived in Los Angeles and secured a job as an overnight DJ, was in search for voiceover work and auditioned to serve as *The Game Game*'s announcer. Barris mistakenly thought he was there to audition for host and gave him the job.

McKrell remembers, "Chuck taught me a lot about hosting. Chuck told me that the host is a traffic cop. My main job was to keep things moving. And he really hammered home the point that I'm not the star of the show. The game is the star. And Chuck could be a little goofy sometimes, but I liked him because I could see how he treated his staff. Chuck, even as the boss, showed loyalty to the people who worked for him. That really stood out to me."

The Game Game, like *The Parent Game*, would expire after only one season. McKrell felt the show deserved a better fate. "I still think *The Game Game* would work today. The core of the game was a 'quiz' very much like you'd see in magazines. 'How romantic are you?' or 'Are you a good judge of character?' And you have three engaging, talkative celebrities talking their way through such a quiz, it could be really interesting. And today, look around social media; look at chain e-mails. Those kinds of quizzes are still all over the place. *The Game Game* should work if a producer wanted to give it another shot."

21

Square Biz

A Nine-Star Revue

 elebrities, trivia, and tic-tac-toe: three unlikely elements fused together for one of the most enduring game shows of all time.

Thinking Inside the Box

Merrill Heatter and Bob Quigley had an idea that they couldn't give up on: a game show that involved a large panel. Their first go at it was a 1963 NBC daytime game, *People Will Talk* with Dennis James, in which contestants tried to predict which members of a fifteen-member panel (some were celebrities, some weren't) had answered an opinion question the same way as the contestants.

The following year, Heatter and Quigley reworked the idea into a CBS prime-time show, *The Celebrity Game* with Carl Reiner. They whittled the panel down to nine famous people, and now the contestants tried to predict how each celebrity would answer a question. This worked slightly better—it survived about a year and a half on the network—but something still didn't feel right.

It was Merrill Heatter who was struck by inspiration one weekend. He grabbed photos of nine celebrities, arranged them in a 3 × 3 formation, and drew a set of lines around them to create a tic-tac-toe grid. He came into the office, showed Bob Quigley what he had done, and they immediately knew they had something special. They named it *The Hollywood Squares*.

CBS was the first one to bite, shooting a pilot on April 15, 1965, with host Bert Parks. The pilot taping went until 2:00 a.m., with Heatter and Quigley paying audience members ten dollars apiece not to leave. Host Bert Parks built suspense and melodrama throughout what was supposed to be a lighthearted game. Fred Silverman, in charge of the CBS daytime lineup at, admitted years later that Bert Parks had been the main factor in his decision not to pick up the show.

Marshall Law

Heatter and Quigley tried another pilot with comedian Sandy Baron, who didn't work either. An actor/singer named Peter Marshall was brought in for an audition because Bob Quigley's wife spotted him in a commercial and thought he might make a good host. Marshall initially declined the offer, but after learning that the

The master of *The Hollywood Squares*, "Beaver Face" to Paul Lynde, and Peter Marshall to everyone else.

producers were also considering Dan Rowan (later of *Rowan and Martin's Laugh-In* fame), Marshall agreed to take the job out of spite for Rowan, against whom he had a personal grudge.

In the meantime, a bit of serendipity helped *The Hollywood Squares.* Larry White was an unemployed television director when Heatter and Quigley called him to direct the unaired *Squares* pilot for CBS. In the months that followed, White became head of daytime programming for NBC. White promptly put *The Hollywood Squares* on the NBC lineup. This move didn't sit particularly well with many insiders; *Variety* skewered White for what it perceived as a political move. But White stood his ground, insisting that he believed in the show and felt it would be a hit, whether or not he had been involved in its initial pitch.

On October 17, 1966, *The Hollywood Squares* debuted on NBC, and for the first time, viewers were introduced to "The Master of *The Hollywood Squares*," Peter Marshall. "Master" was a job title he would earn well. He had briefly hosted a local game show with celebrity guests in Los Angeles. It only ran for ten weeks, but that was just long enough for him to get some invaluable advice from a producer named Tom Naud, who told him how to handle a celebrity panel: "Peter, there are going to be a lot of stars on your show—don't let them intimidate you. Just imagine that you've invited them all to a party at your home. Treat them as you would an honored guest, but always remember—it's your party."

And that's how Peter conducted himself, letting the stars get their laughs but quickly reining them in and getting answers out of them before the game ground to a halt—a concern of Merrill Heatter, who concluded that the first few weeks of games moved too slowly.

If you've forgotten how *The Hollywood Squares* was played, Peter was the man to explain it; his signature catchphrase, if you could even call it that, was his explanation of the rules, a paragraph of info that he rattled off at one hundred miles per hour on each show:

> The object for the players is to get three stars in a row, either across, up and down, or diagonally. It's up for the players to figure out if the star is giving them the correct answer or just making it up; that's how they get the square. Every game is worth $200 and we play a best two-out-of-three

match. In addition, each day we have a Secret Square game, and we'll play that as soon as we finish the game in progress.

The Original Regulars

Merrill Heatter said in 1967, "People enjoy seeing celebrities test their intelligence on the air. It brings the star down to the audience's level. These are no longer actors and actresses playing a role, but real human beings acting as themselves, putting themselves in a vulnerable spot where they might come up with a wrong answer at any time."

It wasn't just the vulnerable spot that the stars were in, though. The true appeal of the game was in the stars and the funny answers they gave to the questions.

Peter: When making a bagel, is the dough molded around the hole, or is the hole punched after the bagel is formed?

Walter Matthau: The bowl is doled around the hole. I mean, the dole is holed around the bowl.

Contestant: I'll agree.

Peter: I don't know what he said!

Walter: I think it's doled around the bowl.

Agnes Morehead, Ernest Borgnine, Nick Adams, and Pamela Mason were there for the first week of shows. In the months and years to come, a steady flow of frequent visitors and semi-regulars would pop in from week to week, including Vincent Price, Martin Landau, Eva Gabor, Allen and Rossi, Michael Landon, and Bill Bixby. But a group of five joined Peter in the early months and helped make *The Hollywood Squares* a homey-feeling game for viewers everywhere: milquetoast Wally Cox, pretty young Abby Dalton, sarcastic Rose Marie, lovable old mensch Morey Amsterdam, and Cliff Arquette as Charley Weaver.

The freshman class of *The Hollywood Squares* in 1966. Top to bottom, Charley Weaver (played by Cliff Arquette), Rose Marie, Peter Marshall, Abby Dalton, Morey Amsterdam, Wally Cox.

Peter: Paul, can you get a pound of feathers out of a goose?

Paul Lynde: Well, I got them in there, didn't I?

The Squarest one of all, the great Paul Lynde.

But the man who would be most closely tied to *Hollywood Squares* over the years was Paul Lynde, who first appeared in the third week of the series and, by 1968, was firmly anchored in the center square on the game board. Lynde was a former stand-up comic who shot to stardom on Broadway in *Bye Bye, Birdie*, crossing to film stardom when the musical was adapted into a movie, and then making his name in television as Uncle Arthur on *Bewitched*.

Lynde, by his own admission, was a script man, considering himself dead weight if he was in an ad-lib situation, but millions of *Squares* viewers never would have guessed it. Of all the panelists, Lynde was the one with the most immaculate timing and delivery; every joke sounded like it had just popped into his head, a mistaken assumption that the show's writers were in no hurry to correct. Peter Marshall cheerfully admitted that Paul Lynde got more fan mail than he and happily gave him most of the credit for *Squares'* popularity. By 1970, it was the number-one show on daytime TV.

Look to the Stars

Booking nine celebrities week after week was a daunting task for the Heatter-Quigley staff, and a big part of the job for the *Squares* team was figuring out every individual accommodation that needed to be made to get the nine stars into the studio for that one big day of taping.

Merrill Heatter told an interviewer, "Our panelists and guest stars often have to travel a considerable distance to studio, and the only way to travel is by car. Also, many of them are involved in simultaneous work, such as making movies or other types of television shows."

Quigley added, "You might say that we pamper our people in our own interest. We provide babysitters when necessary, we supply transportation if it is needed, we act as a sort of telephone answering service, we are in the food catering business—in short, we do anything to make our people happy and available as we need them."

Finding celebrities wasn't difficult—*The Hollywood Squares* was a rare game show blessed with good reviews from the press, and as a result, the "I don't do game shows" attitude didn't find its way to *Hollywood Squares* very often. To the contrary, A-listers like Pearl Bailey, Sonny and Cher, Lloyd Bridges, Mel Brooks, Ray Charles, Alice Cooper, Rodney Dangerfield, Sammy Davis Jr., Redd Foxx, Aretha Franklin, Betty Grable, Helen Hayes, Eartha Kitt, Dorothy Lamour, Mickey Mantle, Steve Martin, Dolly Parton, Lily Tomlin, and hundreds more took their seats in the nine squares to laugh it up for thirty minutes a day.

Of course, that didn't mean they were thrilled to be there. George C. Scott reluctantly agreed to be on the panel with his wife, actress Trish Van Devere, because she wanted to promote her new movie. Scott, a famously gruff, no-nonsense type, walked into the make-up room before the taping and told a staffer, "I want you to know that I'm scared shitless."

So, if the big stars were scared shitless, why did they appear? Heatter said in 1966, "They are glad to have a chance to appear more or less as themselves, as against being 'characters' in other types of shows. They feel that it gives them an extra dimension in the eyes of viewers." He added, "Also, such regular or periodic appearances help keep a performer, who may or may not be on a video series at any particular time, before the public."

Such was the case of Bill Bixby, who found the years after *My Favorite Martian* rather lean. He began appearing on *Squares* semi-frequently and credited the paydays from the show with helping him keep his head above water while he looked for his next big break. He was so grateful that even after *The Courtship of Eddie's Father* went into production, he continued appearing on *Squares* when his schedule allowed it.

Burt Reynolds would credit *Squares* with his rise to superstardom. A talent booker for *The Tonight Show* had seen Reynolds on *Squares* and found him so personable that Reynolds was invited to be a guest of Johnny Carson for the first time. A casting director saw the Carson appearance and ended up casting him for his breakout film role in *Deliverance*. Reynolds was adamant that *Squares* had been the root of his success as a film star, and even as a superstar, Reynolds would carve out one day in his schedule every now and then to tape five episodes of *The Hollywood Squares*.

And for stars who specialized in live performance, *Squares* was good for business. Comics like Bob Newhart and Don Rickles always appeared on the show in advance of upcoming gigs in bigger venues. On a typical episode of *Squares*, a comic may, at most, only have to deliver two or three jokes in a half-hour, all prepared by the show's writers so that comic wasn't using any of his own material. In return, he got some laughs in front of a national audience, and a few viewers might head out to the arena or to the nightclub to see his act live.

But all of the incentives and all of the babysitting accommodations in the world couldn't always prevent the occasional catastrophe. One day, two stars abruptly canceled with just hours to go before taping. The staff desperately tried to figure out a solution until somebody realized that one of the stars appearing during that taping would be impressionist Rich Little. Rather than try to find two substitutions, the *Squares* staff arranged for Rich Little to sit between two empty boxes. Names of other celebrities were posted onto the empty boxes; when a contestant selected an empty box, Rich Little would move over to that box and perform as that celebrity. Crisis averted.

Here, Square, and Everywhere

While *The Hollywood Squares* thrived on NBC daytime, the network was struggling with their lagging Friday-night lineup. A sitcom called *Accidental Family* had crashed against tough competition from *The CBS Friday Night Movie* and NBC needed to cut their losses. *The Hollywood Squares* already had a staff and cast, not to mention a single set already built, game shows were the most cost-effective programming available, so *The Hollywood Squares* got plugged into a Friday-night slot for nine months in 1968.

In the fall of 1968, children's advocates condemned the state of television for America's youth; in particular, Saturday-morning network lineups consisting of what were considered violent or mindless cartoons. The FCC was starting to make it clear that they weren't happy with Saturday mornings, either, so in midseason that year, NBC abruptly dumped two cartoons and replaced them with a nature show, *Untamed World*, and a new but familiar-looking game show called *Storybook Squares*, which premiered January 4, 1969.

Storybook Squares saw the familiar tic-tac-toe grid now housed in a set that resembled a castle. The Guardian of the Gate (announcer Kenny Williams) opened a massive storybook at the opening of each episode, and out walked nine celebrity guests, now dressed as famous characters; some from storybooks and nursery rhymes (Stu Gillam as Merlin the Magician, George Gobel as Little Boy Blue), some from history (Wally Cox as Paul Revere, and Soupy Sales as Henry VIII), some Biblical (Doc Severinsen as the angel Gabriel), and some stars from prime-time series showed up playing the characters they were already known for (William Shatner as Captain Kirk, Carolyn Jones as Morticia Addams, and Arte Johnson usually played one of his *Laugh-In* personas).

Merrill Heatter said in 1969, "It's no secret that most children do not like to be told that they're being educated, even if it's good for them, so we made minor changes . . . to give the kids educational material sugar-coated with entertainment manufactured by some of their favorite people."

Many of the questions of *Storybook Squares* revolved around history, occasionally delving into safety tips. The show ran for only one season; because of the custom-fitted costumes for the stars, *Storybook Squares* was a deceptively expensive endeavor, but the Heatter-Quigley staff and Peter Marshall (who called *Storybook Squares* his favorite TV work that he ever did) loved it so much that for years after, *The Hollywood Squares* would continue doing *Storybook Squares* as special weeks of programs once or twice a year.

The stars, Peter Marshall, and the kids who won the prizes all lived happily ever after on *Storybook Squares*.

Solemnly Square to Tell the Truth

Peter: On television, who lived in Doodyville?

Paul Lynde: The Ty-D-Bol Man.

Heatter-Quigley didn't give any thought to the fact that they had a staff of writers coming up with funny lines, and that the panelists were being fed jokes. It was just a means of making the game more entertaining. But to their surprise, a few people thought it seemed an awful lot like rigging the game. Producer Mark Goodson called it "actionable fraud," and the FCC was suddenly investigating Heatter-Quigley Productions.

Heatter-Quigley reasoned that giving the stars funny lines wasn't really rigging the show. The funny lines didn't affect the game itself; the stars had to follow their jokes by giving a real answer off the top of their heads, either a bluff or their best attempt at the right answer. The contestant had to earn the square by declaring "I agree" on a correct answer or "I disagree" on a wrong answer. Still, though, the process involved telling the celebrities in advance the subject matter of each question as well as the punchline, and occasionally that was enough context for the stars to figure out exactly what question they'd be asked. That detail led the FCC to say that Heatter-Quigley had been misleading the public without NBC's knowledge.

Heatter-Quigley Productions agreed to be more forthcoming about the process. But after this full investigation, the FCC didn't even ask them to stop; they simply wanted the show to disclose it on each episode. *The Hollywood Squares* added this disclaimer to the credits:

> The areas of questions designed for each celebrity and possible bluff answers are discussed with each celebrity in advance. In the course of their briefing, actual questions or answers may be given or discerned by the celebrities.

And Peter Marshall amended his explanation of the show's rules, casually ending each of his rattled-off rundowns with "And remember, although the stars are briefed in advance to help them with their bluffs, they're hearing the actual questions for the first time."

As it turned out, feeding funny lines to the stars bothered the FCC far more than it bothered the average American viewer. *Hollywood Squares* continued unhindered into the 1970s and became a television fixture.

22

Renaissance

Let's Do It Again

G ame shows looked like a dying breed at the end of the 1960s, until some shrewd business decisions by Mark Goodson and Bill Todman led the television business to discover that viewers still wanted game shows. And in some cases, they wanted seconds.

The Ebb Before the Flow

Mark Goodson-Bill Todman Productions was shrinking in the 1960s. In 1965, *The Price is Right* with Bill Cullen ended after nine years. Two years later, *Password* came to a close, as did *I've Got a Secret* and *What's My Line?* In 1968, the word came down from CBS that Bud Collyer and *To Tell the Truth* would be going away after twelve years.

Mark Goodson-Bill Todman Productions were left with only two shows once *Truth* was gone: *The Match Game* with Gene Rayburn was still thriving, and then there was *Snap Judgment* with Ed McMahon, a much weaker game. It was quite a turn in fortunes for what had once been the dominant game show factory in the business.

Ralph Edwards had some success syndicating *Truth or Consequences* five days a week, establishing the precedent that Goodson-Todman would follow, by reviving their demised network properties for new syndicated versions. A few staffers came up with the idea of reviving both *I've Got a Secret* and *What's My Line?* as a single series, by expanding the format of *Line?* to incorporate elements of *Secret*.

What's On the Line

John Daly, who had secured a position at Voice of America, the country's propaganda service, declined to host the new version of *What's My Line?*, although it's unlikely he would have hosted anyway once he learned what was in store for the new version. *What's My Line?* would now include demonstrations of contestants' occupations, much as *I've Got a Secret* had included demonstrations of secrets. Producer Gil Fates, who oversaw both shows in their original weekly incarnations on CBS, actually wanted to do this on *What's My Line?* years earlier, seeking to book a contestant whose occupation was "professional billiards player" and then pulling the curtains open after the game to reveal a billiard table so the contestant could demonstrate trick shots.

Daly dug his heels in as soon as he heard the idea. The stuffy moderator, protective of his reputation as an ABC network newsman, curtly told Fates, "Save this show business stuff for *I've Got a Secret*."

In future years, Fates would repeatedly try to breathe new life into *What's My Line?* by sneaking *Secret*-like segments into the plans, and Daly would repeatedly shoot down every attempt by threatening, "You'd better get yourself a new boy."

Because TV ratings data can't tell you anything about *why* viewers were watching, nobody wanted to take the chance of dismissing John Daly from the program. Daly got to host the staid, straightforward form of *What's My Line?*, while producer Fates grimaced later about how the show suffered from "hardening of the creative artery."

For the five-day-a-week syndicated *What's My Line?*, Washington, D.C., newsman Wally Bruner would host. Arlene Francis would return as a regular panelist, while Bennett Cerf came back for occasional appearances. Madcap comic and kids' show host Soupy Sales signed as another regular.

The new version of the game sped things up by having Bruner drop a hint at the start ("This contestant deals in a product that is worn" or "This contestant needs a telephone to perform her job") which would cause the panel to guess the line faster, or sometimes get stumped faster than they would otherwise. With the extra time gained, the show now followed each game with a demonstration. After a contestant revealed that her line was "Getting Sawed in Half," the magician that she assisted would perform his act. The author of a book about Monopoly strategy gave a brief lesson, using a teacher's pointing stick and a wall-mounted game board (among her tips: the green properties bring the best return on investment). And when a contestant revealed that she sang singing telephone messages, the show played an audio recording of her work the previous day, calling Soupy Sales and wishing him a happy birthday on behalf of the *What's My Line?* staff. Garbage can decorators and chainsaw sculptors would treat viewers to a gallery of their handiwork.

The 1968 model *What's My Line?* openly courted youth. Certainly, the set looked younger, and livelier. The plain, unadorned walls and curtains of the original version gave way to an eye-catching new set, covered with colored spotlights and ornamental avatars representing various lines of work. The game cast for youth too. Heartthrob actors Bert Convy, Gawn Granger, and Alejandro Rey sat on the panel, as did kids' show puppeteer Shari Lewis and improv comic Patti Deutsch. Arlene Francis's husband, Martin Gabel, had played the original *What's My Line?* frequently. For the new, young version of the show, it was Arlene's son, Peter Gabel, who played the game.

The *What's My Line?* syndicated version worked beyond Goodson-Todman's wildest dreams. The show just worked, and to the staff's surprise, they found themselves able to handle what had seemed like too daunting a workload. On CBS, *I've Got a Secret* and *What's My Line?* both had a full week to prepare and plan each episode. Much of the same staff, in 1968, stared at the prospect of doing five of the same caliber programs with the same amount of prep time. When the show was first pitched to local stations, the stations were explicitly told that the show would have Mystery Guests sometimes, but not every day. Talent booker Bob Bach didn't

Newsman Wally Bruner had a new line in 1968, moderating the panel for *What's My Line?*

think he was capable of that. But he was, without fail. By 1975, *What's My Line?* went off the air, and every single episode had a mystery guest.

To Tell The Truth

The success of *What's My Line?* gave Goodson-Todman such a surge of confidence that they took an idea that they had for the 1969 season one step further. The company had been saving the master tapes of the final year of Bud Collyer's *To Tell the Truth*, with plans of selling the show into syndicated reruns. Audience response to the new *What's My Line?* was so overwhelmingly positive that the reruns were called off and Goodson-Todman simply launched a new version of *To Tell the Truth*.

With long-time host Bud Collyer electing not to join the new version due to health problems, Mark Goodson invited Garry Moore to lunch. Moore had been the host of *I've Got a Secret* until 1964, when an argument with CBS president Jim Aubrey compelled Moore to retire from television for a few years. In 1967, he had briefly returned with a prime-time variety show, but the new endeavor was a flop and Moore went right back into retirement. Goodson sensed that Moore was bored with retirement—a sentiment that Moore later admitted was completely true—and when Goodson casually mentioned during lunch that he was reviving *To Tell the Truth*, Moore jumped at the opportunity to host.

Goodson-Todman stuck with what was clearly working. After the real contestant please stood up, a demonstration would follow. A motorcycle racer brought along footage of herself wiping out at the start line. A fashion designer and her impostors were all decked out in her elaborate outfits. For a contestant who designed children's furniture, the game was played while the contestants and the panel were surrounded by very young children using the furniture. One of the children was the daughter of a *To Tell the Truth* staffer; Garry Moore talked to the little girl at the start of the game and told the audience that his young friend's name was Cynthia Nixon. It was about thirty years before *Sex and the City* for her.

One of the most memorable post-game demonstrations involved an undercover police officer named Richard Buggy. All three contestants were wearing costumes, as an undercover officer would. After the real Richard Buggy stood up, the two impostors revealed their identity: one was Kitty Carlisle's son; the other was guest panelist Joe Garagiola's son.

Joining Garry Moore on the 1969 version was a veteran panel: Kitty Carlisle, Peggy Cass, and Orson Bean, stalwarts of the original *To Tell the Truth*, along with Bill Cullen, perennial panelist of *I've Got a Secret*. Despite the familiar, and admittedly not-exactly-fresh-faced talent running the show, *To Tell the Truth* also made a play for the younger audience. The game was presented on a psychedelic set beyond Peter Max's wildest dreams, while the theme music was a soft rock love song that sounded like it had been plucked straight from the songbook of Lennon and McCartney.

But the new version of *To Tell the Truth* stood out in particular with the gutsy and sometimes controversial subjects that the games dealt with. A central subject in one game was a light-skinned black man who toured the country, lecturing about his experiences with "passing," or lying about his race and background to gain opportunities. As a means of emphasizing his point, *To Tell the Truth* had two white contestants as the impostors for the game. A woman who was against Woman's Lib was spearheading the "Fascinating Woman" movement, an effort to teach women to take more pride in making life better for men. Drug use, strippers, and television violence were all addressed in a variety of games.

Getting Back on the Clock

From the sublime to the ridiculous: as *To Tell the Truth* presented a cerebral game tackling heady subject matter, Goodson-Todman revived another game in 1969 involving inflatable dummies, balloons, whipped cream, and tennis racquets. *Beat the Clock* was back.

Bud Collyer, who had hosted the original article until it was canceled by ABC in 1961, declined to host this one, although when Jack Narz got the nod to host, Bud sent him a handwritten note congratulating him and wishing him luck. Collyer died on September 8, 1969. In a strange coincidence, that was the date that many stations began airing the new versions of *To Tell the Truth* and *Beat the Clock*.

On the new version, two couples competed in a series of stunts, assisted by a weekly guest celebrity: Hugh O'Brian, Dick Clark, William Shatner, Leslie Nielsen, Cab Calloway, and Jack's brother Tom Kennedy all joined the fun of the new version.

Giving the program a distinctive sound was the live organist improvising his way through the entire show. Dick Hyman was a revered jazz pianist and composer for numerous classic films, including *The Purple Rose of Cairo*, *Hannah and Her Sisters*, *Mighty Aphrodite*, *Moonstruck*, *Mask*, and *Two Weeks' Notice*. For such an accomplished performer, playing the organ for a game show, and doing so semi-anonymously (he was identified in the credits, but never acknowledged or shown on camera), came off to some of his peers as "slumming it," but he gave the show a distinctive sound, even with a loud ticking clock underscoring his every note.

The first year of the new *Beat the Clock* was taped in New York. In 1970, the show relocated to Montreal, Quebec, to take advantage of lower production costs, and

Allen Ludden was an early '70s fashion plate on the new version of *Password*. Playing the game are Meredith MacRae and Bill Bixby.

to make a little extra money by selling the show for broadcast in Canada, since it now qualified as a Canadian production.

The Canadian production of *Beat the Clock* proved more hazardous than some of the production crew expected. One winter, when California was experiencing an unprecedented heat wave, Jack Narz was in for a shock when he departed from one-hundred-degree temperatures in Los Angeles and landed in Montreal, which had dipped to minus-fifty. A few months later, another blizzard struck, and not only did taping get canceled, but Jack Narz and the crew were stranded in Montreal for three days.

By 1971, Jack Narz had enough, not just with the weather, but because of the prohibitive cost of airfare. Goodson-Todman wasn't paying for his commute to Montreal (Goodson refused to pay for hosts who commuted, reasoning that there was nothing preventing them from relocating to the taping area) and by 1971, costs were so high that Narz quit the show. Announcer Gene Wood was promoted to host, remaining until the show ended in 1974 after Mark Goodson stopped production over a dispute with Canadian TV about profit sharing.

Pass the Word, Password Is Back

When *Password* started to wane in 1966, Goodson-Todman made the decision to save tapes of every episode, and when it went off the air in 1967, it was immediately replaced in some cities by *Password* reruns. The reruns were highly successful and the Password home game from Milton Bradley was still a top seller. It was like *Password* never left.

Meanwhile, ABC had built a strong daytime lineup with *The Newlywed Game*, *The Dating Game*, and *Let's Make a Deal*. When a popular soap opera, *Dark Shadows*, was showing signs of wear and even the show's producer conceded that they were out of ideas, ABC decided to replace it with another game show. What game show?

And then an ABC network executive began considering a question that they had always asked focus groups in the past when they had considered a new game show. When a test audience had watched a pilot for a game show, ABC gave them a questionnaire to fill out. One of the questions was "How does this show compare to *Password?*" The executive reasoned that if ABC had already made up its mind about the pinnacle of quality for a game show, why not air the pinnacle instead of seeking another?

Password arrived on ABC with fresh episodes on April 5, 1971, and the new series secured the game's place in TV history forever. An episode of *The Odd Couple* revolving around a game of *Password*, with Allen Ludden and Betty White guest-starring as themselves, became one of the most popular episodes, and possibly the most frequently rerun episode of *The Odd Couple* for years afterward. In 1974, at the first Daytime Emmys ceremony, *Password* claimed the first Emmy for Outstanding Game Show. It was sweet revenge for boss Mark Goodson, who had surrendered his membership in the Academy of Television Arts and Sciences seven years earlier, outraged that game shows were no longer recognized in the prime-time Emmy ceremony.

And with an A-list lineup of guest players—Carol Burnett vs. Henry Fonda! Peter Lawford vs. Burt Reynolds!—it was apparent that the show wasn't fooling around when announcer John Harlan opened each episode by proclaiming it "the word game of the stars."

Prime Access Time

While Goodson-Todman was producing at full speed in 1971, Goodson-Todman Executive Vice President Giraud "Jerry" Chester was negotiating a big deal directly with the FCC. At the beginning of the decade, network prime-time schedules began at 7:30 p.m. Eastern Monday through Saturday, 7:00 p.m. Eastern on Sundays. Chester compelled the FCC to issue a mandate to the broadcast networks to hold off prime-time programming until 8:00 p.m. Monday through Saturday. The reason Chester presented was that it gave local TV stations access to a larger audience in their own area, and that they could produce their own prime-time-caliber programs.

In his memoirs, Goodson-Todman producer Ira Skutch admitted that this wasn't exactly the goal that Chester had in mind. The 7:30 time slot was, as Chester requested, opened up for local TV stations, but the vast majority of stations lacked resources to produce lavish prime-time programs, so instead, the stations turned to syndicated programs. *To Tell the Truth, What's My Line?*, and *Beat the Clock* got bumped to prime-time slots as a result of this decision. *Truth or Consequences* with Bob Barker got moved around on a few stations too. But these were all five-a-week programs. Many stations, with the mindset that prime-time programs should be weekly programs, like the network schedule had, were building "checkerboard schedules," consisting of once-a-week syndicated offerings. And game show producers immediately began putting together offers for prime-time shows.

The Hollywood Squares produced one extra episode, and then two, at tapings for use as prime-time shows. Although successful in prime-time, the success of prime-time *Squares* served as a cautionary tale for producers and networks who were mulling the possibility of introducing nighttime games. *The Hollywood Squares* had been the number-one game show on daytime TV, but when the nighttime show was introduced, the daytime version's ratings suffered. It wasn't in trouble by any means, still an enormous success, but now everybody had seen that overexposure might be a hazard of prime-time adaptations.

Monty Hall, who had been hosting and producing *Let's Make a Deal* in daytime and nighttime, made a deal behind the scenes with ABC to pull the nighttime version from the network and offer it as a syndicated show, a more lucrative endeavor. The syndicated version would last six seasons.

Good Sports

In 1971, two unusual but extremely popular game shows made their way into the prime access slots on many stations from coast to coast. Game shows had always kept subject matter fairly broad, but for the first time, game shows targeting a particular niche were introduced: sports game shows.

Dick Enberg hosted *Sports Challenge*, a game which he also helped produce along with Gerry Brown. That Enberg even had time to do the show was a colossal achievement, given his duties calling games for the California Angels, the Los Angeles Rams, and UCLA's basketball squad. He usually had to cram tapings of four *Sports Challenge* games into the same day as an Angels game.

Each week, two teams of sports legends competed against each other (sample game: three members of the 1955 Brooklyn Dodgers, including Jackie Robinson, versus legendary jockeys Willie Shoemaker, Eddie Arcaro, and John Longdon) each team playing for a youth charity. Enberg would ask a toss-up question; the team that answered correctly won points plus a shot at two "free-throw" questions involving archival footage of classic sports moments. The winners earned $1,000 and returned the following week; the losers got $500. Joe DiMaggio, Red Auerbach, Bill Russell, Frank Gifford, Billy Martin, Whitey Ford, Y. A. Tittle, Nolan Ryan, Billie Jean King, and Jesse Owens were just a sampling of the sports legends who played the game.

It would be one thing if *Sports Challenge* had just been a parade of sports legends, with the game serving as a flimsy excuse to trot them out there. What made *Sports Challenge* truly special was that these sports legends also proved to be sports fanatics. The games were fiercely competitive, and often high-scoring. According to the producers, far more often than not, the legendary sports figures could be spotted swapping autographs after the game; they were fans of each other.

But by far, one of the oddest game shows of any kind was the other sports game show introduced in 1971: *Celebrity Bowling*. It was exactly what it sounded like. Jed Allan, formerly Ranger Scott Turner on *Lassie*, hosted as two teams of two stars competed against each other in ten frames, with the highest score winning prizes for a randomly selected member of the audience. A stunningly eclectic array of talent toppled the ten pins on the show: Don Adams, Mike Connors, Ernest Borgnine, Gary Owens, Cesar Romero, Hugh O'Brian, Larry Storch, Greg Morris,

One of the best starting lineups ever, on the field or on the stage of *Sports Challenge*.
Photo courtesy of Zane Enterprises

James Farentino, Michele Lee, Dick Martin, Bob Newhart, Rob Reiner, Jimmie Walker, Jack Carter, Leslie Nielsen, Lloyd Bridges, Michael Douglas, Roy Rogers, Adam West, the Lennon Sisters and the Brady Bunch kids all played. From the beloved world of game shows, Tom Kennedy, Wink Martindale, Alex Trebek, Peter Marshall, and Jim McKrell competed, too. The game survived for seven seasons.

Host Allan explained, "You can learn a lot about stars watching them on a show like this. They let their hair down. Most of them are good people, but a few are so competitive—they just HAVE to win—that they're no fun to be around."

23

CBS Names Its Price

The Tiffany Network Comes Out to Play

 ame shows came roaring back in 1972, kicking off arguably the most prosperous period in the genre's history. This is the story of that big comeback.

Game Show Fans Have a Bud

As the calendar switched from 1971 to 1972, CBS didn't have much to brag about in daytime. The schedule included some weak soap operas, *Where the Heart Is* and *Love is a Many Splendored Thing*. Elsewhere, they plugged holes in the schedules with reruns, like *Gomer Pyle USMC*, *The Lucy Show*, *The Beverly Hillbillies*, and *Family Affair*.

In February 1972, B. Donald "Bud" Grant was appointed to head the network's daytime programming department and instantly knew the change he wanted to make. Curiously, he was inspired by a television event that nobody at the time would have considered a viable guideline for appealing to housewives.

Bud Grant explained to a reporter, "Winning is a part of the American culture. The Super Bowl would not be the number-one event in the country if games were not popular."

Grant immediately announced that the prime-time reruns had to go. In their place would be game shows.

Amateur Half-Hour

The Bud Grant regime got off to a bad start with *The Amateur's Guide to Love*, a Merrill Heatter–Bob Quigley Production starring Gene Rayburn. It was a strange hybrid that melded game shows with *Candid Camera*. A celebrity panel would watch a previously filmed hidden-camera prank and try to predict how the victim would handle the situation. That victim—who had since been let off the hook—would then win money based on how accurately the panel predicted the outcome. For example, actor James Darren walked into a book store and approached women about joining him to try on three-legged pants—he said it was an experimental product for couples who wanted to be closer together.

The game didn't work. There were a few drawbacks, chief among them the expense involved in the show—actors and separate production crews had to be compensated for the hidden-camera pranks—and the somewhat low quality of the pranks being played. *Candid Camera* was still the gold standard, and *The Amateur's Guide to Love* never really met it.

Host Gene Rayburn was hammy, outgoing, and quick-witted, but the game deposited him behind a lectern and gave him little more to do than introduce pre-recorded bits and get the panel's reactions.

As TV critic Cynthia Lowry summed it up, "The result was a daily series that came out vulgar, phony, and sort of desperate."

The Amateur's Guide to Love was hastily canceled after only thirteen weeks, with its hole in the schedule plugged by *My Three Sons* reruns; exactly what Bud Grant was trying to avoid. He was unfazed, however, and the network continued moving forward with its plans to reinvent the daytime schedule with game shows. A clean sweep of the reruns happened at the end of summer, and on September 4, 1972, CBS introduced a triumvirate of triumphant game shows.

The Next Game on Deck

Merrill Heatter-Bob Quigley Productions immediately pitched another game show to CBS, one that had actually been pitched to Heatter-Quigley by a CBS stagehand while they were doing *The Amateur's Guide to Love.* Heatter-Quigley never took outside suggestions for game show formats, but they were intrigued enough by the stagehand's proposal, *Celebrity Blackjack*, that they signed him to a deal for royalties, then tinkered with the idea, removing the celebrities from the game, and pitched it to CBS under the title *Gambit*.

Dick Clark auditioned for host, but apparently wasn't quite what Heatter-Quigley was looking for. Jed Allan of *Celebrity Bowling* won the job, but on the day of taping for the pilot, he showed up looking extremely irritated about something, and his attitude was so off-putting that Heatter-Quigley replaced him.

A 1972 interview with Jed Allan lends some clue about what was bothering him. He told a reporter, "I don't want to become typed as a game show host. I want to act. Look what happened to Peter Marshall—he's a very good actor. Since he's been so successful with *The Hollywood Squares*, nobody will let him act."

With *Celebrity Bowling* already putting him on TV screens as a master of ceremonies every week, Allan, it can be speculated, probably reasoned that hosting *two* game shows at once would probably end his acting career, and he probably wanted to get out of *Gambit*.

The job went to Wink Martindale. Martindale was a talented host in search of a hit. In the past decade, he had *What's This Song?*, *Dream Girl of '67*, *How's Your Mother-in-Law?*, *Can You Top This?*, and *Words and Music*, and not one of them made it to a full year on the air. But good things come to those who wait, and Wink had waited long enough for *Gambit*.

The premise was this: Married couples competed against each other in a game that combined trivia with blackjack. Heatter-Quigley, which had previously given the nation a giant board game on *Video Village* and a giant tic-tac-toe grid on *The Hollywood Squares*, now presented a giant deck of playing cards; but other than that, it was always, as Wink Martindale reminded viewers at the top of the show, "a normal deck of fifty-two playing cards."

A correct answer earned a playing card for a couple, with the game going to the couple that came closest to twenty-one without going over; twenty-one on the nose won a cash jackpot. Two out of three games won the match and a chance to pick prizes from a twenty-one-square board. The couple had to draw a card for every prize they picked, and busting meant forfeiting all the prizes won up to that point. Getting exactly twenty-one in the bonus round earned the winner a car on top of everything else. *Gambit* survived more than four years.

Wink says, "Having married couples play the game was a wonderful idea; for some reason, couples bring out something extra in each other, so you had these great personalities on display during the game. And *Gambit* was so utterly simple. It's Blackjack. Everybody can count to twenty-one. And it was even stripped-down Blackjack; there weren't that many rules to our version of the game. Simplify, simplify, simplify. Keep the game simple or else it won't work."

I Have a Wild Idea

While Wink Martindale may have waited through five so-so games to finally land the job on *Gambit*, the man on the CBS lineup who had been waiting longest was Jack Barry, the host/producer who had vanished in disgrace during the quiz show scandals.

In the coming years, Barry attempted to get back on his feet, but suffered a series of personal indignities. He had a hit show on local station KTLA in Los Angeles in 1962 called *You Don't Say!*, but was replaced when NBC launched a national version. He created a game show for ABC, *Everybody's Talking*, but to ensure the program would get on the air, he had to leave his name off the credits. He briefly worked for his former competitors, Mark Goodson-Bill Todman Productions.

Barry, with a $40,000 loan from his father-in-law, put an audacious plan into motion: he purchased a radio station in Redondo Beach, California. Owning a radio station required obtaining a license from the Federal Communications Commission, the very same group that instituted new laws and regulations due to the quiz show scandals. Barry obtained the license and spread the word that the FCC trusted him to conduct himself ethically. Small jobs trickled in—a 1969 ABC game, *The Generation Gap*, needed to replace the host of the show, which was already canceled, and gave Jack the nod to finish the episodes still remaining on the contract. ABC was happy enough with Jack's performance that they tapped him to host a summer replacement quiz, *The Reel Game*, in 1970. Jack hosted a revival of *Juvenile Jury*, a successful early TV effort of his, for one season in 1971.

But the chance to produce and host game shows still eluded Jack Barry. He told a reporter, "I find the immediacy of a game series very exciting. It's something that's happening right now and you can't help but get involved with the contestant."

It wasn't for lack of trying. During his brief tenure at Goodson-Todman, he had conceived a question-and-answer game in which contestants spun a slot machine to determine which questions they'd be asked. After leaving Goodson-Todman, Barry produced a series of pilots for CBS to test the concept. The game was called *The Joker's Wild*, and Allen Ludden hosted the pilots, all bearing slightly different formats. In one, the slot machine displayed photos of guest celebrities, each of whom each represented a designated category. The contestant would hear from the designated celebrity for whichever category was selected. Another pilot removed the celebrities. The slot machine simply displayed categories, with Allen Ludden himself asking the question. In either form, the pilot didn't sell.

Barry reworked the idea into another pilot, *The Honeymoon Game*, an ambitious pilot for a ninety-minute weekly game show featuring married couples. The idea still didn't work, but Barry was persistent. By 1971, he had sold *The Joker's Wild* locally to KTLA in Los Angeles, with himself as host. When CBS

Elaine Stewart deals out the cards for *Gambit*. Her husband, Merrill Heatter, was the game's co-executive producer.

announced plans for a new of game shows, *The Joker's Wild* was picked up for the September 4, 1972 launch date.

Mark Maxwell-Smith, who worked first as a prize coordinator, later as a warm-up man and question writer for *Joker*, remembers, "The day of the first taping, Jack Barry gathered the entire staff into Studio 33 and had them sit in the studio seats, and he gave about a ten minute speech. And the gist of the speech was 'I haven't had a steady job in 13 years, please run this show honestly and don't anybody screw this opportunity up for me."

Two contestants, champion and challenger, competed. Each took a turn pulling a lever to activate a three-window slot machine. Each window displayed a category or a Joker. If a category appeared once, it was worth $50. A pair was worth $100 and a triple was worth $150 or $200. The Jokers could be used to represent any category the contestant wanted. The first contestant to score $500 or more won the game; giving a correct answer after spinning three Jokers won the game automatically, regardless of the score, and the bonus round could add a few grand worth of cash and prizes to the winner's haul.

The slot machine—which host Jack Barry often simply referred to as "wheels"—was actually an impressive bit of machinery. Three wheels had the categories mounted onto them as slides, and then mounted on a frame on the side of each of

Jack Barry chats it up with the families on a special week of *The Joker's Wild* played by children. The children's games were eventually turned into their own spin-off series, *Joker, Joker, Joker.*   *Fred Wostbrock Collection*

three Kodak carousel projectors. There were notches throughout the wheels; when a contestant pulled the lever, a solenoid (a small, tight coil) would extend a small arm that would catch a notch in each projector, bringing the wheels to a stop and displaying three categories for the contestant.

Mark Maxwell-Smith recalls, "The one and only time that the game's honesty was called into question had to do with the slides on the category wheels, and this wasn't even really Jack Barry's fault. The Jokers on the wheels increased the values of the questions, which affected how long it took for the players to reach $500 and win the game. We had an issue where the show was going overbudget because the games went too quickly and we were playing the bonus round too much. So to slow the game down, Jack instructed a stagehand to put fewer Jokers on the wheels—which is perfectly fine. Both contestants are equally affected when you do that, so there's nothing unethical about it. The problem was that the stagehand's approach to this was to remove all the Jokers from the third wheel. So we get to a point in the game where a contestant is way far behind and Jack says 'You can still win if you spin three Jokers!' He didn't find out until after the game that all the Jokers were removed from the third wheel. The Standards and Practices representative scolded him for saying the thing about three Jokers because Jack was touting something that couldn't happen. That got smoothed over quickly, but it rattled Jack. Jack was always on his toes; he was very worried that another scandal might break out some day."

Although Barry was, perhaps unfairly, being hovered over a bit more carefully than other producers, he was doing an honest game, and *The Joker's Wild* was a wild success. It actually led to the demise of Dinah Shore's popular talk show in the same slot on NBC. Three *Joker's Wild* home games were produced, and Jack Barry constantly tinkered with the game to add extra bits of excitement. A special bonus round to be played by members of the audience was introduced. Weeks with child contestants were extremely popular. Special slides were added to the wheels that could pay off with cash jackpots or trips around the world if the contestants spun them in triple. There was just something new happening all the time, and that variety, on top of an exciting, engaging quiz, meant that *The Joker's Wild* survived on CBS for three years.

The Price Pays Off

Mark Goodson-Bill Todman Productions got a nine-year hit out of *The Price is Right* with Bill Cullen, spanning 1956–1965 on NBC and ABC daytime and prime-time. As early as 1967, Goodson-Todman had received offers to put the show back into production, but Goodson resisted, reasoning that it was too soon. He felt the show needed to stay gone for a while to make the audience hungry for a new version.

By 1972, the time seemed right. Goodson-Todman was preparing for a new once-a-week syndicated prime-time version of *The Price is Right*, with plans to tape at the ABC studio that housed the current version of *Password*. But when Bud Grant got word of Goodson-Todman's plans, he made an offer for a daytime version to complete the CBS schedule.

Although 1972 seemed like the right time for a new *Price is Right*, Goodson felt that it wasn't the right show. For one thing, Bill Cullen made it clear he wouldn't host. The new version was taping in Hollywood, and Cullen was committed to an NBC daytime game called *Three on a Match*, the syndicated version of *To Tell the Truth*, NBC's weekend radio show *Monitor*, and a television ad campaign for a chain of department stores, all based in New York.

Besides that, audience attention spans were changing. The era of the remote control had arrived and it meant that the audience needed to be more consistently engaged in order to stay with a program. On *The Price is Right*, the host presented a prize. Contestants placed their bids . . . then placed slightly higher bids . . . then placed slightly higher bids . . . until everyone decided to stop placing bids. This show could not survive in 1972.

So, Goodson went to Bud Grant and said that the show they were going to deliver would be *The New Price is Right*, all right. It just wouldn't be the show that CBS was expecting. Bud Grant trusted Mark Goodson's judgment and told him to make whatever changes he felt were needed to make.

Goodson-Todman came up with a format that drew apparent inspiration from some of the recurring games and features of *Let's Make a Deal*, and borrowed some of the elements of the old *Price is Right* that still worked. The idea took shape slowly. Originally, three contestants called from the studio audience would be shown a prize and place a series of bids, with the host telling them if the correct price was higher or lower after each bid; this would continue until somebody named the right price. That contestant would play one of a series of mini-games, called pricing games. Some games would involve groups of children placing bids. Three pricing games would be played, and at the end of the show, the three contestants who made it onstage were each given a showcase of prizes to bid on; the best bidder won their showcase.

The Goodson-Todman staff meticulously reworked some of their ideas. The game involving children was jettisoned. The three contestants from the audience were nudged up to four, and the higher-lower game to decide who came onstage to play a pricing game was replaced by a one-bid round, identical to a round played on the original *Price is Right*. The three showcases were cut back to two, to be bid on by the contestants who won the most merchandise.

For a host, Goodson-Todman went with veteran master of ceremonies Dennis James, formerly of *The Name's the Same, High Finance, People Will Talk, PDQ*, and many, many others. James won the job when Bill Todman happened to be watching *Let's Make a Deal* on a day that James was guest-hosting; Todman was so impressed that he made an offer on the spot.

But when Goodson-Todman closed a deal with NBC-owned-and-operated stations to air the nighttime version, CBS executives voiced concerns about a perceived NBC-connected star appearing on a CBS show, and insisted on a second host for the daytime version. The job went to Bob Barker, who was initially reluctant to host. Concerned that he wouldn't get along with Mark Goodson, he initially asked CBS if he could host *Gambit* or *The Joker's Wild* instead. CBS held him to *The New Price is Right*, and Barker, in hindsight, was probably grateful for that rejection.

It was an announcer who gave *The New Price is Right* its signature, though. Johnny Olson had been told to call the names of the audience members to come to Contestants' Row. For the first day of taping, he told them "Stand up!" But it was such a stiff announcement that Johnny wrapped it up by saying, "All four of you come on down, you're the first four contestants on *The New Price is Right*."

Johnny liked the sound of it, so he kept calling future contestants to "Come on down!" *The New Price is Right* officially had a hook.

For the first week of shows, the game had a rotation of only five pricing games, so with three played in each half-hour, viewers were very familiar with the games, some of which were indicative, again, of how meticulously Goodson-Todman refined their concepts. The following are some examples.

Bullseye was a game that was intentionally designed never to be won, not that the public was told that. Don't misjudge it, the game wasn't rigged, it was just exceedingly difficult to win. A contestant saw a car and guessed the price; the host would say "higher" or "lower" and the contestant would guess again, with a maximum of seven bids to guess the correct price. Seven just wasn't enough, but the staff noticed a strange quirk in preparation. For some reason, it always worked out that the final losing bid would be just a couple of dollars away from the correct price. It was a close loss, so the rationale would be that the audience wouldn't notice that the game was always lost; the audience would rather just think what a shame it was that the first bid placed wasn't just *slightly* different.

Another was *Grocery Game*. A contestant was shown five grocery items and had to purchase any quantity they wanted, hoping to strike upon a combination that added up to somewhere between $6.75–$7.00. The staff refined this one right before show time. Originally, a prize was to be awarded for going over $6.25, another for going over $6.50, and another for going over $6.75, and losing everything by going over $7.00. In practice games, this created a strange anticlimax, where a contestant could win two prizes but be treated like a loser for not winning a third, so it was whittled down to a single big payoff.

Double Prices was by far the most frequently seen pricing game. A contestant saw a prize and two prices. Picking the right price won the prize. If it doesn't sound interesting, that's fine. It wasn't supposed to be. The game existed as a means of saving time so that longer games could be played, although *Double Prices* was tinkered with in preparation too. Like *Grocery Game*, it was supposed to be played for three prizes, and for much the same reasons, the game was reduced to one prize by show time.

Some of the refining was the result of minor disasters. The wrong contestant once "came on down" due to a similar name; going forward, a cue card (not visible to the home audience) was held up at the same time that Johnny Olson made the announcement, so that the correct contestant came on down. Originally, when both contestants in the Showcase overbid, a buzzer would sound and each of them could bid again. At an early taping of Dennis James's version, production assistant Roger Dobkowitz had so much trouble hearing the second bids that the Showcase was awarded to the wrong contestant, a mistake that nobody caught until after the taping was over. The episode never aired, and the rules were promptly changed. Overbids in the Showcase weren't done over.

Despite all the tinkering and retooling of those early weeks, it was apparent even from the beginning that *The New Price is Right* had hit the ground running. Mark Goodson optimistically told Bob Barker before the first taping that he thought this was a pretty good, solid game, and Bob Barker agreed telling him, "I think we'll be around for a while."

The Big Picture

The games of September 4, 1972, were more important than just giving game show fans three more viewing options. In one fell swoop, the standards for game shows changed that day.

Curt Alliaume, a dedicated game show fan who was just a kid when he watched the premieres of *Gambit*, *The Joker's Wild*, and *The New Price is Right* that day, swiveled the dial to NBC after the new games were over. He remembered, "I noticed that all of a sudden, *Concentration* looked awfully old."

Bob Barker resisted hosting *The New Price is Right* when the offer was initially made, but eventually, it was hard for him to imagine doing anything else.

CBS's Los Angeles complex, Television City, was home to all three of the new games that the network introduced that day. The Television City studios were larger, and they were ground level, which allowed for more lavish sets that could be more easily transported between tapings. *Gambit* had a massive ace and jack that split apart to reveal the twenty-one-space bonus board, surrounded by chasing lights. *The Joker's Wild* had that larger-than-life slot machine separating Jack Barry and the contestants, who seemed miles apart from each other as the game was in progress. And then there was *The Price is Right*, which crammed three sprawling doors, a turntable, a giant price tag, and curtains among its impressive set. The sets were alive, they were colorful, and they were big. Compared to many game shows, particularly those in New York, that used smaller facilities, often converted radio studios, the new CBS game shows had more and did more with it.

It was more than the sets; it was the music. *Concentration*, *Beat the Clock*, and *Let's Make a Deal* all still had live organists providing peppy jingles throughout the show. The new CBS game shows had state-of-the-art synthesized music packages, each one a distinctive and memorable assembly of tunes to introduce the host or underscore the announcer's description of a sofa. The new shows had music so distinctive that you knew exactly what show you were watching just from the sound of the incidental tunes. It was a drastic change from a decade earlier, when game shows plucked their music straight from record albums.

It wasn't just that viewers got new game shows that day. It was that game shows themselves were new. In a single day, the standards changed, and producers, even those running the very shows that CBS introduced, realized that they had ideals that they had to live up to now.

24

Pyramid Climbing

Game Shows Get Their Money Back

Pyramids Weren't Built in a Day

Producer Bob Stewart had departed acrimoniously from Mark Goodson-Bill Todman Productions in 1964 after a dispute in which Goodson refused to let him develop a new idea for a game show. Stewart conceived a spin on *Password* in which one member of a team would give a list of items ("Money, a driver's license, a social security card . . . ") and the other would guess what tied the items together ("Things kept in a wallet"). Goodson balked at the idea, so Stewart walked.

Stewart's first attempt at selling the concept independently was an NBC pilot in 1967, *Celebrity Doubletalk*. It was a somewhat flimsy game in which the players gave clues to their opponents, trying to give clues that were technically accurate, but as misleading as possible—if the category was "Something that is Inflated," a *Celebrity Doubletalk* player would steer clear of clues like "a balloon" or "a tire" and instead give a clue like "your ego." NBC passed, but Bob Stewart didn't throw away ideas that he liked and he was convinced he could make this work.

In 1972, Bob Stewart tried a pilot called *Cash on the Line*. Host Dick Clark would announce a category, with four items that fit hidden on the game board. The players tried to guess all of the hidden items. There was also a category with three items, a category with two items, and a category with a single item. The game board was a large, eye-catching pyramid.

Cash on the Line didn't sell either, but Stewart kept tinkering and came up with a new pitch for CBS. In the main game, a player would give the partner rapid-fire clues to a series of items that all fit the same category, against a thirty-second clock. After each team did this three times, the high-scoring team would play a bonus round where a team member would see a series of categories and rattle off a list of items that fit each category, for the contestant to guess one at a time, in sixty seconds or less.

A CBS executive named Oscar Katz watched a demonstration of Stewart's game and interrupted him to make the surprising point that since the main game used six categories, it should use a board shaped like a pyramid, similar to what *Cash on the Line* had used. Stewart thought it was an odd suggestion, but if it would get the show on the air, fine, he'd give CBS a pyramid.

It was probably a coincidence, but the next demonstration, using a re-shaped game board, went so extraordinarily well that CBS put it on their daytime schedule before they even bothered telling Stewart they were buying the untitled game. The only reason Stewart found out was because he saw a schedule at the CBS New York offices and had to ask somebody what *The $10,000 Pyramid* was. Opening day was March 26, 1973.

Bob Stewart's son Sande says, "None of us had any inkling that *The $10,000 Pyramid* was anything different or special, particularly because we went on the air without shooting a pilot. We weren't able to gauge anything in advance without a pilot. But once in a while, magic happens."

Getting to the Top

The first few days in production were surprisingly stressful for Bob Stewart's staff. In practice games, nobody cleared all ten subjects in the Winner's Circle bonus round, so Stewart hastily ordered some crew members to cover the four bottom boxes with plywood, and the Winner's Circle board was scaled back to a more winnable six subjects in sixty seconds. It proved *too* winnable for the CBS network brass's tastes. June Lockhart and Rob Reiner were the guest celebrities for that first week, with Rob Reiner holding the distinction of being the first celebrity to clear the Winner's Circle, helping his contestant claim $10,000 on the subject "Things with a Hole."

Francine Bergman, who served as the game's contestant coordinator, remembers, "Rob Reiner told us backstage that he didn't think this game was going to be a hit. He said it was too easy!"

Reiner cleared the Winner's Circle so fast that a CBS executive in the Ed Sullivan Theater, watching the show in progress, declared that the fix must be in, and Stewart had to talk him out of stopping the taping. Unfortunately, by the time the five-episode taping had ended, the $10,000 had been claimed a second time. Now CBS was really unhappy; they had budgeted the show for one $10,000 payoff per eight episodes. The show had exhausted three weeks' worth of their budget in only five episodes.

Another problem: the game seemed too hard. For the main game, the writers had concocted categories about monarchs, famous quotations. The celebrities and contestants alike were stumped by answers that they had to convey, about which they had very limited knowledge. Bob Stewart and his staff changed their material to subjects that were more universal: "things you keep in your pockets" or "foods you eat at breakfast." This led to higher-scoring games, but more importantly, the games with the more universal subjects helped the staff figure out what the show was. *The $10,000 Pyramid* didn't work as a test of knowledge. The game worked as a simple game of communication; against a thirty-second clock, the players were free to give whatever clues they wanted, but for a high score, they had to economize their words. Entire games hinged on a contestant using one word too many, only to have the clock run out before the partner could think of the answer.

Francine Bergman says, "*Pyramid* was a fascinating example [of] learning by doing. The game wasn't fully developed when we went on the air, but the longer it stayed on, the better a feel Bob had for what worked. He would just come into the office and announce 'From now on, we're doing it this way . . . ' and explain the change we were making. And it worked, thankfully. Every change we made just made it better."

And there was one element that was exactly perfect from day one: the seemingly effortless hosting of Dick Clark, who immersed himself more deeply in the game than many emcees would have. His trademark was his gentle critiquing of the game in progress. Never obnoxious, never condescending, Dick Clark would just chime in with "A better clue would have been . . . " or "Keep an eye on the clock; if you get hung up on a word like that again, you may want to pass."

But even as Clark tried to maintain a reserved, neutral attitude during the competition in the main game, when it was time for

Dick Clark saved his weekends for the *Bandstand*, but Monday through Friday, he went *Pyramid* climbing.

the Winners' Circle, contestant against the house for ten grand, Clark let his guard down and let the viewers in on the fact that he really wanted these people to do well. He could be heard saying *"Hurry!"* and *"Go!"* as the seconds ticked down. He never got overexcited, never jumped up and down, never shouted after a big win. But when a contestant did claim the $10,000, a warm smile from Dick Clark said a thousand words and more.

Francine Bergman says, "It's easy to forget this about Dick Clark because he became so synonymous with the show. When we hired him, he was a pretty big celebrity. He had a huge following because of *American Bandstand* and he was considered a major figure in the music industry. He had come to us in search of a job because he was going through a divorce. Hosting a game show was only a one-day-a-week job because five episodes were taped at a time, and he needed the extra money. But that was a lucky break for us because Dick's presence attracted some curiosity and drew some extra eyes to the show.

"What Dick brought to the show was a command of the game. Dick had natural instincts for what made the show work, and he just understood the game so thoroughly that when he walked into the studio, you almost felt like he was as in charge of the show as Bob Stewart was. Dick ran that set. A lot of modern game show hosts don't have that quality. A lot of modern game show hosts need help and ask for it. Dick never needed help, he was completely in control."

The result of all this was, according to Tom Shales of *The Washington Post*, "The most watchable and brain-tickling game show ever put on the air."

And the steak had plenty of sizzle to it. Set designer Jim Ryan, instructed by Stewart to use slot machines as a source of inspiration, gilded the pyramid at center stage and surrounded it with dazzling chase lights, topped off by a flashing "$10,000" surrounded by even more chase lights. The eye-popping structure, taken in with the dynamic theme music, "Tuning Up" by Ken Aldin, providing the soundtrack, made *The $10,000 Pyramid* look as thrilling and engaging as it truly was. Every step of the way, the production was perfection.

Catching Up

With *The Price is Right, Gambit, The Joker's Wild*, and *The $10,000 Pyramid* securely in place as hit shows on CBS, suddenly the competition was looking outdated. NBC took notice. At the end of 1972, the Peacock Network appointed brash, outspoken thirty-one-year-old Lin Bolen to head the network's daytime programming. She didn't waste any time either.

Within months of her arrival, on March 23, 1973, the longest-running daytime game show of all time (at that point), *Concentration*, signed off after an incredible fourteen-and-a-half years. The audible clacking puzzle board with the simplistic two-tone rebuses, which had been so charming just a decade earlier, now looked like an antique compared to the slick and shiny CBS games. *Concentration* concluded with a final rebus puzzle—the solution was "YOU'VE BEEN MORE THAN KIND"—and host Bob Clayton gave a hasty goodbye before the organist in the studio played a peppy rendition of "Auld Lang Syne." The following Monday, Clayton started his new job, announcing *The $10,000 Pyramid* with Dick Clark. It was unintentionally a symbolic change in career for the announcer. The old guard was surrendering its post to the new crew on duty.

Concentration lived on for five more years thanks to an unusual business deal in which Goodson-Todman leased the rights to the format from NBC and produced new episodes for syndication. But even the new version of *Concentration* was emblematic of how much game shows had changed in the span of just one year.

Goodson, who was never shy about criticizing games from outside his fiefdom, had once walked into the studio during a taping of the NBC version of *Concentration* and said to producer Norm Blumenthal, "How did I let this show get away from me?"

But even an unabashed *Concentration* fan like Goodson felt there was room for improvement. Goodson amended the rules, adding more wild cards, and allowing the contestants to pick three numbers on each turn, so matches came faster and puzzles were solved sooner. The Goodson-Todman form of *Concentration* even had a bonus round, called Double Play, in which a player had to solve two rebuses puzzles against a ten-second clock to win a car.

Mo' Money

The $10,000 Pyramid had not only made it safe to offer five-figure paydays, but made viewers expect those big dollars. Many game shows hastily looked for ways to infuse more money into their shows. Some changes worked. The nighttime *Let's Make a Deal* added the Super Deal; if a contestant won the Big Deal, that contestant could promptly forfeit it to choose one of three mini-doors. Each of the doors was hiding cash, but if the contestant picked a door hiding $20,000, they got the cash and they got their forfeited Big Deal prizes back. *The Hollywood Squares* now offered a small fortune in prizes and cash, including a new car, for winning five consecutive matches. *Gambit* hid checks for $10,000 on their Bonus Board.

But in some cases, the changes could be awkward. *Password* now held a tournament every three months for $5,000, with the winner returning every three months to defend their title. *Jeopardy!* added a cash jackpot for contestants who answered all five clues in a single category. On paper, it sounded good. In execution, it significantly disrupted the flow of the game, with Art Fleming keeping constant track of each contestant's progress in a single category. *Jeopardy!* had appealed to viewers with how straightforward it was. The cash jackpot was almost too much of a twist for its own good.

Francine Bergman says, "It's silly to think that offering more money would draw more viewers to *Jeopardy!* Nobody cares how much money people win on *Jeopardy!*; that's not why anybody watches that show. They watch to see how well the game is played. That's why *The $10,000 Pyramid* worked. We developed a game that was fun and compelling to watch regardless of how much money was offered. The money was just icing on the cake; it's the game that drew people in."

Wink Martindale adds, "The money on a game show is a funny thing. The money became more of a selling point for the networks than the viewers. Part of the pitch would be, 'The bonus round can pay off up to TEN THOUSAND DOLLARS!' And that would get the executives' attention. But the cash doesn't really do anything for the viewers. A game's popularity is built on the format, and in a small part, on the host. But mostly the format. If it's a bad game show, you can offer $10 million and nobody will watch. If it's a good game show, you can give away $1,000 and the audience will tune in tomorrow. And if it's a bad game show, your host doesn't even matter. If the format is bad, Alex Trebek can't save it. Bob Barker can't save it. Wink Martindale can't save it. The game is most important."

Stud #1: Alex

It had now been about three decades since the first flickering screens began making their way into American living rooms. Television had now existed for a generation, and many performers on television had a generation's worth of experience. Hosts like Bill Cullen, Jack Narz, Dennis James, Bob Barker, Jack Barry, and Art Fleming certainly weren't old fossils, but they weren't exactly kids either. NBC daytime boss Lin Bolen, in search of talent that would attract the eyes of a largely female demographic, began looking for game show hosts who were younger and better-looking. In a remark that lived in infamy, Bolen half-jokingly referred to the new breed of game show hosts she was hiring as "my studs."

The first beneficiary of the Lin Bolen regime was a thirty-three-year-old Canadian journeyman broadcaster named Alex Trebek. The dark wavy hair and heavy moustache were a decidedly different look for a game show host, and the network heavily touted his background—Russian on his father's side, French and

The bushy hair and the moustache weren't exactly a common look for game show hosts until Alex Trebek came on the scene.

Indian on his mother's side—to make him sound like an exotic visitor. As an extra bit of promotion, Alex was booked as a guest contestant on a special episode of *Jeopardy!* with host Art Fleming.

Alex Trebek's game was *The Wizard of Odds*, in which contestants were asked a series of questions about statistics; winners had their names added to The Wizard's Wheel of Fortune, which was spun at the end of the show for bonus prizes. The show's most distinctive characteristic was a dynamic theme song composed by the show's producer, Alan Thicke, singing the praises of Alex the Wizard: *"Who's the man with the money, makes a dark day sunny? Who's the fellow every day, gives a bundle away?"*

The Wizard of Odds debuted on July 16, 1973. Trebek, for his part, hedged his bets; he had moved most of his belongings from Canada to Los Angeles at the beginning of the series, but for three months, he stayed on Alan Thicke's couch, just in case the show got canceled.

The game didn't last, but Trebek did. *The Wizard of Odds* struggled against *Gambit* and *Now You See It* (a word-search puzzle game hosted by Jack Narz) on CBS and ended on June 28, 1974; the following Monday, July 1, Alex strolled onstage as host of Heatter-Quigley's big-dice game, *High Rollers*.

Stud #2: Geoff

Jeopardy! had its apple cart upset by Lin Bolen's youth movement. Bolen had declared that *Jeopardy!* was too stuffy, too old-fashioned, and too stationary to attract the young female demographic. *Jeopardy!* was moved to 10:30 a.m.

In the primo noon slot went a game from Bob Stewart that was more to Lin Bolen's tastes: *Jackpot* was hosted by another young stud, Geoff Edwards, a former news reporter (present at Jack Ruby's murder of Lee Harvey Oswald) and disc jockey who had attracted the attention of game show producers with an impressive turn as host of a local Los Angeles game called *Lucky Pair*, produced by Bob Barker, and guest-hosting *Let's Make a Deal*. In the fall of 1973, he began hosting *The New Treasure Hunt* for Chuck Barris.

Sande Stewart says, "Geoff was hired because he had this air of cool about him. He was a Los Angeles disc jockey, so he was hipper than your average host. It showed in the way he dressed, the way he talked. But he had a knack for hosting. He was one of the most talented hosts ever in this business."

Jackpot was a markedly different game, from the moment the show faded in on a stage with sixteen contestants (whittled down from Bob Stewart's original conception of forty-nine contestants) waiting for the game to start. One contestant, dubbed "the Expert," picked the others one at a time to read riddles for the Expert to solve. Every riddle was worth a different amount of money, every riddle fed the growing jackpot. One was a Jackpot Riddle that paid off the entire haul, to be shared by the person who picked the riddle and the person who read it. If an Expert ever got tripped up by a riddle, the riddle reader became the new Expert. And as a very alluring bonus, if the value of the jackpot ever matched a pre-selected value, the Expert and the riddle reader had a chance to win a Super Jackpot that could reach an astronomical $50,000.

Jackpot was everything that Lin Bolen was looking for. As Sande Stewart explains, "*Jackpot* was the beginning of glitz on daytime game shows. It was 1974 and that's when game shows really started to look like Las Vegas. We put as many blinking light bulbs on the set as possible

Geoff Edwards's leisure suits and open collars were far from the norm in daytime TV.

to appease Lin Bolen, who loved visible light bulbs. And that's what every game show looked like from that point forward."

The game was fast-moving. Contestants got excited, screaming, running across the stage and hugging each other after a big win—something you never saw happen on *Jeopardy!*—on a set that was, at once, minimalist and flashy. There was a gallery for the fifteen riddle readers, a pulpit for the Expert, and a table at which stood Geoff Edwards. But it had just the right amount of glitz and color, and the massive board that calculated the value of the Super Jackpot made it look just spectacular enough.

Geoff Edwards was everything that Lin Bolen was looking for in a host—young, shaggy-haired, open collared, leisure suit–wearing, and with a million-watt smile. He was good at his job too, personable and humorous. If he had been a good-looking dud, he wouldn't have lasted. But to Lin Bolen's ever-lasting credit, the good-looking young guys she was hiring genuinely had talent.

Stud #3: Jim

Texas disc jockey Jim McKrell had been discovered by musician Henry Mancini during a tour stop and, with the composer's urging, he moved to Los Angeles in the late 1960s, hosting *The Game Game* for Chuck Barris and the unsold pilot *The Honeymoon Game* for Jack Barry. By 1973, he had become the go-to guy for NBC game show pilots. He was young, blonde, deep-voiced and handsome; a few executives noted that he bore a passing resemblance to Johnny Carson. In 1973 alone, he hosted

Jim McKrell, a long tall Texan discovered by Henry Mancini.

seven pilots for NBC; the one they finally picked up was *Celebrity Sweepstakes*, a game that turned *Hollywood Squares* into a horse race.

McKrell says of boss Lin Bolen, "She became a friend. We're still in contact. What I found I liked about her was that, unlike some executives, she didn't communicate through a chain of command. If I did something as a host that she didn't like, she wouldn't relay the message to an assistant, who would relay it to a producer, who would relay it to me. Lin would go straight to me, look me in the eye, and tell me what the problem was. I liked that.

"There's something else about Lin that I liked and it applied directly to *Celebrity Sweepstakes*. We taped two pilots for that show. The first pilot was dull. We had celebrities who didn't bring much to it and it wasn't very engaging. Most executives would throw the format in the trash. Lin Bolen watched that first pilot and saw through the dull celebrities. Lin absolutely believed there was something to that game, so instead of trashing it, she asked for a second pilot with a different celebrity panel. Second pilot went much better and Lin bought the show."

Six celebrities were seated at what resembled the starting gates of a racetrack. McKrell asked a trivia question, and each member of the studio audience, equipped with a push-button console, voted for the one celebrity that they thought was most likely to know the answer. Based on the audience votes, odds were posted on each celebrity, and the contestants would pick a star and place a bet. And the bets paid off handsomely; in the show's first weeks on the air, one contestant amassed $27,000, and another collected $19,000.

McKrell says, "We were a hit right out of the box. Placing bets on the stars' knowledge was a new idea, and a different way of using celebrity guests for a game show, so there was some intrigue there. NBC put us on at 11:30 a.m., which was just the right time slot. Some viewers were on their lunch breaks from work and it was a perfect show for a lunch break. The stars were fun and the game was entertaining."

The Prime-Time Pyramid

Although NBC's call to move *Jeopardy!* away from the noon slot was derided by fans, in the short-term it did pay one surprising dividend. It dented the ratings of *The $10,000 Pyramid*. CBS, mistaking the dent for a sign that the show's time had come, canceled *Pyramid*.

Francine Bergman says, "CBS canceled us with a 32 share in the ratings, which should give you an idea of how much television has changed. Today, if you delivered a show with a 32 share every day, the network would throw you a parade."

Bob Stewart knew his creation was something special, and he wasn't ready to let go yet. He immediately shopped it to local stations as a syndicated prime-access-time game show with a prime-time-sized payoff. The prime-time version was called *The $25,000 Pyramid*. Because Dick Clark's contract with ABC for *American Bandstand* prevented him from hosting prime-time shows on other networks, and because the CBS owned-and-operated stations had already expressed an interest in *The $25,000 Pyramid*, he was replaced on the nighttime show by Bob Stewart's perennial first choice, Bill Cullen.

Fortune smiled upon Bob Stewart's creation, though. ABC snapped up *The $10,000 Pyramid* for an afternoon time slot, and the daytime *$10,000 Pyramid* with Dick Clark continued . . . and thrived. By January 1976, it had doubled in size, prize-wise. It was renamed *The $20,000 Pyramid*.

Bergman said, "When we changed the cash prize, we had been on the air for three years, and remember, at the time, daytime TV didn't do season-by-season renewals. Your show was on the chopping block every thirteen weeks, so staying on the air for three years was a big accomplishment. And Bob Stewart simply felt the game needed some kind of facelift, but the game itself worked so well that we doubled the prize money in the bonus round. The money was the only thing we could change, everything else was perfect the way it was."

The Look

The new young games had a way of making the veterans feel squeezed out. It wasn't just that Lin Bolen liked flash and pizazz—she was jokingly called "the woman that owned all the light bulbs in television" because she liked visible flashing lights on the sets of game shows—it was that she liked hosts who fit her mold: youthful, tan, handsome, contemporarily dressed.

Veteran hosts found themselves having to get with the times. Art Fleming, who had sported slick hair on *Jeopardy!* for a decade, switched to the dry look. Dennis James, who had been doing television since the experimental broadcasts of the late 1930s, wore artificial sideburns on *Name That Tune*. Bill Cullen grew his hair to shoulder-length and switched from ties to butterfly collars. And when their games were all canceled, Art Fleming, Dennis James, and Bill Cullen all stayed away from NBC until after she was gone.

But to Bolen's ever-lasting credit, she launched the careers of a new generation of emcees who were extremely talented in their own right, she gave the green light to popular formats like *High Rollers* and *Celebrity Sweepstakes*. Her youth-oriented drive for pizazz gave a distinctive identity to a new game from Merv Griffin (see Chapter 25) that would end up lasting for decades. And she did appreciate the talents of the old guard. Producers like Bob Stewart, Ralph Edwards, Merv Griffin, Jack Barry, and Heatter-Quigley had opportunities to develop programs under Bolen's watch, and when she developed a game show format of her own, *Stumpers!* in 1976, she gave the job of host to silver-haired Allen Ludden. Whatever "infamy" she attained as a network executive was ultimately in the eye of the beholder.

25

Change of Fortune

Merv Griffin Goes for a Spin

Game Boy

Summertime during the Great Depression. Mr. and Mrs. Griffin would load their two kids into the backseat for a road trip. The kids got bored on these long drives and entertained themselves with a pencil and paper game called Hangman. You've probably played it too. One player draws a series of lines to represent the letters in some kind of phrase. Another player guesses letters trying to fill in the blanks and solve the puzzle. Calling a letter not in the phrase would add body parts to the hanging victim until the full body had been drawn.

Mr. and Mrs. Griffin's little boy Merv really didn't like the long car trips, but he enjoyed playing Hangman in the back seat. When Merv grew up, he developed a knack for, among other talents, creating game shows. He daydreamed about those long car trips and thought that Hangman might make an interesting format.

Griffin had another flashback: the annual church bazaar, the social event of the year in young Merv's part of the world. One of the features was a wheel with names of prizes written on the wedges; you could buy a ticket, spin the wheel, and win one of the small prizes up for grabs. As an adult, Merv visited casinos in Las Vegas quite often, and he found that the childhood allure of that prize wheel was a powerful one. Griffin had no interest in the slot machines or the blackjack tables. He wanted to play the game with the spinning wheel. And no matter how often he lost, he kept going for a spin. Griffin struck upon a way to incorporate that spinning prize wheel into a game of Hangman, and he pitched his idea to NBC daytime programming chief Lin Bolen.

Bolen's approval was particularly important to Griffin because of the contract he currently had with NBC had on the air, *Jeopardy!* Bolen made it known that she found the *Jeopardy!* too staid, and with a watchful eye on demographics, she dictated that *Jeopardy!*'s large fifty-and-over audience was undesirable. At the height of the show's popularity, Griffin had scored a plum stipulation during a contract renewal, giving him the right to develop and produce a new series if and when *Jeopardy!* was canceled. With Bolen making it clear that she wasn't a *Jeopardy!* fan, Griffin was keenly aware that the Hangman-with-a-wheel concept he was noodling with was probably going to be shown to Lin Bolen.

Bolen added an idea of her own to Griffin's proposal. Women liked shopping, and while game shows had certainly used elements of shopping, like guessing a price, there hadn't really been a game show that involved true shopping. She suggested adding a wrinkle to the game where contestants used the money they won during the game to buy prizes from an onstage boutique. Griffin agreed to work the idea into his format.

Truly Bazaar

Griffin worked up an unwieldy format, *Shopper's Bazaar*, and prepared for shooting a pilot. In search of a host who fit Lin Bolen's drive for youth, Griffin made a rather off-the-wall choice: Chuck Woolery, an Ashland, Kentucky, native who briefly worked as a salesman for Pillsbury before moving to Nashville and scoring a Top 40 hit with a psychedelic pop tune called "Naturally Stoned." Woolery had moved to Los Angeles to continue pursuing a career as a singer/songwriter, a path that sent him into a spot as a guest on *The Merv Griffin Show*. Griffin chatted on the air with Woolery for fifteen minutes and had a surprising hunch that this singer might make a good game show host.

Woolery said thanks but no thanks, but Griffin wasn't taking no for an answer, and Woolery finally agreed to host the pilot. *Shopper's Bazaar* taped in 1973. The game started with three contestants wandering around the stage and picking the prizes they wanted to win. They compiled their lists, the retail price of those prizes was totaled, and that total essentially became a "debt" that the contestants had to pay off in order to win the prizes they had picked.

To win those prizes, they played Hangman. They faced a puzzle board with a set of pull tabs concealing the letters in the puzzle. Woolery had a button in his hand that controlled a constantly spinning upright wheel. When a contestant yelled, "Stop the wheel!," Woolery would press his button and the wheel came to a stop on a dollar amount. Calling a letter in that puzzle would earn that money; if the letter was in the puzzle more than once, the dollar value was multiplied accordingly. Scattered around the wheel were spaces like BUY A VOWEL (a contestant was forced to spend $250 to buy an A, E, I, O, or U), and YOUR OWN CLUE (the contestant picked up a telephone and heard a hint to the solution that the other contestants couldn't hear).

Lin Bolen, in the control room, didn't like what she was seeing. She felt that the puzzle board and the wheel were too old-fashioned in design, and that the game moved too slowly. Griffin himself agreed; he took stock of the game in progress and realized there was too much going on: the stage was cluttered, the contestants' progress in paying off their debts made the game too confusing (they won money, yet hadn't actually won anything because it wasn't enough money). Even the opening was too strange to be engaging: the show faded in on the contestants already guessing letters while Woolery was explaining the rules and the show's announcer explained what prizes the contestants were playing for, all as the show's theme, a synthesizer-based version of "Chitty Chitty Bang Bang," provided a needless soundtrack to all the business. The game was, at once, too much and not enough.

Back to the Drawing Board

Bolen rejected *Shopper's Bazaar*, but Griffin, again, proved to be a hard man to say no to. He reworked the game inside and out. He hired veteran director Marty Pasetta and set designer Ed Flesh to come up with a more contemporary look. Flesh cast out the Vegas-style upright wheel used in *Shopper's Bazaar* in favor of a horizontal wheel that required contestants to bend over a little bit so they could spin it. The contestants and the wheel faced an enormous puzzle board that lit up as letters were called, so the whole thing got brighter as the puzzle got closer to being solved. Because there wasn't enough time to mechanize the puzzle board the way Pasetta and Flesh had wanted, a modeling agency dispatched a striking blonde named Susan Stafford to turn the letters as they were called. She added so much personality with the way she dashed across the stage to turn the letters, shrugged apologetically if a letter wasn't there, and openly rooted for all three contestants, that everyone decided to keep her onboard if the pilot sold, and plans for mechanizing the board were called off.

Griffin even reworked Bolen's shopping idea into something easier to follow. Contestants simply focused on spinning the wheel, racking up the money, and solving the puzzle. After that was over, everyone turned their attention to a series of small boutiques onstage, and the winning contestant spent their money on whatever prizes they could afford.

Two more pilots were shot with the new title *Wheel of Fortune*. One pilot was hosted by Griffin's choice, Chuck Woolery. The other was hosted by Lin Bolen's choice, Edd Byrnes ("Kooky" of *77 Sunset Strip* fame). The *Wheel of Fortune* pilot went through the roof; test audiences loved it and Lin Bolen was finally satisfied with what she was seeing.

The original set of *Wheel of Fortune*. Near the wheel, one of the boutiques where contestants went shopping for prizes after solving a puzzle.

Jeopardy! with Art Fleming went off the air on January 3, 1975. In accordance with Merv Griffin's contract, *Wheel of Fortune* with Chuck Woolery took over the time slot on Monday, January 6, 1975.

Chuck Woolery's Tomfoolery

When an interviewer asked Woolery what a singer/songwriter was doing hosting a game show, he bluntly answered, "It beats the hell out of me! I was asked, I guess. Listen, it's something I can do that I enjoy and it's fabulous exposure. It's amazing to me how good the exposure is. I don't think it's the ultimate goal for me, but I could make a career out of it."

A lot of people didn't think Woolery could make a career out of it. In the early weeks, executives at NBC couldn't help noticing how awful Woolery seemed to be. He stammered, explained rules incorrectly, asked people offstage for help, mispronounced words . . . that was bad enough, but he also let out a loud laugh every time he made a mistake, drawing even more attention to his all-too-frequent gaffes.

Chuck Woolery in front of the upright casino-style wheel used for *Shopper's Bazaar*, the unaired pilot that would become *Wheel of Fortune*.

NBC summoned a veteran game show host to audit the new guy. *Hollywood Squares* host Peter Marshall was sent to a taping to figure out what Woolery needed to improve. Marshall (who recalled later that there were only six people in the audience) surprised everybody with his opinion.

"He's adorable," Marshall argued. Woolery was mistake-prone, but it didn't detract from the game, and besides, human beings make mistakes. Viewers liked seeing someone on TV who was just as human as they were, especially one who felt so free to draw attention to it and laugh at himself when he slipped up. It may not make sense, but somehow, Woolery's goofs were adding to the show.

Spinning Wheel

Wheel of Fortune wasn't a smash hit right from the start, but it was competitive against tough competition—CBS's established hit game *Gambit*—and helped Merv Griffin maintain a foothold as a creative force to be reckoned with in daytime TV, while establishing a long and successful television career for Chuck Woolery. And that was just what happened in 1975. There was plenty more spinning to come.

26

The One-Hour Experiment

Daytime TV Takes Its Time

A Dramatic Turn of Events

Daytime TV was more than just game shows, of course. For years, daytime TV was defined by another genre: the soap opera. A staple of daytime radio, soaps migrated over to TV at the same time that every other genre migrated, and in the coming years, the popularity of soaps led to some expansion, in more ways than one. It wasn't just that more and more soaps were premiering; it was that they began gobbling up more and more airtime.

In the beginning, the vast majority were only fifteen minutes long, because that had been the standard running length of the radio soaps. In 1956, *As the World Turns* proved that thirty minutes wasn't too long for a soap. Thirty minutes eventually became the standard running time.

In the early 1970s, a handful of soap operas bit the dust and the networks did something unusual. Instead of seeking out new programs, the networks expanded other soap operas from thirty minutes to sixty minutes. It could have stretched other programming thin, but with complex storylines and a deep roster of recurring characters, plus a large staff of writers behind the scenes, many soaps proved to be up to the challenge. Hour-long soap operas worked. So daytime television had hour-long soap operas, hour-long talk shows . . . all while game shows remained thirty minutes.

The Price of Survival

In 1975, *The Price is Right* with Bob Barker was showing signs of wear against tough competition from soaps in the 3:00 p.m. time slot: *General Hospital* on ABC and *Another World* on NBC. *Price* had been on the air for three years, and it could be tough to maintain an audience for a game show after three years. *The Joker's Wild*, one of the other game shows that CBS introduced on September 4, 1972, bit the dust in June 1975, while *The Price is Right* went in search of survival tactics.

The Price is Right tinkered. It introduced a recurring feature called the Do It Yourself Showcase, in which a contestant was given a choice of nine prizes and built their Showcase by selecting three at random by number. In execution, it proved unwieldy and was discarded quickly.

On the other hand, the staff found a way to liven up the Showcases that absolutely did work. They infused the segment with sketch comedy; Showcases now frequently told little stories that unfolded comically and happened to incorporate a series of prizes. There was the day that announcer Johnny Olson donned a garish wig and became Flippity Fleischman, an obnoxious disc jockey who offered a prize every time the lyrics of a Top 40 song mentioned one: "Kodachrome" by Paul Simon led to a camera; "Both Sides

Bob Barker celebrates with the winner of A NEW CAR on *The Price is Right*. The show finished its third season in 1975, with the show's staff little aware that they had only just begun.

Now" by Judy Collins led to Circus World tickets; and the creepy novelty song "Beep Beep" by the Playmates culminated with the revelation of a Cadillac. Another particularly insane Showcase was an involved parody of the film *The Exorcist*. A dinette set, a television set, $500 in cash, and a sports car were woven into a tale of Father Johnny Olson exorcising a demon from a little girl who said mean things about Bob Barker.

The Showcases were also livened up with a new rule: if the closest bidder was within $100 of the price of their own Showcase without going over, that contestant won both Showcases. The Double Showcase win, accentuated by a cacophonous series of whooping sirens and clanging bells, became the pinnacle of excitement on the show.

The Price is Right introduced some fancy new digs, too, switching its earth-toned set after three years to a more vibrant rainbow-colored set. New pricing games were introduced too. Production assistant Roger Dobkowitz created a game called Ten Chances, in which contestants were shown three prizes and the digits in the prices, but not the correct order of any of those digits. The contestant had a total of ten chances to write the correct prices, one at a time, for all three prizes.

Another new pricing game, Golden Road, became one of the truly legendary games seen on *The Price is Right*. Contestants walked along a gold path with four stops, filling in the digits for incomplete prices to win a series of prizes, culminating in a luxury item, like a sports car, a cabin cruiser, or some other mondo-gift with a five-figure price, a rarity in the 1970s.

Anniversary Party

Toward the end of summer in 1975, CBS announced that *The Price is Right* was being taken out of the 3:00 p.m. time slot and moved to a morning slot. Nothing really earth-shattering about that, but CBS made the surprise announcement that *The Price is Right* would be doing a special week of programs to celebrate their third anniversary, and all episodes during that special week would be an hour long. Since the third anniversary of a game show typically wasn't celebrated with such lavish festivities, a few viewers read between the lines and figured out that CBS had something bigger in mind.

Super Third Anniversary Week kicked off on September 8, 1975. Six pricing games were played on each show instead of the standard three. In addition, the shows included a new feature, Showcase Showdown, which the *Price* staff had conjured up to appease a request from CBS bosses to add a wheel to the show. Instead of the original rules that simply stated that the two top winners of the day returned for the Showcase, the game now had two Showcase Showdowns each day. After three pricing games, the three onstage contestants returned to spin a wheel with small money amounts ranging from five cents up to one dollar. The contestants could each spin once or twice; the contestant who came closest to one dollar without going over advanced to the Showcase; scoring one dollar on the nose earned a $1,000 cash bonus.

CBS was so happy with Super Third Anniversary Week that the announcement was quickly made that effective November 3, the show would permanently be an hour in length. The show distributed "HOUR POWER" T-shirts to hype the change, while stars from other CBS shows made cameos on *Price* to tout the impending change and talk about all the excitement that viewers would be seeing on the new hour-long version of *The Price is Right*.

The Peacock Strikes Back!

CBS was excitedly touting *The Price is Right* as the first big hour-long game on television, but when November 3 rolled around, it wasn't the only hour-long game show that day. NBC's *Wheel of Fortune* and *The Hollywood Squares* both did hour-long episodes for that entire week. *Squares* justified it as a tenth anniversary celebration (which was true; autumn 1975 would be the start of the show's tenth season on NBC) and came up with a whopper of a special week featuring fifty stars; every time the show returned from a commercial beak, there was a new celebrity sitting in one of the boxes. Redd Foxx, Peter Graves, Mike Connors, Sally Struthers, Michael Landon, Milton Berle, Ernest Borgnine, Eva Gabor, and Peter Marshall's sister Joanne Dru all dropped in and out throughout that week.

Wheel of Fortune had a jaw-dropping $100,000 worth of merchandise on the stage for the post-puzzle shopping, and instituted a tournament format to its show. A total of six contestants appeared each day, playing two complete games. At the end of the hour, the two winners competed against each other in a single puzzle, with the winner playing a bonus round. The contestant was given a choice of four puzzles, classified as Easy, Medium, Hard, or Difficult, with the prize values increasing accordingly. The contestant chose four consonants and one vowel and had fifteen seconds to solve the puzzle to earn their bonus prize.

Hour-long *Squares* worked short-term, but in the long run, it wouldn't have been the most practical show from a talent-booking standpoint. The program was already taping two nighttime episodes for syndication each week, and a permanent one-hour daytime version would have made it a little trickier to book celebrities for what would have been an extremely lengthy taping session.

Daytime *Wheel* worked a little better, and a month after that special week, *Wheel* expanded to one hour on a full-time basis.

ABC Strikes Out

The ABC network had one game show on its schedule that seemed suited for a one-hour slot. *Let's Make a Deal*, like *The Price is Right*, incorporated a variety of smaller games into every show, and with a skillful master of ceremonies and production staff behind the scenes, a one-hour *Let's Make a Deal* should have worked perfectly. ABC approached Stefan Hatos-Monty Hall Productions and handed down the order for the company to deliver a week of one-hour episodes.

In 2000, Monty Hall told game show historian Steve Beverly, "I never liked [the one-hour *Let's Make a Deal*]. Not that we weren't capable of doing an hour. I felt we were expanding the show just for the sake of expanding it. We didn't have enough time to prepare to do them right."

That preparation time had been crucial to *The Price is Right*. Over the course of three years, *The Price is Right* had built up a roster of more than twenty pricing games, plenty to rotate day after day for some variety, particularly as the staff continued whipping up even more pricing games to sustain a one-hour show. ABC gave Monty Hall's crew two weeks to prepare the one-hour *Let's Make a Deal*.

Hall told Steve Beverly, "ABC wanted us to give away bigger prizes and add that Super Deal (the $20,000 cash bonus game from the nighttime version) . . . I didn't agree for two reasons. Every time we'd tried to kick up the prizes, it didn't make one difference in the ratings. I always said it wasn't how much we give away but the way we give it away. The other reason was, I told ABC, "What if you don't stay with an hour? Then the next week, we come right back with our regular format. How do we do that without looking like we're pulling back?"

The hour-long *Let's Make a Deal* may have actually been the show's undoing. By Hall's own admission, the week was sub-par, owing to lack of prep time, and ratings were actually down for that entire week. ABC lost faith in the show and moved it to a noon time slot, which was fast becoming no man's land in daytime TV, as many, many stations across all the major networks started airing local newscasts at noon instead of the network program. On July 9, 1976, *Let's Make a Deal* aired its final program on ABC, bringing an end to an impressive twelve-year network daytime run.

Monty has a fistful of dough for these people, dressed as they are. Giving away the loot for a full hour of *Let's Make a Deal* was easy; as Monty and ABC found out, the hard part was keeping it interesting.

The Right Show at the Right Time

A shrewd scheduling move by CBS led to total victory in the one-hour experiment. When CBS introduced the permanent one-hour *Price is Right*, it was slotted to begin at 10:30 a.m., immediately following *Gambit*. When NBC announced the one-hour *Wheel of Fortune* was also going to start at 10:30 a.m., CBS flip-flopped their two morning games, so *The Price is Right* now started at 10:00 a.m. and *Gambit* started at 11:00 a.m. By the time *Wheel of Fortune* started each morning, viewers were firmly invested in Bob Barker's fun and games and couldn't bring themselves to change the channel.

Wheel of Fortune was scaled back to thirty minutes after only seven weeks. *The Price is Right* wasn't just the most successful hour-long game on daytime TV, it was *the* hour-long game on daytime TV. And it stayed that way.

27

Talk Dirty to Me

Tell Me You Didn't Just Say That!

What the Blank Did They Say?

During the 1960s, *The Match Game* with Gene Rayburn evolved in a way not typically seen on TV game shows. The game started out as a quiet, *Password*-ish show. Gene Rayburn asked simple questions, like "Name something you pour gravy on."

The show had been on the air for a little more than three years when ratings started to erode, and everyone figured that *The Match Game* had simply reached its expiration date. Everyone, that is, except writer Dick DeBartolo, who also wrote for *MAD* magazine. DeBartolo suggested changing the question style to something sillier, like "Mary likes to pour gravy on John's (blank)."

The change worked so well that ratings suddenly showed signs of life again. *The Match Game* survived on NBC for four more years.

In 1973, Goodson-Todman Productions introduced a revamped version, *Match Game '73* (the title of the show changing every year on the New Year's Eve broadcast, with the massive lighted logo on the stage sweeping away to make way for a new one). Gene Rayburn hosted the new version, which now had contestants trying to match answers with a six-star panel. Initially, the series had the "Name something . . . " line of questioning, but after producer Ira Skutch watched the first few episodes tape, he flatly declared, "This isn't working" and *Match Game '73* resorted to the naughty fill-in-the-blanks.

In a matter of weeks, *Match Game '73* became the most popular show on daytime television, a post that it would hold for nearly four years. Anchored firmly in the 3:30 p.m. Eastern time slot on CBS, the show was a ritual for kids coming home from school, even though much of the humor was unmistakably adult-oriented.

> **Gene Rayburn:** We polled a recent studio audience and asked them to give their best response to this: "Eugene BLANK."
>
> (One of the answers given in the audience poll is "Eugene Roach.")
>
> **Rayburn:** Who is Eugene Roach?
>
> **Charles Nelson Reilly:** Eugene Roach was the inventor of that little clip you use to hold your marijuana.

Get ready to match the stars! Gene Rayburn has a few laughs with Avery Schreiber, Brett Somers, Charles Nelson Reilly, Joan Collins, Richard Dawson, and Patti Deutsch on the rowdy and ribald *Match Game*.

Fred Wostbrock Collection

In a 2014 interview, frequent *Match Game* visitor Orson Bean said, "For better or for worse, all of us who appeared as panelists on *Match Game* contributed to the coarsening of America. In the 1950s, I did shows where everything was censored. . . . And then you look at television decades later, when David Letterman is saying that summer is so hot in New York City that the squirrels in Central Park are putting ice on their nuts. How did we get from the uptight censorship of the 1950s to jokes like that being permitted on television? I honestly think *Match Game* helped a little bit. Because we began to break that down very slowly. There were suggestive words in the questions, and we very delicately would handle it by writing answers like 'tinkle' and 'doo-doo,' and we just kept pushing and pushing it. I'm not sure television is better for it, but at the time, we had a lot of fun playing the game."

Pants on Fire

In 1969, viewers in Los Angeles saw an unusual game with an even more unusual host. *Liars Club* saw a celebrity panel examining an unfamiliar object, each panelist giving a different explanation of what the object was. The simple task for the contestants was to figure out who was giving the truthful explanation. Betty White was a regular panelist; the host was, of all people, Rod Serling, creator and host of *The Twilight Zone*. The game ran for only one season in Los Angeles before being revived in 1976 for a national run, hosted at first by Bill Armstrong and later by, fittingly, Mr. Betty White, a.k.a. Allen Ludden. Betty returned to her old spot on the panel for many episodes.

Ralph Andrews co-produced the national *Liars Club* with Larry Hovis, stand-up comic and former co-star of *Hogan's Heroes*. Hovis frequently served as a panelist, but behind the scenes, he collaborated with the writers, passing objects around the room and figuring out what it looked like this object might do or be. His ribald

Would David Letterman lie to you? Allen Ludden is trying to figure that out, while Dody Goodman and Larry Hovis listen in, during *Liars Club*.
Fred Wostbrock Collection

sense of humor often found its way into the explanations offered to contestants. On one episode, he examined a small, yellow cup, and told the contestants: "Pole vaulters don't have an easy time. Poles are tubes of fiberglass, so the vaulters have to run down the field and stick the tip of the pole into the shoe. That pole can slip sometimes, so they've made this. It's called a butt plug."

Allen Ludden deadpanned, as did a few of the other panelists, but Betty White bowed her head and hid her face from the audience as her shoulders shook in heaves of laughter.

Liars' Club writer Shelley Herman remembers, "Larry loved to sneak in that kind of stuff. He held up an item one day and he said, 'It's for blowing bubbles . . . I think she said her name was Bubbles, anyway."

Tattletales Tell All

In 1974, CBS cleared the 4:00 p.m. time slot for another game from the Goodson-Todman workshop. *Tattletales* was a reworking of a format Goodson-Todman had been tinkering with for a decade. It had started as a pilot called *It Had to be You*, then became a one-year syndicated show, *He Said She Said* with Joe Garagiola, and another unaired pilot, *Celebrity Match Mates* with Gene Rayburn.

Tattletales, as it was finally known, was hosted by Bert Convy, and played by three married celebrity couples. Each couple was playing for one-third of the studio audience, who received equal shares of all the prize money accumulated by their couple (the show installed a check-cutting machine in the back of the studio, and everybody got paid as they headed for the exit). For much of the run, the game was similar to *The Newlywed Game*, with Bert Convy asking deeply personal questions.

> **Convy:** You're in the middle of making love when the room begins to shake. It's an earthquake. Do you think you'd stop or do you keep going?

Mrs. Gene Rayburn: Sure as heck aren't gonna stop—we need all the help we can get.

Convy: You're in a hotel room and you can faintly hear the couple next door making love. Would you try to ignore it or try to hear it better?

Dennis James: If you're hearing it faintly in the other room, I say bring the action into *our* room so you can really hear it!

Mrs. Dennis James: I'd try to hear it better. After all, you might learn something.

Nothing Square About It

Contrary to what the average viewer would think, the standards for daytime television were less rigid than the standards for prime-time programming. The ninety-minute block 7:30–9:00 p.m. was deemed "family time" by the major networks, which all ran tight ships with regards to content. On the other hand, only adults were at home during the daytime, and daytime programming was largely considered less important anyway. There were some standards, but that lack of concern allowed daytime shows to cut loose with occasionally questionable content so. In the months and years before *Saturday Night Live* debuted in October 1975, arguably the naughtiest, wildest jokes on television were being heard on daytime shows, and game shows in particular.

The Hollywood Squares took full advantage, with a team of writers coming up with "zingers" for the stars to fire off before actually attempting to answer the question, and because of how tightly written the jokes were (gags didn't span the length of the show or call back to previous gags; a particular joke began and ended with the question that triggered it), it made *The Hollywood Squares* arguably the most quotable show on television. *Squares* released paperback volumes and even an LP of the funny answers heard on the show.

Peter Marshall: The University of South Carolina offered a class for Lovemaking. Why was the class canceled?

Redd Foxx: Too noisy.

Peter Marshall: True or false . . . Psychologists have found that a man's face registers the same expression for both hunger and passion.

Rose Marie: You mean this whole time, that guy was only hungry?

Peter Marshall: King Lear had three of them, Cordelia, Regan, and Goneril. What were they?

Paul Lynde: King Lear had Goneril?

Bank On It

The reunited Jack Barry and Dan Enright Productions, the phoenix rising from the ashes of the quiz show scandals, introduced their own blend of celebrities and sly jokes. They called it *Break the Bank*, with host Tom Kennedy; the show wasn't related to the original *Break the Bank* of early radio and television; in fact, Barry and Enright paid royalties to Herb Wolf Associates, the company that owned the original series, in order to use the title.

Barry seemed to hold his nose somewhat while acknowledging to one newspaper writer that the jokes on *Break the Bank* were right on the border of good taste. Barry said, "[T]he networks believe that very risqué material is what makes it on daytime television."

> **Tom Kennedy:** You have just bent your epee. What are you doing?
>
> **Jan Murray:** You should know, you were the one who straightened it for me last time.

The jokes were so startling to some ears that when Jack Barry introduced a weekly edition for prime-access-time syndication, which he hosted himself, he had to assure station managers that the nighttime edition would be more suitable for family viewing.

Questions, Questions . . .

Writing a trivia question that had a very definite correct answer, but coming up with a "zinger" answer that worked every time, was a tough job for even the most talented writers. Some *Hollywood Squares* writers would toil at the show for weeks before finally getting a single joke on the air; trivia and jokes were two flavors that could be extremely difficult to mix for a newcomer.

The result was that, every now and then, some of the jokes on game shows sounded awfully familiar. Writer Mark Maxwell-Smith tells this story:

> I was employed by Ralph Edwards Productions as a question writer, but I was permitted to work for other production companies doing audience warm-ups, so by day, I would write clues for *Cross-Wits* and by night, I did audience warm-up for *Break the Bank*.
>
> One of the other clue writers at *Cross-Wits*, a wonderful man named Bob Allen, wrote a great clue. Seven-letter word: Organ of the body that's the size of your fist and it's just below your belt. On the next day we taped *Cross-Wits*, there was a man in the studio that I will identify only as Mr. X. We do the clue for that seven-letter word. Naughty double-entendre, it got a big laugh from the audience, contestant solves the word. It's STOMACH.
>
> The next time I do warm-up for *Break the Bank*, I see Mr. X and I say hello to him. Game starts, and Tom Kennedy reads a question: "This organ of the body is just below your belt and it's the size of your fist. Name it."

And then, I swear to you, a few weeks later, I'm watching *Hollywood Squares*. Peter Marshall says, "Paul Lynde, what organ of the body is just below your belt and it's the size of your fist?"

Don't Even Think About Saying It!

Game shows still had to adhere to some network standards, and occasionally the bleep button was used. If things got really bad, the scissors came out.

On *Tattletales*, Bert Convy was host to Dick Gautier and Barbara Stuart. With Barbara in isolation, Bert Convy asked Gautier, "Which of these TV wives does your wife most closely resemble: Edith Bunker or Maude Findlay?"

Gautier answered, "Well, most of the time she's Edith Bunker, but once a month, she's Maude Findlay."

That exchange didn't air; nor did this answer on *The Hollywood Squares*:

Peter Marshall: Can the puppies in a litter come from different fathers?

Paul Lynde: Why, that bitch!

CBS required a censor to thoroughly examine the questions penned by the *Match Game* writers before the games taped. Usually a slight rewrite was all they asked for, but occasionally, they did just flat-out reject a question. As an example of what CBS deemed unfit for *Match Game*, here's a rejected question from writer Dick DeBartolo: "Whenever the Six Million Dollar Man runs out of energy, he sticks his (blank) in an electrical socket."

Panelist Marcia Wallace stepped away from double entendre and dove headfirst into single entendre when Gene posed this puzzler: "Unlucky Louie said, 'Just my luck. I went on a diet and I lost three inches. Unfortunately, it was three inches off my (blank)."

As Richard Dawson wiped away tears of laughter, Marcia Wallace shamelessly revealed the answer: "Genitalia."

Did She Really Say That?

The queen mother of salacious responses was one that a writer didn't come up with. It was 100 percent from the mind of contestant Olga Perez on *The Newlywed Game*.

The Newlywed Game had concluded its highly successful run on ABC on December 20, 1974. The show returned for a new run in five-day-a-week syndication beginning in the fall of 1977, and many stations aired it in an early evening slot, which raised the ire of parents' groups. In many cities, the syndicated *Newlywed Game* opened with a viewer-discretion warning, while station managers fended off complaints from offended viewers unable to locate the knob that changed the channel.

The question Bob Eubanks posed to Olga was "Where is the strangest place that you and your husband have ever gotten the urge to make whoopee?"

Olga stared at Eubanks nervously, hesitated for several seconds, and said, "In the ass."

The answer become the stuff of legend, literally. Video recorders weren't common yet, there was no coverage of the incident to speak of (single wacky answers on game show episodes tend not to get lots of press), and, save for thirteen weeks of reruns in the summer, there weren't a lot of opportunities to catch another viewing of a syndicated game show.

But the incident stuck like glue in the minds of a few viewers, and over the years, the incident spread like an urban legend. Bob Eubanks had simply forgotten that the incident happened—that one

Bob Eubanks steps onto the stage of *The Newlywed Game*. With thousands of contestants over the years, it's understandable that Bob forgot about Olga . . . but many TV viewers remembered.

day of taping blended in his mind with the thousands and thousands of other off-the-wall answers he had heard over the years, but eventually, he grew so tired of being asked about it that in several interviews during the 1990s, he claimed he would pay $10,000 to anyone who could produce a videotape of the incident.

Game Show Network never inquired about Eubanks's offer, but they did finally unearth the incident in 2000 and air it as part of a *Newlywed Game* marathon.

Tame by Comparison

In 1973, *Match Game*'s naughty fill-in-the-blanks and *The Newlywed Game*'s nosey queries were cutting edge. But as the 1970s wore on, *Maude* did an episode about abortion; *Three's Company* made a running gag out of landlord Mr. Furley's impotence; *Mary Hartman, Mary Hartman* had flashers, peeping toms, venereal disease, and adultery; *Saturday Night Live* did sketches about marijuana, child molestation, and one-night stands; and *All in the Family* covered just about everything else.

By the end of the 1970s, taboos had disappeared from the airwaves one by one, and the game shows once deemed mischievous now seemed almost pure compared to the rest of television. The naughty game shows all disappeared one by one, but they weren't really replaced. Game shows over the next decade just went for pure enjoyment of the game, without any need for comedy writers or the occasional hands cupped over Junior's ears. The humor on game shows once served as a barometer of the American psyche, but now that job was taken over by other television, and game shows just went back to being game shows.

28

Nighttime Is the Right Time

Games You Play in the Dark

The prime access time slot afforded game shows an opportunity to sneak back into after-dark spots on TV schedules during the 1970s. Here's a look at some of the most popular game shows that appeared once a week at around 7:30 p.m. (6:30 central) on your local station.

Barris Hunts for a Hit

Game shows had long compelled TV critics to dig out their thesauri. If they liked what they were seeing, "exciting," "brain-tickling," "suspenseful," "charming," and "engaging" were choice terms. If critics disliked the game, "tacky," "greedy," "obnoxious," "noisy," or "confusing" would seep into the paragraphs. But one game show in the 1970s left critics so speechless that some of them felt forced to use a word that almost never appeared in their reviews of game shows: "Cruel."

The New Treasure Hunt began life as a challenge issued to Chuck Barris by TV executives who had become weary of his relentless pitches for game shows that just didn't feel right. *The Dating Game* and *The Newlywed Game* were off-the-wall ideas that just happened to work, but a string of oddities—*How's Your Mother-in-Law?*, *The Game Game*—had failed. By 1972, television executives were so frustrated by Barris' pitches that several of them began asking him to pitch a more "traditional" game show. *Let's Make a Deal* was invoked by one executive as an example of what they were looking for.

Chuck Barris went back to his office and ruminated on *Let's Make a Deal*. His mind wandered to a drawn-out prank that he and his staff had played on network executives a few years earlier, shortly after *The Dating Game* and *The Newlywed Game* both exploded onto the scene. Barris, who previously couldn't get a meeting, was now being bombarded with requests for new formats.

As a goof on the executives, Barris and his staff came up with a phony game show format; it was deliberately the most tasteless concept they could imagine. They called it *Greed*. Contestants would be shown an elderly disabled man walking on crutches and be offered a sum of money for kicking the crutches away. Each successive offer made to the contestants would be smaller and smaller, with the winner being the contestant who agreed to do it for the least money. For another round, Barris suggested, contestants would be shown a child with a dog and asked how much money they'd need to kill the dog.

Barris later recalled the results of the experiment. "*Greed* was a gag, but we never let on that we were kidding, and one buyer actually left promising to check with his boss to see if he'd like the show for syndication. The moral is, never underestimate what people will do for money."

Barris took the advice about *Let's Make a Deal* to heart, but did something quite unusual. Rather than create a new game show, he dug into television's past and

A wild-eyed *Treasure Hunt* contestant is let off the hook by Geoff Edwards. After a long, slow build towards a Klunk, Geoff reveals that her prize is a new car!

found an old idea that seemed to suit the executives' desires, as well as his own. It was Jan Murray's old game show, *Treasure Hunt*. To Barris's mind, the format also preyed on the innate greed of the average contestant.

Barris bought the rights to *Treasure Hunt* from Jan Murray and produced a pilot in 1972 with host Geoff Edwards. Edwards's negotiations to host *Treasure Hunt* included an unexpected sticking point. Edwards was known for sporting a rather contemporary wardrobe by the standards of the time; on television, he seldom wore neckties, preferring open collars or the occasional turtleneck. When he learned Chuck Barris wanted the host of *Treasure Hunt*, whomever he may be, to wear a tuxedo every week, Edwards balked, not wanting to wear the same black formal wear week after week. Barris made the concession that Edwards would be given a $15,000 collection of ten tuxedos to alternate between, each in a different color.

What's a Klunk?

Chuck Barris didn't have it in him to produce a "normal game show," and even though *The New Treasure Hunt* (as it was officially named) was as close as he could, every part of the presentation made it unmistakably a Chuck Barris offering. Geoff Edwards was welcomed onstage at the start of every show by a bevy of models. Ten women in the audience would hold up the gift boxes they had been handed before the show and open them on Geoff's cue; the three who had numbers in their boxes would run to the stage to play a small game involving three more boxes, two of which were empty and one hiding a jack-in-the-box or a pop-up flower. The audience member who found the hidden surprise selected one of the thirty treasure boxes on stage. They weren't pirate chests, like the original version; just big boxes wrapped in the gaudiest department store wrapping paper designs that 1973 had to offer.

Once the contestant had chosen the treasure box, she (and the contestant was always a she; absolutely no male contestants allowed) was offered cash to forfeit the box and all its contents. After the contestant decided, she found out what she had won (or could have won). That's as much as there was to the game. Just a series of pure luck decisions. And yet viewers would be enamored.

Geoff Edwards explained to reporter Vernon Scott, "There is a certain amount of the voyeur in almost everyone. Watching a show like ours could be compared to listening in on the party line in the old days. We place the contestant in a dilemma. There she stands with, say, $1,500 in her hands trying to decide to gamble it all on that unseen prize in the package. Viewers are fascinated by such decisions."

The New Treasure Hunt's unique presentation was that it revealed the prize hidden in the box through a drawn-out comedy sketch. All thirty of the boxes onstage had a separate and unique set of props and goodies in them, each geared toward a specific sketch. When a contestant selected her box, the show paused for a commercial break, the contestant was escorted offstage momentarily, and Geoff got a briefing from the show's producers about what was in the box and how the upcoming sketch would play out. Taping resumed after the briefing, and Geoff would ad-lib his way for the next five minutes or so.

An improvisational sketch comedy game show? How does that even play out? Geoff explained it to one interviewer. "For example, if a contestant picks a box with a bell in it, I ring it. A butler instantly appears carrying a tureen. Inside the tureen is a piggy bank. We shatter the bank and out slips a change purse. But, when the purse is opened—oh, my!—all that's in it is plain old confetti. So, I throw the confetti toward a door. When that portal opens, the contestant has won . . . a box of Kleenex to cry in."

Many contestants found themselves hopelessly stuck with a Klunk, a booby prize (the word was coined by Geoff Edwards for the show). A contestant played Keno only to learn that her prize was a crummy broken radio. A Russian auto-maker with a heavy accent told Geoff that the contestant's prize included "a pair of vipers" and indeed the prize was nothing more than a pair of inflatable toy snakes.

The emotional toll that the game took on contestants was the reason that men weren't allowed to be contestants; there was a very real fear that Geoff Edwards would take a punch to the face from an angry male someday. Women, meanwhile, were run through the emotional wringer. The series' high point, as it were, was the night that a nervous contestant collapsed and fainted after the reveal of her prize, a restored 1937 Rolls Royce Phantom. The moment alarmed the producers of *60 Minutes* so much that for one segment, they confronted Chuck Barris about the woman's reaction, and Barris was relentlessly proud that she had fainted.

Barris boasted to a newspaper reporter, "Other shows teach other lessons, but *The New Treasure Hunt* is the one to watch to see just how far greed will drive an individual. . . . Some of the contestants are absolutely incredible. There is a hatred in their eyes when they lose a fifty-dollar prize, and we darned near had to pull one housewife off of Geoff Edwards when she felt he hadn't given her enough help in locating a $25,000 cash prize!"

The emotional toll proved too much for Geoff Edwards after four seasons. Edwards had a falling out with Chuck Barris over a series of increasingly mean prize revelations. Chief among Edwards's concerns was a sketch in which a car would be revealed, but the actual prize would be a small trinket barely visible on the roof. Edwards walked in the spring of 1977. Barris shut down production on the show.

Though Edwards escaped, he found that *The New Treasure Hunt* had left some collateral damage on his career path. Friend Sande Stewart explains, "There was a magazine article about Geoff titled 'The Cruelest Quizmaster of All,' and Geoff said that article really hurt his career because he shouldered the blame for carrying out Chuck Barris's bidding. *Treasure Hunt* came off as a mean show sometimes, and there were producers who wanted nothing to do with Geoff because of what he had done on that show."

Nighttime is the Right Time

One of daytime's biggest hits was a smash at night too. The nighttime version of *The Price is Right* with Dennis James premiered in much of the country during the same week that the daytime *Price is Right* with Bob Barker premiered on CBS.

James's wife would admit in later years that his relationship with Goodson-Todman was strained, and that James actually dreaded going to the studio to tape *The Price is Right*. James playfully referred to a shiny new car as "a hunk of junk" and found himself being screamed at by producer Frank Wayne when the show was over. There was also an embarrassing incident during one of the game's most popular pricing games, Cliff Hangers, in which a climber ascended a mountain as the contestant placed bids on small items. The further a contestant was from a correct price, the more likely the mountain climber was to fall over the edge of the mountain and crash. James, in just another attempt to be playful, saw the mountain climber fall off and announced, "There goes Fritz!"

Fritz was the name of model Janice Pennington's husband, who had disappeared two years earlier during a mountain climbing expedition. She left the stage and cried in

Dennis James invites you to "come on down" for *The Price is Right* in the nighttime.

Photo courtesy of Micki James

her dressing room for the rest of the show. (Pennington later learned that the mountain climbing expedition was a front for an espionage operation, and ended up writing a book about her discovery, called *Husband, Lover, Spy*. Her husband was never found.)

As the daytime *Price is Right* grew in popularity, particularly after its well-received expansion to one hour in the fall of 1975, Dennis James began feeling more like the show was looking for reasons to get rid of him. In 1977, Viacom, which distributed the show for syndication, closed a deal that switched the show's homes in many major cities; NBC owned-and-operated stations would no longer carry the program. It would instead air on CBS owned-and-operated stations. The CBS stations insisted on a CBS personality for the nighttime show, and Dennis James was relieved of his duties in 1977. Bob Barker hosted the nighttime *Price is Right* until it expired in 1980.

Matches Lit

CBS's other hit game show, *Match Game*, jumped into nighttime syndication in 1975, despite reservations from the network, which feared that overexposure would harm the daytime version's ratings. Ultimately, daytime *Match Game* would remain number-one in the ratings, and nighttime *Match Game*, or *Match Game PM* as it was officially named, was a smash, too.

The successful game with the suggestive questions was a tricky show to put together for nighttime syndication. All three major networks required their own censor be present for every taping; after the taping, producer Ira Skutch would receive notes from each censor. Editors would make three different versions of the program, one edited to accommodate each network's standards, and the tapes were carefully coordinated so that only affiliates from a specific network would see the edit made for that network.

The other reason *Match Game PM* was a tricky show to put together was because of the economical way that Goodson-Todman went about putting it together. It would be taped immediately following a five-episode taping session for the daytime *Match Game*,

Gene Rayburn and the *Match Game PM* regular panelists: Brett Somers, Charles Nelson Reilly, and Richard Dawson.   *Fred Wostbrock Collection* using the same panelists. Because *Match Game* famously had its open bar available to the panel throughout that taping day, a handful of panelists had to be poured into their seats before *Match Game PM* started taping.

Tune In

Harry Salter created *Name That Tune* in the 1950s, but in 1974 television syndication mogul Sandy Frank snapped up the rights to the format and sent the word to numerous producers that he wanted to put a new version on the air, but not with the same game, with contestants racing to ring a ship bell before naming that tune. Ralph Edwards took the challenge and worked with his staff to tinker with the game, adding to *Name That Tune*'s legend in the process.

In 1974, Edwards prepared two new versions, one for network daytime, and one for prime-access-time syndication. After auditioning a handful of actors for host, Edwards went with more traditional casting, Dennis James on the daytime version for NBC, and Tom Kennedy of ABC's *Split Second* to host at night. Dennis James's version languished in the ratings—by his own admission, he was a bad fit for the show, and a bad fit for NBC daytime at that time; NBC boss Lin Bolen was actively hunting for young viewers, and fifty-seven-year-old Dennis couldn't feign the youthful vim and vigor that Lin Bolen demanded. NBC's *Name That Tune* was gone in six months.

Nighttime *Name That Tune* was a drastically different story. Tom Kennedy, forty-seven years old but looking at least a decade younger, brought the youthful vitality and energy to spare; it wasn't that hard, he maintained years later. He found that the show's set design alone gave him all the energy he needed. The studio audience surrounded the stage, and Tom hosted directly in front of a sixteen-piece orchestra. He admitted at the time, "It's not difficult for me to be cheerful and happy for every show. It comes naturally. I hear the music and shift gears to my television personality."

Name That Tune pitted contestants against each other in a variety of games: for Melody Roulette, a spinning wheel determined the payoff for identifying the song; for the Money Trees, contestants plucked dollar bills from trees belonging to the opponent, and kept plucking until the opponent named a tune. The contestant with the most money left on the tree won the round (the game was eventually discarded because players kept cutting their hands on the clips that held the bills onto the tree).

But the most famous round of *Name That Tune* was the brainchild of writer Mark Maxwell-Smith, who explains, "The original third round of the show, as Ralph Edwards envisioned it, was a little bizarre. The idea was that there would be two cars on one side of the stage and a finish line on the opposite side. Each contestant got in a car, and instead of a steering wheel, the cars had typewriters. The contestants heard the orchestra play tunes, and had to type the names of the tunes on the typewriters. With every correct word typed, the car would inch forward, and the first contestant to cross the finish line won.

"For some reason, I had poker on my mind one day and I thought a game with bidding might be intriguing. So, I suggested a round where the contestants bid on how much of the tune they got to hear before they guessed."

The idea became Bid-A-Note, in which the host would read a clue to a song title, and the contestants bid on how few notes they needed to supply the correct answer. "I can name that tune in *one* note" would invariably draw Ooooh's of admiration from the audience. Contestants almost never said it nervously; it was the boldest declaration heard on any game show.

The big winner of the night listened to the Golden Medley, a series of seven songs played in thirty seconds. Naming all seven tunes with time to spare was worth a cool $15,000 worth of cash and prizes.

Ralph Edwards Productions would tinker with the show in the coming years to keep it fresh. The game would introduce a new round called Sing-a-Tune, in which contestants heard a professional singer perform the chorus of five songs and write their guesses for each title. The "La-La Lady," so named because she'd sing "La" instead of the song's title to avoid giving it away, was Kathie Lee Johnson, who eventually married a pro football player and became better known as Kathie Lee Gifford.

Changing Their Tune

The biggest alteration to the show came in the fall of 1976, when the show was rechristened *The $100,000 Name That Tune*, and the show gutsily introduced some new elements that bore a striking resemblance to the rigged quiz shows of the 1950s that many in the business were still trying to forget.

Tom Kennedy doles out the dough for a big winner on *The $100,000 Name That Tune*.

A contestant who won the Golden Medley returned the following week to step into an isolation booth that was wired so that the contestant could hear only the keys being struck by a nearby pianist. After hearing the song for twenty seconds, the contestant got a single guess at the exact title of the song. A correct guess was worth $10,000 per year for the next decade.

Preceding that moment was some of the most high-security and high-drama effort on a game show. As Tom explained at the start of the season, that was by necessity. "Let me tell you, the security is so tight that NBC (which oversaw the owned-and-operated stations that aired *Name That Tune* in many major markets) has written a whole book of procedures just for our show. All of us working on the set have to get clearance from an armed guard when we come in from rehearsals.

"On taping days, we arrange for a member of the production staff to keep the contestants occupied when they are not before the cameras. They are taken out from morning till night, to a movie, the zoo, lunch, dinner. . . . Then we bring them to the studio and assign them to isolated quarters where even their bathrooms are separated from the regular network facilities. There is an NBC Compliances and Practices official who even stands guard in the make-up room, just to be sure there is no conversation between the make-up artist and contestants. . . . We have to be absolutely sure that the public knows the show is on the up-and-up."

The contestant was escorted into a room supervised by executive producer Ralph Edwards, several members of the staff, the NBC Compliances and Practices representative, and security guard Jeff Attis. Attis would open the safe, which contained sixty unmarked manila envelopes. Each envelope contained unlabeled sheet music, and a smaller envelope containing the history, copyright information, and exact title of the tune. Once the contestant picked an envelope, it was handed over to the show's pianist, who would enter a protected rehearsal hall to practice the song briefly (and out of earshot of the contestant). The contestant was then escorted onstage, and led into the isolation booth for that once-in-a-lifetime crack at $100,000.

And why did *Name That Tune* make such a grandiose effort involving a massive grand prize? Simple. To stay ahead of the competition.

The Biggest Question of All

Early in 1976, Viacom had announced that it was shopping a revival of a famous—or infamous, depending on how you looked at it—quiz show of the 1950s. They were offering a new version of *The $64,000 Question*.

There were a couple of flies in the ointment to start. The first was that the CBS owned-and-operated stations agreed to air the new version, only to have the network pitch a fit about that plan because the network itself imposed a maximum of $25,000 in winnings for game show contestants. The next was an ambitious, but ultimately failed, plan by Viacom to try to get every station that signed up for the show to agree on a single night of the week for broadcast, in hopes that they could air the program live via satellite and give it an extra shot of excitement lacking from most game shows, where pre-recording had become standard operating procedure.

But the biggest problem was that Ralph Edwards Productions blindsided everybody by boosting the grand prize on *Name That Tune* to $100,000. Viacom had planned to tout the new *$64,000 Question* as having the biggest cash prize on television and now, obviously, Ralph Edwards had totally taken the wind out of that sail. To get it back, Viacom hastily changed the title of the show and made a slight alteration in the format. The game was renamed *The $128,000 Question*. Any contestant who won $64,000 would return at the end of the season for a play-off quiz that would pay an additional $64,000.

Like the original show, *The $128,000 Question* sought people with disparate fields of knowledge: a minister specialized in the category of Human Sexuality; a cab driver was an expert on the works of Michelangelo; a New York cop fielded questions about wine; a model answered questions about the Supreme Court; a nine-year-old boy dealt with Scriptures; and one oddly appropriate series of episodes saw a contestant named Susan B. Anthony answer questions about the history of the women's movement.

Anthony told her hometown newspaper, *The Palm Beach Post*, about her experience. "I loved every moment of it. . . . It was worse than preparing for my doctoral oral exam and that was like an inquisition. The worst part is the isolation booth—this horrible, vertical, airless booth that looks like an oxygen tank on end. There's no air, there's no air-conditioning. The lights are beating down on your head and up from your feet and you're trying to keep from stepping on them while they're playing this clanging music, which no one in the world could think under or over."

The suspense was still there, the isolation booth was still there, even the original music was still there. The only thing that changed was that the game was now on the level. Viacom pledged that *The $128,000 Question* was run under some of the tightest precautionary measures ever used for a television show. Among them was the unique way that questions were asked. Host Mike Darrow didn't have question cards; he had a set of computer cassettes that had to be fed into a special readout device that would automatically type the questions onto a sheet in front of the contestant, ostensibly so that nobody could read them before the game started.

For the second season, the process was somewhat streamlined. New host Alex Trebek read them from question cards like a normal game show host. The high security measures were still there, but not heavily hyped the way they had been. People had simply reached a point where they trusted game shows again. *The $128,000 Question* would expire after its second season.

29

Bang the Gong Slowly

Talentless Show

S ome ideas are so firmly etched in time that it's hard to remember the true beginnings. Fans of rap music don't realize that a performer named Pigmeat Markham was rapping on television and records in the 1960s. Likewise, fans of *American Idol* and *America's Got Talent* don't realize that the era of the anti-talent show that occasionally actually found good performers began much earlier than the 2000s. In 1976, Chuck Barris brought reality TV to our screens before anybody knew what to call it.

Major Talent

Edward Bowes was a former real estate agent whose business was wiped out by the 1906 San Francisco earthquake. In search of new revenue, he pursued the thriving theatrical business in New York City, becoming a conductor, composer, and producer for various shows, and assuming the role of managing director for New York's Capitol Theatre. Bowes ran the theatre so efficiently that a number of people compared it to a military operation, and Bowes liked the comparison so much that he began referring to himself as Major Bowes, insisting that everyone around him address him that way.

Several times while he was running the theatre, he would put together special "amateur night" broadcasts for smaller radio stations. They were so well-received that, by 1934, he introduced a regularly scheduled series, *Major Bowes' Amateur Hour*, on radio station WHN. The following year, the show went national on NBC.

Major Bowes' Amateur Hour wasn't a clever or cute title in any way; it delivered exactly what it advertised. Aspiring entertainers in search of their big break auditioned for a spot, and then performed on the radio show. Among the careers launched by an appearance on *Major Bowes' Amateur Hour*: comedian Jack Carter, opera singer Beverly Sills, and Ol' Blue Eyes himself, Frank Sinatra.

But Major Bowes could annihilate a career just as quickly as he could build one. Major Bowes hosted the program while seated next to a gong. If an act wasn't performing to his satisfaction, or if he felt it wasn't meeting the expectations of the audience, he would bang the gong, bringing the act to an abrupt and embarrassing end. After a large number of complaints about how it seemed too mean, however, Bowes eliminated the gong.

The Great American Talent Search

In 1975, Chuck Barris approached ABC with a pitch for his most forthright concept ever. The man who had specialized in off-the-wall concepts like men engaging in competitive flirting to win a date, and married couples revealing embarrassing secrets about themselves to win a sofa, simply wanted to do an old-fashioned amateur hour.

He told the network, "We need a great talent show."

He reasoned that there weren't really any more venues for talent to be discovered. The talent shows of radio and early television had all disappeared, and the number of nightclubs across the country was dwindling. The clubs that remained open didn't book a broad range of acts, either; mostly a singer and a comedian. Barris wanted to introduce a talent show in search of good acts, hoping that his new series would be a stairway to the stars. All types of acts were welcome, and the exposure from the show would allow performers to launch their careers.

Barris needed to produce a pilot, so he held the first *Gong Show* auditions and made them an open call. Anybody with any kind of act, amateur or professional, was welcome to try out. And Barris was struck by how truly dismal the auditions were. The big revelation, after several days of enduring tone-deaf singers and dancers with three left feet, was that there apparently wasn't as much talent out there as Chuck Barris thought.

Barris tried to take his mind off his troubles by going to a hockey game with a friend, variety show writer/producer Chris Bearde. Barris couldn't help venting his frustrations and laid out what he had hoped the show would be, and what it was turning out to be. From Bearde's point of view, though, this didn't sound like a problem. He told Barris to flip the idea; instead of being a stairway to the stars, this talent show would be a downward-spiraling chute to the abyss. It would be an anti-talent show, presenting bad performers, bizarre performers, and once in a blue moon, somebody with actual talent.

The Great American No-Talent Search

Barris revitalized the "too-mean" element of *Major Bowes' Amateur Hour* for his own spin on the concept. It would ultimately give Barris's creation a name and an identity: *The Gong Show*.

The pilot was taped at the studios of KGO, the ABC network affiliate in San Francisco. The host was Gary Owens; Barris and Bearde thought that *The Gong Show* acts would be funnier if the host was somebody who gave off a pompous air, and Owens, a tall man with a rich, booming voice known for his humorless delivery of the ridiculous introductions on *Rowan and Martin's Laugh-In*, seemed like the ideal straight man. The panelists for the pilot were Richard Dawson, Jo Anne Worley, Arte Johnson, and Adrienne Barbeau. The common bond connecting Owens, Dawson, Worley, and Johnson was not a coincidence; they all did the pilot for free as a favor to Bearde, a mutual friend of theirs stemming from their time on *Laugh-In*. Bearde promised to have them escorted by limousine everywhere they went during the weekend in San Francisco and treated them all to dinner at the city's finest Chinese restaurant in lieu of payment. In perhaps a curious omen for the endeavor, it snowed on San Francisco that night. *The Gong Show* was so off-the-wall that even the weather got a little goofy.

Dawson expressed his reservations about doing the show, saying that he couldn't bring himself to bang a gong on any act. Once the show began and Dawson saw the actual caliber of the acts being presented, he changed his tune drastically. Here's Dawson, immediately after banging the gong on a balloon artist.

> **Richard Dawson:** You don't have an act! You give birthday parties a bad name!

> **Balloon Artist:** Let me ask you a question, who makes balloon animals like this?

> **Dawson:** Let me ask *you* a question! Who makes a sound like this? (Bangs gong again) *Me!* That's who!

The pilot went almost-well. The show used a specialized type of light called a carbon-arc spotlight. In the middle of taping, the carbon was changed and it caused audio problems for the rest of the night. But what they had taped was enough to give ABC an idea of what *The Gong Show* would be . . . and the network wanted no part of it.

But NBC did! Madeline David, now in charge of daytime programming, wanted something different, looking to break out of the mold of game shows in the morning and soap operas in the afternoon. You could make the argument that *The Gong Show* was a game show, but it sure didn't feel like one.

The Gong Show began production in June 1976; there would be an NBC daytime version hosted by John Barbour (a local Los Angeles TV personality, later a correspondent on *Real People*), and a syndicated prime-access-time version hosted by Gary Owens. After taping five episodes with Barbour, it was apparent that it wasn't working. He didn't seem to grasp the tongue-in-cheek nature of the show, chastised judges for being too quick to gong acts; it wasn't working. Chuck Barris, watching from offstage, became angrier and angrier as the taping sessions went along. Barbour wasn't getting the job done.

Madeline David pointedly told Barris that if he had such a firm idea in his head of how the show should be hosted, he should be hosting it himself. The premiere date for the show was looming and the studio time had already been committed; she made it clear that she wouldn't allow them to cancel tapings. There was no time to audition a new host. Barris, firmly trapped between the proverbial rock and a hard place, reluctantly donned a tuxedo and walked onstage himself at the next taping. Chuck Barris was the host of *The Gong Show*.

The One and Only Chuckie Baby

The Gong Show premiered on NBC on June 14, 1976, with Gary Owens's version bowing in September across most of the country. Both shows were successes. There were a couple of prevailing theories as to why:

- Theory #1. Like *Queen for a Day* in the previous decades, people were watching it to feel better about themselves. Watching a ventriloquist with moving lips get gonged made viewers with no talent of their own feel relieved that they weren't the poor schlub on stage.
- Theory #2. From minute to minute, there was something different. *The Gong Show* presented a wide array of skill levels, but with Ed Sullivan long gone, *The Gong Show* was really the only forum on television where you could see a full gamut of acts: a man who played the sink, Count Banjola who played the banjo while hanging upside-down, puppet shows, poetry, singing owners and their howling dogs, magicians, acrobats. You never knew what you were getting, but you knew it was going to be different from yesterday's episode. A regular viewer was almost afraid to miss one.

Jaime Klein, who served as a joke writer for the show, penning the tongue-in-cheek introductions for the contestants ("Our next contestant doesn't have a lot of trouble making ends meet . . . she's a contortionist. Get it?"), offers his own insight: "*The Gong Show* was a hit because it was honest. It was naked and unabashed. It felt real, it felt unprepared. Chuck is famous for game shows but if you look at all of his output, the game show element is secondary. They were comedy shows. And they took their comedy from some form of truth. *The Gong Show* was like that. There was no posing, no façade. It was a chance to see what ordinary people were willing to do if it meant a chance to be seen on TV."

But late into the show's first season, Gary Owens received a note from Chuck Barris. As Owens recalled, the note read something like, "Dear Gary, I want you to know that when your contract is up, I'm going to be taking over the nighttime as well as the daytime show, because I feel I have better chemistry for the show."

Chuck Barris's strange word choice notwithstanding, he later told the Archive of American Television that he had a fairly altruistic reason for wanting to host both versions. Barris was very hands-on with the show. He conducted the auditions himself. He conducted call-backs himself. He conducted rehearsals himself. By the time an episode of *The Gong Show* was ready to tape, the contestants had all got a chance to know Chuck pretty well, and they had a friendly relationship with him. And then it was time for them to go onstage with Gary Owens, the intimidating celebrity judges, a studio audience that seemed out for blood, and it was a daunting atmosphere. Barris reasoned that he was better off always being there as host because it meant every contestant had at least one friend within a few feet of them.

And Barris himself had arguably given the show more of an identity than Gary Owens had. Owens's straight-man style had worked, up to a point. But then you had daytime host Chuck Barris, who smiled blankly, shuffled his feet, read from cue cards poorly, looked down, looked up at the lights, clapped his hands and generally came off so bizarre that most of America suspected that he was either drunk or extremely high (Barris would always maintain that he was totally sober on *The Gong Show*, and that his seemingly inebriated performance was actually just his natural style).

The Family That Gongs Together

Early on, the show struggled to find and maintain a rotation of celebrities to sit on the judges' panel for the same reason. Nobody wanted to be mean. Avery Schreiber blamed the audience when he reluctantly gonged one act, and then never appeared on the show again. Joyce Bulifant did a week, and then appeared on *Match Game* and admitted that she was too embarrassed to try it again. Other panelists in the early weeks of the show looked desperate to crawl offstage and sneak away, appalled to realize what they were a part of.

M*A*S*H cast member Jamie Farr, who was there for the first taping with John Barbour, clearly had no such inhibitions. He banged that gong loudly and proudly, mocking the acts as they skulked offstage.

Singer Jaye P. Morgan was glad to do the honors, too. In 2002, she told *E!*, "It was nothing. You just had to be outrageous and say stupid things, and I can do that. That's my forté! . . . And I gonged every chance that I got. I was doing my civic duty to keep them out of show business."

Comedian Rip Taylor told the channel, "I really felt terrible in the beginning . . . but then we couldn't wait to beat the hell out of them!"

Phyllis Diller chimed in, "*The Gong Show* was a breakthrough in comedy. . . . We love to laugh at our fellow human beings."

Film critic Rex Reed, who always sat with a dour expression on his face and gave only very reserved words of praise for the few acts that he didn't gong, seemed on the surface to be having a miserable time. But he appeared on the show constantly. He finally explained to author Jerry Bowles, "Everyone from Barbara Walters to Joshua Logan to Lotte Lenya to Walter Cronkite's wife Betsy has called to tell me they are totally hooked on the show. I have developed new legions of fans who never knew I was alive, renewed old fans who always thought I was just an intellectual critic, and received literally scores of letters from people who are seeing me in a brand-new light. The show has been a whopping success."

The Gong Show began doing something interesting as weeks went along; it slowly introduced a cast of recurring characters. Brief comedy sketches and character pieces crept into the show. Suzanna was a too-quiet singer whose performance was always interrupted by a marching band. Rhett and Scarlett, dressed as the *Gone With the Wind* characters, tested the

Gary Owens, the original choice to host *The Gong Show*, helmed the nighttime version for one season.

censors with filthy jokes; virtually none of their punchlines actually made it on the air. Writer Larry Spencer was a bungling musician whose instruments always fell to pieces before he had played one note. A struggling comedian named Murray Langston put a paper bag on his head and rocked the show as The Unknown Comic, who irritated Chuck Barris with insults ("I have a joke that's going to make you look like an asshole. . . . Oh, you must have already heard it") and obnoxious jokes (his "impression of an Eskimo going to the bathroom" consisted of unzipping his fly and squeezing an ice cube out of his hand).

Jaime Klein remembers, "I was on the show a few times . . . and remember, this is the 1970s we're talking about . . . as a Chinese philosopher named Confusion, and all of my words of wisdom were silly jokes. What I remember about Chuck was the way he screwed with you with absolutely no warning. One of my jokes was supposed to be that I'd say 'In the words of my brother, How-Long—' and then Chuck would interrupt me and say, 'Your brother was How-Long?' and I'd say 'About six feet.' That was the gag we rehearsed. On the air, I said 'In the words of my brother, How-Long,' and Chuck grins at me and says 'Your brother was named How-Long?' What am I supposed to do with that line?"

Klein was far from Barris's only victim. A stagehand would occasionally dress in Catholic priest garb and, as "Father Ed," perform a few religious gags. One day, as Father Ed delivered his sermon, Barris instructed the cue card man to turn the cue card upside-down. Father Ed went silent, then giggled nervously as the bit went down in flames.

Shelley Herman was a young page at NBC who found herself involved in a bit once. "One of your jobs as a page is to give guided tours. I was giving a tour one day, and a member of Chuck's staff comes running down the wall and says, 'Shelley, Chuck needs you!' and pulls me away from my tour group. He's pulling me into the studio and he puts me onstage, where the contestants perform. I said, 'What does Chuck need?' And Chuck runs out at that point and takes me by the arm and pulls me to the stage. He says, 'Don't worry, when the curtain comes up, you'll know what to do.'

"And he dashes offstage and just leaves me there. But I loved Chuck and the whole staff. And he ended up being right, it was a really short, simple bit, I got the idea right away, and I was done in twenty seconds. But to just be thrust out there with no warning and get a laugh, how great is that?"

But by far, the best-known recurring star on *The Gong Show* was a tall, burly stagehand named Gene Patton, whose arrival, always heralded by Milton DeLugg and the Band with a Thugg's rendition of "Jumpin' at the Woodside," got audiences revved up and out of their seats. "Gene Gene the Dancing Machine" would dance his heart out as he was pelted with debris from all directions.

The show grew so popular that NBC agreed to a prime-time special, *The All-Star Gong Show*, featuring some of the best—and worst—acts from the show's first ten months on the air, plus surprise performances by Alice Cooper and Tony Randall. The special was so well-received that the following winter, NBC introduced a prime-time variety hour, *The Chuck Barris Rah Rah Show*, which featured performances by special guest stars like Milton Berle, Ray Charles, and the very best acts from *The Gong Show*.

Accidentally Famous

The endless parade of hefty ballerinas and singing conjoined twins would occasionally give away to true emerging talent. A local improv comic named Paul Reubens appeared as a contestant on the show and learned that the show's policy about contestants was that a person could audition as many times as they wanted, no limit. But they had to perform a different act and use a different name every time. Reubens would appear on the show dressed as a cat burglar and performing a scat rendition of the song "Alley Cats"; saluting old radio with brief comedy sketches while his partner provided sound effects; wearing a headdress and doing a rain dance; and performing as part of a dance troupe. All in all, Paul Reubens appeared on *The Gong Show* nine times; he would later shoot to stardom as Pee-Wee Herman.

A young comic named Michael Winslow got some of the loudest applause ever heard on the show for his impressive act in which he mimicked turning the knob on a television set and supplied the sound effects of static, electric guitar, and other noise; in the 1980s, he'd become a star in the Police Academy movies. Comedian Robert Schimmel was on the program in 1979, playing the piano with his nose.

This Time You've Gong Too Far!

The Gong Show didn't seem to know any boundaries. It welcomed strippers, a flasher who exposed his genitals while singing a folk song, a man who sang "Please Release Me" while tied to a crucifix, and an endless parade of dogs who would bury their noses right into Barris' crotch as soon as he came near them (Barris later revealed that he was rubbing dog food on

Some of the performers who came out of the woodwork for their chance at stardom on *The Gong Show*.

his crotch whenever the show had a dog act, because he knew the audience would laugh at the dog's behavior).

The NBC censors weren't particularly happy with Barris, who had made a science out of his dealings with them. There were some acts who auditioned for the show that Barris absolutely knew would not meet the censors' standards. There were some that were borderline; Barris thought they *might* be safe, but the act pushed the envelope of good taste just enough to concern him. Barris's strategy when he had a borderline act that he liked was to book another act that he knew for sure wasn't fit for broadcast, and use them both on the same episode; generally, the censors would object so strongly to the filthier act that the questionable act would slip through the cracks and make it on the air.

For one taping, Barris booked a for-sure-unsuitable act consisting of two women who consumed popsicles. On paper that didn't seem like much, but once you saw these two women slowly licking every side of the frozen treat and then pushing it in their mouths as far as they would go, the, er, symbolic nature of the act would sink in. To Barris's amazement, the NBC censor, who apparently didn't get the joke, had absolutely no objection to the performance, and the popsicle lickers made it on the air, at least on the East Coast. NBC executives in New York were so aghast at what they saw on *The Gong Show* that day that a rerun was aired on the West Coast. Combined with a recent incident in which Jaye P. Morgan flashed the camera while Gene Gene the Dancing Machine was performing, and NBC had enough. *The Gong Show* was canceled, airing for the five hundredth—and final—time on NBC on July 21, 1978. That fall, the syndicated version expanded to twice a week and continued airing for two more years.

Shelley Herman says, "Chuck was sort of a victim of his own success. *The Gong Show* was heralded as this zany, unpredictable, anything-can-happen show, and when you develop that kind of reputation, you feel pressure to deliver it constantly. Chuck kept trying to top himself with every episode, and seeing what boundary he can push this time. And Chuck and the show self-destructed from that."

You Asked for It!

Chuck Barris would endure criticism from all sides in the coming years about the relentlessly "cruel" nature of the program. Richard Dawson would make sport of *The Gong Show* with off-the-cuff jokes on *Family Feud*. Bob Barker called *The Gong Show* hell on earth. *Match Game* host Gene Rayburn once vowed in an interview that he would never work for Chuck Barris.

Jaime Klein says, "Every show gets criticized. If you're going to work in television, somebody hates your show, it comes with the territory. But the criticism of *The Gong Show* just annoyed me. They said we were cruel to the contestants. We didn't con these people to come on the show! It wasn't a ruse! They signed up for it, they were coming to us. We'd have the auditions at Old World Restaurant, just up the street from the offices, and people would audition at the restaurant while being videotaped. We called the people who worked at Old World 'shock troops' because they had to see everything. And they rejected a lot of acts that weren't

Chuck Barris emphatically leads a round of applause for Daddy-O, a fifties cover band, on *The Gong Show*.

suitable for television at all. These people signed up and auditioned knowing that they'd be on national TV, and that these judges were ready to bang a gong and tell them that they were no good. And they went right ahead and did it anyway."

Shelley Herman adds, "Chuck did not deserve the reputation he wound up with, especially when you saw how he ran his company behind the scenes. I was a teenager when I first appeared on *The Dating Game* and started getting to know his crew. And what I always noticed was how valued the women were in that company. The women who worked for Chuck Barris rose in the ranks, they were given important duties, and Chuck trusted them to do it. He never looked over their shoulders. Chuck was Peck's Bad Boy on camera but away from the show, he was just a wonderful, sweet man."

Lights, Camera, Gong!

The Gong Show came to an end in unique fashion in 1980, concluding four years of wacky, tacky shows with a full-length movie. *The Gong Show Movie* was a strange blend of farcical comedy and documentary (the film uses actual footage of *Gong Show* auditions) starring Chuck Barris, who penned the screenplay himself and used it as his own therapist couch. The film's story actually came from a number of personal issues Barris was dealing with; *The Gong Show* left him feeling burned out; he was tired of the constant attention and constant criticism; he was having issues with his daughter (who appears as herself in the movie) and girlfriend (also appearing as herself), and he was fed up with the constant pressures of his television bosses involving censorship and ratings.

Barris vents all of those frustrations in the film, which is loaded with cameos by the most popular acts from the past four years of *The Gong Show*, plus odd-ball scenes involving the show's regulars—Rip Taylor plays a French waiter, the Unknown Comic briefly appears nude (but with a strategically placed second paper bag), Jaye P. Morgan wakes up in a giant bed surrounded by Milton DeLugg's band. And even a not-yet-famous actor named Phil Hartman has a brief scene in an airport. The film climaxes with full-cast musical number, "Don't Get Up," in which everyone encourages Chuck not to come in to work anymore, and one by one, they all say goodbye to their time on *The Gong Show*. The movie came and went in a weekend in some theaters, a firm bomb at the box office.

Barris's attempts to follow the success of *The Gong Show* with more of the same didn't help the company. *The Chuck Barris Rah Rah Show*, a prime-time variety show that mixed *Gong Show* acts with actual name performers, failed in a matter of weeks. *The $1.98 Beauty Show*, a faux-pageant hosted by Rip Taylor, hung on for two seasons, but didn't really make waves.

Jaime Klein says, "I think what happened with *$1.98* was that the audience actually saw through it. It was striving to be *The Gong Show*, and even fans of *The Gong Show* looked at it and figured out that we were just trying to deliver more of the same, but in a different package. *$1.98* had this 'It's been done' aura to it through the whole thing. And at the same time, even *The Gong Show* was losing its luster anyway. In the beginning, the fun of the show was that all of these bizarre acts emerged out of nowhere, and you'd ask yourself where these people crawled out from. But more and more people began developing acts specifically for the purpose of appearing on *The Gong Show*, and I always felt that took some of the magic out of it."

But according to Chuck Barris himself, the show that really did his empire in was *3's a Crowd*, which host Jim Peck colorfully described as "*The Newlywed Game*

Rip Taylor hosts *The $1.98 Beauty Show*, a make-believe pageant with *Gong Show* sensibilities.

with fangs." The game, which Barris had pitched to ABC a decade earlier, only for them to emphatically reject it, welcomed three groups of contestants; each group consisted of a man, his wife, and his secretary; the object of the game was to determine which woman knew the man better.

Jim Peck, in a 1996 interview, recalled that a total of twelve couples got divorced after appearing on the show, and at least one secretary got fired. Peck himself found the show so cringe-inducing that Chuck Barris's staff granted his request that, at the end of each taping, all of the contestants were to be kept onstage until he was safely inside his dressing room with the door locked, so he wouldn't have to face what he had been a part of.

Barris had enough. Between the constant bagging on *The Gong Show*, the bombing of *3's a Crowd* (which, it turned out, viewers truly hated), and the wane of *The Newlywed Game*, the Duke of Daytime abdicated his throne in 1980. Chuck Barris Productions shut down for a time, while the boss snuck off to Europe for a few years, decompress, and write a book in which he claimed to be a CIA assassin. (The author conducted a careful investigation into Barris's claim of being a hired gun for the Federal Government, but is unfortunately not at liberty to divulge his findings.)

In a few years, Barris would relaunch his empire, mounting new versions of *Treasure Hunt*, *The Dating Game*, *The Newlywed Game*, and *The Gong Show* for syndication before retiring to the quiet life of an author and occasional recording artist. He died at the age of eighty-seven on March 21, 2017.

Jaime Klein says, "Chuck Barris left a positive imprint on television, and I hope that deep down, he knows that. He brought candor and honesty and spontaneity to television and those are qualities that this medium doesn't have nearly enough of."

Barris would attempt to revive *The Gong Show* in 1982 under the title *Million Dollar Talent Show*, a weekly hour-long version in which winners collected $10,000 (a huge leap from the $516.32 of the NBC version of the $712.05 of the syndicated version) plus a chance to return for a chance at $1,000,000. The 1980s and 1990s belonged to a kinder, gentler talent show, *Star Search*, and the 2000s and 2010s belonged to *American Idol* and *America's Got Talent*. All captured the public's imagination, all launched careers, but television would never again see anything like Chuck Barris and *The Gong Show*.

30

The Redemption of Barry and Enright

Back in Business

T he producers who suffered the greatest consequences for fixing quiz shows in the scandalous fifties made an unexpected comeback, becoming one of the most successful game show packaging companies of the 1970s.

Let's Get to Work

Jack Barasch was a Long Island native who quickly grew bored working for his father as a handkerchief salesman and broke into radio as an announcer. Dan Ehrenreich was a former radio engineer and Signal Corps member who went into the production end of the radio business, and ended up hiring Barasch for a job at station WOR in New York. They first joined forces as producers in the 1940s, when Barasch, who changed his name to Jack Barry, created a radio program called *Juvenile Jury*. Barry served as panel moderator, reading letters from listeners who wrote in with personal problems. The show's panelists, all children aged twelve and under, gave cute, precocious advice.

A concerned mother wrote in, complaining that her son liked to climb fences and he kept ripping his pants. One of the jurors pointedly told her, "Sew them up!"

Another kid suggested, "Better yet, when a kid climbs a fence, he should take his pants off, climb over the fence, and then put his pants back on." It would get picked up for a television run on NBC, becoming the first sponsor-supported series on the fledgling NBC network and running for seven years.

Barry and Ehrenreich, who eventually changed his professional name to Dan Enright, followed that success with a similar program, *Life Begins at 80*, where the wise and witty kids were replaced by wise and witty octogenarians, and still another show that merged both panels called *Wisdom of the Ages*.

Barry and Enright would try to expand their horizons beyond panel shows. They produced a detective show, *The Adventures of Michael Shayne*; in 1950, they secured the rights to author Faith Baldwin's collection of sixty novels and fifteen hundred short stories in an attempt to develop them into an anthology series.

Barry would make a considerably successful foray into children's programming as host of *Winky Dink and You*, a whimsical early go at developing interactive TV. Children wrote in for a kit consisting of magic crayons, magic erasers, and a magic window. The magic window was a sheet of transparent plastic that a child could attach to the television screen. As the program's storyline played out, Winky (a cartoon pixie) and Jack would get into predicaments and Jack would ask the children to draw objects on the screen that would help them resolve the problem.

It was a tricky proposition that required Barry, Enright, and business partner Ed Friendly to develop several innovations, among them an adhesive plastic sheet, a machine that would allow Jack to interact with a cartoon character in real time (Jack would carry on conversations with Winky and other characters throughout the program, and although they were cartoon characters, their lips could keep up with the voice actors' ad-libs), and they had to invent a crayon that could be easily erased from plastic. CBS was so worried that they'd be caught short-stocked that they wouldn't allow *Winky Dink and You* to premiere until 100,000 kits were made. The requests were so overwhelming that those 100,000 kits were gone in four months.

Think Big

By 1955, the Barry and Enright panel advice programs were fading away and Jack Barry made himself available as a host-for-hire. Entertainment Productions, Inc., the company that developed *The $64,000 Question* for CBS, created a $100,000 jackpot quiz for NBC, *The Big Surprise*, and Barry got the nod to host. After only six months, he was fired.

The dismissal wasn't particularly graceful either. Producer Steve Carlin bluntly told the press that he considered Barry's hosting style boring and saying that the sponsor "couldn't get rid of Jack fast enough."

Barry admitted in October 1956, "About four months ago, I was all set to chuck everything. I had had it. I had lost *The Big Surprise*. We had a couple of other disappointments in the shop here, and I was thinking of buying a little radio station, somewhere far from New York, and closing the book. It seemed as if the battle was hardly worthwhile. But television is like a seesaw. You may be way down one minute and way, way up the next . . . and here I am, raring to go again."

That was because in the summer of 1956, NBC bought two new formats from Barry and Enright. One was *Tic Tac Dough*, a daytime game that premiered on July 30, 1956. Contestants added X's and O's to the nine-square game board with every correct answer; money was added to a pot with every answer, too, and getting three in a row won the game and all the money in the pot. In the often-likely event of a tie game, the symbols were erased, but the money wasn't, and the pot would swell well into the thousands before the cash was won.

All by Myself

Dan Enright attempted to transition into the film production business. He oversaw two low-budget features, *Blast of Silence* and *Idyll*, before going north to Canada and producing shows there. During the 1960s, Barry and Enright optimistically made several attempts at rejoining forces and trying to go back to work as producers.

Barry put on a brave face for reporters during the early 1960s. A number of writers wrote stories detailing what had become of the people involved in the fixed quizzes, and Barry earnestly told writer Harold Stern, "I'm about ready to return to TV. I'm going to pursue the plan I've had for the past two years. First, I'll make several appearances on radio and television interview shows and, concurrent with those appearances, I'll be showing four or five program ideas to the top ad agencies . . . I'll produce everything myself and under my own name. One of the TV show ideas is a variety program which I'd produce and star in."

None of that happened.

Barry referred to the 1960s as a period of purgatory. He later told the *Los Angeles Times*, "I didn't work. It became the old story of people who I used to know intimately walking across the street just to avoid saying hello."

He later elaborated, "In retrospect, I think I can understand; they couldn't help me and they were embarrassed and they just didn't want a confrontation. So, they ducked."

Barry moved to the West Coast to try to rebuild his television career in Los Angeles. He tried launching a revival of *Juvenile Jury* called *Kidding Around*, but it got dumped after only six weeks on a single station. He hosted a successful game show, *You Don't Say!*, on Los Angeles station KTLA, but embarrassingly, when NBC picked it up as a national series, Barry got booted because NBC considered him tainted. He remained at KTLA until a change in ownership; as Barry explained it, Gene Autry bought the station in 1965 and fired him the same day.

It wasn't just NBC and KTLA. Jack would do consulting work for various producers in the 1960s as they developed new shows, but Barry had to agree to leave his name off the credits for anything he had his hands in. Barry briefly worked for Mark Goodson-Bill Todman Productions, but quit because of a disagreement with his competitor-turned-bosses. He created a game show format called *Everybody's Talking* for Jerome Schnur Productions, but yet again, he had to keep his name off the credits.

The Boys are Back in Town

But Jack's strategy to win over the FCC finally paid off in 1968; he had been forced to sell his Florida station for $350,000 and after a few years of sitting on that money, he put in a $200,000 bid for a station in Redondo Beach, California. The FCC granted him a license and allowed him to buy the station, and as Barry anticipated, work began trickling in. He was hired to replace Dennis Wholey for the remaining weeks of an already-canceled ABC prime-time game, *The Generation Gap*, in 1969. Then came another summer series, *The Reel Game*. And then a brief role in the Woody Allen film *Everything You Wanted to Know About Sex (But Were Afraid to Ask)*. And then a full-season revival of *Juvenile Jury*.

By 1972, Jack Barry was fully back in business as creator, producer, and host of his own series, *The Joker's Wild* on CBS (see Chapter 23). In 1973, Jack added to his portfolio with *Hollywood's Talking*, a star-packed revival of *Everybody's Talking*. In 1974, Jack developed *Blank Check*, a short-lived guessing game in which contestants

Jack's back! Jack Barry created and hosted the long-running hit *The Joker's Wild.*   *Fred Wostbrock Collection*

had to pick the digits that appeared in the value of the eponymous check. The show was gone in thirteen weeks. Host Art James later admitted that he and many staffers found the game so stupid that they jokingly referred to the show as "Blank Mind," but for host Jack Barry, it was a source of pride, short run notwithstanding. What mattered most to him was that *Blank Check* had been purchased and aired by NBC, the very network that had fired him and seized control of his creations. With *Blank Check*, as far as Jack Barry was concerned, sixteen years of struggle and resentment had washed away.

"It's funny," he mused at the time. "All that is over now. I'm even back on NBC, the network where it all happened, and they've welcomed me back with open arms."

The year 1974 also marked Dan Enright's reuniting with his former partner, taking over as executive producer of *The Joker's Wild*. From that point on, it was like old times. Barry and Enright were developing formats and pitching them left and right.

Ron Greenberg, who had worked on Barry and Enright's *Dough Re Mi* in the 1950s, says, "It didn't surprise me that Jack and Dan were able to rebuild their empire. It was bound to happen, eventually, that scandal had to blow over and the people involved had to come back. There were so many people involved in that scandal, and television needs people who know what they're doing. So, yes, they broke the rules, but they had the necessary knowledge for the business."

Barry told interviewer Dick Kleiner, "[Television is] like a treadmill. Once you get started it's almost impossible to stop. Besides, you're almost forced to have more than one show going for you. If you have only one show on the air, you're very vulnerable. If that one show gets canceled you're out of work. With two you have a more secure position. Three or more and you can stand a cancellation very easily. I don't know what will happen tomorrow, but for the time being, we're living it up."

Presently Tense

The return of Dan Enright didn't make everybody in Barry's staff happy. According to question writer Mark Maxwell-Smith, director Richard Kline was put off by the reunion. "Jack Barry was very hail-fellow-well-met to his employees, and needed somebody to be, in essence, a more hard-nosed counterpart. And Richard Kline filled that role. But Dan Enright arrived and started functioning the same way. Kline felt supplanted, and it caused a rift in the company. Everybody had to pick a side, you sided with Jack Barry and Richard Kline, or you sided with Dan Enright."

Enright also carried himself in a way that struck Maxwell-Smith as insecure, not just in his attitude toward his own staff, but his attitudes toward the competition: "I have a vivid memory of Dan Enright standing at a studio monitor that was carrying a feed of the *Wheel of Fortune* taping that was happening. And Dan Enright broke down, point by point, every single reason that *Wheel of Fortune* didn't work. You prove nothing by doing that to another show. If it doesn't work, it gets canceled after thirteen weeks and everyone sees that it doesn't work. If it's a hit, which is what happened with *Wheel*, then you look a little silly for the dissertation that you went on about why it didn't work."

Here's the Twist

During the 1970s, Barry and Enright had a rather interesting assemblage of games and a method for developing them. Many of their shows seemed somewhat inspired by game shows from other packagers. Barry and Enright's games certainly weren't rip-offs, but a viewer could draw a parallel between many of them and other games on the air.

The Hollywood Squares seemed to inspire Barry and Enright's *Break the Bank*, which likewise featured a panel of nine celebrities who fired off quick jokes before giving answers to trivia questions. The difference was it utilized a game board similar to Battleship; right answers helped contestants claim spaces, and claiming three like spaces would win the game.

Match Game apparently led to *Hollywood Connection*, in which contestants tried to predict the written answers given by a panel of six stars. The difference was that on *Hollywood Connection*, the blanks were replaced by either-or questions, with the contestants guessing what answer each individual panelist had written down.

Barry and Enright also produced *We've Got Your Number*, an unaired, unsold CBS pilot for a dice game that bore a slight resemblance to *High Rollers*. *Decisions, Decisions* had contestants guessing the results of public surveys, like *Family Feud*. Even Jack Barry's own creation, *The Joker's Wild*, got revamped and tinkered with. An unsold pilot called *Double Cross* also involved a set of three spinning wheels that determined the categories, as did a 1980 syndicated offering, *Bullseye*, which ran for two seasons.

Barry reasoned to one reporter, "In picking a show, I look for, and rarely find, originality. Almost everything has already been done. Failing to find originality, I look to see if the idea is compelling enough to make it exciting to the audience."

Tic Tac on Top

But by far, Barry and Enright's two most popular game shows were wholly original creations from the duo: *The Joker's Wild* and *The New Tic Tac Dough*. After CBS canceled *The Joker's Wild* in 1975, Barry and Enright put together a package of episodes from the final year on the air and made them available for syndication. The *Joker* reruns performed so well that Barry and Enright put *The Joker's Wild* back into production as a five-day-a-week syndicated game in 1977, with former staffer Ron Greenberg returning to the fold to serve as producer. They followed that up in 1978 with a revival of *Tic Tac Dough*, starring Wink Martindale.

Tic Tac Dough and *The Joker's Wild* were a match made in heaven. In many ways, they were almost two shows in one. Most of their stations aired the shows back-to-back. They taped in the same studio, even using the same basic set design (host stage left; contestants stage right; game board in the middle) and sharing some of the same incidental music. Behind the scenes, they were even treated as the same show. *Tic Tac Dough* and *The Joker's Wild* both included a daily announcement of a phone number to call if viewers wanted to be contestants. Whichever show a person called, they were brought in to take the same test. Contestants who scored high were used for *Tic Tac Dough*; contestants with more average scores played *The Joker's Wild*.

In a way, *Tic Tac Dough* and *The Joker's Wild* likely represented a greater source of redemption for Barry and Enright than the deal for *Blank Check* a few years earlier. After the quiz show scandals, the major networks instituted strict limits on how much a contestant was allowed to win on a TV game show. During the late 1970s, ABC limited winnings to $20,000. The CBS cut-off point was $25,000. NBC was more lenient, with a $50,000 limit.

Because *Tic Tac Dough* and *The Joker's Wild* were syndicated, they weren't beholden to any network rules and took full advantage of that, allowing contestants to stay on until they were defeated. As it happened, *Tic Tac Dough* and *The Joker's Wild* had rules that gave the returning champion a built-in advantage. On *Tic Tac Dough*, the returning champion always got the first turn. On *The Joker's Wild*, where contestants played to a $500 goal, if the challenger reached that amount first, the champion got a final turn to try to catch up.

The result of all that were some hefty paydays for contestants on both shows. On *The Joker's Wild*, Frank Dillon amassed cash and prizes totaling more than $175,000. In the 1979 Tournament of Champions, he was felled by Eileen Jason, who won $250,000. But Dillon and Jason were both left in the dust by a big winner on *Tic Tac Dough*, U. S. Navy Lieutenant Thom McKee, who defeated forty-three opponents and collected winnings of $312,700; $200,000 of that was cash, the rest of the haul included eight cars. (McKee gave one car to a missionary friend in Africa, traded the rest in for a single Cadillac, and got the vanity license plate TIC TAC.)

A winning combination, host Wink Martindale and *Tic Tac Dough*, a long-running game created by Jack Barry and Dan Enright.

Wink Martindale says, "Dan Enright referred to Thom McKee as the quintessential game show contestant, and he really was. He had a brilliant mind, he was young, he was handsome, he was wearing his country's uniform, he had a beautiful wife, and as a bonus, his wife was pregnant. He was everything that you wanted to root for."

McKee's winning streak in particular got a great deal of press. America was captivated by the show, wondering if his run would ever end. But remarkably, the fact that Barry and Enright were in charge of *Tic Tac Dough* was almost an afterthought in all the newspaper articles written about the big winner. The press and the public were completely satisfied that the two men who had been most implicated in the 1950s were now running an honest operation; there was no suspicion, no finger pointing. Even Joseph Stone, the district attorney who had conducted the investigations in 1958 that led to Senate hearings, had watched *The New Tic Tac Dough* and was completely satisfied that it was an honest endeavor. (In his memoirs, Stone cynically observed that he found the questions on the new version so easy that he couldn't see a need to rig it.)

Greenberg remembers, "When I was producing *Joker*, I could see first-hand that Jack and Dan were never quite able to shake off the dust from those scandals. I went with them to NATPE, which is the annual convention where producers sell the new shows that they're offering to local stations for syndication. Jack saw someone from across the room, points him out to Dan, and says, 'I can't remember, are we still talking to him?' They had a good laugh, but there was truth there. There were people that they never regained contact with, even all those years after the scandal."

Regrets, I've Had a Few

In a 1991 PBS special documenting the quiz show scandals, Dan Enright said, "[Herbert Stempel] was taken from obscurity, came from rather impoverished circumstances . . . and then exposed to the light of celebrity. Became, for some six weeks, a celebrity, and then just as quickly was cast back into obscurity. We at the time deluded ourselves into believing that what we were doing was not that wrong . . . and I'm sorry. I should have been far more mindful and more sensitive."

But interestingly, no apology would ever come forth from Jack Barry. In fact, he was quite open about how much he resented the fall-out from the quiz show scandals, and that he felt he didn't deserve the consequences.

He reasoned to reporter Cynthia Lowry, "It was a long-time established industry practice. It was done long before I was even in broadcasting. Answers were always given to certain contestants, and with the advent of the big, big money, it was thought to be necessary for dramatic purposes—to ensure that interesting contestants were carried over from week to week. Sure, it was wrong and unfair and deceptive—but we didn't see it that way then; it was purely a show business device."

He told another interviewer, "Everybody was doing it, not just Dan and I . . . I felt then and I still feel now that I was being punished for the sins of other people. There's a certain poetic justice in our coming back the way we did. Our company is much stronger, much more important, and much more successful than before."

Jack Barry died in 1984, while *The Joker's Wild* was still on the air; he would be replaced as host on that program by Bill Cullen. Dan Enright died in 1992.

Mark Maxwell-Smith remembered, "Dan Enright always struck me as angry, impatient, frustrated, judgmental, too smart for the room. Every once in a while, you got a flash of another side to him, you got some indication that he had a generous side and a caring side. At his funeral, a bunch of celebrities that Enright struck up a friendship with away from work spoke, and all these stars talked about how wonderful he was, and the Barry and Enright Productions employees in the room looked at each other wondering if we were at the right funeral. That dual nature always made me wonder what the quiz show scandals did to Dan Enright, mentally and emotionally. You saw so much of Dan's dark side at work, but hearing these stories about how kind he was, you wondered if the stress of that scandal did something to him. It always made me wonder."

Marc Summers concurs. "I was the warm-up man for *Tic Tac Dough*. The computerized game board malfunctioned one day and taping stopped for forty-five minutes. It's every warm-up man's nightmare and it happens to all of us eventually. You look for anything to talk about and ultimately, you find yourself showing the audience photos of your kids. Out of the corner of my eye, I see Dan Enright, and I think 'Okay, this will buy me a minute,' so I introduced Dan to the audience. 'Ladies and gentlemen, one of the preeminent game show producers of television history, part of the team that brings you this program and *The Joker's Wild*, Mister Dan Enright!' And I have the audience give him a round of applause. He got so angry that out of earshot from the audience, he threatened to fire me for that."

Both men left a rather mixed legacy as a result of the scandals; both of them were characters in the 1994 film *Quiz Show* about the scandal. But scandal or not, they had a track record of success, and sustaining success, in a fickle and stormy business. Both of them could be, and were, proud of what they had accomplished.

31

Putting the Games Back on the Shelf

Let's Play Something Else

Ruffled Feathers on the Peacock

I n the late 1970s, NBC was ailing. Aside from its impressively strong late-night offerings (*The Tonight Show Starring Johnny Carson*, *Saturday Night Live*, *Tomorrow*, *The Midnight Special*), the network was desperately searching for new shows that would win back viewers who were far more interested in what ABC and CBS had to offer. In a gutsy move, the network lured Fred Silverman to assume the position of president and CEO of NBC. Silverman had started the 1970s at CBS, where he was responsible for greenlighting a slew of successes, including *All in the Family* and *M*A*S*H*; he had then defected to ABC and launched the perpetual third-place network to number 1 in the ratings for the first time in its history. Silverman arrived at NBC in 1978.

In that year, NBC's track record with game shows was hit and miss. *The Hollywood Squares* was a rock, still bringing in big and loyal audiences after a dozen years on the air. *Wheel of Fortune*, a mere baby at the time with only three full years behind it, was doing just well enough to justify getting renewed every thirteen weeks. A word game from Heatter-Quigley Productions, *To Say the Least* with Tom Kennedy, had fizzled after twenty-six weeks, as had an oddball Q&A game from Ralph Edwards, *Knockout* with Arte Johnson.

Old Friends

In 1978, NBC increasingly built its daytime schedule with familiarity instead of new frontiers. *Jeopardy!* with Art Fleming was dusted off, a mere three years after being iced by Lin Bolen for attracting too many old viewers. According to one anonymous NBC executive at the time, it was an impressive stack of mail that led to the show's revival. When any show is canceled, letters from unhappy viewers come in for several months afterward. Viewers complained about the demise of *Jeopardy!* and nobody at NBC was really surprised by that, but the eyebrows raised higher and higher as the mail wouldn't stop coming.

The unnamed exec told *Chicago Tribune* writer Gary Deeb, "With *Jeopardy!*, the bellyaching continued for years. It was clear to us that the complaints weren't an organized campaign. They were mailed in by real human beings acting on their own."

A full three years after *Jeopardy!* was canceled, word got to the network that CBS had taped a pilot for a revival in 1977 and elected to pass, and NBC snapped up the new version.

The reincarnated *Jeopardy!* tinkered with the rules considerably; the low-scoring contestant was eliminated after the Jeopardy round, so only two players advanced to Double Jeopardy. Final Jeopardy was cast aside in favor of a bonus round, Super Jeopardy, in which the day's top scorer tried to win a cash jackpot by giving five correct responses in any line or row on a twenty-five-square board. *Jeopardy!* had always appealed to viewers who weren't that interested in game shows, and with a big cash jackpot and a flashy set, the game just seemed too stereotypical. The newer, slicker, modernized *Jeopardy!* expired after only twenty-six weeks.

NBC also dusted off *High Rollers*, a moderately successful Heatter-Quigley game with Alex Trebek. *High Rollers* was based on an old-time dice game called Shut the Box, sometimes sold as a board game but often played with mere pencil and paper. In Shut the Box, players wrote down the numbers one through nine on the paper, and then rolled dice, using the number they rolled to eliminate the numbers on the paper. For example, with a roll of eleven, a player could remove the two, four, and five, because $2 + 4 + 5 = 11$.

When *High Rollers* was first introduced in 1974, contestants answered trivia questions for control of Ruta Lee's next dice roll. Every number was hiding a prize, and the game ended when a contestant either rolled the last remaining number on the board (collecting all of their own prizes and winning the game) or rolled a number that couldn't be removed in any combination (losing the game to the opponent).

On *The New High Rollers* for 1978, Heatter and Quigley infused an extra layer of strategy into the game by mixing the numbers and arranging them into a 3×3 grid for each game, with each column representing a jackpot of prizes. Eliminating the last number in a column captured all the prizes in that column, provided that contestant went on to win the game. Each of the three columns could swell to a maximum of five prizes; the potential for a big payday was realized on only the twentieth episode of the series, when a contestant accumulated more than $40,000 on a single roll of the dice, capturing three maxed-out columns of five prizes apiece. The game deftly fused quick wits and luck, and with the laid-back hosting style of wisecracking Alex Trebek (*High Rollers* wasn't bound by time restrictions; if the show ended in the middle of a game, everyone would just come back to finish it at the start of the next episode, and Trebek kept a much looser grip on the game with no clock to keep an eye on), *High Rollers* just worked.

Early in 1979, Allen Ludden was back with *Password*, in a rejuvenated form called *Password Plus*, in which each series of five passwords now served as clues to the Password Puzzle, a famous person, place, or thing. The goal of the game was now twofold: first to guess the password, and then to solve the puzzle. The winner played Alphabetics, a new twist on the original show's Lightning Round in which ten passwords were arranged in alphabetical order, the first letter of each password

Allen Ludden came back with *Password Plus*. Joining him are one of *Password*'s favorites, Lucille Ball and Dick Martin.   *Fred Wostbrock Collection*

was given to the contestant, and solving all ten in sixty seconds paid five grand. Though a number of fans would admit over the years that they actually preferred *Password Plus* to *Password*, the new version never attracted such a big audience. Producer Robert Sherman admitted years later that there were many renewal periods when the Goodson-Todman staff was actually surprised that NBC was asking for thirteen more weeks of *Password Plus*.

Shark Attack

Another game that just worked, that premiered on the same day as *The New High Rollers* and one that would have been just as well suited for a table at a casino, was *Card Sharks*, an elegantly simple game from Goodson-Todman Productions. The job of host went to Jim Perry, a New Jersey–born ex–disc jockey and straight man for Sid Caesar, who had gone on to considerably more success as a broadcaster by going north of border. He had become a ubiquitous presence on Canadian TV screens, hosting *Bingo at Home*, *Headline Hunters*, *Definition* (the longest-running game show in Canadian history), and the annual Miss Canada pageant. At the time he got *Card Sharks*, he jokingly called himself the most experienced unknown in America. Funnily enough, one of the candidates he had beaten for the job was Nelson Davis, a Canadian actor attempting to build a career in America.

Though not widely known in America, Perry came to Goodson-Todman highly recommended. He explained in 1979, "When I was working with Sid Caesar, my manager took me to (*Name That Tune* creator) Harry Salter. He had a new show that maybe never worked out, but he asked me to audition. . . . A year later, another fellow named Howard Felsher (formerly a producer on *Tic Tac Dough* and later *Family Feud*) remembered me and introduced me to two other people and they had me do a pilot film which never sold. From that, I was asked to be the emcee of a game in Canada called *Fractured Phrases*. It's kind of remarkable that my first show came from an audition I did a full year before and a guy who remembered me."

Card Sharks pitted two players against each other. Each player had a designated deck of fifty-two cards to use through the entire match; five cards were dealt at a time, and the object was to correctly predict whether each card in the row was higher or lower than the one that preceded it. Clearing your row won the game.

There was a catch in that modest goal, though; a player couldn't tackle the cards without first winning a "high-low toss-up," in which the players heard a question previously posed to a specific group of 100 people (sample question: "We asked 100 police officers, 'Do you believe that marijuana should be legalized?' How many said yes?") One player guessed a number; the other would guess if the correct answer was higher or lower.

Jim Perry shows off his massive deck on NBC's *Card Sharks*.   *Photo courtesy of Zane Enterprises*

Bob's Big Secret

Bob Eubanks would always be known as a game show host, but the truth is he always had quite an entrepreneurial spirit. He owned nightclubs, he promoted concerts (he held the distinction of being the man responsible for bringing the Beatles to the Hollywood Bowl), and even competed in rodeos. After so many years of hosting game shows, he got an urge to create and produce his own formats. He developed a not-exactly-a-game-show called *Smart Alecks*, a prehistoric form of *Shark Tank* in which an inventor presented his or her newest creation to a celebrity panel. The panelists would give a blunt assessment of what they thought of the invention, and members of the studio audience voted on how much money to give the inventor. *Smart Alecks* never got on the air. Neither did a pilot called *Ask a Silly Question*, hosted by a young comic named David Letterman.

But Bob finally got a game on the air called *All-Star Secrets*. Three contestants faced a group of five celebrities. Eubanks, serving as host for his own creation, would announce a secret that one of the celebrities disclosed in an interview with the show's staff. The contestants won money for correctly guessing which celebrity, with a bonus prize going to the top money winner at the end of the day.

Eubanks's staff managed to wring some remarkable mysteries out of the celebrities. Among the fun facts disclosed by the guest stars: Phyllis Diller always travels with five pencil sharpeners; Pat Boone was once arrested for breaking and entering; Greg Morris, a believer in reincarnation, felt he had been King David in a former life; LaWanda Page, "Aunt Esther" on *Sanford and Son*, was a former stripper; Bill Cullen considered Evangelism "the biggest rip-off in the world"; and Jamie Farr, at the height of his popularity as Klinger on *M*A*S*H*, revealed he had won the title of Miss Congeniality in a beauty pageant.

Each show ended with one of the guests getting a surprise. Arte Johnson, who revealed he had been pelted with garbage by a woman who mistook him for

Bob Eubanks listens as another star prepares to tell all on *All-Star Secrets.*

Photo courtesy of Zane Enterprises

chauvinist tennis player Bobby Riggs, was surprised by the real Bobby Riggs. Ross Martin, who said he had long dreamt of conducting a symphony orchestra, was surprised when Eubanks handed him a baton and the stage split apart to reveal a full orchestra waiting backstage. Martin held back tears as he waved the baton through a stirring performance that Eubanks called the best moment of the series.

Those secrets and those fun moments just weren't enough to ensure a long run, however. *All Star Secrets* was gone in only thirty-nine weeks.

Game Show Death Day

In 1980, Fred Silverman took stock of NBC's fortunes and made the same assessment that Lin Bolen had made in 1973: the game shows they had on the air were attracting the wrong demographic, and NBC needed to think younger. Unlike Bolen, who wanted to update the look of game shows, Silverman's approach was to eliminate as many as possible. He was adamant that game shows attracted older demographics no matter what.

At the same time, David Letterman had put himself into Silverman's good graces with a dynamite stand-up performance at a dinner where the producer was being honored. Silverman thought that a ninety-minute daytime talk show starring the thirty-two-year-old Letterman would spruce up his network nicely, and word was handed down from on high: on June 23, 1980, *The David Letterman Show* would premiere on NBC, and that to make room for it, three NBC daytime games would bite the dust on June 20, a date that fans would later refer to as "Game Show Death Day."

The first on the chopping block was *The Hollywood Squares.* Peter Marshall later pointed out that when the original *Squares* pilot was produced for CBS in 1965, Fred Silverman had made the call not to buy the show. Marshall speculated in his autobiography, *Backstage with the Original Hollywood Square,* that when Fred Silverman arrived at NBC a decade later, he was annoyed that the show he didn't want had done so well without his blessing. Silverman began playing with the show's time slot, moving it from 11:30 a.m. to 10:30 a.m. to 1:00 p.m. to 12:30 p.m. and back to 10:30 a.m. Five time slots in under four years was more than even the most ardent fans could handle, particularly that 10:30 a.m. slot, which put the show head-to-head with *The Price is Right* on CBS. *The Hollywood Squares* went out with an R-rated bang. Ventriloquist Wayland Flowers and his dummy Madame sat in the center square for that final episode (Paul Lynde had left the show in September 1979). Flowers and Madame caught everybody off-guard with an F-word-laced tangent that rattled Peter Marshall so much that he sent the show into a commercial break without finishing his question, because he needed to collect himself. When the episode aired, the show had deftly inserted the word "Fool" into Madame's remarks.

High Rollers with Alex Trebek signed off that day too, but the third game show biting the dust proved to be the source of some confusion. The game that was initially canceled was *Wheel of Fortune*. Ratings-wise, the game had always stayed just above that line to justify keeping it on the air, but after five-plus years of so-so ratings, the feeling at NBC was that it was time to move on to something else. The fact that *Wheel* had recently attempted to mount a once-a-week nighttime version for the prime-access time slot, but couldn't get enough stations to sign up, seemed to reinforce this belief. *Wheel of Fortune* received the death sentence.

But then it got a reprieve. NBC suddenly decided that it would be a relatively new show, the twenty-six-week-old *Chain Reaction* with Bill Cullen, that would go off the air. Although *Chain Reaction* would eventually be brought back to life (see Chapter 36), it would be end of the line for *Chain* in 1980, and it was proving to be particularly dismal time for Bob Stewart Productions. Stewart was supposed to serve as producer for the new *David Letterman Show*, but after a disagreement with the star, he abruptly quit. The following week, ABC would air the final episode of *The $20,000 Pyramid*, which left *Family Feud* as ABC's last remaining game show. The nighttime *$25,000 Pyramid* with Bill Cullen had come to an end in 1979, and Cullen and Stewart's daily syndicated offering that year, *The Love Experts*, expired after only one season. Game shows were fast becoming an endangered species.

Chain Reaction's departure caused a happy problem for *Wheel of Fortune*; the staff, along with host Chuck Woolery and hostess Susan Stafford, were literally in the middle of a wrap party when they were interrupted by the announcement that they needed to report back to work the following Monday; the show wasn't canceled yet. The episodes that they had just finished taping were all hastily edited to remove Woolery's references to "our final week on the air," and the final segment of Friday's episode was deleted altogether because it included a lengthy goodbye from Chuck and the assembled staff.

CBS Runs Out of Breath

The late 1970s saw signs of trouble for the game shows of CBS too. CBS affiliates had gradually been dropping the network's feed at 4:00 p.m. in favor of airing syndicated programming, which triggered the demise of *Tattletales* with Bert Convy. CBS's other afternoon game, the dominant *Match Game '77*, was moved out of the 3:30 p.m. time slot, where it had thrived for its entire run. In November 1977, the show was moved to a morning time slot to form a solid ninety-minute game show block with *The Price is Right*. On paper, this was a brilliant idea; another game show with a large celebrity panel, *The Hollywood Squares* had done well in a morning time slot for years.

The problem was that the 3:30 p.m. time slot that *Match Game* had up until that point meant that they were attracting a large but very specific type of audience: kids coming home from school. *Match Game* had been a daily ritual for children throughout the 1970s, but moving the show to a morning time slot meant that *Match Game*'s largest and most loyal audience was literally not capable of seeing it anymore. CBS caught the mistake in judgment quickly, taking *Match Game* out of the 11:00 a.m. time slot after only six weeks, but their solution was puzzling: they didn't put it back at 3:30 p.m. They put it at 4:00 p.m., which meant it was subjected to the same local station dropouts that had wrecked *Tattletales*. *Match Game* fared no better, leaving CBS on April 20, 1979.

The following Monday, CBS unleashed a freshly shuffled daytime schedule, complete with a new game show boasting the nearly unpronounceable title *Whew!* The game was created by two former Goodson-Todman aide-de-camps: Bud Austin, who had been the company's executive vice president for a number of years and had been a master at negotiating high fees from networks for Goodson-Todman's shows; and Jay Wolpert, a former *Price is Right* producer whose job duties included interviewing all 330 members of the studio audience for each taping and deciding which nine would get called to come on down.

The host of *Whew!* was Tom Kennedy, who found the show's title tricky enough that he usually sidestepped it by calling it "our show" as each day's game played out. The other noteworthy on-air talent was *Whew!*'s announcer, a former shock jock from Texas who had become a familiar voice to prime-time viewers over the 1978–1979 TV season as the narrator of the controversial sitcom *Soap*. His name was Rod Roddy; *Whew!* was his first game show.

The staff of *Whew!*, with host Tom Kennedy front and center.

Fred Wostbrock Collection

Bob Stewart once said that a good game show was one that could be explained in one sentence. *Whew!* didn't exactly pass that test, but it adroitly combined knowledge, strategy, blind luck, and even a little comedy into one package that won over a small but loyal following. *Whew!* today is largely thought of as a cult favorite among game show fanatics.

Two contestants competed against each other. For each round, a category was announced for the board of twenty-eight boxes. Each box was hiding a "blooper," a statement with a mistake that needed correcting. (Sample blooper: "The boy who walks down the aisle at a wedding is traditionally called the pill bearer.") One contestant would be designated the Charger; the Charger's job was to clear the board by solving a blooper on each of the six levels of the game board in sixty seconds or less. The other contestant, designated the Blocker, tried to inhibit the Charger's progress by hiding six secret blocks on the board; uncovering a block required the Charger to stop playing for five seconds.

Richard Dawson once opened an episode of *Family Feud* by checking his watch and wisecracking, "Tom Kennedy should be finishing the rules to *Whew!* right about now."

Clocking Out

A month after *Whew!*, CBS introduced a retooling of an old favorite, *Beat the Clock*. But the new version was nobody's favorite. Goodson-Todman originally pegged Jack Narz (who hosted the show in syndication at the start of the decade). But CBS had Monty Hall, a frequent competitor to Goodson-Todman, locked into a contract and insisted on justifying it by having Hall host the show.

This decision didn't make anybody happy. Certainly not Monty Hall, who disliked the zany stunt show to begin with and didn't like being shoved into it. He later said, "I hated it with all my heart."

Goodson-Todman tried to placate the displaced Jack Narz by making him the show's announcer and giving him a second job title, associate producer, and a second paycheck to go along with it, to get his salary close to what it would have been as host. Narz didn't want to do anything but host the show.

Beat the Clock and *Whew!* both limped along for several months, and managed to fend off cancellation for a little while by attempting the same quick fix for both shows: infusing the games with celebrities. The shows became *All-Star Beat the Clock* and *Celebrity Whew!* The star treatment ultimately didn't help either patient. *Beat the Clock* went off the air in February 1980; *Whew!* followed it to the exit in May. Both shows were replaced by prime-time sitcom reruns, with no new game shows forthcoming from CBS.

Down But Not Out

When *The Hollywood Squares* was canceled, it was regularly pulling in a 20 rating and a 27 share in its time slot. Three months later, David Letterman was averaging a 9 rating, with dozens of NBC affiliates dropping the show altogether in favor of syndicated programs. The audience Letterman did have was loyal, but even his own fans, and critics who otherwise praised the show, observed that the show he was delivering felt like a late-night show. Silverman reluctantly canceled *The David Letterman Show* after eighteen weeks and held Letterman until a better time slot opened up.

Silverman may not have liked the older audience, but the problem was it was a larger and more profitable audience in daytime, so Silverman gave the go-ahead to replace Letterman with game shows.

Heatter-Quigley introduced an old favorite in a new home with *Las Vegas Gambit*. Wink Martindale now hosted the blackjack quiz from the Tropicana Hotel/Casino in Las Vegas; the game was fundamentally the same except for one change midway through the run. *Gambit* switched from its original bonus round (picking hidden prizes from a board, taking a card for every prize, and trying to stay under 21 to keep everything) to a strangely familiar one. A craps table was now onstage, a very familiar pair of large dice showed up, and the winning couple now played the bonus round from *High Rollers*.

Blockbusters with Bill Cullen followed. Based on the board game Hex, *Blockbusters* was touted as the game that determined if two heads were better than one. A solo player and a family pair faced a grid of twenty hexagons, answering questions to capture each hexagon with the goal of making a connection from one end of the board to the other.

Las Vegas Gambit was canceled and replaced by Regis Philbin after only a year. *Blockbusters* survived only slightly longer, and only because its replacement kept getting delayed. NBC wanted to plug a soap opera into the time slot, but when technical problems kept holding up production, NBC kept calling the Goodson-Todman staff and asking for two more weeks of *Blockbusters* . . . and then two more . . . and then two more . . . and then two more . . . until ultimately, *Blockbusters* had managed to sneak an extra six months of life out of this soap opera's problematic start. But finally, everything was ready to go and *Blockbusters* was off the air in April 1982. By that time, *Card Sharks* and *Password Plus* had gone off the air, too. In 1982, each of the major networks had whittled down their game show schedules drastically: CBS had *The Price is Right* and a new version of *Tattletales*, though at 4:00 p.m. *Tattletales* was subject to pre-emption from local stations and was seen across much less of the country than *Price*; ABC had *Family Feud*; and NBC had *Wheel of Fortune*, which was just barely hanging on by its fingernails.

32

Out of Their Prime

"Feud" Holds Down the Fort

Don't Mess with the Family

When Goodson-Todman realized the extent to which *Match Game* was dominating daytime TV ratings in 1974, a few staffers began kicking around the idea of a *Match Game* spinoff based on the Super Match bonus round. For part of the Super Match, the contestant played a game called Audience Match. A simple fill-in-the-blank had been presented to a previous studio audience, who individually wrote their answers and handed them in before leaving the studio; the contestant saw the fill-in-the-blank on a board hiding the three most frequently given responses. The contestant gave an answer and won $500 for matching the most popular answer, $250 for the second most popular, and $100 for the third most popular. This would be the basis of Goodson-Todman's new game.

Over the next two years, the Goodson-Todman staff fleshed out the idea considerably; it started off as a format that the staff called "On a Roll," a contest between two players. But as the staff debugged the idea and reworked it, it gradually swelled into five players against five players. Feeling that sticking five strangers together to form a team wasn't a terribly compelling idea, one staffer suggested that the opposing teams be families, and *voila*! *Family Feud* was pitched and sold to ABC for a summer launch. *Match Game* regular panelist Richard Dawson, who had a clause in his contract allowing him to host a Goodson-Todman game show, exercised that clause to become the game's host.

Family Feud premiered on July 12, 1976, as a replacement for *Rhyme and*

The dashing Richard Dawson gets to know the contestants on *Family Feud*.

Reason, a game curiously similar to *Match Game*. In his autobiography, *Rhyme and Reason* host Bob Eubanks speculated that Mark Goodson, who exerted incredible clout in daytime television, had made that show's cancellation a condition for ABC putting *Family Feud* on the air.

The game pitted two families against each other in a series of questions that had previously been asked of 100 people. The top-ranking answers were on the board (sometimes as few as the top three or as many as the top twelve—generally, the show put the answers on the board that had been given by at least two people).

Family Feud zoomed to number 1 in the daytime ratings, even surpassing its parent, *Match Game*. It had the shout-at-your-TV factor that home viewers crave; as families onstage furrowed their brows over questions like "Name something you do with your nose," people across America were firmly attached to their TVs and hollering "Blow! *Blow!*" It was a game that anybody could play, and every day, millions did.

There was one other factor undeniably contributing to *Feud*'s success, the inimitable Richard Dawson. The British accent and the distinctive hand gestures would have been enough to make Richard stand out in the field of TV game shows, but everything about his performance was truly different.

He openly took contestants to task for poor answers: "I said name a time that most people get up. And being the Einstein that you are, you said, '*Morning.*' That's what time I get up. Survey said . . . ZIP. If that wasn't bad enough, I said name a time that most people go to bed. You said, of course, '*Night!*'"

And he was relentlessly affectionate, even flirty. He calmed down a nervous contestant one day by giving her a kiss right on the lips, little realizing it would be his trademark. Kissing the contestants might have seemed obnoxious if he was selective about it, but part of his charm was that he kissed every woman on the show; the pretty ones, the plain ones, the young ones, the old ones, and, to the dismay of several arch-conservative sponsors and ABC affiliate managers, he kissed minorities, too.

Richard opened one episode by announcing that a sponsor complained about his kissing a black contestant and said that he didn't want that sponsor backing *Family Feud* anymore. He later told the Archive of American Television, "I kissed black women daily and nightly on *Family Feud* for eleven years and the world didn't come to an end, did it?"

Feud became so popular that it actually leapfrogged the once-a-week nighttime syndicated version that had become standard operating procedure for hit game shows in the mid-1970s. ABC actually contracted Goodson-Todman and Richard Dawson for a series of one-hour *Family Feud* specials in prime-time, featuring celebrities—often co-stars of other prime-time shows—competing on behalf of their favorite charities.

A prime-access-time *Family Feud* was introduced in the fall of 1977. It started off as once a week, like nearly all of the other prime-access-time offerings, but *Family Feud* was so white-hot that the show quickly expanded to twice a week. In 1980, with no signs of waning, the nighttime show expanded to five nights a week.

ABC put *Family Feud* in prime-time several times each year for hour-long specials pitting the casts of TV shows against each other. Here, Loni Anderson of *WKRP in Cincinnati* faces off against Fred Grandy of *The Love Boat*.

Losing the Feud

Barely a decade after Goodson-Todman's attorney had lobbied the FCC to create prime access time, the company effectively killed it in one fell swoop. *Family Feud* was already the highest-rated prime-access property, and stations didn't bat an eye when it swelled to five nights a week. Of course, if *Feud* was airing five nights a week, that meant the station had to bump four other prime-access shows off the schedule, and with fewer and fewer stations carrying them, the shows vaporized. *The $100,000 Name That Tune* went off the air in 1980. Even Goodson-Todman's other properties weren't safe. *Match Game PM* and the nighttime *Price is Right* were both canceled, while an attempt to mount a nighttime *Card Sharks* never got off the ground.

And to be clear, it wasn't just game shows. It was virtually all other weekly prime-access-time programs that bit the dust. Variety shows like *The Muppet Show* and *The Lawrence Welk Show* withered in *Feud*'s wake; the prime-access-time shows that followed were predominantly "strip" (meaning five-a-week, like *Feud*) offerings, which made competition for those plum time periods extremely fierce. *Family Feud* was the top game show at the beginning of the 1980s, but it was the top of what had unexpectedly become a very low mountain.

33

Spinning Wheel

The Boom Begins

The Eye and the Pyramid

In 1982, CBS was in nearly exactly the same position it had been in 1972. It was drifting aimlessly in the morning with prime-time reruns; ABC didn't have anything on the national schedule during the 10:00 a.m. hour. NBC had reruns of *Diff'rent Strokes* and *Wheel of Fortune*, which was approaching eight years but had always been "just kind of there" as far as general audiences were concerned. Across all three networks, nobody seemed to give any thought to the 10:00 a.m. hour.

And so, CBS did exactly what it had done ten years earlier: it turned to game shows and came out swinging in the fall.

On September 20, 1982, CBS introduced one new game show and one revival of an old favorite. The new game was *Child's Play*, a cute idea from Mark Goodson Productions (Bill Todman died in 1979 and the company changed its name in the summer of '82) starring Bill Cullen. Contestants would watch pre-recorded interviews with children in which the kids supplied definitions, and the contestants had to guess the word. The children, ages five through nine, tended to go quite adrift with their definitions. A child threw the game into total confusion once by giving a lengthy description of the recent labor strikes in Poland that he had seen on the news; the word he was defining was "slavery." Another child was given the term "Three Wise Men" and spoke reverently about Ronald Reagan, New York City Mayor Ed Koch, and New York Governor Mario Cuomo.

> **A Child Defines "Rude"**: When you're sitting in class, you just sit there quietly while the teacher talks. You don't interrupt her and shout, "Hey teacher! I have to make doody!" Because that's not polite. You wait for her to finish talking and then you shout that.

Child's Play would only survive for one year, but that year would be an impressive showcase of success to come. *Child's Play* didn't recruit child actors to appear on the program; they went to area schools in Los Angeles and New York and just sought out chatty, outgoing kids. But a surprising number of the kids would, in fact, go on to stardom when they got a little older: Jeff Cohen, who played Chunk in *The Goonies*; actress Tara Reid; *Man vs. Food* host Adam Richman; *All That* cast member Lori Beth Denberg; *The Adventures of Pete and Pete* star Michael Maronna; and Devin Ratray from the film *Home Alone* were among the cute kids who cracked up audiences during that one-year run.

Also premiering on September 20, 1982, was *The $25,000 Pyramid*. Creator Bob Stewart's legendary game was last seen in a six-month syndicated incarnation called *The $50,000 Pyramid* that expired in the summer of 1981; at the time, it was notable for being the last daytime game show to emanate from New York. Stewart would move his whole operation to Los Angeles in the next year, under pressure from the major networks, who really didn't want to do business with any producers who weren't by then living full-time in Los Angeles.

On Independence Day in 1982, Stewart got a call from NBC, saying that they wanted to mount a pilot for a new version of *Pyramid* for a considered spot on the daytime schedule. Bob Stewart enthusiastically said yes. But word of

Bill Cullen is back with another game; it's *Child's Play* on CBS.   *Fred Wostbrock Collection*

NBC's plans spread quickly somehow, and a few days later, CBS called with a counter-offer; they were offering to buy a new version of *Pyramid* outright, without shooting a pilot first.

The $25,000 Pyramid aired before *Child's Play* in the 10:00 a.m. Eastern time slot, putting Bill Cullen, who hosted the nighttime syndicated *$25,000 Pyramid* in the 1970s, in an interesting spot: his *Child's Play* aired on CBS directly between two shows that he had previously hosted; *Child's Play* was followed by *The Price is Right*.

At the same time, reruns of Bill Cullen's *$25,000 Pyramid* were being sold in syndication, which created some confusion for viewers. To clear things up, Dick Clark's new version was retitled *The New $25,000 Pyramid* and stayed that way for three years.

The $25,000 Pyramid tinkered with the rules of the original version and created arguably a better game in the process. Contestants stayed for the full half-hour, switching partners halfway through the show and playing a full game with each celebrity guest, meaning that nobody was completely at the mercy of a weaker celebrity guest. The money earned in the Winner's Circle served as the contestant's score in the overall game, and the contestant who won the most in the Winner's Circle was the day's champion. And the show would give away plenty of money in the years to come because the celebrities and contestants alike had mastered the game so artfully after eight years of watching it on CBS, ABC, and in syndication.

During the 1980s, *The $25,000 Pyramid* was arguably the best-played game on television. Day in and day out, teams delivered riveting seesaw battles that seemingly always came down to the wire.

Contestant coordinator Francine Bergman says, "We were doing a television show, so of course we needed outgoing people with likeable personalities. But Bob Stewart always made it very clear that top priority was the ability to play the game. If they couldn't play, we couldn't put them on the show, no exceptions."

So meticulous was Bob Stewart about making sure the game was the star that, much as he had done when he was producing *Password* under Goodson-Todman's watch, he insisted on bringing celebrities in to audition for the show before he would bring them on to play the game. Smokey Robinson, a fan who actually called Stewart's office asking to be invited, made it onto the show. Richard Simmons, who had the perfect personality for a big-money game show but just couldn't get the hang of it, was politely thanked for his time and never booked for the show.

Francine Bergman says, "A celebrity I'll never forget would be Maureen Reagan. We only used her for one week of shows, but I'll never forget her. She was President Reagan's daughter so it was a big deal to have her there. We had Secret Service agents surrounding the stage. We had a woman win $25,000 and her husband runs up onstage to congratulate her, which happened hundreds of times. It was part of our show, we were used to it. Well . . . we were so used to it that it didn't occur to us to tell the Secret Service that audience members will occasionally jump out of their seats and run to the stage. So, the Secret Service saw this man jump out of his seat and run right toward Maureen Reagan, and those agents had their guns drawn immediately. That was an awkward moment."

Though *The $25,000 Pyramid* would never dominate the ratings in years to come, it would dominate the Emmys, collecting the Outstanding Game Show trophy every full year it was on CBS, with Dick Clark taking two Emmys of his own for hosting. The game of quick wits and word communication also joined that elite group of games to become critical darlings. Even critics who held their noses at all other game shows would breathe easier in the presence of *The $25,000 Pyramid*.

Aaron Solomon was just a kid obsessed with game shows in the early 1980s, and *The $25,000*

Dick Clark gives a pep talk to a team in the Winner's Circle preparing for television's tensest minute.
Photo courtesy of Zane Enterprises

Pyramid caught his eye. "To me, word communication in general is an interesting idea. When you're playing a word-association game, it's not so much a matter of raw knowledge, it's a matter of ingenuity. The players are trying to figure out how best to convey a specific word and a specific idea to their partners.

"What I've always found so intriguing about word-communication games is that, like other game shows, there's a play-along factor, but it's different from a trivia game. When you watch *Jeopardy!* and *Wheel of Fortune*, you're trying to figure out the correct answer along with the contestants on the show. What shows like *Password* and *Pyramid* have done is show the correct answers on the screen throughout the game. As a viewer, there's never any doubt about the correct answer, and yet, there's still a play-along factor. You're shouting a better clue at the screen, you're thinking about how there's a better way to tackle that word than the way they're doing it."

Solomon would go on to serve as executive producer of ABC's *The $100,000 Pyramid* in 2016. Who better to run things than somebody who gets the game?

Man, Oh, Man

NBC's attempt to drift away from game shows had gone just as poorly. *The Regis Philbin Show*, *The Doctors*, and *Texas* hadn't enamored viewers, and the network conceded that viewers wanted game shows. As a result, January 3, 1983, would be a surprisingly busy day for game show fans; NBC was unleashing three shows to join *Wheel of Fortune* for a solid two-hour block.

One of the new games on the lineup was a concoction of Jay Wolpert, whose unconventional *Whew!* had been a part of CBS's ill-fated 1979 daytime makeover. His new game was just as unusual and, like *Whew!*, it would attract a cult following among game show fans. It was called *Hit Man*.

Hosted by former commercial actor Peter Tomarken, who took the job because his agent told him, "You'll make six figures and you'll only have to work four days a month," *Hit Man* was a memory game that made use of "mini-movies" made especially for the show. They were short films, consisting mostly of stills, music, and occasionally some very basic animation. The movies all revolved around specific subjects, with Tomarken serving as narrator and providing rapid-fire fun facts and history, organized into a short story. "The History of Blue Jeans" told the tale of how Levi Strauss Co. used to put copper rivets into the crotches, until a Levi executive went on a camping trip, stood too close to a campfire, and discovered to his horror that copper is an excellent conductor of heat.

Bowing to the trends of the early 1980s, the set, designed to resemble the tops of arcade cabinets, used "Hit Men" instead of points to keep score. For the first round, the Hit Men ran a race on behalf of the contestants, advancing one space per correct answer until two Hit Men crossed the finish line. For the second round, the survivors competed against the previous day's returning champion in a game where correct answers zapped your opponent's hit men, one at a time. A challenger could win by zapping the champion's last hit man; the champion won by zapping all of the challengers' collective hit men.

Peter Tomarken is surrounded by the cute little hit men of *Hit Man*.

Unconventional? Yes. Maybe even too much so. *Hit Man* was gone in thirteen weeks.

Men, Oh, Men

Debuting in the noon time slot for NBC on January 3, 1983, was a show that was so unconventional that even its own announcer seemed unsure of what to call it. Sometimes, the voice of Steve Day announced it as "a new game show," sometimes "a new talk show," and sometimes, "the most unusual new game show and talk." It was to be called *Studs*.

Rick Rosner, a former *Hollywood Squares* staffer, developed *Studs* with the intention of doing some unconventional casting for the master of ceremonies—he wanted a woman. Betty White half-heartedly accepted the offer after having been rejected for such a job thrice in her career; she was considered for *Make the Connection* in the 1950s, *Get the Message* in the 1960s, and *Hollywood's Talking* in the 1970s, rejected each time because executives felt that in the long run, a female game show host just wouldn't work. Quite frankly, Betty White figured the same thing would happen when she was offered *Studs*.

She explained the problem to newspaper columnist Vernon Scott: "The networks said women at home want to look at men, not females. They also were convinced viewers were tired of hearing feminine voices, that they preferred the more authoritative male sounds."

Betty, a youthful sixty at the time, also thought she'd be miscast on a show where she'd be surrounded by male celebrities. She told Scott, "I told them they should get someone young and gorgeous. But NBC wanted experience, a woman who could think on her feet."

Betty, it's worth noting, had started on television in the late 1940s with a daily series called *Hollywood on Television*, which was five-and-a-half hours long and almost entirely unscripted; Betty White's experience and ability to think on her feet were well spoken for. That still didn't mean she expected to make it on the air. Either the show was going to be rejected, or surely the executives would say it needed a male host, the way they always did.

But then NBC President Brandon Tartikoff saw the proposal; not only did he like the show enough to buy it, he explicitly said that he thought having a female host it had been a stroke of genius. The only objection he raised was about the title *Studs*, which Rosner happily agreed to change. *Just Men!*, starring Betty White, premiered at noon.

Two contestants, always women, competed against each other in a game of intuition involving a panel of seven celebrities, always men. Betty would ask a personal question, and the contestants predicted how a specific man on the panel answered.

> **Betty:** What's the last part of your body to wake up in the morning?

> ***Days of Our Lives* actor Josh Taylor:** Depends on what they were doing the night before.

A correct prediction earned that panelist's key. The woman with the most keys at the end of the game selected one of the keys she earned and attempted to start the car onstage. If she could start the car, it was hers to keep.

A fascinating grab bag of men sat on the panel to field Betty's questions: David Hasselhoff, Leif Garrett, Dick Van Patten, Tim Reid, Jeff Altman, Los Angeles Dodger Steve Sax, Mr. T, Garry Marshall, Herve Villachaize, Pat Sajak, Gene Rayburn, and Peter Tomarken all joined the fun.

But *Just Men!* had three strikes against it:

- Strike One: NBC Chairman Grant Tinker, fighting a bad cold and staying home from work one day, watched the show and didn't like it.
- Strike Two: It was on in the noontime slot, which an increasing number of NBC affiliates weren't carrying in favor of airing a local newscast. Much of the country didn't even have a chance to watch *Just Men!*
- Strike Three: The noon time slot also meant it was airing directly against ABC's *Family Feud*.

So, after thirteen weeks and three strikes, *Just Men!* was out.

Now on Sale

But NBC did manage to unleash one hit game on that January day.

Sale of the Century had been a modest hit for the network, originally premiering in 1969, first with host Jack Kelly and later Joe Garagiola. The new series would be hosted by Jim Perry, returning to NBC less than two years after signing off from *Card Sharks*. When *Sale of the Century* premiered, however, the show had an interesting problem. Goodson-Todman sold reruns of *Card Sharks* to local stations, and several aired *Card Sharks* in direct competition with Jim Perry's new game. Perry was particularly proud, though, of the NBC station in Detroit, which aired *Card Sharks* back-to-back with *Sale of the Century*. Jim affectionately called the Detroit NBC lineup "A Morning Festival of Jim Perry."

Three contestants competed against each other, spotted $20 at the start of the game and answering trivia questions worth five dollars apiece. Along the way, there were Instant Bargains, in which Perry would offer a prize to the leader, and then haggle over the bargain price that would be taken out of that player's score. ("I'll tell you what, this trip to Tahiti is priced at $8. What if I knock it down to $6?

Sale of the Century's Jim Perry and Summer Bartholomew.

I'll even throw in a hundred dollars cash for spending money on the trip.")

Jim Perry stuck around for the entire run, but the lovely assistant joining him each day proved to be quite a revolving door early on. Sally Juian, Lee Menning, and Lou Mulford all came and went in *Sale*'s first two years, but the show finally found a capable co-star in Summer Bartholomew, a former Miss USA who had been searching for a game of her own for a while. She had appeared on *The Price is Right* in 1975, and then found her way onto *Wheel of Fortune* for a special wedding-themed week, dressed as a bride as she modeled the prizes; she returned to *Wheel* for a week in 1981 as an audition to be the show's new letter turner (more on that later in the chapter), but settled into *Sale*, and, after a self-admitted rough start, her chemistry with Jim Perry and her warmth toward the contestants made her a keeper.

Wheel's Turn at the Big Time

But the game show renaissance truly began in the fall of 1983, with the most unlikely suspect: *Wheel of Fortune*. *Wheel* was closing in on nine years on the NBC schedule at that point, but really, at the time, *Wheel of Fortune* was probably the most insignificant show ever to stay on the air that long. If you were to imagine TV ratings as a single line, with everything above the line staying on the air and everything below the line getting canceled, *Wheel of Fortune* had spent most of its run seated directly on top of the line, always performing exactly well enough to justify getting another thirteen-week commitment from NBC.

Making *Wheel*'s survival even more remarkable was that its two stars had both departed recently, and both had been replaced by virtual unknowns. Chuck Woolery left in a salary dispute, departing from *Wheel* on Christmas 1981. He was replaced by Pat Sajak, best known to viewers in Los Angeles as the KNBC Channel 4 weatherman with the bone-dry sense of humor. Game show producers had been keeping one eye on Sajak for a while. Merrill Heatter of *The Hollywood Squares* saw a lot of Wally Cox in Sajak's demeanor and off-the-cuff jokes during the weather report. Mark Goodson recruited him to host a pilot called *Puzzlers*, a *Price is Right*–style collection of mini-games under the umbrella of a larger game; in the case of *Puzzlers*, they were all word games. Ralph Edwards tapped him for *Press Your Luck*, a game show adaptation of the popular memory toy Simon.

Sajak's approach to game show hosting was a different one; he seemed cool and detached sometimes, but that dry wit made him stand out from the pack considerably, and he made his mark on *Wheel*.

Hostess Susan Stafford departed from the show less than a year after Woolery. *Wheel* conducted auditions on air, with several hostesses appearing on the show for a week at a time. The job went to the one that Sajak personally considered the dark horse candidate, a shy, quiet, and visibly nervous model from South Carolina with the distinctive name of Vanna White. Merv Griffin hired her for the perfectly bizarre reason that she had a large head; he had a theory about attractive women with large heads. He thought they attracted more attention, and that people were more prone to remember them.

Sajak and White's customary thirty-second chats at the end of each episode seemed to bring out the best in each of them. Sajak's own dry sense of humor and White's reactions, which seemed to fall somewhere between amused and bemused, were, again, unique in the world of game shows. Hosts and models either maintained their distance (like Bud Collyer and Roxanne on *Beat the Clock*), or had a flirty relationship (like Geoff Edwards and Jan Speck on *Treasure Hunt*). Sajak and White's chemist ry was such that a rumor began swirling that she was his kid sister.

In 1983, Merv Griffin made an unusual deal with NBC. The network, which owned the right to sell the show for a syndicated nighttime version, made a deal to sell Griffin that right. As part of the deal, NBC agreed to renew *Wheel* for a full year instead of the customary thirteen weeks. Griffin recruited a small television distribution company, King World, to sell the nighttime *Wheel of Fortune* to local stations. King World's primary product up to that point had been rerun packages of the *Our Gang* short subjects of the 1930s. Founder Charles King's children had since gone to work for a different syndication company, Colbert Television Sales, where they had become the company's star salesmen with their successful handling

The breakout hit of 1983, nighttime *Wheel of Fortune*.

of *Tic Tac Dough* and *The Joker's Wild*. After being denied raises, they returned to their father's company and went to work distributing the nighttime *Wheel of Fortune*. And that's when everybody in the television business found out just how good the King brothers were at selling television shows.

Wheel of Fortune debuted in syndication in September 1983, airing in direct competition with *Family Feud* in most markets, which led most to anticipate a quick one-season death for the nighttime *Wheel*. But when February rolled around, the impossible happened: *Wheel of Fortune* was number 1. A 14.3 rating and a 25 share meant that it was outdrawing *Family Feud* and the other grand champion of syndication, *M*A*S*H* reruns.

Pat Sajak's own theory, in 1984: timing is everything. He told a reporter, "I think it was a matter of timing and the general state of the syndicated market. Let's face it, there isn't very much out there. And *M*A*S*H* is getting a little weary. I love that show as much as anyone, but it's gotten so we can all say the lines with the characters. I think we filled a nice void at the right time."

Feud Cools Off

Sajak tactfully avoided slinging any speculative mud at *Family Feud* during his interview, but January 1984 had been a particularly bad month for the show, owing to a damning *TV Guide* cover story about game show hosts. The cover featured six members of the game show hosting fraternity: Bill Cullen, Jack Barry, Wink Martindale, Monty Hall, Bob Barker, and Pat Sajak. The article bluntly disclosed that Richard Dawson had been invited to appear on the cover but said he would only appear if he was alone. The article included candid quotes from Wink Martindale, Barker, and Hall, all of whom had conspicuously low opinions of Dawson, calling him "arrogant." Even Mark Goodson, who stood to benefit the most from a positive depiction of Dawson, admitted to suffering from heartburn whenever he had to deal with the problematic host.

It triggered an Arthur Godfrey–like fall from grace for Dawson and *Family Feud*; in the 1950s, Godfrey had watched helplessly as the TV audience abandoned him in droves after the seemingly down-to-earth Godfrey fired singer Julius LaRosa on the air. In 1984, Richard Dawson looked at the ratings for *Family Feud* and realized that there was nothing he could do, either. The syndicated *Feud* aired its last episode on May 17, 1985. The ABC daytime *Feud* followed it through the exit door a month later. It was difficult to have a moment of silence for *Feud* by that point, though; every studio in Hollywood had buzzers and bells blaring. The TV game show was back.

34

Mr. Know-It-All

Nowhere-Near-Final Jeopardy!

What Do You Want to Do When You Grow Up?

George Alexander Trebek spent a great deal of his childhood in Sudbury, Ontario, trying to figure out what he was going to do when he was older. At times, he considered being a pilot, a doctor, a priest (a calling he lost interest in once he became a teenager and discovered girls), or possibly prime minister. A shy child when he entered boarding school at age twelve, he immersed himself in books and built his brain considerably, though at the time, he never thought of himself as an intellectual.

Trebek attended University of Ontario, considering medicine or law as a career, but when he needed to scrape together money for his junior year tuition, he applied for a job at radio station CBO-AM in Ottawa; when he graduated, he didn't leave the station. He did a little of everything: commercials, news, weather, sportscasting.

Trebek on TV

CBO was an affiliate of the Canadian Broadcasting Corporation, which maintained a television station anywhere they also maintained a radio station. This gave Trebek an opportunity to build a television career rather quickly. Only two years after graduating college, he hosted a music show for teens, *Music Hop*. He even sang a few times on the program.

Trebek told the Archive of American Television, "I don't know if you'd call me a natural, but I enjoyed it. I wasn't too intimidated by it. I wanted to have fun, and I did."

Trebek had a variety of duties for CBC television. In addition to hosting *Music Hop*, he was co-anchoring the local news in Ottawa, a duty that he didn't take particularly seriously; he would play pranks off-camera to try to make other reporters laugh, and sat behind the anchor's desk wearing a sport coat, tie, and—knowing the home viewers wouldn't see—shorts and sneakers.

He got a career-changing assignment in 1966, getting tapped by the network to host *Reach for the Top*, a Canadian version of America's popular *College Bowl*. It was low-key, it was fast-paced, thirty-minute bombardment of tough trivia. It was a sign of things to come.

When he was initially seen on Canadian TV, Alex was clean-shaven, with relatively short hair, but as the 1960s wore on, he developed a distinctive new look that would serve his career well. The hairdresser at the CBC would always straighten Trebek's wavy locks before he stepped in front of the camera, but as men's hairstyles grew longer and thicker later in that decade, Trebek tried to keep up with the trend. Attempting to grow his hair longer made it more difficult for the hairdresser to straighten it, and it just grew thicker and fluffier. Trebek let it grow into a full afro, which, combined with the mustache he grew during that period, gave him a swarthy, countercultural look that perhaps belied his true nature.

Due South

Trebek hosted a daytime talk show called *Afternoon* that was fundamentally the same format as a late-night talk show; guests, a live band, and Trebek even performed a monologue at the opening of the show. Trebek struck up a friendship with a musical guest who appeared on one episode, Alan Thicke, who left Canada shortly after to seek his fortune in Hollywood.

Thicke's career took an unlikely detour and he found himself working on the

production staff of a game show in development for NBC, titled *The Wizard of Odds* (see Chapter 24). The set designer had come up with a theater-in-the-round set for the show, which looked so snazzy and different that the production staff wanted to use it, but the problem was theater-in-a-round sets were counterproductive to any show that used cue cards, which meant finding a host for *The Wizard of Odds* would be a tall order. Thicke gave a glowing recommendation for the *Afternoon* host that he had encountered in Canada, and with NBC daytime boss Lin Bolen on the hunt for new young talent, thirty-two-year-old Alex Trebek was deemed just right for *The Wizard of Odds*.

And Trebek later admitted that it wasn't just ability and youth that got him the job; it was that unusual afro/mustache combination. "I had a full head of hair and a pretty big mustache, and that was one of the reasons they

Alex Trebek's afro and moustache made him stand out in his first endeavors on American TV. Later TV viewers who only knew the professorial, gray Trebek would be startled by his original look.

liked me," he told the Archive of American Television. "I was the first game show host since Groucho Marx to go on the air with a mustache."

And *The Wizard of Odds* was just the right job at the time for Alex Trebek. He was such a workaholic at CBC that he had never used any of his paid vacation time, which accumulated every year that he failed to use it. When he got the offer to host *The Wizard of Odds*, he was able to take a sixteen-week paid vacation without leaving his job. Since *The Wizard of Odds*, like most network daytime shows, would only get an initial commitment of thirteen weeks, it afforded Trebek the opportunity to take a career risk without actually quitting his job.

But when *The Wizard of Odds* got renewed for another thirteen weeks, Trebek tendered his resignation for CBC, crashed on Alan Thicke's couch for a few weeks, and then moved into his own place in Los Angeles. The jobs would keep coming; Alex hosted *High Rollers*, the show that replaced *The Wizard of Odds*.

Then it was on to *Double Dare*, a hard quiz from Goodson-Todman Productions that looked like something out of quiz shows past; the two contestants sat in isolation booths and listened to a series of clues to the identity of a person, place, or thing. The contestants pressed buzzers to ring in; pressing your buzzer would also cut off your opponent's view of the game board and their audio feed. A right answer would allow a contestant to dare the opponent for extra money if the opponent was stumped by additional clues.

Trebek, looking back on the show, said, "It was probably too cerebral for the audience in daytime in that period."

The ratings seemed to indicate that; it was gone in twenty-six weeks. Trebek enjoyed hosting what he called "an intellectually stimulating show" like *Double Dare*, and eagerly signed on to do another hard quiz, *The $128,000 Question* (see Chapter 28). He returned to *High Rollers* for another run on that show from 1978–1980, but even by that point, Trebek's preferred realm was becoming apparent to many around him.

Art Alisi, a producer on *High Rollers*, suggested to a friend once that Alex Trebek would make a great host for *Jeopardy!* if it ever went back on the air.

In Pursuit of a Hit

Merv Griffin always maintained a sweet spot in his heart for *Jeopardy!* and wanted to keep it on the air. It seemed like he wasn't the only one. Milton Bradley continued producing *Jeopardy!* home games through 1982, three years after the show was last seen on NBC. Milton Bradley even created a version for the Omni Entertainment System, a short-lived electronic pushbutton console.

But the unlikely impetus for the revival of *Jeopardy!* was the unlikely success of a board game that had been slapped together by some friends on a whim in 1979. They wanted to play *Scrabble*, found that some of the pieces were missing, and suddenly decided to just make a board game of their own. They named the game *Trivial Pursuit*, and it was a blockbuster when it hit U. S. toy shelves in 1982. America suddenly craved trivia; Mark Goodson loved the game so much that he asked his staff to come up with a game show format that had "Trivia" in the title and utilized similar questions. Goodson's game, *Trivia Trap*, didn't work; it premiered in 1984 and disappeared after only twenty-six weeks on ABC. But there was another trivia game show that premiered in 1984, and the other one absolutely did work.

Merv Griffin had produced a pilot for a new version of *Jeopardy!* in 1983. Right or wrong, Art Fleming had taken the blame for the failure of the 1978–1979 revival of *Jeopardy!* on NBC and the feeling among Griffin's staff, even though they liked Fleming, was that they should probably try *Jeopardy!* with a new host if they wanted a network to bite. Griffin hired Alex Trebek.

The 1983 pilot for *Jeopardy!* was an odd attempt to make the show look new, but it was oddly stuck in the past. The set was designed to look like a series of giant computers. The game board, contained within a giant "monitor," still had the old-fashioned cardboard slabs with answers printed on them, as on Art Fleming's version. The contestants sat at an area decorated to resemble a keyboard, and wrote their responses to Final Jeopardy with Magic Markers on cue cards. But the show still somehow looked like a relic from the past. The networks weren't interested.

When *Wheel of Fortune* caught fire in early 1984, Griffin was strongly encouraged by his staff to introduce another game that could be paired up with *Wheel* and sold as a one-hour block. Griffin strongly resisted using *Jeopardy!* for this purpose—syndication, despite its high-profit margin, was seen as less prestigious than network television, and Griffin felt that *Jeopardy!* was "too classy" a game to sell in syndication. His staff eventually won that battle, and even compelled Griffin to shoot a second pilot with a better set than the one used in 1983. The cardboard slabs went in the trash can, replaced by a monolithic bank of thirty television monitors. The players used Telestrator pens, the kind used by sportscasters for drawing across an instant replay, for Final Jeopardy! The dollar values from Art Fleming's version were increased tenfold. *Jeopardy!* finally looked like it belonged in 1984. King World, which distributed *Wheel*, agreed to offer *Jeopardy!* to local stations too.

A Weird Promotion

Jeopardy! got the unlikeliest help promoting the new version of the series, thanks to a silly singer who was only trying to sell a single. "Weird Al" Yankovic, who had burst onto the music scene in the early 1980s by mocking top songs with absurd parodies like "My Bologna" and "Another One Rides the Bus," unveiled a parody of Greg Kihn's "Jeopardy," a song about a man venting his frustration with an untrustworthy lover. Yankovic's version was titled "I Lost on *Jeopardy!*," the saga of a disastrous day when the protagonist is a contestant on the show and draws a blank on the Daily Double, his score dipping further and further into negative numbers as he battles and loses, against a plumber and an architect, both with a Ph.D. The music video was filmed on a faithful recreation of the original NBC version's set, and included Art Fleming rolling his eyes and blowing a raspberry at Weird Al for his dismal performance, plus announcer Don Pardo reading a list of all the prizes Al wouldn't receive as a result of his meltdown.

"I Lost on *Jeopardy!*" was a hit, arguably more so than the Greg Kihn song that inspired it, and the music video in particular served as a reminder of the wonderful game that was about to hit airwaves once more. Merv Griffin loved the song so much he had Yankovic on his talk show for perform it live, thanking him afterward for helping spread the word about the impending revival.

Getting Out of Jeopardy

It would be a surprise to a viewer today to learn that *Jeopardy!* didn't look like there was a long future beyond its fall 1984 unveiling. Critics who had adored Art Fleming's version turned on the new Alex Trebek version with a vengeance. Among their key complaints: It was hosted by the former host of *High Rollers*, which was not an intellectual quiz show and therefore Alex Trebek must not be a qualified host; a number of writers also complained that the subject matter was easier than Art Fleming's version. The fact that they were kids when Art Fleming's version premiered, and that they had since completed high school, college, grad school, and worked as professional journalists for several years did not, for some reason, sufficiently explain why they suddenly found *Jeopardy!* easier than they had as children.

The contestant hopefuls who came out in droves to take *Jeopardy!*'s audition test certainly didn't think it was easy. An October 1984 article about the *Jeopardy!* audition process described the way potential contestants were given a forty-question written test, with an unstated minimum score needed in order to meet with contestant coordinators for another try-out, a mock game played similarly to the actual show. The staggering ratio given by reporter Mark Dawidziak: For every 150 people who took the written test, three would achieve passing scores and be invited to a mock game.

Trebek didn't think it was easy, either. At least not any easier than Fleming's version. "I think we're a victim of faulty memory," he said. "I don't think the questions are any easier. A lot of people remember the old show being tougher than it was. I could show you tapes, and you'd be surprised at what you thought was tough. And if you make it too difficult, people aren't going to watch."

And in key cities, *Jeopardy!* had awful time slots. During that first season, it aired at 1:30 a.m. in New York. Los Angeles initially aired it at 4:00 p.m. Alex Trebek recalled with embarrassment giving an interview to a reporter when 4:00 p.m. rolled around and they switched on a TV to watch *Jeopardy!* together. They instead saw a *Quincy* rerun. The Los Angeles station had dumped *Jeopardy!* with no notice.

Trebek remained optimistic in the face of countless comparisons to Art Fleming and the old guard. He said in those early days, "If this succeeds, one of the reasons will be Art Fleming, Don Pardo, and the old series. No doubt about that. But the old *Jeopardy!* didn't become a hit overnight. It developed over the course of twelve years. I hope we're given that chance."

In numerous cities throughout the Midwest, *Jeopardy!* was pulling in strong ratings on stations airing it at 7:00 or 7:30 p.m. King World began pulling more strongly for stations to put it in one of those time slots. Not only did the tactic work, it worked so well that it altered network television for decades. Hundreds of local TV stations across the country aired the network newscasts, *NBC Nightly News*,

Alex Trebek's natural habitat, the set of *Jeopardy!*

ABC World News Tonight, or *CBS Evening News,* at 7:00 p.m. *Jeopardy!* proved to be such a wildly successful show at 7:00 p.m. that one by one, stations caved in, and 6:30 p.m. became the standard time slot for the network news in the Eastern and Pacific time zones.

'Pardy All the Time

"I'm just a guy who comes out and does his job," Alex Trebek insisted in 2011.

But in doing that job, Alex Trebek left his fingerprints all over a game that had already secured its place in pop culture. It's a rather interesting and rare case of a game show host reinventing himself. Fans of *High Rollers* in the 1970s who remembered the loose, freewheeling Alex Trebek who hosted the show with only one hand on the steering wheel would be surprised to see the Alex Trebek of *Jeopardy!*—quieter, with no truck for tomfoolery, moving full speed ahead from clue to clue. Alex Trebek fully recognized that the star of *Jeopardy!* was, in fact, *Jeopardy!,* and his greatest strength as a master of ceremonies was in letting the game speak for itself.

35

Game Glut

They're Everywhere! They're Everywhere!

If You Were a Game Show Fan in the Fall of 1984 . . .

Y ou could turn on NBC, for *Sale of the Century, Scrabble, Wheel of Fortune,* and *Super Password.* Or you could turn on ABC, for *Family Feud* and *Trivia Trap.* Or you could turn on CBS, for *The $25,000 Pyramid, Press Your Luck, The Price is Right,* and *Body Language.* Or you could watch first-run syndication offerings, like the nighttime *Wheel of Fortune,* nighttime *Family Feud, Jeopardy!, Tic Tac Dough, The Joker's Wild, The New $100,000 Name That Tune, Anything for Money,* and *The All-New Let's Make a Deal.*

The Difference Between Night and Day

Although "prime access time" had pretty well died off by 1984, it was still a goal of many game show producers to launch a daytime game successful enough to merit a nighttime version. Because *Family Feud* changed the standards for a nighttime version, all of the 1980s nighttime games were five nights a week instead of six, which meant that if you wanted that nighttime slot, you were walking a fine line. For a nighttime show, you didn't just need a good game . . . you needed a game that people wouldn't get sick of.

In the case of *Wheel of Fortune* and *Family Feud* (although *Feud* was fading away, and would be off the air by 1985), both shows met those needs. They were good games, and their viewers were seemingly insatiable. For a time, ABC aired *Family Feud* reruns in addition to the new episodes of *Family Feud* on its daytime schedule, all as the nighttime *Family Feud* continued airing in syndication. That was fifteen episodes in a standard week, more if ABC was doing one of its occasional hour-long *Family Feud* prime-time specials.

Wheel of Fortune would drench the marketplace even beyond the standards set by *Family Feud.* It had a daytime edition, and a nighttime edition, and a syndicated newspaper feature, right alongside the crossword puzzle and the Jumble. It inspired the most successful line of slot machines in the history of Las Vegas, as well as lottery tickets and arcade machines. *Wheel of Fortune* would be the first game show adaptation for the original Nintendo Entertainment System. Vanna

White starred in made-for-TV films, and her autobiography, *Vanna Speaks*, was a best seller.

The only game show that seemed capable of giving the nighttime *Wheel of Fortune* a run for its money was *The Price is Right*. Competing against the NBC daytime *Wheel* for much of its run, *The Price is Right* had been the firm number 1 network daytime show since 1979, thanks to the effortless charm of Bob Barker, the friendly team of Barker's Beauties assisting him—Dian Parkinson, Janice Pennington, and Holly Halstrom—plus charming milquetoast announcer Johnny Olson, and a wide variety of engaging and eye-catching pricing games that wrung maximum entertainment out of the same basic concept of guessing a price.

A nighttime version of *The Price is Right* was announced for the fall of 1985, but Bob Barker just as quickly announced that he'd be sitting that one out. Barker, who had gladly hosted the nighttime version in the 1970s, when it was only once a week, strongly opined that a thirty-minute weeknight version plus an hour-long weekday version was simply "too much of a good thing." There was also the case to be made that everything about *The Price is Right* clearly worked better when the show was expanded to one hour back in 1975, and that, by nature, a version of the show shrunken back to thirty minutes was going to be weak.

Veteran host Tom Kennedy (see Chapter 22), who was hosting *Body Language* for CBS and Mark Goodson at the time, added the nighttime *Price is Right* to his workload, with tapings starting in April 1985. Kennedy would later refer to it as a frustrating experience, owing to the sheer amount of information that an emcee had to have in the back of his head to host *The Price is Right*.

Kennedy's nighttime version, which played three pricing games per night, had twenty-seven games in rotation. Each had its own set of rules, a specific spot on the stage where Kennedy and the contestant had to stand to play it, and unique language for walking the contestant and the player through each game. Kennedy handled it well, but referred to himself as "a slow learner" and later admitted he made far more mistakes during the season than he would have felt comfortable with.

In a 2003 interview, he conceded, "Barker's a genius."

Kennedy's version failed, likely for reasons that really didn't have anything to do with his performance. Syndication can be a flighty business. Although the nighttime *Price is Right* was intended to be aired in that sweet, sweet 7:00 hour, New York City saw it, or didn't see it, rather, at 2:00 a.m. Other cities were just as erratic with their scheduling, and the nighttime *Price is Right* expired after only one season.

If You Were a Game Show Fan in the Fall of 1985 . . .

You could turn on NBC and watch *Your Number's Up*, *Sale of the Century*, *Scrabble*, *Wheel of Fortune*, and *Super Password*. You could turn on ABC and watch *All Star Blitz*. You could turn on CBS and watch *The $25,000 Pyramid*, *Press Your Luck*, *The Price is Right*, and *Body Language*. Or you could watch first-run syndication offerings, like the nighttime *Wheel of Fortune*, *Jeopardy!*, the nighttime *Price is Right*, *The New Newlywed Game*, *Tic Tac Dough*, *The Joker's Wild*, *The All-New Let's Make a Deal*, *Break* *the Bank*, the nighttime *Sale of the Century, Catch Phrase, Every Second Counts*, and *Headline Chasers*.

Hang-Over

In the 1950s, NBC executives would strongly recommend to television producers that children's games should serve as a primary source of inspiration, which is how game shows like *Tic Tac Dough* and *Concentration* originally came into existence. Thirty years later, that mindset had seemingly remained, because Hangman was absolutely everywhere in the 1980s.

There was, of course, the grand dame of Hangman game shows, *Wheel of Fortune*, but funnily, in 1984, Chuck Woolery, the show's original host, re-emerged with a new spin on Hangman that made use of a years-old title: *Scrabble*.

The classic crossword-based board game, introduced in 1938, would sell its one hundred millionth copy by the end of the 1980s. Scrabble tournaments had become annual events in multiple locations; a designated Scrabble players' diction-ary, and as of July 2, 1984, a Scrabble game show. The game show had an unusual origin story. Exposure Unlimited, a firm that acquired prizes for game shows, secured the television rights to Scrabble from game manufacturer Selchow and Righter. Exposure Unlimited then closed a deal with Reg Grundy Productions, an Australian-based group which had taken its first steps in American television the previous year with the new version of *Sale of the Century*.

Scrabble had name recognition and was highly popular, but a game that's fun to watch is not necessarily a game that's fun to play, and *Scrabble* was the quintes-sential example of that. So, the TV version, despite its name, really wasn't going to be Scrabble.

The show's executive producer, Robert Noah, candidly told a reporter, "Board games do not lend themselves to TV. [The game show format] is a shotgun marriage."

Reg Grundy Productions concocted a game that was fundamentally Hangman, but with the trappings of Scrabble. Contestants viewed a Scrabble board and were shown blank spaces representing a word. Woolery read a clue to the answer, usually in the form of a misleading pun ("A nine-letter word: People are always talking behind his back") and the two contestants would draw Scrabble tiles that would reveal either letters in the word or "Stoppers," letters that weren't in the word and would cost a player a turn, and this continued until one of the players solved the word ("CHAUFFEUR"). The pink-and-blue-colored bonus squares on the Scrabble board offered cash on the new version, if a player solved a word immediately after placing the proper letter in that space.

Scrabble not only took a popular old board game and spun it into an exciting new game, it put a very fresh look onto the old favorite. *Scrabble* was an ornate presentation; the game board was a 12′ × 12′ × 12′ cube that rotated as the game progressed; inside that cube were thirty-three slide projectors, a video projector, light boxes, and more than four hundred neon tubes. And all that was primarily for the benefit of just the contestants and the studio audience; the home viewers

Three years after leaving *Wheel of Fortune* under acrimonious circumstances, Chuck Woolery had reason to smile. He returned with a new game show, and audiences loved it.

kept track of the game primarily through state-of-the-art computer graphics and animation superimposed on the screen. For perspective, numerous other game shows were still printing their graphics on paper and then fixing a camera on the paper. *Scrabble* also made use of arguably more sound effects than any other game show. A total of sixteen unique noises accentuated the game: a "ping" when a contestant selected a tile, a "worble-worble" as a letter was inserted into a word, and a video game-inspired "POW" when a Stopper cost a player a chance to win.

ABC had its own version of Hangman . . . and its own ersatz version of *Hollywood Squares*, too. In fact, they were the same show. *All-Star Blitz* was created by Merrill Heatter, the same man who had whipped up *Hollywood Squares* twenty years earlier. At the show's peak, Heatter and partner Bob Quigley (who died in 1981) sold the rights to *Squares* to Filmways, which meant that when the original version of *Squares* went off the air, Heatter and Quigley lost control over it.

Heatter smartly went about creating game show formats that were as close as he could come to *Squares* without being sued by Filmways. He switched his inspiration from tic-tac-toe to another children's game, Dots and Boxes, and used it to create *Battlestars* for NBC, in which contestants captured the dots surrounding a star's triangular "battle station" by agreeing or disagreeing correctly with the star's answer. For ABC, Heatter expanded on the idea by having the stars sit underneath the grid of boxes instead of inside it. The contestants again had to agree or disagree with the stars' answers, this time with the goal of revealing hidden letters in the grid forming a Hangman-style puzzle. The *Blitz* twist on Hangman was that there were always exactly six boxes in the puzzle, but no consistency about how many letters were hidden in each box; some hid just one, others hid up to five. *All Star Blitz* lasted only six months.

Elsewhere in 1985, Wink Martindale left *Tic Tac Dough* after seven seasons to host a show of his own creation. Wink was reading *The Los Angeles Times* one morning and came up with an idea for a game.

"There was a banner headline," he explained that year. "And I thought, if I took some of those letters out, could I still come up with the headline? I tried it on my wife when she got up and she said, 'I don't know what the headline says, but that would make a great game show.' I said, 'I'm glad you said that because it's exactly what I had in mind.'"

Wink was able to sell the show into first-run syndication through King World television distribution, the same firm that distributed *Wheel of Fortune* and *Jeopardy!* The heads of King World had previously been the salesmen at Colbert Television Sales, in charge of selling *Tic Tac Dough* to local stations, before quitting to start their own firm. As creator and host of *Headline Chasers*, Wink stood to make $30 million during the 1985–1986 TV season.

Headline Chasers pitted married couples against each other. The couples were shown incomplete headlines based on actual news events; letters were gradually added until one couple rang in and solved the headline, and that couple could answer follow-up trivia questions about the news event for extra money. *Headline Chasers* failed; syndication is a tricky business, and despite aligning himself with King World, Martindale found himself at the mercy of local station managers' scheduling. In some cities, *Headline Chasers* aired in direct competition with *Wheel of Fortune* or *Jeopardy! Headline Chasers* went off the air after only one season.

Martindale remembers, "I wanted the material to be somewhat difficult, because we were part of the same company that was putting *Jeopardy!* on the air, and because the material on the show was based on actual events. We were a history game show. When the ratings were flagging, I went on a promotional tour to try to drum up interest. In Miami, I met with a station manager who asked me if I could dumb down the show a little bit. And the moment he asked me that, I knew my show was doomed. Not a good feeling."

Lorimar Telepictures attempted to flatten *Wheel*'s tires with their own version of Hangman, and for added good measure, they opened the Lorimar purse strings quite a bit to offer the richest prize on television. In 1986, they introduced *The $1,000,000 Chance of a Lifetime*. Based on a rejected 1979 pilot called *The Letter Machine*, Jim Lange hosted as married couples played two layers of Hangman, first having to solve a single word, then having to solve a much larger puzzle for which the single word served as a clue. The bonus round had the contestants choosing a category and having to guess six words in that category in sixty seconds or less. If a couple won the bonus round three consecutive days, the payoff was $50,000 a year for the next twenty years.

The cash prize alone was enough to entice viewers to tune in for the opening week, which actually did the unthinkable and topped *Wheel* in the ratings. But viewers lost interest quickly, and the show just faded away after a season and a half. A cash prize only carries a game so far. Meanwhile, Merv Griffin was offered a multi-million-dollar chance of a lifetime

Who's the man with the fistful of dollars? It's Jim Lange on *The $1,000,000 Chance of a Lifetime.*
Photo courtesy of Zane Enterprises

himself, and on May 5, 1986, he sold *Wheel of Fortune* and *Jeopardy!* to Coca-Cola Television for $250 million.

If You Were a Game Show Fan in the Fall of 1986 . . .

You could turn on NBC and watch *Sale of the Century*, *Wheel of Fortune*, *Scrabble*, and *Super Password*. Or you could turn to ABC and watch *Double Talk*. Or you could turn to CBS and watch *The $25,000 Pyramid*, *Card Sharks*, and *The Price is Right*. Or you could watch first-run syndication offerings, like the nighttime *Wheel of Fortune*, *Jeopardy!*, the nighttime *Card Sharks*, *The New Hollywood Squares*, *The $100,000 Pyramid*, *Cross-Wits*, *The New Newlywed Game*, *The All-New Dating Game*, and *Split Second*.

USA! USA! USA!

The 1980s saw a new avenue opening up for game show producers. Cable television, little more than an experiment for most of the 1970s, had become a viable entity in the 1980s, not just for new programming, but for game show reruns.

For decades, the prevailing mindset, among network executives and even some game show producers, was that nobody would want to watch reruns of game shows, on the logic that there's no fun in watching a game knowing who will win. Never mind that the average rerun viewer knows every time that the Vitameatavegimin will make Lucy drunk but they watch anyway.

With that attitude, game show tapes were indiscriminately erased and reused after broadcast. Many of Goodson-Todman's prime-time game show broadcasts survived on kinescopes, but nearly all of their daytime output up until the 1970s was gone. Goodson-Todman was actually the first production outfit to figure out that game show reruns might be a profitable venture; the company saved the tapes from the final year of *Password* on CBS and sold the reruns to local stations successfully for four years. The final year of *You Don't Say!* made its way into reruns too. Jack Barry sold reruns of *The Joker's Wild* into syndication after CBS canceled the series, and the reruns were so popular that Barry switched out the reruns for new episodes a year later.

Those were the exceptions to the rule, however. Game show erasure continued into the next decade, until cable channels began signing on the air and realized they needed shows to fill all that precious airtime.

The two channels leading the chairs were CBN (Christian Broadcasting Network, later known as The Family Channel and then ABC Family) and USA Network. Christian Broadcasting Network offered reruns of *Treasure Hunt*, *Face the Music*, and *Blockbusters*, among others. USA Network would, over the years, offer a sizable menu of game show favorites, like *The Gong Show*, *Liars Club*, *Chain Reaction*, *Let's Make a Deal*, and *Name That Tune*.

Beginning in 1986, USA Network teamed up with Canada's Global Television Network to produce original game shows, to air in both countries on their respective channels. There was *Love Me, Love Me Not* with Ross Shafer, in which contestants tried to "capture" panelists of the opposite sex by guessing if the stories they told were true or false. USA and Global also dusted off the 1970s favorite *Jackpot* with host Mike Darrow. Original *Jackpot* host Geoff Edwards already had a gig of his own, hosting *The New Chain Reaction*.

Sande Stewart, who helped his father Bob produce *Jackpot* and *The New Chain Reaction*, says, "We had a low budget for both shows. There were two things that helped us get the most for our money. One was that USA and Global agreed to split costs; the other thing that helped us get the most bang for our buck was that we taped the shows in Canada instead of in the USA, which meant we were only obligated to pay out the cash prizes we were announcing in Canadian dollars, and because of the exchange rate at the time, that meant that when we had a $10,000 winner, we were only paying out $8,000 U. S., and after a while, that adds up."

Wink Martindale had concocted his game *Headline Chasers* by thumbing through a newspaper. Thumbing through a magazine gave him the inspiration for his next game. He happened across an advertisement depicting license plates from all fifty states, which led to a train of thought about some of the distinctive vanity license plates he had seen. He created a game called *License 2 Steal* and joined forces with his former *Tic Tac Dough* bosses, Jack Barry and Dan Enright Productions, to sell the show to USA and Global. Under the new title *Bumper Stumpers*, Wink Martindale had another hit. Canadian newsman Al DuBois hosted the show in which contestants were shown a vanity license plate and had to decipher it after being told who it supposedly belonged to (for example, the license plate "KCNO" belonged to an odds-maker; the contestants had to figure out that KCNO had to be pronounced "Casino").

If You Were a Game Show Fan in the Fall of 1987 . . .

You could turn on NBC and watch *Sale of the Century*, *Classic Concentration*, *Wheel of Fortune*, *Win Lose or Draw*, *Super Password*, and *Scrabble*. You could turn to CBS to *The $25,000 Pyramid*, *Card Sharks*, and *The Price is Right*. You could turn to ABC and be sorely disappointed. The network got out of the game show business entirely . . . an omen, of sorts. Or you could turn to first-run syndication offerings, like the nighttime *Wheel of Fortune*, *Jeopardy!*, *Hollywood Squares*, *The New Newlywed Game*, *The $100,000 Pyramid*, and *High Rollers*.

An Old-Fashioned Revival Meeting

While the late 1980s offered a gallimaufry of games, a large number of them were recycled concepts. In 1987 alone, *Squares*, *Pyramid*, *Jeopardy!*, *Concentration*, *Card Sharks*, *Password*, *High Rollers*, and an extremely short-lived NBC revival of *Blockbusters* were reigniting engines built in the 1960s and 1970s. Mark Goodson Productions, meanwhile, had virtually ceased developing new game show formats, building most of its business around the properties that were established hits. In 1987, Goodson told a reporter that the company was working on a new version of

Wink Martindale hosts *High Rollers*. In the late 1980s, everything old was new again, and many TV game shows, *High Rollers* among them, were updates of previous shows.

What's My Line? Trade publications printed advertisements for *Match Game '87*, set to premiere in the fall.

In a 1987 syndicated special, *The Game Show Biz*, Art James zeroed in on the reason that genre was successful, yet seemingly uninspired. As he explained, "In the last fifteen years, there have only really been three new successful formats. *The Price is Right*, *Wheel of Fortune*, and *Family Feud*."

Game shows in general are low-budget offerings, which means it's easy for networks and producers to turn a profit. But a new idea could be a bust, so reviving even a modest success from past years was more likely to generate maximum profits for the investment. Case in point, Mark Goodson was, in fact, developing a new *Family Feud*. Goodson went in an unconventional direction initially, considering football great Joe Namath to host the new version. Instead, the job went to Ray Combs, an up-and-coming stand-up comedian widely gaining a reputation in show business for being the best warm-up man in the business, coming out and performing for the audience before tapings and during stopdowns for virtually every hit sitcom of the late 1980s.

If You Were a Game Show Fan in the Fall of 1988 . . .

You could turn on NBC and watch *Sale of the Century*, *Classic Concentration*, *Wheel of Fortune*, *Win Lose or Draw*, *Super Password*, and *Scrabble*. You could turn to CBS to *The $25,000 Pyramid*, *Card Sharks*, and *The Price is Right*. If you had cable, you were a happy viewer . . .

Kids' Stuff

One of the complaints that executives have had about game shows for years is that they attract too old an audience. Younger is better. When Lin Bolen took over NBC daytime in 1972, she complained that *Concentration* and *Jeopardy!* skewed too old. When Fred Silverman wiped out three game shows in 1980, it was because he felt game shows attracted too old an audience. But in the late 1980s, the two capable networks most aggressively targeting young viewers used game shows to do exactly that. And they succeeded.

Nickelodeon, which had emerged in 1979, approached building its schedule as if for any other network, just one that happened to target kids. In late 1985, Nickelodeon executives and producers looked at their schedule to see if anything was missing. Their assessment: the channel didn't have any game shows.

Geoffrey Darby, a produce r who, according to one newspaper writer, looked like a big kid himself, teamed up with a young NYU graduate, Michael Klinghoffer, and co-created a game called *Double Dare* (having no connection to the Goodson-Todman game show from a decade earlier). A classmate of Klinghoffer's, a film and television major named Dana Calderwood, came onboard to direct. Marc Summers, a young former writer for *Truth or Consequences* who had since become a warm-up man for *Star Search*, got the job hosting, beating out an impressive field of candidates that included Dana Carvey and Soupy Sales.

Summers says, "Timing is everything. I was thirty-four when I was hired but I looked like a teenager. And that had been a problem for me for years. I had been auditioning for such a long time to host game shows, but conventional wisdom at the time was that you wanted your host to have crow's feet around the eyes and some gray around the temples. Nickelodeon was looking for a host that kids could connect with, and I guess I looked more like an older brother than an authority figure. It was really the first time that the way I looked had helped me instead of hindering me."

Dana Calderwood remembers, "*Double Dare* was everybody's first job in the post they were assigned to. It was the first show that Michael Klinghoffer produced. It was the first show I directed. It was the first television show that our announcer, John Harvey, worked on. It was the first show that Marc Summers hosted. And I think that gave the show some extra energy. We all wanted to show what we were capable of."

For production facilities, Nickelodeon made an off-the-wall choice, opting not to tape the show in Los Angeles or New York. To attract "real kids," the show opted to tape in the studios of WHYY-TV in Philadelphia, Pennsylvania.

Summers says, "Taping in Philadelphia was the best decision anybody made in the development of *Double Dare*. I honestly believe it's the big reason the show was a hit. Taping in Philadelphia meant that we didn't have actors, we didn't have 'professional children.' We didn't have what I call 'Disney Channel children.' We had real kids in all shapes, all sizes, sometimes crooked teeth, sometimes acne. Kids across the country watched *Double Dare* and saw themselves."

Although the show had been developed to fill that supposed game show gap that Nickelodeon found in their schedule, hopes weren't high. Marc Summers admitted that he was expecting to tape sixty-five episodes and then be done with the show forever, but instead, *Double Dare* proved to be the highest-rated show in the short history of Nickelodeon.

Touted as the game show where "getting sloppy can win you a mess of cash," *Double Dare* pitted pairs of kids against each other in a battle of trivia. You could opt not to answer a question, instead daring your opponents to answer, which doubled the value of the question. The team could double-dare you back, which quadrupled the original value.

And if you truly didn't know the correct answer at that point, you could try to earn the money with a physical challenge, a messy stunt played against the clock, like smearing peanut butter and jelly on a pancake, flipping it over your shoulder without looking so your partner can try to catch it on a plate (Marc Summers stood back and held an umbrella over his head while that one was played). One of the most famous challenges, "Pie in Your Pants," had one teammate wearing clownish baggy pants, with the partner trying to toss pies into the pants from a distance.

The winners of the day contended with the Obstacle Course, eight rapid-fire stunts all to be completed in sixty seconds or less, with a prize awarded for each one completed. There was Pick-It, in which the kids had to find the flag hidden inside a massive nose (created because the show reasoned that kids just automatically find body parts funny), and the One-Ton Human Hamster Wheel, where a contestant had to climb inside and turn it until six lights on the side had illuminated. That one was the brainchild of Nickelodeon director of creative planning

Millions of kids wanted to take the physical challenge, but here's a lucky pair that got their chance at it: the contestants on *Double Dare*, hosted by Marc Summers.

Dee La Duke, who admitted that running in a giant hamster wheel had been a strange little fantasy of hers as a child, and as an adult, *Double Dare* became her excuse to actually pursue it.

Then there was The Tank, a large plexiglass container that the kids would have to wade through from one end to the other to capture a flag. Sometimes, The Tank was filled with balloons, which wafted and burst as the kids rushed through; other times, it was filled with Styrofoam packing peanuts. And during one very ambitious week, it was filled with baked beans. The beans were poured into the tank to the very top, and then used through five days of tapings, even as the beans were exposed to five days' worth of open air in the large studio, and left to simmer under the hot studio lights. By the end of the week, the show's crew quickly realized that cleaning out The Tank this time around was a job they weren't prepared for. They had to hire a professional septic tank cleaner, who told everybody after he was finished that removing all the baked beans had been the grossest job he had ever done.

Dana Calderwood says, "From the very beginning, I thought this show was going to be a lot of fun to work on. The whole basis of the show was a series of meetings where we would sit around and ask, 'As a kid, what would be the most fun thing to do?' Having a food fight without getting in trouble, trashing a room, making a mess. And that's what we delivered."

But between all the ransacking, there were trivia questions. Even the trivia questions were strategically written to draw in kids. *Double Dare* asked things that kids would know—that doesn't mean the questions were easy. To the contrary, a number of parents looking in would go cross-eyed trying to ferret out the correct answers. But that was the point. The questions were easy *if* you were a kid.

Calderwood says, "We asked questions about rock music, video games, Disney characters, slang words. We asked things that your average adult, adults who didn't work on a kids' game show, wouldn't know. The whole point of that was we wanted parents to feel left out. And we wanted their kids to feel like the show was a secret clubhouse. There have been dozens of kids' game shows since then and that's a detail that almost all of them miss. When we changed the show to *Family Double Dare*, we made it a point not to change that question style, because it presented these constant scenarios where the parents depended on the kids to come up with the correct answers, and we loved that."

Although the show was ambitious, it languished with a basic cable TV budget in the mid-1980s. One episode, an "all-holiday special," was produced with only a $200 budget for set decorations. With the show struggling to make maximum mess from minimal money, Casio came knocking with an eye-popping offer: $1 million, in exchange for having Marc Summers open every physical challenge by saying, "Let's put thirty seconds on the Casio Clock!" To the show's dismay, Nickelodeon rejected the offer.

While the staff certainly noticed their lack of funds, viewers certainly didn't. Night after night, they tuned in, not just kids, but college students, who got hooked because the show's time slot happened to coincide with meal time at most dormitories.

Calderwood says, "As a kid, I watched *Rocky and Bullwinkle*, which was ostensibly a kids' show, but they would throw in jokes that clearly went over their target audience's heads. And even as a kid, I would say to myself, 'I know that was a joke, I don't get it now, but I can't wait until I'm old enough to get it.' The way we manifested that idea on *Double Dare* was multiple-choice questions. Every fourth or fifth question was a multiple-choice question, and the third choice was always a really bad joke that kids wouldn't get. Every once in a while, it would actually trip up the kids. We once asked the question 'What is kohlrabi?' And one of the kids actually guessed that the correct answer was 'C.' The act of stealing fossil fuels.'"

A Remote Chance

When Nickelodeon's target audience was enamored by *Double Dare*, another Viacom-owned cable channel, MTV, took note. MTV executives came to a *Double Dare* taping, liked what they saw, and decided that their channel needed a game show, too. Nick at Nite had launched in 1985 and found an audience for TV nostalgia right away, which convinced MTV that television trivia was the way to go. In 1987, the channel unleashed *Remote Control*, an off-the-wall quiz show hosted by Ken Ober. The show's premise was that Ober still lived with his parents and built a game show in his basement, inviting a neighborhood girl, Marisol Massey, to be the show's model, and a buddy, cement mixer-voiced Colin Quinn, to announce.

Howard Blumenthal, identified in the show's credits as "High-Priced Consultant," describes the origins of what he and MTV called the anti-game show: "MTV wanted to start doing more than music videos. I was brought in to look at three ideas for shows that MTV was considering. Joe Davola, a producer at MTV, really, really wanted the network to develop a game show. *Remote Control* was one of the ideas I looked at. And that was the one I went with."

Susan Bolles, charged with designing a set, looked at MTV's target audience, teenagers, and gave them a set pulled straight from their world: a basement rec room, with Barcaloungers, a big-screen TV manufactured by Zenith (a company chosen by Blumenthal because they were considered "old" at the time, and he thought it might be funny if the show looked outdated), and even a washer-and-dryer combo. Bolles's final set design was ridiculous, yet impressive; it even provoked the imagination of the show's staff. Ideas for categories and recurring characters were spawned by merely looking at the world she created.

A host of potential hosts were considered, including Danny Bonaduce, comedian Kevin Meaney, and magician Amazing Jonathan. But the job went to comic Ken Ober, whose delivery was so dry and low-key that he genuinely came off as a slacker who lived in his parents' basement.

Dana Calderwood says, "There's a problem that you usually have when you hire a comedian to host a game show. They get how to interact with contestants, they get how to pull a laugh out of the situations, but generally, comedians forget to play up the horse race aspect of the game. Ken didn't have that problem. Ken would emphasize how close the scores were; he would get excited when the contestant in third place gave a correct answer. So, you had this host who had a real spark, who was funny, and creative, and he was a good host. He knew how to make the game exciting."

But the true star may have been announcer Colin Quinn, whom Blumenthal calls the unsung hero of the series. "Colin Quinn was hired first," he recalls. "And he just *got* that show. Before we had a set, before we had a show, Colin managed to lock into exactly what we wanted and bring it to us. And he wound up giving so much of himself that his spirit really was intertwined in everything we did once the show went on the air. He was wonderful."

Director Dana Calderwood says, "We all expected Colin to be a big star. He was so funny offscreen, completely fearless, and just a genuine guy. He was fantastic."

Remote Control appeared to be doomed before it even started. In keeping with the show's premise of Ober living in his parents' basement, and the notion that the whole show was a nod to old television, *Remote Control* was originally conceived to be part game show, part sitcom. Every episode would have a title and a plot. For example, one episode would have Colin suspecting model Marisol Massey of stealing from the prize closet, a story that would unfold as the contestants played the game. When focus groups were completely confused by the show's pilot, the sitcom elements were eliminated, and it was just a straight game show—albeit one that took place in the Ober family's basement.

Contestants on *Remote Control* found themselves thrust into what Blumenthal called a glued-together game. Virtually the entire staff offered input and got ideas on the show to some degree. The end result was a wildly bizarre array of challenges for the players to navigate. They would channel-surf around nine channels in each round, battling such categories as "Dead or Alive" (Ober named a celebrity who had faded into obscurity, contestants had to guess if that star was still alive), "Brady Physics" (difficult science questions, framed as *Brady Bunch* storylines), and "Public Opinion Channel" (sample question: "What's the worst thing about getting sand in your bathing suit?" Any plausible answer is worth ten points).

Some of the categories were games within a game—Survey Says was a category that ripped off *Family Feud*, complete with a slapdash gameboard that borrowed heavily from the genuine article. In Beat the Bishop, a clergyman did a fast-stepping walk through the studio, with the contestants trying to solve a math problem before he had walked a complete lap around the studio. There was even a channel where contestants tried to identify a celebrity from viewing a recent X-ray. What kind of game show *is* this?

Howard Blumenthal recalls standing in the control room and watching the first taping. Everyone looked at each other in bewilderment, and Blumenthal said, "Either this is going to be a massive hit, or none of us will ever work in television again. I can't tell which."

Happily, it was the former. *Remote Control* became the highest-rated show on MTV, even introducing a national touring version for a time, with Ober and Quinn performing stand-up between rounds of an actual game played onstage. Teenagers couldn't get enough of it. Meanwhile, their younger siblings flocked to Nickelodeon, and *Double Dare* remained perched on that channel's throne. Young people will watch game shows. You just have to invite them.

36

Changing Fortunes

For Every Flow, An Ebb

NBC Cleans House

In 1987, NBC's daytime lineup included three straight hours of game shows, carrying over from the morning into the early afternoon. Just two years later, the network's landscape looked starkly different, with one or two shows at a time fading away.

On March 24, 1989, NBC bid adieu to *Sale of the Century*. The game show that had heralded the genre's comeback at the beginning of 1983 was disappearing; the series came to an end on an intentionally undecorated center stage, looking as if Sale got a head start on moving out of the building. Summer Bartholomew opened the show with a warm goodbye and a thank you to NBC. Jim Perry wrapped up with the show's final cash and prize tabulation—they had given away more than $8 million during almost two thousand episodes in the past six years. Viewers on the East Coast actually missed Perry's goodbye because of a news bulletin—the Exxon-Valdez oil spill in Alaska.

That same day, Bert Convy signed off from *Super Password* after four-and-a-half years. *Super Password* had enjoyed a stunningly long run given its terrible time slot: noon on the East Coast. Because many NBC affiliates chose to air local newscasts in that time slot, the noon show on the network schedule didn't air at all in many cities. Previously, *Just Men!*, *The New Battlestars*, *Go*, and *Hot Potato* had all come and gone in a matter of months. *Super Password*, on the other hand, was able to strike an unusual deal in many of the cities that aired noon newscasts—independent stations would air *Super Password* instead in those cities, and *Super Password* held on far longer than the rest as a result.

Bert Convy emotionally promised the audience that he'd "be brave" for the final show. Betty White, in a fit of pique, destroyed the prop used for the show's daily Cashword bonus (a portion of the game that she openly disliked), and Convy closed the show by dedicating the series to Betty. Because of her marriage to original Password emcee Allen Ludden, Convy said that it was "Betty's show."

Wheel of Fortune was the next casualty, on June 30, 1989; if NBC had kept it on the network just two months longer, it would have become the longest-running game show in NBC history, beating the run of the original *Concentration*. Daytime *Wheel of Fortune* had begun crumbling in January of 1989 after the departure of

Pat Sajak, who was giving up the daytime version to focus on *The Pat Sajak Show*, his late-night talk show on CBS.

Sajak continued on the nighttime version, but was replaced on daytime *Wheel* by a most unlikely candidate, former San Diego Chargers place kicker Rolf Benirschke. Benirschke himself thought he had done a poor audition—he even said so on his first episode!—but Merv Griffin often made unconventional casting choices for his hosts and had faith in a newcomer. Ratings for daytime *Wheel* slid, however, and the show was off the network by June. It was actually picked up by CBS, which by this point had canceled *Card Sharks* and its replacement, *Now You See It*. For CBS daytime *Wheel*, a more conventional choice for host, Bob Goen (formerly of the short-lived games *Perfect Match* and *Blackout*), took over the show.

Next on the chopping block: *Win, Lose or Draw*. The show had only been on the network for two years, but in that brief period, *Win, Lose or Draw* had left an amazing pop-culture footprint. The game achieved fad status for a time. The nighttime version (hosted by Bert Convy, who developed the show along with Burt Reynolds) was popular; the NBC version, hosted by Vicki Lawrence, was successful, too. The Disney Channel even introduced a kids' version hosted by Marc Price ("Skippy" from *Family Ties*) that ran concurrently, for a whopping fifteen episodes of *Win, Lose, or Draw* each week. The home games sold well, too. All of them—the regular edition, the Party Edition, the Travel Edition, the Nintendo version, the computer version, and even the specially marked boxes of Raisin Bran that had smaller home games packaged in them. But just as quickly, the novelty of the picture charades game seemed to wear off. The daytime show disappeared in the summer of '89. The nighttime version and the teenagers' version ended a year later.

Scrabble hung on a bit longer, disappearing on March 23, 1990. An attempt at relaunching the show in syndication for the fall didn't come to fruition.

What is Loni Anderson trying to draw? Only Bert Convy knows for sure on *Win, Lose or Draw*. *Photo courtesy of Zane Enterprises*

Sale of the Century was replaced by a soap opera, *Generations*. *Super Password* was replaced by nothing; NBC finally took the hint and stopped scheduling the noon timeslot altogether, ceding it to local affiliates. *Wheel of Fortune* was replaced by *Golden Girls* reruns. *Win, Lose or Draw* was replaced by reruns of *227*. *Scrabble* was replaced by *The Marsha Warfield Show*. When one game show went away, another one no longer followed. Game shows were on the wane, but it looked like it might only be a temporary condition. A wave of new game shows was slated for the summer and fall of 1990.

ABC in Its Prime

ABC elected to introduce a one-hour block of Saturday-night game shows in the summer of 1990, one a familiar show and one a new entry. *Super Jeopardy!*, with Alex Trebek hosting, was a thirteen-week tournament welcoming back many of the champions of previous seasons, and even a champion from Art Fleming's tenure, with the ultimate winner collecting $250,000.

The other game was *Monopoly*, a game show-ized version of the iconic board game. There had been numerous attempts made to get a Monopoly game show on the air for at least three years, including a stunningly complicated pilot hosted by Marc Summers that was produced and rejected in 1987.

Summers remembers, "It would take me about seven pages to explain the rules of the game for the *Monopoly* pilot in 1987. Going into that pilot, I already knew it was going to fail, because the best game shows of all time have all been, 'Ask question, give answer, get your check, the end.' The version that made it on the air improved on the format of my pilot a little bit but not enough. It was still too much."

Merv Griffin got his hands on the game and drastically altered it to a game played in two rounds. In Round 1, players claimed properties on the Monopoly board by solving crossword clues. In the second half of the game, dice were rolled and a neon light circled the board; wherever the light landed, the owner of that property had a chance to win the value of the property by solving another clue.

The original pilot, hosted by Peter Tomarken, didn't have the neon light circling the board. Instead, a female dwarf was adorned in a top hat and tuxedo and circled the board. Peter Tomarken complained to producers about the dehumanizing treatment he felt the dwarf was being subjected to—chief among his objections: producers had told him explicitly not to speak directly to the dwarf, which seemingly reduced her to the role of giant prop.

When Griffin failed to sell the show into syndication, he successfully paired it up with the *Super Jeopardy!* tournament and offered it to ABC for their prime-time block. With Tomarken out of the picture, Griffin made another famously unconventional pick for master of ceremonies, Mike Reilly, a former *Jeopardy!* champion and contestant on Tomarken's unaired pilot who was working as a waiter when Griffin called him and asked if he'd come in and audition for host.

Michael King, CEO of King World, which was helping Griffin produce *Super Jeopardy!* and *Monopoly*, told the *New York Times*, "Game shows are a very effective way to counter-program what's in the marketplace, and ABC has learned through

America's Funniest Home Videos and *20/20* that you don't have to have a sitcom in prime-time to work."

That was true, but Ted Harbert, ABC's executive vice president of prime-time programming, told the newspaper, "The experiment is going well. The good news is it does represent an improvement for us in the time period, [but] the best success still comes from situation comedies, dramas, and occasional reality shows like *America's Funniest Home Videos*."

The ratings were good, but not good enough, and more importantly, the ratings didn't stay there. Particularly in the case of *Monopoly* (which really was a flawed and convoluted game), viewership declined precipitously week by week over the thirteen-week commitment, and when the summer run was over, it was clear that neither show was coming back for another go.

Over at CBS, another attempt at getting a game show in prime-time ended before it even started. The network attempted to counter-program ABC's game block with a prime-time version of *The Price is Right*. The network had presented *The Price is Right Special* on Thursday nights in 1986, but the summer version of the daytime classic fizzled against reruns of *The Cosby Show* and *Family Ties*. But the bigger issue, for Goodson, was that when CBS had asked for a prime-time *Price is Right* in 1986, they had given Goodson so much notice that the show began working on ways to make *The Price is Right Special* a little more special. Glitzier set pieces were assembled to give the show more pizzazz. Some of the pricing games got totally rebuilt and refurbished sets. The prize coordinators rounded up grander goodies to give away. But in 1990, Goodson candidly told CBS that they hadn't given him enough notice to prepare anything worthy of prime-time television.

Tic Tac is Back!

"In a moment . . . the game that intrigued a nation . . . " Those were the imposing words with which announcer Larry Van Nuys reintroduced an old favorite in the fall of 1990. The game would have some familiar personnel behind the scenes. Executive producer Dan Enright was still running the show, with the questions being written by Scott Wyant, a former champion from the 1970s version of *Tic Tac Dough*. Henry Mancini even came onboard to compose a dynamic new theme.

But there was a startling change in front of the camera. Wink Martindale, who was synonymous with the show during the 1970s and 1980s, would not be hosting the new version. The new host was actor Patrick Wayne, the son of John Wayne who, like his father, had amassed a long résumé of roles in western and war flicks. But in 1980, he had served as master of ceremonies for *The Monte Carlo Show*, a syndicated variety program taped in Monaco, and he found performing as himself to be far more enjoyable. He began actively seeking work as a game show host during that decade—he nearly became the host of *Card Sharks*, but lost out in the final round of auditions to the more experienced Bob Eubanks. But in 1990, he finally secured his dream role of game show hosting.

Being a game show host may have seemed like a strange aspiration for someone with the pedigree of a legendary A-lister, but Wayne told reporter Ron Miller that his father's level of fame, and the effect it had on his life, affected his own career aspirations.

He said, "It's something I always struggled with—watching my father and realizing his life was so restricted. Later, when I was old enough to learn what it was all about, I had to go back and figure out how to deal with it."

The new *Tic Tac Dough* failed. The show became something of a running joke in the years to come among game show fans for all the things they found wrong with it—chief among them, the bonus round included a rapping dragon, an amazingly awful "special" week pitting divorced couples against each other, and Wayne's own performance—an actor by trade, he often came off as an actor playing the role of a game show host—were a few of the problems hampering *Tic Tac Dough*. In the syndication business, most programs that get picked up are guaranteed a full season on the air. *Tic Tac Dough* flopped so badly it was gone in thirteen weeks.

Wildly Different

Richard Kline, formerly the director for most of Barry and Enright's game shows in their '70s and '80s heyday, had left the company in 1984 to launch his own production company, Kline and Friends. As Dan Enright revved up *Tic Tac Dough* for its ill-fated return, Kline and Friends joined forces with Jack Barry's sons to mount a new version of Barry and Enright's other signature show, *The Joker's Wild*.

A small plaque on the giant slot machine dedicated the series to Jack Barry, but the format was actually drastically different from the game Barry created. Jokers and categories no longer appeared in the windows. There were now various monetary amounts in the windows; the third window contained a Joker which could triple the money in the other windows if it appeared. Contestants were now asked rapid-fire "definitions" and had to supply the correct answer to collect the money, but as long as the answers were correct, they would keep getting definition after definition until they finally made a mistake, bringing an end to their turn.

The monumental change to the game actually came in response to *Jeopardy!*'s enduring popularity. The show fed viewers questions and answers at a rapid-fire pace, sixty-one per half-hour, and Kline's team reasoned that the sheer amount of content was what drew in so many viewers. *Joker* was drastically overhauled to maximize the amount of Q&A in each episode.

In search of a new host (Jack Barry died in 1984; Barry's replacement, Bill Cullen, was terminally ill when the new *Joker* was in development and had died by the time production started), Kline and Friends found Pat Finn, a rookie host who made friends in high places.

Finn told *Gannett News Service*, "When they were replacing Pat Sajak as host of the daytime version of *Wheel*, I was one of the two finalists, along with Rolf Benirschke. I actually taped an audition show, with players, Vanna White, and everything. Of course, Rolf got the job, but Vanna introduced me to her agent, who later recommended me for the *Joker's Wild* job."

The new format didn't appeal to viewers, who strongly preferred the old *Joker's Wild*. A marketing survey conducted during the series found that *The Joker's Wild* had shockingly strong name recognition: 95 percent of respondents said that they had either watched or at least heard of the original *Joker's Wild*. When ratings for the new version weren't up to snuff, the format was changed to something of a middle ground between the old version and the new; they had categories and Jokers on all the wheels now, with the dollar value being determined by how many of each appeared on each spin. The contestants still got rapid-fire definitions in each category, with only a wrong answer ending their progress.

It was all for naught, though. The new *Joker* outlived *Tic Tac Dough*, but not by much. It was done after a single season.

A Challenging Endeavor

Producer Ron Greenberg, whose résumé included the early years of *Jeopardy!*, *The Joker's Wild*, and *Tic Tac Dough*, had found some success as an independent producer in the '60s and '70s, creating a quiz for NBC called *The Who, What or Where Game* with Art James. In 1989, he took a job at Dick Clark Productions for the opportunity to pitch and produce a new version of *The Who, What or Where Game*.

Pat Finn in front of the Joker Machine on *The Joker's Wild*. Viewers adored the classic version, but this drastic overhaul was a bit too much for them.

Dick Clark hosted the pilot himself and collaborated with Buena Vista (Disney's television distribution wing) to distribute the new version for syndication. This revival of *The Who, What or Where Game* had a scaled-down title, *The Challengers*, and an ambitiously different way of assembling its Q&A.

The Challengers was a current-events quiz. Because game shows for the previous thirty years had been mostly pre-recorded, they largely steered clear of current events. *The Challengers* boasted that it would be almost entirely current events. The questions would be culled from, among other sources, the current issue of *Newsweek* magazine.

Despite a formidable team like Dick Clark and Disney overseeing the project, *The Challengers* failed to gain any traction. *Jeopardy!* was still regarded as the hard quiz of record, and *The Challengers* seemed trapped in the large shadow being cast by Alex Trebek. *The Challengers* was canceled after one season.

Creator Ron Greenberg says, "I had bad luck. *The Challengers* wasn't a runaway smash, but the ratings were fine. That's the word I would use, 'fine.' But as we got close to the end of the first season, there was a change in management at Buena Vista, the new boss didn't settle for ratings that were just fine, and we were off the air."

Quiz Kids Grow Up

An updated version of a radio classic (see Chapter 4), *Quiz Kids Challenge*, hosted by Jonathan Prince, pitted a team of three children against a team of three adults. It was gone in sixteen weeks.

Bob Boden explains, "On paper, child geniuses versus average adults is a great premise. But here's the issue *Quiz Kids Challenge* had. The truth is, no matter how smart a child is, adults will always have a significant advantage in a trivia contest. Life experience gives adults a degree of knowledge that the smartest child will never have without reaching adulthood. So, you had very one-sided games. That's not interesting television. So, the material began getting skewed to give the kids a more competitive shot, and it became so skewed that the game still wasn't interesting television. No matter what they did, it would create a new problem that had to be dealt with."

Make America Change the Channel Again

Trump Card, adapted from a British quiz called *Bob's Full House*, emanated daily from the Trump Castle Casino Resort by the Bay in Atlantic City. Hosted by former football star Jimmy Cefalo, the game was part of a marketing strategy by Donald Trump's entertainment staff, who hoped that a national game show taping on the casino stage would draw interest to all three of Trump's Atlantic City properties. Donald Trump's staff was wrong. *Trump Card* was gone in one season.

Game show producer Mark Maxwell-Smith, who was not involved with *Trump Card*, remembers, "The sales pitch for that show was such a bizarre thing, they were touting that Donald Trump himself would occasionally appear on the program. Wow, this real estate investor will occasionally come onstage and take a bow; I'd better circle that in *TV Guide*. Are you kidding?"

Truth of the Matter

NBC, which had wiped out so many game shows in 1989, gave the genre another crack in the fall of 1990, with a new version of *To Tell the Truth*. It failed, but it was a fascinating failure only because of how cursed it seemed to be from the get-go.

Advance publicity for the show made note of the new host for *To Tell the Truth*, Australian-born broadcaster Gordon Elliott. But when *To Tell the Truth* debuted on Labor Day 1990, Gordon Elliott wasn't there. It was actor Richard Kline, formerly of *Three's Company*.

Kline had hosted the pilot earlier in 1990, and when NBC introduced the new version of *To Tell the Truth*, they aired that pilot by mistake. Kline himself didn't realize what was happening until he got a confused phone call from his mother, saying "I thought you said you didn't get the job!"

Kline called Mark Goodson Productions and learned what had just happened on the East Coast. He revealed to NPR in 2014 that, although it had been a total accident, and one that Goodson had no control over, the following day, Mark Goodson sent him a check for $10,000 and a gift basket.

But within a matter of weeks, Gordon Elliott wasn't hosting the show either! Earlier in 1990, he had hosted a game show pilot called *Get the Picture*. A condition of his contract for that pilot was that he had to wait a specified length of time before agreeing to host another game show. Hosting *To Tell the Truth*, a judge ruled, was a violation of his contract, and Elliott was slapped with an injunction that prohibited him from even entering the studio where *To Tell the Truth* was taped.

The queen of *To Tell the Truth*, Kitty Carlisle, and host Gordon Elliott, who lasted for only a few weeks in 1990 before being forced out of the show.

Football great Lynn Swann, who had made a strong impression as a panelist in those first few weeks, took over as host, but made it clear to Goodson that he could only be an interim host, due to his travel commitments as a sportscaster. Swann hosted the show for literally as long as he could and then was replaced by Alex Trebek, who was still hosting *Classic Concentration* for NBC and *Jeopardy!* for syndication. *To Tell the Truth* gave him a third daily television game, a level of ubiquity not seen on TV game shows since Bill Cullen's prime.

Trebek ended up missing two episodes himself, however, when his wife went into labor during a taping. Trebek's understandable but abrupt departure left Mark Goodson with no choice but to host the show himself, a job he had done twenty-four years earlier when Bud Collyer fell ill. *To Tell the Truth* would be the only game show on television that Goodson hosted himself.

Reviving *To Tell the Truth* was a tricky proposition. Even Goodson admitted that taking a game show that was created in 1956 and presenting it in 1990 was going to be difficult without modifying it somehow, but, as he told a reporter, it was hard to do that with *To Tell the Truth* without drastically altering the core game.

The analogy Goodson used: "You can't really turn a waltz into rock and roll."

Rock and roll might not have been terribly apt for the new *To Tell the Truth*, which used an orchestral theme and a set composed mostly of brass and glass; it looked more like a museum than a game show set.

Match Strikes Out

One concept show that Goodson did significantly overhaul was *Match Game*. It was actually Mark Goodson's son Jonathan who oversaw the new version of *Match Game*, introduced by ABC on July 16, 1990.

Originally pitched for syndication with host Bert Convy, ABC expressed interest when syndication fell through. Convy, unfortunately, fell ill when preparations for the ABC daytime version began (he died in 1991). Original host Gene Rayburn was briefly considered, but was heartbroken when he was rejected; he was so insulted that he refused Goodson's offer to appear on the show as a panelist for one week. Bob Eubanks was briefly considered for the show, but the game ultimately went to Ross Shafer, former host of *Love Me, Love Me Not*.

Mark Goodson excitedly said of the new *Match Game*, "It's been sped up, tightened, changed, and new elements put into it."

All that was true. Two rounds of classic *Match Game* were played each day, along with two rounds of a new feature called "Match-Up," where the contestants were given rapid-fire fill-in-the-blanks and tried to match stars against the clock as many times as possible.

Match Game had been popular for its free spirit, its spontaneous goofing around and banter among the stars. But because the new *Match Game* had so much game that had to be crammed into each thirty-minute episode, the stuff that really made *Match Game* was eschewed.

Gene Rayburn, original host of Match Game, was replaced for the 1990 revival. It was a slight that Gene didn't forgive easily.
Photo courtesy of Zane Enterprises

Match Game regular Charles Nelson Reilly lamented to former regular Brett Somers, "It's really not the same."

Combined with a noon time slot (ABC was the last network still putting shows in that slot; the others had given up), and *Match Game* was doomed from starting line. It was canceled in thirty-nine weeks.

No Big Deal

An ambitious new version of the show appeared on NBC on July 9, 1990, with new host Bob Hilton taking the torch while Monty Hall co-produced the show with Dick Clark.

Hilton's dressing room was adorned with an enormous pair of sneakers, given to him by a friend. He glibly told a reporter, "A friend of mine sent me those, to remind me that I've got a big pair of shoes to fill."

Unfortunately for Hilton, the joke wasn't really a joke. This version, which taped at Walt Disney World, lagged in the ratings, and NBC abruptly pressed Monty Hall into service to take over as host. The move didn't work. *Let's Make a Deal* was zonked by NBC on January 11, 1991.

In 1996, a reporter for *People* magazine suggested that, when the time came, an appropriate epitaph for his Monty Hall would be "Let's Make a Deal." Hall winced and said, "You put that on my tombstone, and I'll kill you."

Monty Hall died at his home in Beverly Hills on September 30, 2017. He was ninety-six years old.

The Wheel Goes Flat

Wheel of Fortune's daytime switch to CBS only lasted about a year and a half. On January 14, 1991, daytime *Wheel* departed from the CBS network (although it would continue taping in the CBS Television City complex) and returned to NBC. The reunion was short-lived. Daytime *Wheel* was canceled for good on September 20, 1991, after nearly seventeen years.

The 1990–1991 TV season was a disaster for game shows, and one from which the genre never fully recovered. It was, unfortunately, a result of crossed wires between viewers and TV executives. The message viewers sent that year was "We don't like these particular game shows." Executives heard "We don't like game shows anymore," and in the next few years, they responded accordingly.

How is it that a wave of game shows could premiere in a single year and all fail miserably? One theory is that too many games premiered at once. Time slots in syndication were actually precious few for game shows in 1990. The 1980s had been an enormously successful decade for situation comedies, all of which were selling their reruns into syndication. Given a chance to air reruns of *The Cosby Show, Night Court, Cheers,* and *The Golden Girls,* or air an unknown format, or an unseen tweaking of a prior format, many stations went with sure things. For the stations that carved out space on their schedules for the syndicated games, the audiences cannibalized each other. With audiences divided among all these new offerings, no one game had a chance to build a respectable viewership.

The daytime network games all failed for a variety of reasons, while at the same time, networks were running out of room for them. Economic factors of daytime television were changing, and syndicated programming was more enticing for local stations than the

The fourth and final host of the daytime *Wheel of Fortune*, Bob Goen.

network schedule. Little by little, the networks gave back time slots to their local stations. The 4:00 p.m. Eastern hour of network programming went away. Then Noon disappeared. Then 10:00 a.m. Eastern disappeared. And networks were, after all, in the business of giving the public what they wanted. Talk shows were hot in the 1990s, and so were some soap operas. But game shows were out. And as network schedules eroded and syndicated television, a far harder-to-predict realm of the industry, took over daytime television, game shows got squeezed out.

Lose or Winfrey

There was one other reason that game shows were suddenly falling out of favor in the early 1990s, and it had to do with the unexpected boom in popularity for a local Chicago talk show that went into national syndication in the late 1980s.

Francine Bergman, Bob Stewart's contestant coordinator who was among many feeling the squeeze in the early 1990s, elaborates: "Television is a business. You follow the money, and that makes sense. You can't begrudge television executives for wanting a hit show, that's the whole point. Oprah Winfrey went on the air in 1986 and gained a lot of momentum, and by 1990, it was the big show on daytime TV. *The Oprah Winfrey Show* was a giant. And the reason game shows fell out of favor was because every network and every syndicator was looking for the next Oprah."

Well, Well, Well

Game show writer and producer Mark Maxwell-Smith says, "The death of network daytime game shows really was preventable. In the 1960s, westerns reached a saturation point and died off because there's only so much you can do on a western. The same happened in the 1970s with too many detective shows. The saturation point shouldn't happen with game shows because there's so much you can do: panel game, wacky stunts, word games, trivia.

"Here's where game shows start to go wrong. Look at the network lineups in the 1980s. On NBC, there's *Classic Concentration* and *Super Password*, both produced by Mark Goodson. Over on CBS, there's *Family Feud*, *Card Sharks*, and *The Price is Right*, all produced by Mark Goodson. Mark Goodson, Bob Stewart, Monty Hall . . . all very talented men, all very deserving of their success, I don't begrudge any of them at all. But every network and syndication executive in the business had it in their heads that if you wanted a game show, there was a list of only four or five people you could call about it. There could have been two hundred viable ideas for game show formats from dozens of producers, and none of them were ever heard because they didn't come from the five people that the networks depended on for game shows.

"The decision makers in television didn't realize how many wells they had to draw from. They really didn't. So, when Mark Goodson, and Dan Enright, and Monty Hall put shows on the air in 1990, and they fail, rather than call the other producers, everybody said, 'Well, if these guys aren't succeeding, then game shows must be passé.'"

37

Drought

Where Have All the Game Shows Gone?

Bored Games

Much in the way that game shows had owned daytime television in the 1970s, the end of the 1980s and the early 1990s belonged to the daytime talk show. Phil Donahue had been the undisputed king until being overthrown by a new queen, Oprah Winfrey. In the 1990s, Geraldo Rivera, Sally Jesse Raphael, Maury Povich, and Jerry Springer all joined the fray. And because of the disastrous 1990–1991 season, nobody in power was in a hurry to give game shows another shot.

Dick Clark explained to one reporter, "We live in a tabloid world at the moment, and the spotlight is thrown on the bizarre, the unique, and the unusual, and talk lends itself better to that than games do."

In one of the more unusual programming moves the genre had been subjected to, *Classic Concentration* remained on the NBC schedule going into 1993, but had not produced a single episode since September 1991. NBC was content to just leave the reruns on the network lineup, with no interest in new episodes. Mark Goodson Productions even tried to prod them by preparing and pitching a new format called *Classic Concentration II* that tinkered with the game's format (an extra round involving word puzzles was added), but NBC was uninterested, and *Classic Concentration* reruns continued.

But at the start of 1993, NBC decided that, yes, it would like some new game show episodes—just not of *Classic Concentration*. While those reruns remained, NBC and Reg Grundy Productions revived the network's popular *Scrabble*, and introduced a new board game–inspired offering, *Scattergories*. *Scattergories*, hosted by Dick Clark, could possibly have been described as "Don't-Match Game." Clark would read a question and a letter, like, "Name something you toss, starting with the letter C." A team of four contestants would give six answers (coin, cookies, etc.) and score a point for every answer they suggested. Clark would then turn things over to five celebrities whose gameplay had been pre-recorded. The team would score additional points for every star who gave an answer other than an answer that the team gave.

The game was somewhat engaging, but smacked of cheapness (the stars weren't actually in the studio, and their pre-recorded interviews sometimes looked as if they had been shot with home movie cameras).

Meanwhile, *Scrabble* was back, and while the game was largely the same as before, and with Chuck Woolery once again at the helm, something about the whole thing seemed off. It was conspicuously cheaper. The Bonus Sprint end game had a jackpot that started at a bargain basement $1,000. Players no longer received cash bonuses for the pink-and-blue squares on the Scrabble board; rather, those squares would feed the value of the jackpot that the contestant *could* win at the end of the show. The game was also played on a much sparser set than its predecessor. It was *Scrabble*, and it was played like *Scrabble*, but it just didn't feel like *Scrabble* anymore.

In March, another game show was added to NBC, *Family Secrets*. Taped at Walt Disney World, *Family Secrets* saw host Bob Eubanks playing a somewhat familiar game. He asked personal questions of children and their parents, with the families scoring points for matching answers.

Scattergories ended production in May after only four months. *Scrabble* and *Family Secrets* barely held on longer, getting canceled the following month.

Despite the failure of *Scrabble*, Bob Boden, a former daytime executive at CBS, was optimistic about the future of his personal favorite form of television programming. In 1993, as *Scrabble* and *Scattergories* lagged, he told the *Los Angeles Times*, "Game shows were weakened a couple of years ago because of the failure of a few syndicated shows that were too similar and too derivative for the industry's good, but now there is a groundswell of activity that will ultimately lead to a strong return of the game show."

The Fizzling *Feud*

During 1992, the changing fortunes of game shows led CBS and Mark Goodson to pursue an unusual reinvention of one of the producer's most popular games. The increasingly desirable menu of syndicated programs up for grabs by local stations meant many CBS affiliates were starting to drop the 10:00–10:30 a.m. slot on the network in favor of syndicated shows. Rather than fight this change in strategy, CBS surprisingly accommodated it with a new concept called *Family Feud Challenge*, a reformatted one-hour version of the show that was structured in such a way that an affiliate wouldn't even have to carry the first half-hour.

On each *Family Feud Challenge*, a total of three families competed. For the first half-hour, two families battled it out while the returning champion family from the previous day waited on the sidelines. The winning family from the first half-hour would face the champions during the second half-hour, with no acknowledgment made during the second half-hour that a game had already been played.

To draw a little attention to the repackaged show, a new feature was added to the start of each game, the Bullseye Round, in which Combs asked five survey questions and only the most popular answer counted. The family that gave that answer added money to the jackpot they could win in Fast Money at the end of the show. The nighttime syndicated *Feud* added the Bullseye round too, and changed the title of the series to *The New Family Feud*.

The format change came at a tumultuous time for the show and for the production company. The big boss, Mark Goodson, died on December 18, 1992. Meanwhile, host Ray Combs, becoming stir crazy after four years of hosting the show (and a result of the format change, hosting more of it than ever) increasingly butted heads with the production staff, seeking to make changes to *Family Feud*.

As Howard Felsher explained Combs's suggestions to E!, "We were making *Family Feud*, and Ray wanted to make it *The Ray Combs Show*."

The Family Feud Challenge left the CBS schedule in the spring of 1993, while *The New Family Feud* continued in syndication . . . for the moment.

Not to Praise Caesar, But to Bury Him

NBC gave the genre one last chance in the summer of 1993, giving a whopping thirty-week commitment (thirteen was the norm) to *Caesar's Challenge*, a rare game show effort from Stephen J. Cannell Productions (*The Greatest American Hero, 21 Jump Street*, and lots more). Executive producer Rick Rosner, formerly in charge of *Just Men!* and *The New Hollywood Squares*, developed the game, which emanated from a showroom at Caesar's Palace in Las Vegas. The grandiose set and the lavish prizes up for grabs made it an unusually expensive endeavor—Rosner told one reporter that a single episode cost as much as $175,000—but the game itself was not without charm. A scrambled word appeared on a nine-letter slot machine. NBC

sportscaster Ahmad Rashad asked trivia questions, with a correct answer earning some cash and the right to spin the slot machine, which would cause a single letter to fall into the correct position, until one of the players solved it. In the show's bonus round, lettered balls would roll from a colossal bingo cage hovering over the stage, until the letters in a nine-letter word had all rolled out (with the sound of a gong and a deep-voiced command of "Caesar says *stop!*" to end the letter drawing). The contestant was shown which letters drawn were actually in the word, and the contestant had to unscramble those letters and form the word to win a car.

But daytime talk shows were a runaway train, and shortly after the arrival of 1994 came the departure of *Caesar's Challenge*. NBC introduced a revamped daytime lineup with two hour-long talk shows, and *Caesar's Challenge* would go down in history as (at the time of this writing) NBC's last daytime game show.

Ahmad Rashad presents the most exciting game on the strip, *Caesar's Challenge*.

Photo courtesy of Zane Enterprises

Trial and Tribulations

In 1994, Jonathan Goodson, now in charge of his father's empire, saw that the ratings for *The New Family Feud* were freefalling and hired a consultant to figure out what changes could be made to salvage the syndicated series. To the shock of Goodson's staff, the consultant recommended firing Ray Combs and bringing back Richard Dawson.

"That is the very worst thing you could do," *Feud* producer Howard Felsher told Goodson.

Combs concluded the 1993–1994 season of *Feud* with a brutally uncomfortable final episode. As a contestant fared poorly in Fast Money, Combs quipped, "I thought I was the biggest loser here today."

After signing off, Combs curtly walked past the winning family in an awkward display, walking straight out of the studio even as the credits were still rolling. It was the start of a tragic downward spiral for Combs—a car accident the following month left him temporarily paralyzed, and he became consumed by depression for months after, finally culminating in his tragic suicide on June 2, 1996, at the age of forty.

Richard Dawson's acrimonious relationship with his former employers had become somewhat warmer in recent years. The company allowed him access to contestant files so he could search for one contestant he had become enamored with in 1983—Dawson finally found her and asked her out on a date in 1989, and by 1994 they were married and had a toddler. For Mark Goodson's final birthday, Dawson seemed to let bygones be bygones, participating in an elaborate birthday video prepared for Goodson, in which Dawson affectionately wished his old boss well.

Dawson agreed to come back to the show so long as, in his words, "we make it the *Feud*" again. Dawson hadn't cared for the Bullseye Round from *Family Feud Challenge* and wanted it eliminated. A compromise was struck in the form of the Bankroll Round, a very similar round scaled down to three questions and played much faster.

Curiously, for all of the talk about "making it the *Feud* again," the *Family Feud* seen when the season premiere rolled around in the fall of 1994 was almost unrecognizable. The folksy, iconic set was replaced by a computer-generated gameboard and glass tile walls. The banjo-and-fiddle country theme was cast aside for a jazz rearrangement of the tune. Four family members competed instead of five.

Feud inflated to a full hour, as the CBS version had, and was structured in the same accommodating fashion. The first half-hour had two families battling it out, with the winners playing a champion family from the original ABC network version. Local stations each had the option of carrying *Feud* for an hour or for thirty minutes; the stations that opted for thirty minutes were given the second half-hour.

Dawson himself was different in many respects. The Goodson staff was aghast at how heavyset he was when he first arrived at the meetings for the new series—Dawson acknowledged the weight gain, saying that he had quit smoking when his daughter was born, and that he had much more of an appetite when he didn't smoke. The Goodson staff asked him if he would try to shed forty pounds before tapings started, but Dawson didn't bother. Dawson had also developed a quirk of talking much more softly. *Feud* was inundated with calls and letters from viewers complaining that they couldn't hear Dawson and asking if he could be told to speak up.

Jonathan Goodson also wanted to give a significant facelift to one of the company's signature shows, *The Price is Right*. A thirty-minute nighttime version of *Price* was introduced that same season, but even the most loyal viewers would have trouble recognizing a show that didn't look, sound, or feel like *The Price is Right*.

Bob Barker and announcer Rod Roddy both opted to sit this one out (Barker again maintained that a five-night-a-week version of *Price* in addition to the daytime show would always be a bad idea). Doug Davidson of *The Young and the Restless* would host the nighttime version, with announcer Burton Richardson (best known for his iconic introductions of "Arseniooooooooooo Hall!") filling Rod Roddy's shoes, if not his glittering jackets.

A high number of staffers involved in the daytime show elected not to participate in the nighttime version; Jonathan Goodson was altering the show so much that many of them didn't feel comfortable with what they were hearing. Goodson commissioned a new set consisting largely of dark colors, a black floor, and a sixteen-monitor video wall. The Contestant's Row round, where contestants bid on a prize for the chance to come onstage and play a pricing game, was eliminated entirely, with audience members called to "come on down" and go straight to the stage for a pricing game. The big ticking clock was eliminated from Clock Game, replaced by a digital graphic superimposed on the screen. The famous Plinko board was altered, and in most episodes, the famous big wheel of the Showcase Showdown was replaced by a new game called "The Price WAS Right"—contestants saw old commercials and bid on how much the product advertised was worth at the time the ad originally aired.

Feud and *Price* were so drastically different from the comfort-food trappings that made them hits that one viewing was just too jarring an experience for many. And the world outside game shows just made it even harder to succeed. It wasn't just the onslaught of talk shows; *Price* and *Feud* were experiencing very real and very insurmountable competition from the trial of the century. On November 9, 1994, the jury was sworn in for the O. J. Simpson double-murder trial, kicking off nearly a year of round-the-clock TV coverage, with start-to-finish live video

The nighttime *Price is Right* from 1994, a far cry from what viewers had come to expect from such a familiar favorite.

coverage of the actual hearings, usually preceded and followed with minute-by-minute breakdown and analysis by a ceaseless parade of talking heads. America was captivated, to the detriment of nearly everything else on television that year. *Family Feud* and the nighttime *Price is Right* were both rendered nearly invisible, with the handful of eyes that were looking in being turned off by the nearly unrecognizable repackaging of games that they used to like. *Price* was gone in thirteen weeks. *Feud* lasted the season, but barely, and it wouldn't be back in the fall of 1995. Game show fans and producers alike were hoping that things would rebound after 1991, but instead, it all somehow got worse.

38

Youth Movement

Letting the Kids Out to Play

hief among the reasons that the networks got rid of game shows was that they attracted older audiences. But as game shows for adults dried up, the early 1990s were arguably the golden age of game shows for children.

Where in the World is Carmen Sandiego?

Prior to 1989, PBS, the Public Broadcasting Service, was a surprisingly informal operation. Despite being thought of as a television network, it never really formally functioned as one until that year, when PBS appointed its first head of programming. Her name was Jennifer Lawson. At a press conference, when asked what her plans were for the network, she pledged not to be beholden to any customary attitudes about what kind of programming PBS would or wouldn't do. She said she what hear pitches for all sorts of shows.

She concluded by off-handedly saying, "Heck, I'd even hear a proposal for a game show."

The headline in the paper the next day was: PBS ANNOUNCES PLANS FOR GAME SHOW.

Fortunately, a company called Broderbund Software had one cooking. Gary, Cathy, and Doug Carlston, a trio of siblings in Silicon Valley, had founded Broderbund Software in 1980, just as computers were starting to enter the home and the classroom. Their library of releases included *Mavis Beacon Teaches Typing*, *Reader Rabbit*, and a 1985 breakout success called *Where in the World is Carmen Sandiego?*, a game that taught geography by leading the player on a chase around the globe in search of a criminal mastermind and her henchmen. Kids learned geography from clues about the cities and countries that the bad guys were suspected to have entered, and the pilfered priceless treasures that needed to be recovered.

Although the game was a success, it wasn't really commercially popular. It sold well, but primarily to classrooms. Broderbund wanted to make a Carmen Sandiego TV show to draw in young viewers in an effort to sell the game for use in the home. Howard Blumenthal, the son of *Concentration* producer Norm Blumenthal and a successful producer in his own right, was recruited by the company to help them put it on the air.

Howard Blumenthal explains, "They had already shot a pilot when I came on board. It was families answering trivia questions on a set that looked a lot like

The Newlywed Game. It tested terribly and they asked me how to repair it. I said the only repair to make was to throw it in the trash and make a new game, so that's what we did."

Blumenthal instantly figured out that straight trivia wouldn't work; he used an atlas to write a batch of questions, but found, for example, that out of 150 people he surveyed, only one correctly named the capital of Australia (Canberra; virtually everybody guessed Sydney or Melbourne). Having figured out what wouldn't work, Blumenthal went to local schools and talked to classes; most of them were familiar with the computer game, and Blumenthal picked their brains about what a TV version should have. What the kids told him, in so many words, was that it should be funny, have some animation, have music and pictures, that only kids should be contestants, and that they shouldn't "make anything that looks like a documentary."

Who in the World is Carmen Sandiego?

Now that he had guidelines to work with, Blumenthal, who had previously helped develop *Remote Control* for MTV, reached out to a few veterans of that program to help him develop his new series. And as a result, the game took shape as an educational children's version of *Remote Control*. Like that program, it would be an "anti-game show" that incorporated wry humor, skits, characters, a story, and an overarching motif into the game.

The game's premise would be that the host was a police detective in charge of training "new recruits." The set would look like a film noir detective's office in the middle of a big city, complete with a newsstand in the alley near the back-entrance door.

The computer game had players taking orders from a teletype machine, which spawned the idea that the host and the contestants on the game show should have a boss they had to answer to. Blumenthal, who had crossed paths with actress Lynn Thigpen years earlier for a Showtime cable TV special, wrote a script for a character named "The Chief" and realized that he was hearing Thigpen's voice in his head as he typed the dialogue. He reached out to her, and after some initial reluctance, she took the role.

Director Dana Calderwood remembers, "Lynn Thigpen was a professional, and she didn't suffer fools. There was a feeling that we needed to be very prepared when she came on board."

As for the host, an eclectic mix of talent would show up to audition, including Al Roker, Ron Palillo ("Horshack" from *Welcome Back, Kotter*), Kathy Ireland, and Greg Kinnear. But the job ended up going to a dark horse, Greg Lee, a production assistant on Nickelodeon's *Double Dare* who had been itching to host a game show. He even said during his audition, "I'm sleeping with an atlas. That's how serious I am about this."

A lot of candidates gave good auditions, but Lee's earnest desire for the job won everyone over. He became host, or as he'd be known on the show, "ACME Crimenet Special Agent in Charge of Training New Recruits."

But there was still the matter of live music for the show. Nearly every voice in Blumenthal's ear was telling him that the show should use rap music, but Blumenthal resisted for three reasons: 1) At the end of the 1980s, it still wasn't clear if rap had staying power or if it was just a fad; 2) Rap music had too fast a tempo, and for educational TV, Blumenthal insisted on music that was slow enough to be fully understood; and 3) Rap was strictly American at that point. For the "global chase" concept, Blumenthal wanted music that was accessible in multiple cultures.

And that's when a friend showed him a laserdisc of a recent HBO special, *Spike Lee Presents Do It A-Capella*. Blumenthal was intrigued; a-capella music had been around for thousands of years; it could be done at a slow tempo; and it was found in many cultures. A group featured in the Spike Lee special, Rockapella, captured Blumenthal's attention, and they agreed to come onboard, performing live music throughout each episode and singing what proved to be one of the most iconic theme songs in the history of TV game shows, "Where in the World is Carmen Sandiego?"

What in the World is Carmen Sandiego?

The computer game dealt with world landmarks being stolen by a thief, with clues being given to a succession of locations that the contestant had to travel to in a search for more evidence and clues to find the thief. After capturing so many thieves, you might eventually track down the eponymous Sandiego. The show followed this basic idea, with a game that sent contestants on a search for Carmen's henchman in the main game, and a bonus round where the winner tried to capture Carmen herself.

Carmen's henchmen were the product of one of Howard Blumenthal's many focus groups in classrooms. A handful of kids in one discussion said that the characters in the computer game, aside from Carmen herself, weren't that interesting, and if the TV show made you sit through a pursuit of a henchman before getting to Carmen, then the henchmen needed to be fun and memorable. Blumenthal, a talented artist, walked up to the chalkboard and just began drawing characters, encouraging the kids to give suggestions as he doodled. He kept going until he had whipped up ten characters, like Vic the Slick, Eartha Brute, RoboCrook, Double Trouble, and Patty Larceny.

After learning about the crook and the loot they were searching for, the contestants would play a series of . . . well . . . it would be hard to call them questions. Rockapella might sing a parody of the song "Brandy" loaded with clues to the city of Bloomington, Minnesota. Penn and Teller, agents from ACME Magicnet, would perform a simple magic trick loaded with hints to a body of water. The Dying Informant, a recurring character, staggered into the room, collapsed onto the floor, and gave some pertinent info about a Canadian province with his dying breath. The Running Informant, in front of a green screen, might be desperately giving as much help as possible while running away from a rhinoceros stampede or a herd of elephants. Plastic Diver Guy, a small aquarium toy (pressed into service as a clue-giver because, Dana Calderwood admits, the show had a low budget)

The cast of *Where in the World is Carmen Sandiego?*, Lynn Thigpen, Greg Lee, and Rockapella.

might give some details about a peninsula. A "Phone Tap" would allow the kids to listen to some info being given by Carmen to the henchman during a conversation. It would change up from day to day. Sometimes it was Peter Graves or Walter Cronkite or Kathie Lee Gifford giving the clues. And sometimes the portrait of ACME Crimenet founder Agnes Acme would come to life and offer a clue. Every episode offered a new mix of songs, skits, and stars to help unravel the mystery.

The low-scoring player would be eliminated, the two remaining would go to a train depot and play a memory game using fifteen actual sites in a world city, searching for "the loot, the warrant, and the crook," in that order. The first contestant to find those items hidden on the board, and find them in that specific order, went searching for Carmen Sandiego.

A thirty-five-foot unmarked map of a continent awaited the contestant. (Blumenthal originally wanted a massive globe, with the contestants traveling from one country to another through a system of chutes and ladders, but that proved to be prohibitively large and unshootable.) Using a series of police sirens on poles, the contestant ran around the map, trying to mark countries as Greg Lee announced them. Marking eight countries in forty-five seconds or less earned the lucky winner a trip anywhere in North America.

Where in the World is Carmen Sandiego? brought the world to kids in the liveliest way imaginable every day. The show's staff, comprised of people born in a total of twenty countries, brought their own knowledge of individual cultures to the program, and viewers appreciated it.

One of those viewers, Stad St. Fleur, grew up to work in game shows himself, on shows like NBC's *Hollywood Game Night*, where he served as associate producer. As he recalled, *Carmen Sandiego* was one of the shows that made him fall in love with the genre. "What I appreciated, even as a five-year-old, was the respect given to everybody. I was a black kid with a weird name. And I loved watching this show because the contestants came in all colors and shapes. They didn't cast these kids because they had the right look. You were seeing real kids. And on every show, at least one kid had a name that was almost unpronounceable, you know? Everybody was welcome. And Carmen Sandiego was almost pure knowledge. You won the game by being smart. And the show not only rewarded smarts, but they rewarded it with humor and music and all these celebrity guests. That show taught me that it was okay to be smart. And that it was fun to be smart."

What was the magic ingredient? Why did the show deliver such strong results? Howard Blumenthal answers, quite simply, "Freedom. PBS had never done a game show before. They knew I had. And so, when PBS decided they wanted a game show, instead of micromanaging and giving us pages of notes, they left us alone and allowed us to find our way. First of all, that enabled us to grow and to learn by doing. Second of all, that made the job more fun, and I truly believe that when you're having fun off-camera, it comes across in the finished product. Freedom is so important for a TV show, and thankfully we had it."

Arcade Game

The year 1991 was one of the most eventful in the history of video games, with the launch of the Super Nintendo and stiff competition from the Sega Genesis wearing out the thumbs of kids across America. Capitalizing on the craze, Nickelodeon unleashed a game show for the 16-bit generation, *Nick Arcade*.

The game was co-created by James Bethea and Karim Miteff, two high school buddies who had attended Bronx High School of Science before moving to Orlando to become producers at Nickelodeon. The first series they worked on was the short-lived three-hour-long variety show *Total Panic*, for which Bethea and Miteff developed the earliest version of what would become *Nick Arcade*. A recurring segment of *Total Panic* was a game called "Eat a Bug," in which contestants stood in front of a green screen. Superimposed behind them were a number of animated insects. The insects would actually react to whatever the contestants did. Swinging your arm at a fly would swat and kill it, for example.

Here's how the "Eat a Bug" technology worked. Computerized graphics of the time were largely "sprites," or objects comprised of 8 or 16 bits. In an interview with the website Splitsider, Bethea credited Miteff for being the one who made the initial discovery: virtual reality software called Mandala that could run on a Commodore Amiga, a common model of computers at the time. Mandala had a feature called edge detection, which could discern where sprites were and detect when different sprites made contact with each other, so a user could program the way sprites should react when they collided.

If you're even slightly interested in television production, you're probably familiar with the term "chroma key," or as it's simply sometimes known, "blue screen" or "green screen." An image is shot in front of a solid color, almost always blue or green, the colors that just work best for the process. That image can now be superimposed over whatever graphics the user desires. Think of your local weatherman's reports. That's chroma key.

Miteff found that Mandala could react to images being shot in front of a chroma key and instantly convert them into sprites, and that the edge detection feature would react to those sprites. A camera could shoot a live human for a chroma key shot. At the same time, a series of sprites, essentially a video game, would be playing in the Mandala software. The live human's image was shot and instantaneously converted into a sprite for the purposes of the software. The viewer at home would see the live human inside the video game, with all elements of the game reacting to the contestant's movements thanks to the edge detection.

Bethea and Miteff concocted a show about video games; interviews, comedy sketches, news features, all revolving around video games. Nickelodeon was cool to the idea. In the early 1990s, the network was still coasting on the success of *Double Dare*, and even though Nickelodeon executives maintained that they were open to any and all ideas, Bethea and Miteff were frustrated to find that, apparently, the executives were only interested in ideas about game shows.

Around the office one day, Bethea kept repeating, "All they want to do is game shows!"

And finally, the light bulb flickered for both men, and they realized that was exactly what their technology was meant for.

Video Games

Bethea and Miteff took it a bit further and pitched a video game–immersed format for a game show to Nickelodeon. Nickelodeon loved the idea so much that they allowed Bethea, Miteff, and their newly hired staff a whopping sixteen months to fine-tune the more elaborate elements of their ideas. Nickelodeon Studios (and their offices) were, at that time, part of the Universal Studios Florida theme park complex in Orlando, which proved amazingly helpful for research and development. As the game's elements became more fleshed out, Bethea and Miteff would leave the office, walk into the theme park, and just randomly approach families and ask if they could come over to the office so the kids could test an idea.

"I can't believe we can do that!" was the enthusiastic reaction from many of the kids as the production staff demonstrated their game show idea and the kids saw what was actually possible with the computer software the show was using. In some cases, even the parents wanted a turn, and the staff happily complied.

A series of pilots was produced and very well received, and the channel moved forward with *Nick Arcade*, a game show for the times, almost wall-to-wall focused on video games. When Nickelodeon picked up the pilot, the search started for a new host. That search led to Phil Moore, a kindred spirit for Bethea and Miteff; he was an egghead who had accidentally wandered into show business. A graduate of an aeronautical school, he worked as a data center computer librarian before accepting a job at AT&T. During a labor dispute, Moore took it upon himself to keep morale up for his co-workers by entertaining the crowd of striking workers, and was shocked to discover that he loved it. He began doing stand-up comedy. At a time when game shows began leaving the cozy confines of California studios to do special weeks from other locations, Phil Moore became the go-to warm-up guy for every game show that drifted into Florida for a special week: *Wheel of Fortune*, *Remote Control*, but most importantly, the 1990 revival of *Let's Make a Deal*, which taped full time at Disney-MGM Studios in Orlando. A glowing endorsement from executive producer Monty Hall set Moore on the path for a show to call his own. *Nick Arcade* started taping in December of 1991, at the same time waves of Super Nintendos were being snapped up by parents preparing for Christmas, and the series premiered the following month.

The game started with contestants playing an arcade game developed specifically for the show (most were either very simple races between characters or variations on Pong), with the reward being control of Mikey, the video game adventurer. Each round saw contestants navigating Mikey through a game board hiding "The four P's: Points, Puzzles, Pop Quizzes, and Prizes." Depending on where the contestants made Mikey walk, they might end up having to answer a trivia question, solve a picture puzzle, or encounter a Video Enemy who would attack Mikey and cost the team their turn.

What most of the teams were probably hoping for was that they'd encounter a square hiding a Video Challenge. Stationed each day on the Nick Arcade set were five video games in current release; uncovering a Video Challenge allowed teams to wager their points and select one of those games. A team had thirty seconds to meet or beat a pre-determined goal to add the wagered points to their score.

The high-scoring team for the day went on to the unforgettable Video Zone bonus round, in which the kids actually entered a video game, through the use of green screen technology. The end result didn't look anything like a weatherman reporting on an incoming storm. The kids were shrunk down to about Super Mario size on the television screen, totally surrounded by obstacles, bonuses, attacking enemies, and everything else you'd expect to see in a video game. Beating three levels, including the final boss, a Wizard—Merlock, Scorcha, or Mongo—won the day's grand prize.

What made the Video Zone particularly special was that the kids actually had total control over their environment. "Virtual reality" was in its infancy in 1991 and it was dazzling to see the way the animated graphics reacted to the living, breathing kid in the middle of it. In the Alien Moonbase, the nuclear reactors actually shut down when the kids slapped them. In the Food Fight, the kids got whacked by flying pizza slices and ice cream cones in a school cafeteria. The kids even had health meters, and their power would drain when attacked by the enemies in each level. Each level had floating objects, like orbs and Super Mario–style coins, the spin from *Nick Arcade* being that they were worth actual cash, fifty bucks for each one collected. And as the producers boasted to the reporters who asked, the show didn't have, in their words, "A Wizard of Oz" backstage who decided what would happen to the kids; they really did have total control over the game they had been dropped into, and the technology developed for the series allowed for total interaction between the living beings and the animated sprites.

"D-D-D-Do You Have It?"

That was the question belted by Rick Witkowski's hard-hitting theme at the opening of every episode of *Nickelodeon GUTS*, an intense battle between three kids that wasn't so much a game show as it was a P.E. class with a "don't try this at home" warning; there just happened to be a trophy at the end.

Twenty-five-year-old actor/comic Mike O'Malley, familiar to Nickelodeon viewers by this point from his stint hosting the short-lived photo-puzzle game *Get the Picture*, served as host, play-by-play commentator, color analyst, and post-game interviewer; in auditions, he had beaten out Robin Marella, Marc Summers's long-time assistant on *Double Dare*.

Assisting him was Moira Quirk, an Irish-born budding actress who had just moved to the U. S. and was working at Universal Studios Florida when she auditioned for the role of the *GUTS* referee, who explained each of the events taking place each day in the Extreme Arena, the sprawling pseudo-gymnasium where the show was taped.

Among the events regularly seen on *GUTS*: Basic Training, a military-grade obstacle course; Slam Dunk, in which the kids were attached to bungee cords to perform high-jumping basketball shots (a game inspired by show creator Albie Hecht's own inability to play basketball well); and White Water, in which the kids attempted to row an inflatable raft across a swimming pool, while jets of water caused the raft to veer off course.

Each episode culminated in a climb up the show's "radical rock," the Aggro-Crag, a studio-high ascending labyrinth of angled rails, foam, and latex that formed a simulated mountain. What viewers didn't see on the air was the array of cables, infrared beams, and activators that would trigger the Aggro-Crag's special effects. As the kids raced up the mountain, a foot crossing just the right beam would trigger an avalanche of foam rocks obstructing the kids' progress, or confetti cannons that interfered with everyone's vision.

The winner of the day received a piece of the Aggro-Crag, mounted onto a base for a glorious trophy; with sweaty red faces and puffed-out chests, every kid that collected a piece of the rock looked like they had earned it.

Nickelodeon GUTS' events were so enticing to viewers' eyes, and ratings were so indicative that the show was onto something, that Nickelodeon introduced a touring *GUTS* attraction, with Mike O'Malley criss-crossing the country and allowing kids at every venue to try the stunts themselves.

Legendary

If a confused channel surfer saw a camera weaving through a jungle before coming to a stop on a giant stone carving that came to life, and was surprised to realize it was a game show, then mission accomplished. Stone-Stanley Productions, which had entered the kids game show fray with *Fun House* in the late 1980s, switched from a wild and wacky factory to a spooky abandoned Mayan temple for the atmosphere-oozing Nickelodeon game *Legends of the Hidden Temple*. The company's mission statement: adapt the fun and adventure of the *Indiana Jones* movies into a game show.

Hosted by Kirk Fogg (although the show's preferred term for his job was "guide"), each episode started with six teams—the Orange Iguanas, Green Monkeys, Silver Snakes, Purple Parrots, Blue Barracudas, and Red Jaguars—had to cross a large, dry ice-laden moat.

The four teams that completed the journey first would hear Olmec, the show's massive stone head mascot, tell the Legend of the Day: a lengthy story actually based on history or well-known mythology and culminating in the revelation of an object from the story now supposedly hidden in the show's temple—the key that Benjamin Franklin tied to his kite, or the nose ring from Paul Bunyon's ox, Babe. The teams then stood on the Steps of Knowledge, a staircase consisting of lock-out buttons that were activated when stomped upon. The teams were subjected to a memory quiz, with all of the questions coming directly from the story they had just heard.

The first two teams to finish descending the staircase advanced to the Temple Games, a series of three stunts played against the clock, usually in the form of a race or an effort to collect multiple objects. The reward for the team that won each stunt was either a half-Pendant of Life or a full Pendant, with the most Pendants winning the game and the right to search the Temple. The Temple was a two-level, twelve-room arrangement. Upon entry, the doors into the adjoining rooms were locked and a contestant had to solve a different goal in each room in order to unlock a door. In the Observatory, a sundial had to be spun to open a door. In the Crypt, three skeletons were clutching books; pulling on the correct book opened the door. The Jester's Court had a variety of paintings of clowns in different poses; pressing one's body against the correct painting and mimicking the pose correctly would grant access to the next room.

TV's biggest stoner, Olmec, along with guide Kirk Fogg, on *Legends of the Hidden Temple*.

But the most unexpectedly vicious challenge in the Temple came in the form of a simple three-piece puzzle. The Shrine of the Silver Monkey housed three pieces of a monkey statue; assembling the pieces unlocked a door. Simple, right? Not simple enough. Kids would lay the bottom part halfway off the platform, or put the torso on upside down, or not secure the head, or drop the pieces.

Also impeding the show's progress: The Temple Guards, three terrifying masked warriors who would emerge in three different rooms and required a Pendant of Life before they would go away. Being caught in a room without a Pendant would get a kid removed from the Temple.

Who Figures?

Summer Sanders, a gifted swimmer who had collected two Gold Medals, a Silver, and a Bronze at the 1992 Summer Olympics, was host of a Nickelodeon game that celebrated the extraordinary and odd achievements of other kids. *Figure It Out* was an idea that borrowed heavily from the panel shows of the 1950s; the kid contestants all had secrets about themselves (one budding entrepreneur had invented a remote-controlled vacuum cleaner; another had discovered dinosaur bones with his toy truck). The panelists had to not only guess the secret, but also avoid committing the Secret Slime Action (touching your face, saying "uh") for each game, which triggered a release of green slime from an ominous pipe looming over their heads. Each game was, of course, followed by a demonstration of the secret (the demonstration of an invention called Talking Toilet was surprisingly suitable for television).

Director Dana Calderwood says, "It makes sense to dust off old ideas because your audience outgrows it every five or six years, and then it becomes a new idea. And when you're doing a show for kids, you can really dust off a lot of old ideas. All *Figure It Out* was, was *I've Got a Secret*. Our audience did not realize they were seeing a 1950s premise."

39

Cable Guys

Taking the Game Somewhere Else

Wink on the Phone

Wink Martindale observed during the late 1980s, "Technology is very important to the audience now. You've got to have that modernistic stuff."

And Wink went modern in the early 1990s with an extremely ambitious idea for a twenty-four-hour game show cable channel, simply called The Game Channel. A 1992 press kit laid out the idea: twenty-four hours of game shows, a mix of original programs and reruns, and between shows, "Playbreaks" that would allow home viewers to call a 900-number and play the games at home for prizes.

The Game Channel never got off the ground, but the notion of Playbreaks would. In 1993, Wink began a successful partnership with The Family Channel, with *Trivial Pursuit*, an adaptation of the board game that featured ten Playbreaks per afternoon, allowing home viewers to call in and play *Trivial Pursuit* at home for prizes ranging from telephones to cruises. The Family Channel quickly introduced three more interactive games: *Boggle*, *Jumble*, and *Shuffle*. All four were hosted by Wink. The economics of the Playbreaks were enough to induce some salivating for the production company and the channel. The 900-number charged a flat rate of $4.98 per call, with a computer system designed to accommodate 2,500 players at a time. With ten Playbreaks each afternoon, a full complement of players would net $124,000 in a single day.

If there were high rewards involved for all involved, there were high risks. The Playbreaks were so lengthy that to accommodate them, The Family Channel aired only six minutes of commercials per hour (about half of the typical amount of commercial time in an hour during 1993) and that cost needed to be offset by a high volume of calls from viewers, many of whom, admittedly, didn't want to spend five bucks on a phone call. As an enticement, Martindale emphasized that callers would be offered coupons for deals that would offset the $4.98.

Wink, looking back today, says, "The expense of those phone calls did us in. You could reasonably ask an average viewer to call in and spend that much money on a phone call once. But asking 2,500 of your viewers to spend that much money every day was asking too much of them. Interactive games that you play on your telephone was a neat idea on paper, but the charges that the callers rack up just killed it completely."

By the summer of 1995, the phones stopped ringing. All of the interactive games were off the air. But by that point, game show fans were already dialing another channel's number.

Game Show Network

Game show fans have no idea how much entertainment they were provided thanks to a Tulsa, Oklahoma–based satellite dish service provider, United Video, in the early 1990s. United Video wanted to expand their horizons beyond just providing service; the company wanted to launch their own programming. The original plan was a 24/7 cartoon channel. But when Ted Turner beat them to the punch with the introduction of Cartoon Network, United Video had to find an alternative. That was when the CEO of the company came home from work, sat down on the couch with his wife, and turned on his TV to relax a little. *Wheel of Fortune* was on.

He instantly knew his plan B. It was time to mount a game show channel. He contacted Dick Block, a broadcasting business consultant who was doing some unrelated work for United at the time, and Block pounded the pavement, going to the offices of every game show production company he could think of to tell them about the idea.

Block remembers, "The response I got was a bit tepid. What I heard over and over again was 'You're not the first guy that's come in here about this.' Pat Robertson had been trying to mount an all-game show channel for a while and those plans fell through. And besides that, during the late 1980s and early 1990s, USA had an afternoon block of game shows for three hours or more every day and it got incredible ratings. The Family Channel did the same thing. They ran game shows for several hours in the afternoon. And the ratings report showed that a lot of people were watching the full block from start to finish every day. So, it was that sell-it-by-the-pound logic at work; if an audience will watch three hours of game shows, they'll watch twenty-four hours of game shows. Well, it became the idea that every cable programmer in the business had in the back of their head—'Hey, we oughta have a channel that's nothing but game shows'—but nothing ever came of it. So, when these game show producers were giving me an unenthusiastic response, it was only because they had heard this proposal repeatedly and it never went anywhere."

An unsung hero for game show fans, Dick Block was the man who got Game Show Network off the ground and on the air in 1994.

Block was surprised to discover, however, that tens of thousands of hours of videotape were lying in these producers' vaults, collecting dust. The more he learned about the sheer volume of the archives, the more he realized that programming this potential channel would be shockingly easy. He wrote a ninety-one-word letter to a friend, Mel Harris, a former Paramount employee who had since moved on to Sony. Dick Block simply asked his friend if Sony would be interested in helping United Video launch a game show channel.

On December 1, 1994, Vanna White, Alex Trebek, and Merv Griffin threw a symbolic switch at the Western Cable Show in Anaheim, California, to christen the launch of Game Show Network. Viewers at home saw second-by-second countdown to launch that final reached zero and gave way to a dizzying six-minute montage of clips from nearly everything in the channel's expansive library, from beloved favorites like *Match Game*, *Family Feud*, and *Tic Tac Dough*, to blink-and-you-miss-it titles like *The Perfect Match*, *All About the Opposite Sex*, and *Ruckus*.

Among the shows that viewers saw on that first day: *What's My Line?* with mystery guest Jackie Gleason; *Family Feud*, in which one of the contestants was Richard Dawson's future wife; *Password* with guest Jerry Lewis; the final episode of the original *I've Got a Secret*; *To Tell the Truth* with baseball legend Don Drysdale as a contestant; and the first episode of the nighttime *Wheel of Fortune* from 1983.

Game Show Network, in the beginning, was a celebration of the genre's glory days. Even its original content revolved around the greats from the past. The channel's answer to *The Today Show* was a program called *Club AM*, in which Laura Chambers (a one-time contestant on numerous shows, later a staffer for several) and Steve Day (formerly the announcer for *Just Men!* and *Caesar's Challenge*) interviewed a very familiar lineup of guests, like Jack Narz, Gene Rayburn, Bob Eubanks, and Bob Stewart. Former *Press Your Luck* host Peter Tomarken hosted the channel's interstitial programming, and ubiquitous announcer Gene Wood provided some voiceovers.

Peter Tomarken and Laura Chambers hosted Game Show Network's original programs during its first few years. *Photos courtesy of Zane Enterprises*

Francine Bergman, longtime staffer for Bob Stewart Productions, says, "I was completely mystified by the success of Game Show Network. I am very grateful and very flattered to be clear, but very mystified. To my way of thinking, we were just cranking these shows out and once they were played, they were done, no looking back. I never thought of them as having a nostalgia factor. So, this channel took off, and they add *Pyramid* reruns to the schedule, and not only are people watching, a lot of people are watching. That blew me away. I still can't understand it!"

Sweep Up

In the otherwise disastrous year of 1990, the sole success story was on Lifetime, which revived an eccentric little ABC game from the 1960s and turned it into a modern-day classic. *Supermarket Sweep,* created by Al Howard, who had the idea while grocery shopping with his wife, had originally distinguished itself in the '60s by getting out of the studios and taping in supermarkets across the East Coast. The pilot for the 1990 version taped in a supermarket, too, but when Lifetime picked up the series, it moved into a studio that looked uncannily like a fully functional supermarket.

Three pairs of contestants (usually married couples or friends) competed against each other in a series of small games revolving around grocery items—sometimes guessing prices, sometimes completing short poems using brand names, among other challenges—with rewards for right answers in the form of time; all the time earned was time that the teams could spend roaming the aisles at top speed in the thrilling Big Sweep. The players raced through the aisles, grabbing literally anything on the shelves (the only restriction—no more than five of any one item) and loading it into their carts. Scattered throughout the supermarket were additional chances at bonuses—grabbing and filling a small candy bag paid $100, stopping to grind some coffee paid $100, going to the Manager's Special bin and finding a marked can was worth $200, among many, many other incentives. Everybody's purchases were rung up during the final commercial break. The contestants all got their grocery bills in cash, but the top scoring team went on a final sweep, solving clues to locate three marked items somewhere in the supermarket for $5,000.

It would be difficult for a casual viewer to spot the differences between the simulated studio supermarket and the true thing—hams and turkeys were actually convincing plastic replicas, and it was seemingly the only supermarket in the world without a bread aisle.

Shelley Herman, a writer for *Supermarket Sweep,* explains, "Fresh bread stays fresh for a little bit, after a few days it goes stale, and a day after that, your studio has a roach problem. So, we tried having fresh bread in the studio for a little while, but the bugs put an end to that. Another thing that we faked, in a sense, was the detergent boxes. We had the big twenty-dollar boxes of detergent, and contestants loved grabbing those because they were expensive. The problem is it's costly for the show if the detergent spills out. We came up with a solution. We just asked the detergent companies to send us empty boxes. We filled them with rice so that the

Did you hear the beep? David Ruprecht and these contestants are ready for their *Supermarket Sweep*.   *Photo courtesy of Zane Enterprises*

contestants wouldn't just fling the boxes into the carts; that wouldn't look right, so we did it to make sure it was the same weight. And then, if a box accidentally spilled, it meant we lost a few cents' worth of rice instead of a few dollars' worth of detergent.

"When *Supermarket Sweep* wrapped up each taping session, all the groceries were given to a guy whose job was to distribute our inventory to 99-cent stores. Well, the distributor didn't know what we were doing to the detergent boxes, so somebody bought a huge box of detergent at the 99-cent store, poured a bunch of rice into their washing machine, and destroyed the washing machine. And that's why I don't go shopping at 99-cent stores. I know what happened to that food before it got there."

Drop In

Lifetime logically paired up their supermarket with a shopping mall in 1991 when they introduced *Shop 'til You Drop*, with host Pat Finn and assistant Mark L. Wahlberg. Each day, teams would compete for points by doing stunts against the clock and going head to head in a ninety-second trivia quiz. The high-scoring team at the end of the game played the *Shop 'til You Drop* round for a dream vacation. The team opened six packages containing prizes and had to decide whether to keep the prize or exchange it for a package at the entrance of one of the fourteen stores in the shopping mall (the name of each store served as a clue to the prize hidden in the packages). Once the team had settled on six packages after making all of their exchanges, the mystery packages were opened, the retail values of all the prizes was tallied, and a total of $1,000 or more (later, $2,500 or more) earned a dream vacation as a bonus.

From the *Supermarket* and off to the shopping mall . . . Pat Finn hosts
Shop 'til You Drop.   *Photo courtesy of Zane Enterprises*

In the Red

Hey, it's that Wink guy again!

In the mid-1990s, crooner Tony Bennett unexpectedly experienced a surge
in popularity among Generation Xers thanks to a concert aired on MTV. Wink
Martindale received a phone call one afternoon from his agent, Fred Wostbrock,
offering him "a game show that will do for you what MTV did for Tony Bennett!"

Wink's new game was called *Debt*. Buena Vista Television built a game show
that was part parody and part actual game, with just a dash of social commentary
thrown in. In 1995, consumers had amassed a total of $1 trillion in personal debt,
a selling point that Martindale emphasized while promoting the show in interviews; it was the unlikely core premise of the show. Each episode opened with the
three contestants holding up slates with their names and personal debts, arranged
to look like the contestants were posing for mug shots. Each contestant fearlessly
revealed what it was that caused them to go so far into the red—a car, back taxes,
student loans, and, in one case, a bald man who remorselessly admitted he had
spent a fortune on a toupee—and then Wink would make his entrance to inexpli-
cable disco music on a set with 1950s-inspired décor.

"Men Who Wear Dresses," "Must See TV If You're Three," "Deodorant and
Antiperspirant" were some of the categories that the contestants navigated on the
game board, with correct answers knocking money off their debt (with their debts
actually on display and treated as their scores).

Debt was an overnight hit for Lifetime, no surprise to Wink Martindale
because, he reasoned at the time, "*Debt* is something everyone can relate to." The
show won a CableACE Award, and the first season's contestants were happy with
the $850,000 worth of personal debt that the show erased in its first year. *Debt's*

contestant line rang off the hook with hopeful players getting in line for their shot. Theoretically, you could pay off your debt by doing well on *Wheel of Fortune*, *Jeopardy!*, or *Supermarket Sweep*, but there was something surprisingly enticing for many about going on a show called *Debt*, announcing your struggle to the world, and winning the chance to dig yourself out.

Executive producer Andrew Golder told the Associated Press, "Getting out of debt in some weird way is almost a new version of the American Dream. Since we're attaching the winnings to their debt and personalizing it, a big burden is lifted off their shoulders. It's not just 'Here's $6,000, go do something.' It's tangible, we know how you got there."

Debt managed to make a few enemies in high places, however. It was slapped with a lawsuit from Visa after only a few weeks on the air, arguing that the show's logo was far too similar to the credit card giant's logo. *Debt* designed a new logo, only to get hit with more litigation from the producers of *Jeopardy!*, who felt that the game's rules bore a few too many strikingly similar to their game, forcing *Debt* to change its first round quite a bit before launching its second season.

Ben Pay

Al Burton developed one of the most all-around unusual premises for a game show and sold it to Comedy Central. *Win Ben Stein's Money* starred Ben Stein, a former speechwriter for President Nixon and later a law professor for Pepperdine University who later had an unexpectedly successful career as an actor, playing an endless parade of dullards and nerds in movies like *Ferris Bueller's Day Off*. The insane premise of *Win Ben Stein's Money* was that Stein was both host and contestant, and that the grand prize was his own paycheck.

Three contestants competed against each other, facing categories with names like "Who Uppercut One?," "George Bush Whackers," and "Shrunken States Not Caused by a Cold Swimming Pool," that were actually hiding pretty tough trivia questions—one critic said *Win Ben Stein's Money*'s grand prize was the hardest $5,000 to win on television.

The $5,000 in cash was Stein's payday for hosting, with every correct answer from a contestant chipping away $50–$200. Halfway through the show, the low-scoring player was eliminated—with Stein eagerly taking back the money that

Ben Stein tempted players with the hardest-to-win $5,000 in game show history; you could only collect by outsmarting him.

player had snapped up until that point—and Stein became a contestant, with the show's hosting duties now assumed by announcer Jimmy Kimmel. Kimmel, a journeyman radio personality, needed to supplement his income a few years earlier and took a job writing questions for a failed game show project called *Gossip*. During run-throughs, Kimmel volunteered to stand in as host (*Gossip* hadn't hired one yet) and dazzled executive Fred Silverman so much that he landed the job for real. *Gossip* didn't go anywhere, but Michael Davies was so impressed that when Burton pitched *Win Ben Stein's Money*, Davies offered the announcer spot to Kimmel.

Brash, sarcastic, soot-mouthed Kimmel had inexplicably strong chemistry with older, stuffy conservative Stein, often tripping up Stein with fake questions ("Do you like carrots, and if so, where?") or tossing off blunt quips during the contestant interviews—he told a woman with the last name "Organ" that she had "a porn star name."

The smart-but-snide quizzer had winners all around. It would be the first Comedy Central show to win an Emmy Award, collecting a grand total of seven throughout its run, including an Outstanding Game Show Host trophy shared by Stein and Kimmel. Kimmel became a star in his own right, departing to co-host *The Man Show* for Comedy Central before going to ABC to mount *Jimmy Kimmel Live!* Filling the announcer spot was screenwriter Nancy Pimenthal and, later, Kimmel's cousin Sal Iacono.

40

The Comeback Kids

Everything Old is New Again

oward the end of the 1990s, a very familiar lineup of game shows appeared in syndication.

The Dating/Newlywed Hour

Sony, the parent company of Game Show Network, had purchased Chuck Barris Productions early in the channel's existence and quickly spread the word to stations across the country that they were looking to put *The Dating Game* and *The Newlywed Game* back on the air.

But when *The Dating Game* and *The Newlywed Game* resurfaced in the fall of 1996, the wheels had been so thoroughly reinvented that they were practically hexagons. Sony seemed to be putting a stronger emphasis on the "game" part of each show's title than Chuck Barris ever had. Whereas Barris's formats were jumping-off points for showcasing personalities, *The Dating Game* and *The Newlywed Game* now moved at a faster pace, with more variety to the way each was played.

Brad Sherwood hosted *The Dating Game*, which now separated its game into a Looks round and a Personality round. For the Looks round, the bachelorette would see each of her potential suitors one at a time, without being told their names or any other information. She would choose, by number, the one she thought was best-looking. The bachelors would then sit on the other side of a partition for the Personality round. The bachelorette would see a list of brief statements, and select them one at a time. Each statement referred to a specific bachelor, who would speak up and explain the story related to the statement. The bachelorette would make her choice for best personality, and then have to decide if she wanted a date with her Looks choice or her Personality choice. (And if she had chosen the same man for Looks and Personality, she got a $500 bonus.)

The Newlywed Game, now helmed by *Saturday Night Live* alum Gary Kroeger, had drastically expanded a simple game of questions from the host and answers on cue cards into a four-round battle. First, the contestants would see tapes of prerecorded interviews with their mates and try to predict how specific sentences were completed. Then the couples tried to match answers in a multiple-choice quiz. Then there was "That's My Wife!/That's My Man!" where Kroeger read rapid-fire odd facts about contestants, and a contestant held up a paddle if they heard a fact that they believed was specifically about their spouse. The game closed with a

Meet the new guys: Brad Sherwood, host of *The Dating Game,* and Gary Kroeger of *The Newlywed Game.*

Photo courtesy of Zane Enterprises

this-or-that game where the contestants tried to predict which of two choices ("Hamburgers or hot dogs?") their spouse would select.

After a shaky first season, the shows were reinvented into something far more familiar. Chuck Woolery, whose vaguely *Dating Game*–inspired series *Love Connection* had ended in 1994 after eleven seasons, was now at the helm of *The Dating Game,* which had gone back to basics, with the Looks and Personality round eliminated in favor of the flirty questions that had made the original show a sensation.

The Newlywed Game went completely back to the drawing board; not only reverting to the original format, but bringing back Bob Eubanks, whose own entrepreneurial spirit over the years had kept him somewhat synonymous with the game. Over the years, Eubanks had toured the country, hosting a live version of *The Newlywed Game* with local couples and attracting audiences that numbered in the thousands to shopping malls and convention centers.

Losing Match

Perhaps the most notorious game show flop of the late 1990s was rooted in the biggest smash of the 1970s. *Match Game* was on its way back for the 1998 fall season.

This was a risky proposition. Host Gene Rayburn had always been the first to say that the classic *Match Game* was, at heart, "a rotten format." But it succeeded because of a variety of factors that propped it up: panelists like Richard Dawson, Charles Nelson Reilly, and Brett Somers had chemistry and vibrancy that gave the show life beyond its own means. Gene Rayburn was, himself, a high-energy goofball who hammed up reading questions and collecting answers, and made himself seemingly indispensable to the show. The questions were off-the-wall, pushing the envelope as far as the standards of the 1970s would allow.

For the 1998 *Match Game,* Gene Rayburn, now eighty years old and in declining health, was understandably sitting out. Michael Burger, who had made his mark on TV viewers in the 1990s as co-host of the talk show *Mike and Maty,* would serve as master of ceremonies. A pitch tape was sent to stations across the country that was actually somewhat indicative of the problems with relaunching *Match Game.* The pitch tape consisted of Burger introducing clips of the 1970s version of *Match*

Game—a show with so many X-factors guiding its success that the pitch seemed to serve as a reminder of a performance that the new version couldn't possibly deliver.

The new version whittled the size of the panel down from six to five, with regular panelists Vicki Lawrence, Judy Tenuta, George Hamilton, and Nell Carter. That there was only one guest on each panel demonstrated another lesson that the new version didn't take from the classic. In addition to the regular family, the show rotated a wide swath of guest panelists in and out. As classic *Match Game* producer Robert Sherman explained in a 2013 interview, the constant rotation of guests meant new viewpoints and new things to talk about, not allowing the show to fall into a rut.

In an era of television where Jerry Springer and the onslaught of anything-goes cable offerings had violated every taboo one right after another, *Match Game*'s once titillating fill-in-the-blanks were no match, pardon the pun, for the rest of television, and the panelists frequently resorted to single-entendre answers. On at least one occasion, Michael Burger asked a question for which every panelist's answer was bleeped. *Match Game* crashed, vaporizing after only one lackluster season.

Starting from scratch: Chuck Woolery hosted *The Dating Game*, and Bob Eubanks returned to *The Newlywed Game*.

Square Off

The other star-studded '70s game show fared slightly better in its new incarnation. King World, the syndicator backing *Wheel of Fortune, Jeopardy!*, and *The Oprah Winfrey Show*, offered a new version of *Hollywood Squares*. The latter show had been in the works for a while. An attempt at a revival called *Planet Hollywood Squares*, intended to be a promotional tie-in for the restaurant chain, fell through earlier in the decade. This new *Hollywood Squares*, from Moffit-Lee Productions, was hosted by Tom Bergeron, formerly of FX's off-kilter morning show *Breakfast Time*, with Carolyn Rhea and comedy writer Bruce Vilanch signing on as regular panelists, but the Center Square would infuse the new version with a surprising amount of star power. A true A-list star, Whoopi Goldberg, was seated in the middle box, and helped the show as much as she could by calling in some favors from fellow mega-stars. Robin Williams, Billy Crystal, Whitney Houston, Sharon Stone, Patrick Swayze, Bernadette Peters, Melanie Griffith, Antonio Banderas, Nathan Lane, and Vanessa Williams all joined the game.

The star power didn't exactly translate to boffo ratings. *Squares* would always get good-not-great audiences, which was the source of quite a bit of backstage tension. Goldberg was increasingly called upon to call in more of her famous friends to play the game and felt as though full blame (and rarely full credit) fell on her for the show's ratings. The mounting animosity between Goldberg and the producers led her to depart after four seasons.

A New Kind of *Family*

When the new *Match Game* debuted in 1998, Pearson Television, owners of Mark Goodson's formats at that point, announced that their long-term plan was to revive *Family Feud* in 1999 and offer *Match Game* and *Family Feud* as a one-hour package for stations. *Match Game* bombed but Pearson went through with their plan anyway, introducing a new *Family Feud* in the fall of 1999 with host Louie Anderson.

Anderson secured the job in a highly unusual way, taping a home movie of himself playing the *Family Feud* home game with his own family. It would be a stormy three seasons for *Feud* and Anderson. Anderson was frequently, and transparently, unhappy at the show; a *Feud* parody on *MADtv* depicted Anderson grousing about doing "the same thing that we did yesterday, a remake of a remake of a bad show," telling the contestants to shut up, and getting bored and trailing off in the middle of explaining the rules. Anderson departed the show in 2002, predicting that the show would meet its demise the following season. As of 2018, this incarnation of *Feud*, although on the receiving end of a few facelifts, has survived without him.

41

Is That Your Final Answer?

Ask the Audience, and They Want More

A Million-Dollar Idea

In early June 1999, *The Los Angeles Times* quietly announced that ABC was instituting "an unusual programming move." In late August, for thirteen nights over the span of only two weeks, the network would air an American adaptation of a popular British game show. Regis Philbin would be the host, and the unconventional title was *Who Wants to Be a Millionaire?*

Nobody really sensed that there was anything special about the upcoming show. Rather, it just seemed to be emblematic of a recent trend at ABC network. The Alphabet had a surprise hit with an adaptation of the improvisational comedy pseudo-game *Whose Line is It Anyway?* hosted by Drew Carey. The network was also mulling a current-events-driven comedy game called *Have I Got News for You*, to be hosted by Norm MacDonald. It appeared ABC was just looking to Great Britain for cost-effective gap-filler shows to put on their schedule, and *Who Wants to Be a Millionaire?* was just one step in that plan.

It was a bizarre game show, from all outward appearances. The set didn't look enough like a game show; the lighting was dim, the colors dull. The music didn't sound like a game show; a Gregorian chant and throbbing heartbeats underscored the questions and answers. Everything moved at an agonizingly slow pace; whereas *Jeopardy!* bombarded viewers with questions and answers, a question on *Who Wants to Be a Millionaire?* could lead to minutes of steady deliberation without resolution. The counterintuitive choice for host: Regis Philbin, the high-energy sixty-seven-year-old talk show host whose previous two game shows, *The Neighbors* and *Almost Anything Goes*, had a combined run of thirty-nine weeks way back in the 1970s.

On August 16, 1999, America tuned in to *Who Wants to Be a Millionaire?* for the first time. And for the next two weeks, the entire nation stopped everything they were doing for thirty minutes a night to see if anyone could win the big money. Everything about the show—the imposing set, the brooding music, the snail-crawl pacing, Regis's good humor, and the game itself all blended in a way that no chemist could comprehend. Every word of the show's vocabulary entered the national lexicon. "I'd like to use a lifeline" was how you said you

"Who wants to be a millionaire?" asks Regis Philbin. "Me!" was the final answer for Americans in 1999.

couldn't answer your teacher's question. "Is that your final answer?" was your incredulous response when your co-worker gave you an explanation that you didn't believe. No game show, not even *Wheel of Fortune* or *Jeopardy!*, had become a cultural touchstone with the speed that *Millionaire* accomplished it.

Big Bucks, Big Brains, Big Hearts

Executive producer Michael Davies boasted that *Who Wants to Be a Millionaire?* was the most wide-open game show on television. Unlike virtually every other game on television, which recruited contestants with the caveat "If you're going to be in the Los Angeles area . . . ," *Millionaire* would recruit its contestants via a 900-number. Making the $1.50 call and answering a series of questions correctly and quickly was enough to qualify you to be on the show, and if you were nowhere near "Little Rock," ABC's studio complex in New York City, the show would even cover your travel and accommodations.

Each night, ten contestants circled the stage and answered a "fastest finger" question, in which four choices had to be arranged in a specific order, using a set of pushbuttons in front of each player. The contestant who gave the correct order in the least time made it to the famous Hot Seat in center stage for a chance at a million dollars. The contestant was asked up to fifteen multiple choice questions. The first correct answer was worth $100, with values escalating until the fifteenth and final question, worth a cool mil. A contestant risked everything on every question, but answering five questions guaranteed $1,000 no matter what, and ten questions guaranteed $32,000 no matter what. A contestant could also elect to quit any time after reading a question and leave with the value of the last correct answer.

"We want you to win as much money as possible," as Regis put it, so the show also spotted the contestant three Lifelines, the 50/50 (eliminating two wrong answers, leaving a player with just one wrong answer and one right answer to choose from), Ask the Audience (the audience votes on what they think the correct answer is), and Phone a Friend (AT&T would let the contestant call anybody in America to ask for help).

Millionaire had a peculiar pedigree, a far cry from the polished game show factories of Goodson-Todman and Barry and Enright that launched format after format in the previous generation. David Briggs, the fifty-seven-year-old director of a radio station in Great Britain, approached a small up-and-coming production house called Celador with a format that he originally called *Cash Mountain*. Paul Smith, the head of Celador, liked the idea and roped in two comedy writers, Steve Knight and Mike Whitehill, to refine Briggs's concept a bit. The men recruited Chris Tarrant, a British television personality and, Smith and Briggs discovered, a mutual friend, to serve as master of ceremonies. They secured a meeting with ITV in Great Britain and walked into a meeting holding envelopes marked with different amounts of money, selling the show by simply playing the game with the executives.

The show everyone wound up with was markedly different from the show they were expecting. Chris Tarrant admitted in an interview with ABC that everyone, himself included, was expecting a fairly conventional game show. But actually playing the game altered the expectations considerably.

Tarrant explained, "None of us had any idea, really, how big this thing was going to be. None of us had a clue. When we went on the air, we were just going to do a big glitzy sophisticated million-pound-giveaway show, and that's what it was about. It was about the money. It was only really early in one of the pilots we started thinking, 'God, this is really tense! This is serious stuff!' We slowly sussed that there was going to be this other element. There was going to be this huge soap opera, which is why it works."

Paul Smith told interviewer Richard Alleyne of *The Telegraph*, "We came up with the Holy Grail of game shows, one where you could give away the ultimate prize of a million pounds. I personally don't think that the million pounds is the draw. It's the emotional drama unfolding on the screen that people love."

The million dollars was great, but it was that heart of gold buried in the show. And that's what drew in Michael Davies, expatriate British television executive now toiling in the United States. Davies saw the breakout hit from his homeland and raved, "This is the best television format I've ever seen . . . and more dramatic than I could imagine. More real, and more edgy."

The soap opera emerged on opening night of the American version, when contestant Hilary Daw was asked, "What is the capital of Iraq?" and elected to use her Phone-a-Friend to call her brother Tom.

Tom confidently blurted out, "Baghdad."

Daw, trying to maintain her composure, told her brother, "Timmy, it's kind of important."

Tom assured his sister it was Baghdad. Hilary voiced her doubts, Timmy repeatedly assured his sister it was Baghdad, and the argument was abruptly cut off when the thirty-second time limit for the phone call ran out. Hilary, sounding not entirely convinced, had enough faith in her brother to declare that Baghdad was her final answer . . . and her brother was right.

Two weeks later, it was over, but one look at the ratings sheets told ABC it had only just begun. *Millionaire* returned for a second two-week run the following November. John Carpenter would make world history by being the first contestant of any version of *Who Wants to Be a Millionaire?* to clear all fifteen questions and win the top prize. Not only did Carpenter do it, he made it look easy, knocking out the first fourteen questions without using any Lifelines and then using his Phone-a-Friend on the final question only to call his father and let him know he was about to win a million dollars.

The audience was still there, and it was insatiable. ABC announced that in January, *Who Wants to Be a Millionaire?* would return as a regular series, airing for an unheard-of three nights per week in prime-time.

"Final Answer"

The distinctive game and its repetitive nature led to a catchphrase that saturated the country. "Final answer."

"I'll have the #4 with extra cheese." "Is that your final answer?"
"I'm going to the corner of 4th and Maple." "Is that your final answer?"
"Will you go to the prom with me?" "No. And that's my final answer!"

As explained in the show's official rules:

> When answering a question, the Contestant must lock in their answer by stating their answer choice and saying the word(s) "final" or "final answer." Once the Contestant has said "final" or "final answer," the answer is locked and cannot be changed. If the Contestant does not say "final" or "final answer" the answer is not locked. The Contestant must also say "final" or "final answer" to confirm (and lock) his/her decision to walk away from the Game. The Contestant may change his/her answer, walk away, or use an available lifeline until the Contestant says that the answer given is their final answer.

It was a notable breech in the way things had normally been done on TV game shows. Countless contestants had blurted out an answer and corrected themselves, only to wince helplessly as the emcee said, "I'm sorry, we have to accept your first answer." *Who Wants to Be a Millionaire?* was seemingly offering contestants a get-out-of-jail-free card, a chance to explore every possible answer without actually committing to one until they had said the magic phrase.

It was an elegant way of avoiding potential ugliness down the road with contestants. A person going for a life-changing amount of money who blew it could have potentially said, "That wasn't really my answer! I was just thinking out loud!" And *Millionaire* certainly went for maximum drama by encouraging contestants to verbalize every thought. When a contestant said, "Final answer," they were saying more than that. They were acknowledging that they had given as much thought as they were going to give, and that they knew the potential consequences.

It worked so well that the big-money quizzes that came after followed suit. Contestants on other games would say, "I accept that answer," "My answer is . . . " or "Lock it in." Many had buttons to punctuate the process. But the purpose of the act is the same. It puts the contestant in a position to acknowledge that they know what they're doing, and that there's no going back.

Not that *Millionaire* was made of stone. Contestant Ed Toutant reached the $16,000 question: "Scientists in England recently genetically altered what vegetable so it glows when it needs water? A) Potato B) Tomato C) Cabbage, D) Carrots."

Toutant, reasoning that you wouldn't light potatoes or carrots because they grow underground, answered "Tomato." He was ruled incorrect. Regis Philbin sent Toutant on his way, and then, during a stopdown in taping, asked a production assistant about the question.

A blogger in the audience that night later wrote, "As clear as if I were still sitting there in Seat 9 right now, I can vividly envision Regis stomping around the studio, flailing his hands up in an obvious hissy fit for the entire audience to take in, and screaming, 'What are we trying to do now . . . *Trick the contestants*?!?!?'"

Philbin had been told that the answer was a matter of semantics. The question asked "What vegetable . . ." Tomatoes are technically fruit and therefore couldn't possibly be right. A visibly annoyed Philbin went on with the taping, performing for an audience that was also rather unsatisfied with the outcome of Toutant's game.

Toutant, whose curiosity had been piqued by the losing question, found two faults with it when he conducted his own research later: the glowing potato experiment happened in Scotland, not England; and an Oxford scientist had, indeed, developed a glowing tomato. The way the question had been written, neither potato nor tomato was a correct answer, but Toutant's answer was arguably more correct than the show's, in a matter of speaking. Toutant wrote what he described as "a very polite e-mail" outlining his findings. He was brought back to the show for another shot, and walked away with $1.8 million.

Shelley Herman, a question writer for many games, opines, "There's a type of question that I see more and more often on the prime-time quiz shows that I find very unsatisfying. It's one where the question is written in such a way that there's an obvious answer implied, and then the correct answer is something entirely different. That, to me, is bad television. If you need a question that's hard enough that it'll save your prize budget, fine, but to me, it's more satisfying when you have a genuinely hard question, and after the contestant has blown it and you explain the correct answer and why it's correct, it makes you say, 'Ooooooh, that makes sense.'"

Fox Gets Greedy

It was hardly surprising that other networks were so eager to follow in ABC's footsteps, but Fox's footsteps were surprisingly loud and fast-moving. Fox prepared a new game show for a November 1999 launch, which was quite remarkable because it truly was a new game show. Mike Darnell, Fox executive vice president for alternative and special programming, saw *Who Wants to Be a Millionaire?*'s success and anticipated that other networks would not only mount their own big-money game shows, but that they would follow ABC's lead by adapting or reviving existing formats. Darnell wanted Fox to stand out from the crowd by offering a truly new game show, even if it meant rushing the developmental process.

Bob Boden explains, "*Who Wants to Be a Millionaire?* premiered on a Sunday night. On Wednesday, after the first few days' ratings came in and everyone saw what a monster this thing was, I got a call from Dick Clark Productions asking if I could formulate a game show in the style of *Millionaire* that could become the next *Millionaire*. I pitched a format to Dick Clark and his lieutenants that I called *All for One*. Five players answered questions together, but the answer didn't count unless a majority of players agreed to it. The following Monday, we went to NBC, but NBC was already preparing *Twenty One*, which was a format that the network owned, so it was going to take something extraordinary for them to say yes to an outside idea. They passed on *All for One*. We showed it to Fox. Fox wanted some changes, and Dick Clark didn't like the title *All for One*, because he felt it wasn't provocative enough. I said, 'Well, the core of the show is greed, so we could call it *The Greedy Bunch*, or *The Greedy Group*...' And Dick said, 'Let's just call it *Greed*.'

From there, we refined the rules until we had something everyone was happy with, and the show premiered nine weeks to the day that I got that first phone call from Dick Clark Productions."

November 1999 marked the debut of *Greed: The Multimillion Dollar Challenge*, Fox's own take on the modern, dimly lit, gloomy-soundtracked big-money quiz. The host was Chuck Woolery, who beat out lead candidates Phil Donahue and Keith Olbermann for the job.

Greed used a question with a numerical answer to whittle a field of six contestants down to five to play as a team, and eventually play against each other. Team members took turns answering four questions for up to $100,000. From that point forward, every question would have four correct answers. The team could also be whittled down by Terminator questions, in which members competed against each other head-to-head, with the survivor taking the loser's share of the winnings. The top prize was $2 million (originally a jackpot that started at $2 million and grew $50,000 per game until claimed; the jackpot was never awarded before switching to the flat top prize).

Greed had the drama, too, and like *Millionaire*, it boiled to the surface early on. In the third episode of the series, a team of three—Daniel Avila, Curtis Warren, and Melissa Skirboll—reached the final question, for $2.2 million. The team members were allowed to choose individually if they wanted to play, or take their money and go home. Melissa and Curtis both quit with $400,000 apiece and went home. Avila gave up $200,000 to go for the big one.

"According to a Yale University study of the most recognizable smells, which four of the following nine topped the list? Baby powder, peanut butter, moth balls, tuna, coffee, dry cat food, chocolate, cinnamon, Vicks Vaporub."

Avila selected peanut butter, tuna, coffee, and Vicks Vaporub. Peanut butter, coffee, and Vicks Vaporub lit up correct. Woolery asked the legendary question, "For $2.2 million ... is it *tuna*?"

A pause.

A red light around the word "tuna." It was wrong. Chocolate was the $2.2 million answer.

Some of the people from behind the scenes emerge to take a photo on the set of *Greed*: Dick Clark, supervising producer Jeff Merkin, host Chuck Woolery, creator Bob Boden, and Dick Clark Productions Executive Vice President Barry Adelman.   *Photo courtesy of Bob Boden*

Greed, while not a mega-hit, was performing respectably in its Thursday night time slot. NBC had owned that night previously, but the end of *Seinfeld* had opened up the field a little bit and Fox posted considerably better numbers on Thursday night when they introduced *Greed*.

The show received a somewhat mixed response, too. Critics who swarmed to *Millionaire* either outright dismissed *Greed* as a clone, or as a mean-spirited, nasty entity. Over the years, game shows had fought the contention that the genre was a vehicle for showcasing avarice, insisting that it was the personalities and the game itself that drew in viewers. Here now was a show that unabashedly named itself for the very characteristic that had tar-brushed the entire genre. Even Woolery delighted in holding up stacks of money and inviting players to smell them before making crucial decisions.

Strangely, *Greed* would be undone by another quiz show on the same network. On June 5, 2000, Fox introduced another new entry into the fray, *It's Your Chance of a Lifetime*, a variation on *Millionaire* in which a contestant answered a question to pay off their entire credit card bill, then answered another question for $5,000 worth of stake money, and then used that money to wager on each subsequent question. Fox aired five episodes of *It's Your Chance of a Lifetime* during that week, with the intent of having the show go to a once-a-week offering after. When the show tanked in the ratings, Fox not only called off future episodes, but then, shockingly, canceled *Greed* too.

Bob Boden laments, "When we were on the air, we were under constant pressure to deliver big ratings. Fox was never completely happy with the ratings we delivered. But I'll tell you something. In all the years that have passed since, Fox has never performed better in that Friday night time slot than we did. We were the strongest show they ever had in that slot."

On the Line

CBS jumped into the big-money quiz craze in exactly the way that Fox predicted, adapting another format from Great Britain, this one called *Winning Lines*. The host was Dick Clark, a surprising choice given that his production company was overseeing *Greed* for Fox—his son was that show's executive producer!

Clark gleefully told reporter Gail Shister, "Years and years ago, when I was a kid in my twenties, I always knew when I got to a certain age, I'd no longer be sought out as an on-camera person. To protect myself and stay in the business, I became a producer too. All of a sudden, somebody offered me a performing job as opposed to me offering one to someone else. Few people get that lucky."

Winning Lines started the game with a field of forty-nine contestants, narrowing it down with a series of six trivia questions with numerical answers. Contestants typed in their answers on keypads, with the contestant who was correct the fastest advancing to the second round. A final elimination round whittled the six down to one player, who competed against the Wonderwall. The Wonderwall was an imposing array of forty-nine answers. With a five-minute clock ticking away, Clark would ask questions rapid fire, and the contestant would have to give not only the answer, but its numeric location on the Wonderwall.

Winning Lines crashed and burned, a victim of a dead time slot (Saturday night, network TV's dumping ground) and a hostile home—of all the major networks, CBS was the most notoriously unenthusiastic about big-money prime-time quiz shows becoming a craze.

The Skeleton in NBC's Closet

"Who wants to be a millionaire . . . when you could win a lot of money?" The NBC promo taunted the competition with a menacing voice, as the network jumped into the big-jackpot quiz fray with what was arguably a shocking choice: a program that, decades earlier, the network wanted to forget.

Twenty One, one of the shows most infamously implicated in the quiz show scandals of the 1950s, had faded in the public consciousness over the decades until 1994, when the Robert Redford film *Quiz Show* re-opened television's old wound with a dramatization of the events surrounding Charles Van Doren's illegitimate championship reign on the series.

Aaron Solomon, a question writer for the new *Twenty One*, remembers, "We wanted to make it very clear that the one thing that *Twenty One* was remembered for was the one thing our show wasn't going to have. The writers were prohibited from being in the studio at the same time as the contestants. Once the questions had been written and printed out, the questions were placed in an attaché case, and Phil Gurin, the executive producer, would actually connect the case to himself with a set of handcuffs, and walk them to the stage with a security guard accompanying him."

Twenty One returned to NBC on January 9, 2000. The timing of the premiere wasn't a coincidence; it was two days before *Who Wants to Be a Millionaire?* assumed its permanent spot on the ABC schedule. In a surprising display of good sportsmanship, talk show host Maury Povich revealed the big news that he would be hosting the new *Twenty One* during an appearance on *Live with Regis and Kathie Lee*. Povich and Regis Philbin amiably wished each other well in the impending war of the prime-time quiz shows.

In many ways, the new *Twenty One* was a throwback. Each episode began with Maury Povich, in a totally dark studio, giving some information about the contestants and what happened in the previous game, the same as Jack Barry had opened each episode some forty-four years earlier. A live orchestra led by Tom Scott provided the soundtrack for the game, on a set that looked very much set in the past.

The game was strangely influenced by its competition, however. A rather pointless segment in which the champion selected the next challenger from a pool of contestants was an underwhelming copycat of the Fastest Finger element from *Who Wants to Be a Millionaire?* The contestants had what was fundamentally a Lifeline; they could each bring a friend to the studio to help them answer one question per game. All questions were multiple choice, and arguably much easier for a show touted in its fixed heyday as having some of the most challenging questions on television; perhaps this version was trying to sidestep allegations of rigging by making the questions so easy that it was obvious that rigging wasn't necessary.

But the show's eagerness to give away as much money as fast as possible was perhaps its undoing. Whereas *Who Wants to Be a Millionaire?* shone its bright spotlight on the contestants going for that big prize, on *Twenty One*, all eyes were apparently fixed squarely on the dollars at stake. Instead of awarding cash per point separating the winner and the loser, as the original show had done, the new *Twenty One* awarded escalating amounts to the winners of each game. A first-time winner received a jaw-dropping $100,000 for that single game, *and* played a bonus round involving a series of true-false questions that could pay off an additional $210,000. Winning a second game added $200,000, a third game $300,000, a fourth game $400,000, and then the money reset to $100,000. If the questions were generally challenging and the games suspenseful, those cash payoffs could have seemed worth it. But the idea that a contestant could win $400,000 for knowing which Nickelodeon series starred Melissa Joan Hart probably seemed downright obscene to many viewers.

Aaron Solomon remembers, "Our first big winner was Rahim Oberholtzer, whom the staff nicknamed 'The Accidental Millionaire,' because the way he amassed his fortune gave away how flawed our show was. We had structured the program in such a way that a contestant could win a million dollars with very little personal effort. We allowed the contestants to bring a friend or family member to help them answer a question for each game, so Rahim's father essentially won one of the games for him. We also had a three strikes rule, where a contestant automatically lost the game on their third wrong answer, which meant a win of six figures by answering softball questions while your opponent just buried himself by missing questions. If you watch the tape of Rahim's fourth win, which was

The results are in, and you ARE the millionaire! Maury Povich gave away the money—a little too much, in the eyes of many—on NBC's *Twenty One*.

the game that brought his winnings up to $1 million, his facial expression is pretty interesting, because you got the sense that he was thinking, 'I didn't really earn this.'"

Povich was forced to admit as much a short time later, when he actually opened an episode by admitting that many viewers had complained that it was too easy to win a million dollars. The show was now adopting a somewhat more conservative money ladder, with the first game paying $25,000 and escalating to a million-dollar payday for winning a seventh game.

Solomon says, "In a way, that change hurt us even more. The right way to do a game show is to test the game in run-throughs and in pilots, check for any bugs, and fix them before it goes on the air. When *Who Wants to Be a Millionaire?* took off, there was a mad rush by other networks to combat it with their own big-money game show. So, NBC put us on the air without shooting a pilot first, and a pilot would have enabled us to discover these flaws. NBC put us on the air without shooting a pilot first. So, we gave away a million dollars without the contestant having to do much fighting to win it, and then we announce all these rule changes. When you award such a huge payday that quickly, and then immediately introduce new rules to prevent it from happening like that again, what you've done is you've just exposed to viewers that you didn't do your job. Even a viewer knows you're supposed to spot these things before they do. And the prevailing theory that 'bigger jackpot equals bigger ratings' was immediately disproved."

Under the new rules, a *Twenty One* contestant named David Legler briefly enjoyed a reign as the top winner in game show history by accumulating $1,765,000 over the course of six games, but not many contestants had the chance to top him. The show came to an end in May 2000, after barely four months on the air.

Goodbye.

While every other competitor tried putting *Millionaire* leftovers in a microwave and expecting the public to eat it up, NBC served up a cold dish called *The Weakest Link*. It was an adaptation of a British quiz—Oh, of course it was, they were just copying *Millionaire*, a cynic might think at first—but nobody could mistake the NBC big-money quiz that premiered on April 16, 2001 for *Who Wants to Be a Millionaire?*

NBC shot two pilots for *The Weakest Link* in January 2001, one with the ice-cold Anne Robinson, host of the original British version, and another with the freshly infamous Richard Hatch (see Chapter 43). Robinson didn't just bring experience to the job, she brought humorless, relentless and remorseless severity to *The Weakest Link*, so NBC began dispatching airplanes for Robinson's exhausting commute from London to Los Angeles to host the American version.

"She's cold, she's ruthless, she's rude. She's everything that makes a great TV executive," quipped NBC Entertainment boss Jeff Zucker. "There's nothing else like her on American TV."

Zucker reasoned that without Robinson specifically as host, viewers would just see *The Weakest Link* as one more version of *Millionaire*, that her style alone was enough to separate it from the pack.

Robinson, who had a "Rudest Woman on Television" award from a British magazine among her many career achievements, defended her approach to the job: "Game show hosts are usually cheesy. They're terribly, insincerely sweet. It's like bathing in treacle and wearing velvet. It's very Andy Williams."

And so, Robinson eschewed that style for what she considered a more direct approach, told reporter Gail Shister, "I hope I don't go beyond that line. If I was that cruel, I would have complaints. I haven't seen anyone leave the set . . . I'm not there to crush people beyond what they can take. You hope they have the experience to know the beast they're battling."

"You are the weakest link! Goodbye!"

NBC viewers were alerted to the impending arrival of a new pop-cultural catchphrase with the earliest promos for the new game, offering little more than a harsh glance of Robinson barking out the declaration. On *The Weakest Link*, a group of eight strangers came together as a team to answer trivia questions and attempt to build a bank that could potentially reach $1 million. Potentially. In execution, teams didn't come close; the highest bank awarded during the series was $188,500; nothing to sneeze at but less than one-fifth of the potential winnings offered by the series.

"Out of a possible $125,000, you banked a limp $8,000," scorned Robinson.

That shortcoming proved to be the show's charm, ultimately. At the conclusion of every timed round of rapid-fire Q&A, Robinson would verbally dismantle the team members one by one.

Robinson: What do you do?

Contestant: Well, I forecast the weather for the number-one ten o'clock news in Charlotte, North Carolina.

Robinson: Do you ever get it right?

Contestant: Like my batting average so far today, yes.

Robinson: Will you be missing any questions?

Contestant: Nobody's perfect.

Robinson: Certainly not weathermen.

Each round concluded with the team members turning on each other by casting votes on which one should be forced out of the game. Ideally, as the title suggested, the players would attempt to vote off the weakest link on their team. Frequently, however, the game saw contestants acting against their own self-interest, voting off the players who racked up the most money and provided the most correct answers, out of fear that this contestant would knock them off in the end. What this meant was that games were often reduced to duh-offs between poorer contestants who had eliminated the ones who could have helped them build up their banks.

This didn't seem to bother viewers, though. The object of a game show is to make the television audience shout at their TVs. It just happened that more often than not, the television audience was shouting, "You *idiots!*"

That's Too Much!

"You are the weakest link! Goodbye!" did indeed become a national catchphrase in America over the next few months, just as it had become in Great Britain (at least once, it had been shouted on the floor of Parliament), but by August 2002, the network version had quickly run out of steam. Two months earlier, ABC had dumped *Who Wants to Be a Millionaire?* The overwhelming consensus was that overexposure was the cause of death. During an interview on NBC's *Today*, legendary game show host Tom Kennedy lamented that ABC had "trampled" *Millionaire*, while Bob Boden, executive producer of *Greed*, invoked the name of his own show during an interview to explain why every one of the big-money game shows had disappeared.

Millionaire had once occupied three hours a week of prime-time television . . . and then four. Sometimes five. When ABC felt it was underperforming in one of its many time slots, the network thought nothing of rescheduling it, often with little or no warning. *Who Wants to Be a Millionaire?* was on too often, and ironically, nobody knew when to watch it.

Likewise, NBC had strangled its golden goose with too much *Weakest Link* too soon. Multiple airings per week and gimmick after gimmick—one of its final episodes on the network saw Anne Robinson facing a team of eight Elvis impersonators—brought that show to an untimely end.

Game show host Marc Summers says, "That's a tendency that hasn't gone away either. At the first whiff of success for a game show, a network will just beat the crap out of it. If ABC had just kept *Millionaire* on once a week, it would probably still be on ABC today. Once a week is fantastic, but then suddenly it feels like it's always on and it stops being fun. What your average network executive doesn't realize is that game shows are like a porno movie; it's the best thing ever for about twenty minutes but then you feel like you're never going to want to watch a porno movie for the rest of your life. Game shows are the same way, they're fun for a little while but you need some space before the next time you watch it."

For the fall of 2002, *Millionaire* and *Link* both resurfaced as thirty-minute Monday-through-Friday offerings for first-run syndication. Journalist Meredith Vieria hosted *Millionaire*, and George Gray—who beat out Richard Hatch in another round of auditions—hosted *The Weakest Link*. *Link* expired after only one season in syndication, while *Millionaire* proved to be the little game show that could. Nowhere near the cultural phenomenon it had always been, *Millionaire* hung on to just enough viewers day after day to sustain for over a decade, and even survive a revolving door of emcees, including Cedric the Entertainer, Terry Crews, and Chris Harrison.

The demise of big-money quiz shows, for a second time, may have disappointed some ardent game show fans, but the true experts were hardly surprised. At the height of *Millionaire* Mania, Bob Barker prognosticated in an interview with *Dateline NBC*, "There used to be westerns all over TV and then people wondered where all the westerns went. In a few years, people will be asking, 'What happened to the big-money game shows?'"

42

Reality Biting

The Tribe Speaks

I Will Survive

Although CBS famously detested the newfound game show craze entering the year 2000, the network lucked into the most enduring hit of the bunch, one that wound up spanning more than twenty seasons and created more than its share of memorable moments and contestants-turned-stars. But don't you *dare* call it a game show—CBS called it a "reality show," a term for game shows that didn't look or feel like game shows. *Survivor*, which abandoned slick studios for the sprawling, scenic outdoors, would be the show that defined the newly coined genre.

Jake Tauber, then-executive vice president of Game Show Network, assessed the swath of game shows hitting the airwaves in 2000 and said, "The shows that will work will follow the same rules that have always been successful for game shows—there must be a strong play-along factor for audiences at home, and they must feel that it could be them up on stage."

Or in the wilderness. Whatever. But *Survivor* became a national phenomenon in part because of that same immersive quality. Viewers watched as sixteen contestants—or as the show called them, castaways—were divided into a pair of tribes forced to sustain themselves on a tiny island or similarly desolate space, thrust into competition against each other in a series of physical and mental competitions. One of the show's favorites, for example, is having the tribes navigate an obstacle course to retrieve puzzle pieces. The winning tribe would be rewarded with creature comforts from civilization, like hot pizza and cold sodas, or blankets and comfortable chairs. Sometimes, it might even be items essential for survival, like fishing equipment.

The losers, meanwhile, laid their disappointment bare for the cameras—not disappointment in themselves, but in their teammates. Assessing blame for catastrophe, taking credit, and making it known who shouldn't be allowed to stay. The losing team gathered for a Tribal Council and cast their votes for the teammate who should be kicked off the island, and once the votes were tallied, the loser was told "the tribe has spoken" and was forced to extinguish his or her ceremonial torch on their way out of the game. As players were whittled away from the competition, the tribes would merge into a single group, and the

Survivor was no passing fad . . . viewers would carry a torch for the show and host Jeff Probst for years.

competitions were individual efforts instead of team games, often endurance challenges, like holding a Totem pole while precariously perched on a wobbly balance beam, with everyone participating in the final vote. With two players remaining, a jury of castaways already eliminated decided the winner, who collected a cool million.

And that's when things got tricky. You had to remain likable enough to win what was essentially a popularity contest, even after your opponents and teammates had watched you spite and snark your way out of getting eliminated.

As Sarah Pekkanen of the *Baltimore Sun* put it, "It's *Gilligan's Island* meets *The Real World* meets your worst high school nightmare."

Access Hollywood correspondent Jeff Probst, no stranger to game shows after a stint hosting VH-1's *Rock and Roll Jeopardy!*, would oversee *Survivor*, often sounding more like an authoritarian character in an old novel than a master of ceremonies. ("I bring news of tomorrow's challenge!")

Survivor came to the U. S. by way of producer Mark Burnett, who had seen a Swedish show called *Expedition Robinson* that he found crudely produced and mean-spirited . . . but surprisingly compelling. He pitched it to CBS executive Les Moonves as much more than a game show with a gimmicky setting. It was a drama and a social experiment all rolled into one. Viewers initially tuned in more likely for morbid curiosity than anything else—someone might drown or get bitten by a snake—but were in for a surprise at how riveting it was to watch teammates building a small raft, or seeing the disappointment in a player getting to know someone, growing fond of them, and realizing that their new friend was such a weak player that they were the obvious choice for elimination when the time came.

Arguably, the contestant that made the show what it is today was a conniving nudist named Richard Hatch, who came into season one with, like the rest of the castaways, no familiarity with the original series, no frame of reference for how to approach it. And yet, somehow, he solved it seemingly before he ever arrived. He assembled a small alliance with three other contestants, who would agree on whom to vote for before the Tribal Council without really giving regard to how anybody played the game. They just settled on a name, cast their votes, and dumped them. When one member of that alliance, Sue, found herself getting dumped late in the game, she vented her poison in a legendary speech, calling out her opponents/teammates for their transgressions: "If I were ever to pass you . . . and you were lying there, dying of thirst, I would not give you a drink of water. I would let the vultures take you and do whatever they want with you."

Hatch collected the million dollars, from a jury of defeated contestants who seemed almost awestruck at how skillfully he had used all of them for his own benefit, and in the process, altered the show's core premise. Virtually every contestant that followed would attempt to duplicate Richard's political, self-serving approach to the game, and instead of being a human drama of simulated survival among the players, *Survivor* became a competition to see who was willing to do what in order to win. It wouldn't be quite the same as shouting the correct answer at the TV, but pondering who you'd cast your vote for while wishing the worst person in the world would finally get eliminated provided that vicarious thrill that drew so many to more traditional game shows.

Survivor would dominate the summer of 2000, reaching number one in the Nielsen ratings and knocking *Who Wants to Be a Millionaire?* off its lofty perch. But while ABC's greed would cause *Millionaire* to bleed to death within two years, CBS exercised admirable restraint with its hot property, and *Survivor* wouldn't succumb to poisonous overexposure.

Game show writer Shelley Herman says, "I want to see people having fun, learning new things, and coming away happy. I do not understand the appeal of *Survivor*, especially given the central theme of the show. There really are people who are suffering in extreme weather conditions, struggling to find food, sleeping in dirt . . . should we be making a game out of something that people are actually trying to endure in the outside world?"

Oh, Brother!

CBS stayed busy in the summer of 2000, introducing a second reality show that was something of an introverted form of *Survivor*. On *Big Brother*, there were no castaways, but houseguests, living together under constant surveillance in a house filled with cameras. As a bonus, *Big Brother* wasn't just limiting its viewers to a one-hour show every week. Live feeds of the cameras in the house were available 24/7 online, allowing fans to look in whenever they wanted. It was a voyeuristic touch that really made it the perfect show for the year 2000. At the tail end of the millennium, Jennifer Ringley's groundbreaking website JenniCam was attracting millions each day who just wanted to see what was going on in her apartment, and Jim Carrey had a box-office blockbuster with *The Truman Show*, the story of a man who didn't know that his entire life was being broadcast on TV.

The host was *CBS Morning News* anchor Julie Chen, whose acceptance of the *Big Brother* gig surprised viewers and CBS co-workers alike. Chen was quick to point out that Hugh Downs and Mike Wallace were both game show hosts in addition to being journalists, and even Downs himself publicly defended Chen's choice of night job.

The freshman season of *Big Brother* was a disaster marred by an unexpected onslaught of controversy—CBS spent over $100,000 on background checks for the *Big Brother* houseguests but failed to catch an outstanding warrant for one and membership in an anti-Semitic group for another. Still another used the household cameras to vent her feelings about the rocky state of her marriage, which led to even louder criticism of Chen for attaching herself to such an intrusive circus.

Still, CBS Television President Les Moonves stood by his new series, admitting "[CBS is] flying without a net on this one, [but] I'm not going to apologize for this show."

While he wouldn't apologize for it, he made it clear that the network was open to tinkering. After being lambasted for a lackluster first outing—the Associated Press said the show "proved that reality television could be simultaneously offensive and dull"—the show would be significantly revamped the following year. More emphasis was placed on the games that the housemates played for the right to become Head of Household, the recipient of luxury household items and the one who decided which two houseguests to nominate for elimination.

Behind the scenes, the man appointed to run the second season was veteran TV and film producer Arnold Shapiro, who rose to prominence in 1978 with his Oscar- and Emmy-winning documentary *Scared Straight*, about a group of juvenile offenders forced to spend three hours with prisoners. Shapiro accepted the job while diplomatically criticizing the overwhelmingly unpleasant tone of the first season, promising to deliver a more crowd-pleasing show for the next outing.

Starting in season two, the show instituted more of a game, instead of just leaving it up to America to vote in a popularity contest. The show introduced the Head of Household competition, with the winner getting their own bedroom complete with a lock on the door, while everybody else endured shared quarters. The Head of Household would also be charged with making two nominations for potential eviction, with the rest of the housemates casting their votes at the end of the week. To spice things up further in season three, a competition for veto power was introduced, with the winner having the option of vetoing a nomination and forcing the head of household to pick a new potential victim.

Big Brother's voyeuristic extra, the 24/7 live feed, continued to captivate viewers for years after, with onlookers following the show every day throughout the summer as though it was part of their own lives. With a more lighthearted tone and arguably more of a game sensibility than *Survivor*, *Big Brother* found its niche, and its audience, keeping fans looking in for summer after summer.

Simply Amazing

While *Survivor* and *Big Brother* isolated its contestants from civilization by cramming them into houses and on desert islands, CBS's next foray into reality TV did just the opposite, sending them into the great big world and relying on their brains, their bodies, and, occasionally, the kindness of strangers to lead them to victory.

The Amazing Race was partly a scavenger hunt and partly a race around the world, a race lasting generally about twenty-five to thirty days, leaving Phileas Fogg in the dust. Eleven pairs of contestants started the race, vying to reach designated checkpoints by way of planes, trains, and automobiles, plus the occasional boat and even a literal race by foot at times. They also had a stipend to cover expenses along the way, although some crafty and outgoing contestants would resort to begging on the streets wherever they ended up to round up extra funds. Phil Keoghan would greet the contestants at each "pit stop" on the race to give them a task or to let them know that they were the last ones to arrive, and that it was time to go.

The Amazing Race premiered on September 5, 2001, six days before the terrorist attacks on New York City and Washington, D. C. that brought America to a standstill. In a strange turn of fate, however, Koeghan would reluctantly admit in an interview with the *Indianapolis Star* that the September 11 attacks may have drawn viewers to the show. After the show's debut broadcast, critics and early viewer feedback suggested that the show came off "too nice" in the field of reality TV. There was no conniving, no scheming or backbiting, so prevalent in the other reality shows.

Koeghan told the *Star*, "If there was any criticism about our show . . . it was maybe that it was a bit soft. I remember a couple of people made comments to me, 'Where's the edge?' That's what people tended to think about prior to September 11. And now, the fact that our show is a feel-good show and people walk away with the experience of a lifetime—that's the worst thing they end up with—I think has made it a show that more people have connected with because it doesn't have that edgy, sinister element."

The teams worked individually from the start, which meant no need to build alliances to topple their opponents. They just had to worry about themselves, which meant that the only thing anybody was trying to accomplish on the show was helping their partner. The program had an uplifting spirit that attracted family audiences as well as Emmy voters. It became the darling of the Academy of Television Arts and Sciences, which introduced a Reality TV category in 2003 and awarded it to *The Amazing Race* for seven consecutive years.

Attitude Problem

Countless critics have weighed in about the perceived nastiness of the reality TV genre, with drama that feeds from some of the less redeeming traits of human beings.

Game show producer Mark Maxwell-Smith weighs in with what seems to be, in a nutshell, the prevailing attitude toward reality TV from those who could do without it.

"I hate reality TV," he said emphatically. "I hate the name because it's not reality. Reality TV is notoriously manipulated. The people are compelled by the production staffs to say what they say and do what they do.

"And I'll admit I'm painting it with a broad brush, but so many reality TV shows venerate the worst things. The first big reality TV star was Puck on MTV's *The Real World,* and he was only famous for being such a prick. On *The Apprentice,* the star contestant was Omarosa, who complained, bossed everybody around . . . just completely nasty. Richard Hatch on *Survivor* was an awful human being. We're celebrating people that I don't want my grandkids to go anywhere near. I'm flawed—I've looked at a porno magazine, I've craned my neck when I overhear an argument in a restaurant, but you know what? Nobody was giving me cash and prizes for doing that. We're rewarding really unacceptable behavior. And after so many years of being desensitized to that, we had a presidential election and voted for the star of a reality TV show. What does that say?"

43

Shiny Floor Games

When Game Shows Became an Event

Waxing About the Term

Game show producer and TV executive Bob Boden rolls his eyes when he hears the term. "I can think of no other genre in the history of the television medium that is classified by how clean they keep their floors," he says.

After a moment, he adds, "There's a strange mindset now about game shows and set design. If your game show is in daytime, you need a shiny white floor. If your game show is in prime-time, you need a shiny black floor. In fact, when certain daytime games have had prime-time specials, they've actually installed black floors in place of the white floors so that they look right, that's how strong this mindset is."

Nobody's quite sure who coined the term, but at some point in the 2000s, the childlike expression "Shiny Floor Games" began popping up more and more when referring to TV game shows. There was arguably a necessity to the term—as reality competitions that put its contestants in a giant house or the great outdoors became more prevalent, "shiny floor games" was a good way to get the point across quickly that this was a traditional game show. And while most game shows had a nice shiny floor, the lustrous surfaces that prime-time game shows of the 2000s were played on gave the programs a subliminally uniform look; seemingly every prime-time game had those well-waxed walkways.

Producer Aaron Solomon elaborates, "Game shows became more cinematic in the years after *Who Wants to Be a Millionaire?* The set designs were made to look futuristic, and post-apocalyptic, and a bit abstract, with the lighting and coloring designed to look like the sets went into an infinite void, plus the constant soundtrack underscoring the entire game. Prime-time game shows definitely took on very similar looks, and central to that was that the floors gleamed."

Producer Sande Stewart laments, "In the beginning, I loved the *Who Wants to Be a Millionaire?* approach to presentation, but then everything looked exactly the same. Every game show had the same lighting, the same floors, the same large screens on the set, mood music. Network executives insist on that look, but it's hard for any one show to make an impact when they all look exactly the same."

Shelley Herman, a writer for many games of the modern era, says, "I don't care for shows where the contestant needs an inspirational story. That's become such a trend. We have contestants giving us their life stories; deaths of family members, the time their house went into foreclosure, their military records, they have their families with them and we get these long segments where we have to listen to the family talking over what number to pick. It's a game show, get on with the game! Nobody cares about these back stories. Give these people thirty seconds to talk about themselves at the beginning and then play the game."

Big Deal

Howie Mandel, actor/comedian best known for putting a rubber glove on his head and imitating a chicken, was the unexpected choice for host for the next overseas phenomenon to cross the ocean and appear on American television screens: *Deal or No Deal*, created by Dick De Rijk, was a sensation in the United Kingdom and Australia before it first appeared on NBC on December 19, 2005, and like *Who Wants to Be a Millionaire?* six years earlier, became an overnight hit.

Mandel told a reporter, "It's not really a game. It's a study of humanity and what level of calculated risks somebody will take to possibly change their lives."

Mandel wasn't completely correct when he said *Deal or No Deal* wasn't a game show. It was barely a game show, a shinier, glitzier, more polished-looking form of the grab bag perfected by *Let's Make a Deal* and *Treasure Hunt*. Twenty-six leggy models wielding twenty-six briefcases stood before a lone contestant. Each brief-

case contained a different cash amount, as low as one penny or as high as $1 million. The contestant selected one briefcase, and then eliminated the other twenty-five briefcases one by one by selecting them and having each model reveal the hidden money amount.

Looking over this basic game was The Banker, a sinister-looking figure shrouded in shadows high over the studio, who communicated with Mandel only, and only by telephone. Throughout the game, The Banker would make offers to the contestant to buy their chosen briefcase, preferably for as little money as possible. If the contestant had opened the unchosen briefcases and revealed high-end amounts, like $200,000 and $300,000, the offer would probably be a lowball. If the contestant had been fortunate enough

Howie Mandel has twenty-six cases waiting to be opened. Which one do you want?

to eliminate paltry amounts like the penny or one dollar, The Banker's offers could grow to six figures.

What the game lacked in skill, it more than made up with pure drama. A contestant could reject a life-changing $187,000 offer from The Banker, only to open the next briefcase, reveal $500,000, and see the Banker's offer nosedive to $20,000 . . . or maybe that contestant, visibly suffering "rejecter's remorse" after saying "*No deal!*" to the banker, would open a $10 briefcase and hoot with joy at getting the next offer of $235,000.

It was laughably simple on paper, but in execution, it was a nail-biter. Mandel had taken the job when he met with producers over lunch; one producer produced a deck of cards with different money amounts printed, asked Howie to pick a card without turning it over, and then played the game with the remaining cards, asking Mandel if he'd be willing to sell his card back to them. It was fake money; Mandel felt his heart pounding anyway. NBC executives held focus groups with episodes of the international versions of the show and were shocked at the way people screamed at the screen as the game played out.

The game was briefly a fad and was treated as such, with video games, board games, card games, scratch-off games, arcade games, casino games, and every other type of game getting a layer of *Deal or No Deal* chrome across it. NBC, apparently having learned some lesson from the early death of *Who Wants to Be a Millionaire?*, avoided overexposing the show, although opening briefcase after briefcase after briefcase seemed to necessitate some bit of occasional tweaking to keep viewers engaged. There were plenty of theme nights, like Spring Break Night, Mardi Gras Night, Breast Cancer Awareness Night, "Going Green" Night, special guest banker Donald Trump, and a *Star Wars*–themed special with all of the models in Princess Leia's slave garb from *Return of the Jedi*, plus Darth Banker.

But the show's most famous gimmick was the well-publicized Million-Dollar Mission. It had been a source of frustration for some viewers that the million-dollar briefcase hadn't been won after a year and a half on the air, so in 2008, the show began adding more million-dollar briefcases. Every time a game played out without a million-dollar winner, another million-dollar briefcase was added, until one contestant finally hit the big money, a payoff that NBC shipwrecked by announcing the night it would happen in its promos for *Deal or No Deal.*

Not everyone was a fan. The game itself was legitimate but the production was treated very much like a dramatic show or a feature film. Contestants and the family supporting them were fed lines, there would be re-takes of briefcases being opened, and contestants would even be asked to react to the opening of a briefcase again if their elated shouts of joy weren't quite jubilant enough. To some well-trained eyes, the fakery seeped through.

Game show writer and producer Mark Maxwell-Smith grimaced, "You did not have to look into Howie Mandel's ear to figure out he was being fed lines. It was such an artificial presentation and it was so removed from what a game show is about—game shows are about the game, they are not about a close-up so tight that the audience at home can count the number of beads of sweat on the contestant's forehead."

A daily syndicated version of *Deal* appeared in the fall of 2008; the NBC prime-time incarnation expired on May 18, 2009, after a perfectly respectable three-and-a-half year run on the network.

1 in a Million

NBC and Endemol, the network and production house overseeing *Deal or No Deal*, imported another game, this one a Netherlands original called *1 vs. 100*. *Full House* dad-turned-crass comic Bob Saget was master of ceremonies. One contestant stood before a looming ten-tiered panel of one hundred opponents, dubbed The Mob. Saget would ask multiple-choice questions, with The Mob using pushbutton consoles to answer the question and the contestant giving verbal answers. If the contestant answered correctly, they won money for each Mob member who answered incorrectly; those Mob-sters were also eliminated from the game and the show. If the contestant was wrong, the surviving Mob divided all the money earned to that point.

Among the notable mob members who sat in on the show was *Jeopardy!* mega-champ Ken Jennings. After his stunning seventy-four victories on Alex Trebek's quizzer and a grand total of $2,522,700, his performance on *1 vs. 100* left something to be desired; he was knocked out of the Mob after two episodes (he didn't know that the 1 on a roulette wheel is red) and left with $714.29, part of a contestant's missed $35,000 jackpot that he split with forty-eight other members.

If you're thinking that organizing 101 contestants for a single game was tricky, you would be right. Producer Aaron Solomon remembers, "The studio complex was an absolute madhouse on the days that we taped. That show actually used two soundstages. One was the stage we used for the game, and then we had a whole soundstage that was used just as a holding area for contestants. We had several hundred people standing by at the start of each day.

"Other game shows screen potential contestants with a test when they audition, and if they get low scores, they aren't called back for the show. Obviously, with 101 players per game, you can't be too picky, so we weren't. In fact, having some lesser-intelligent contestants in the Mob helped. We wanted to increase the likelihood that with each correct answer the One gave, a number of Mob members were eliminated, so there was a sense of progress. Otherwise the odds would have been statistically prohibitive that the One would ever knock out one hundred people of the same aptitude. So, we actually came up with a system. We came up with four subsets of game-playing ability, of intelligence really, and we'd put every player in one of those subsets. We devised a formula for how many contestants from each subset we needed for every game, and that kept it interesting."

Although it was modestly successful, the game didn't make waves the way *Deal or No Deal* had. Some light tinkering was done with the show—instead of being paid per Mob member eliminated, the contestants got a flat payoff per ten eliminations. The show *1 vs 100* expired after fourteen months on NBC.

Who's That?

Undaunted, NBC and Endemol kept churning out more and more formats. An original concept snuck through the cracks on December 19, 2006, *Identity*, hosted by Penn Jillette. The show was symptomatic of how derivative prime-time game shows had become since the dawn of *Who Wants to Be a Millionaire?* Like *Millionaire*, it had brooding music and dim lighting. Like *Millionaire*, a contestant had three Lifelines—er, "helps," as the show called them. Like *Millionaire*, the show had a ladder of money that grew and grew with every correct answer. Like *1 vs. 100*, one contestant faced a large field of challengers. Like *Deal or No Deal*, the contestant had their family to the side of the stage cheering them on.

The contestant faced a group of twelve strangers. To their side was a list of twelve identities—for example, Pickpocket, White House Intern, Music Video Dancer, KO'd Mike Tyson, etc.—and the contestant picked identities one at a time and tried to match each one to the correct person onstage. One of the tricky things about the show was how utterly impossible it was to stagger the level of difficulty: The contestant selected the identity "KO'd Mike Tyson" and picked the one person of the twelve onstage who was most obviously Buster Douglas.

Identity crashed and burned after only twelve episodes spread out over five months. NBC "put it on hiatus" after April 2007, but the hiatus never ended, and *Identity* went into the dustbin of forgettable game show ideas.

This Game is Shat!

William Shatner experienced a strange career renaissance in the 2000s by settling for becoming a parody of himself, releasing an album of his trademark talk-singing method of performing songs, and becoming Priceline's hammy Negotiator in a popular ad campaign. In 2006, Shatner sank his teeth into the set of a new prime-time game show on ABC, *Show Me the Money*.

ABC touted the game as a variety show, a category verified by the presence of the Million-Dollar Dancers, thirteen gyrating babes who danced their way onto the stage at the start of the show. Each Million-Dollar dancer wielded a scroll containing a different money amount, ranging from $20,000 to $200,000. Yup, a large number of attractive women hiding amounts of money. Sound familiar? It should, Dick De Rijk created this one too.

Shatner would ask a question; the contestant gave an answer, then selected a Million-Dollar Dancer, who opened her scroll. A right answer earned the money, a wrong answer took the money away, even if it took the player below zero. The game continued until the player gave either a sixth correct answer or a sixth incorrect answer. One of the Million-Dollar Dancers had a Killer Card, which could cost a contestant all their money with a single wrong answer. *Show Me the Money* ran for five episodes—it taped seven—with reruns being sold to Game Show Network, which aired only two reruns before pulling it from their schedule. ABC and Game Show Network might have tried to show you the money, but that didn't mean anybody was looking.

I'll Have a Fifth

Three adults, Barry Poznick, John Stevens, and Mark Burnett, developed a game of child's play with the very grown-up grand prize of one million dollars. "You might be a redneck" comic Jeff Foxworthy hosted the game show with one of the best titles ever devised: *Are You Smarter Than a 5th Grader?*

And behind the great title was actually a pretty great premise. All the question-and-answer material for each contestant's eleven-question climb to a million dollars was grade level-appropriate material culled from textbooks from first to fifth grade.

Although the idea that fifth grade-level educational material merited a million-dollar grand prize might have seemed like evidence of a shocking decline in American intelligence, it was more like evidence that the average adult didn't retain much of what they learned after taking their tests a few decades earlier.

David Mikkelson, co-founder of the urban legends website snopes.com, wrote in 2007, "Just about *any* test looks difficult to those who haven't recently been steeped in the material it covers. If a forty-year-old can't score as well on a geography test as a high school student who just spent several weeks memorizing the names of all the rivers in South America in preparation for an exam, that doesn't mean the forty-year-old's education was woefully deficient — it means the he simply didn't retain information for which he had no use, no matter how thoroughly it was drilled into his brain through rote memory some twenty-odd years earlier. I suspect I'd fail a lot of the tests I took back in high school if I had to re-take them today without reviewing the material beforehand."

Jeff Foxworthy loved the premise of *Are You Smarter Than a 5th Grader?* so much that he agreed to commute from Atlanta to Los Angeles for each taping.

For proper context, Mikkelson wasn't even writing about *Are You Smarter Than a 5th Grader?*, or even about game shows at all, when he typed those words, but he unintentionally presented a viable explanation of what made the concept such a fantastic TV quiz. Adults might like to believe that they're smarter than a ten-year-old child, but when it's time to put the pencil to the test sheet, any kid has a distinct advantage—at this moment in their lives, they have to know this stuff.

So, contestants contended with questions like, "True or False: A turtle is an amphibian" and "How many sides are on a heptagon?" And just to make them sweat harder, actual fifth graders were onstage. Not child geniuses, Foxworthy emphasized. They were kids who simply performed well in school, and they were there to bail out the adult contestants, who generally didn't feel a whiff of embarrassment about asking the kids to tell them the correct answer to the question.

Though not a smash, the game performed respectably on the Fox prime-time lineup. Education blogger Alexander Russo saw the appeal: "Most parents are, effectively on this game show every night."

Just a Minute

Identity, NBC's big-cash flop, had borne an uncanny resemblance to "Who's Who," a small game seen on the later seasons of the venerable *What's My Line?* with a grand prize of $25. It was played pretty much just for fun in its first life, and NBC and Endemol had tweaked it into a big-money game show. In 2010, NBC and Universal Television dusted off another oldie-but-goodie from the Goodson-Todman playbook. They turned *Beat the Clock* into a million-dollar game.

TV chef Guy Fieri (*Diners, Drive-Ins, and Dives*) hosted *Minute to Win It*. Like *Beat the Clock*, contestants battled, not really against each other, but against a loud, ticking clock. Like *Beat the Clock*, they had to complete stunts in sixty seconds or less to win the cash and advance to the next stunt. Like *Beat the Clock*, the stunts used common household objects, like cups, balls, balloons, and soda bottles.

Very unlike *Beat the Clock*, *Minute to Win It* was drowning in the gimmicky hype of a prime-time game show: dark set, moody music, and a weirdly serious tone for a game show involving balloons and balls.

The *Los Angeles Times* griped, "It's the show's construction that we find most unsettling. From the coldly hyper-stylized set to the instructions delivered by a soothing faux-robot voice, the show feels like a campy, sci-fi depiction of a dystopian future—except it's actually happening."

Minute to Win It, it seemed, had taken the fun out of a game played for fun.

The Chase is On!

Game Show Network started life in 1994 as a haven for vintage game shows. As the years progressed, the channel tackled original game show formats with mixed success, but always on a modest budget. The channel's biggest hit, *Lingo*, awarded a grand prize of $5,000 for most of its seven-season run.

In 2013, Game Show Network launched arguably its most ambitious game ever, a weekly, prime-time, big-jackpot quiz. They missed the fad by about a decade, but that didn't make the show any less special. It would be the highest-rated game show in the channel's history: *The Chase*.

Based on a hit British game show (Great Britain sure seems to have a lot of great game show ideas), *The Chase* pitted a team of three players against Mark "The Beast" Labbett. Labbett, wielding a masters in mathematics from Exeter College and a job as a question writer for a quiz company in Great Britain, became known as The Beast (a play on not only his six-five, 385-pound frame, but also on his last name, which sounds like "La Bete," the French for "The Beast") on the original British version of *The Chase*.

Each team member played a Cash Builder round, individually answering as many of host Brooke Burns's questions as possible against a sixty-second clock, with $5,000 going in a jackpot for every right answer. The team member then competes against Labbett in *The Chase*. Labbett starts *The Chase* eight spaces away from the bank. The contestant starts five spaces away. Labbett offers the contestant less than the jackpot to take a step closer to the jackpot (farther away from Labbett), or more than the jackpot to take a step farther from the jackpot and closer to Labbett. After the contestant's decision, Burns grills both the contestant and Labbett with a series of questions, with each of them taking a step toward the jackpot on the right answer, or staying still on a wrong answer. If the contestant reaches the jackpot before being caught by Labbett, the money goes into a bank that the team can claim at the end of the night. If Labbett catches the contestant, they're eliminated from the game and the team gets nothing.

For the Final Chase, the surviving team members compete for whatever money is in their bank. The contestants have two minutes to ring in and answer as many questions correctly as possible. The Beast, working alone, must beat that score.

The Chase had something for everybody: for trivia buffs, it was certainly the proverbial bag of peanuts; an average episode of *The Chase* contained more than 100 questions and answers. The sneering Beast was an instantly irresistible villain, with brains to back up his considerable bravado. GSN saw something special in the show too. It initially ordered eight episodes for its opening season, but advance buzz for the series was so positive that the channel picked up *The Chase* for a second season before any episodes had aired.

By January 2015, new episodes of *The Chase* were pulling in 749,000 total viewers, significantly above GSN's average for prime-time programming, about 447,000 pairs of eyes. But even a hit show is vulnerable in the volatile field of television. At the end of 2015, *The Chase* was canceled despite still ruling the ratings at GSN.

44

Social Superstars

When Game Shows Became an Event

#winning!

Did you hear what happened on *Wheel of Fortune*? The answer to the puzzle was PROFESSIONAL GENEOLOGIST, but a contestant guessed that it was "Professional Gynecologist!" What Pat said next will leave you speechless!

On *Family Feud*, Steve Harvey asked "What was the last thing you put your finger into?" What this contestant said, nobody expected!

OMG! The model on *The Price is Right* grabbed the wrong price tag during the game and accidentally gave away the price of the car! Check it out!

Alex Trebek asked a contestant about her interest in nerdcore hip-hop and called fans of nerdcore losers. Twitter melted down! Follow the link!

In years past, game shows aired, funny moments happened, the viewers chuckled, and then everyone moved on with their lives. But in the era of social media, a single funny moment on a game show can generate three or four days' worth of free advertising, maybe more, as the video clips go viral and the word-of-hashtag spreads across cyberspace. But what impact has social media actually had on game shows?

Harvey-Har-Har

Arguably the most significant fruit reaped from social media has gone to *Family Feud*. Since being revived in 1999 with host Louie Anderson, *Feud* was something of a "just-kind-of-there" property on television. Actors Richard Karn and John O'Hurley would have their turns at hosting. By 2010, the modern incarnation of *Family Feud* had survived for eleven seasons, but without making any significant waves. It was just a nice little show that channel surfers might look in on if they happened past it.

But in 2010, when comedian Steve Harvey became the new host, he would unexpectedly rocket-launch the show to a newfound wave of popularity, even doing the impossible and soaring it past *Wheel of Fortune* and *Jeopardy!* in the ratings. What happened?

Part of what happened was the gradual switch to salacious questions that *Feud*'s ancestor, *Match Game*, had used to become top dog in the ratings decades earlier.

"Name something most women do not do as well as they think they do," "Name a part of your body that was bigger when you were sixteen," and other lurid fare found their way into the game. Steve Harvey would develop a reputation for being the most easily offended game show host on television, reacting to every naughty answer with a deadpan stare, a hanging jaw, a bit of scolding and head-shaking, only easing up when he decided he'd milked this insanity for all it was worth.

One moment after another made its way onto YouTube and other sites, and after being saturated with so many clips of what happened last night or last week, apparently, viewers began trickling into *Feud* to be part of the moments as they first aired.

Executive Bob Boden opines, "Traditional marketing strategies have been flung out the window in recent years. There's a need to generate buzz, there's a need to make people talk about your show. And because of that, there's a strong desire now to try to get those viral moments. I don't think it's necessarily mandatory, but it's important particularly if you want to get a young audience."

Although there's no arguing with success, a few observers found *Feud*'s path to prominence a bit hamfisted. Among them, former *Feud* staffer Aaron Solomon, who observes, "*Family Feud*, in the years since Steve Harvey became host, has developed this odd fondness for editorializing their survey responses in a way that you know that the people taking the surveys didn't actually phrase them. The number-one answer to a question will be 'Her Hangin' Hooters,' for example. You know full well that forty-two people did not say 'her hangin' hooters,' but it will be phrased that way on the board, Steve Harvey acts shocked by it, and it gets a giant laugh. There's a better way to get those laughs and get those viral moments, and there's a real art to it. You need to write material that feels natural and organic, but find a way to slip in some key extra element that can be used as a prompt to trigger a funny answer or a reaction."

Getting Interactive

For years, game shows have boasted about the play-along element, the ability for a viewer to get immersed into the show, to the point that they're shouting answers, in effect playing the games themselves.

But that's evolved to a desire to literally play along with the game. Family Channel viewers in the 1990s called a 1-900 number to play game shows hosted by Wink Martindale. Game Show Network, at its inception, used dial-in-and-win games to draw in viewers.

Bob Boden, formerly of Game Show Network, explains, "We had a game called *Decades*. Viewers would dial in and be given historic events from the 20th century, and you pressed buttons on your phone to guess what decade the event took place in. And the concept has really evolved from there. In the early 2000s, viewers could go to the Game Show Network website and play along with our prime-time game shows, playing the same questions, same puzzles, facing the same game boards, taking risks and making decisions, and at every commercial break, we would show a leader board with the top 10 players' scores in the online games. And to be honest, it surprises me that it hasn't evolved further than that. It's a realm that really needs to be explored more."

But while interactive games haven't really gone much further than they went in the early 2000s, the subsequent boom of social media left its mark on the game show world in the eyes of some observers. Boden says, "It allows shows to reach out to a far bigger and more targeted pool of potential contestants, so in a strange way, social media has helped us do our jobs behind the scenes much better. It also helps out with getting feedback. The [number] of letters and phone calls you got from viewers in the past was always a tiny, tiny percentage of your audience. Now, social media allows enough voices out there that you can truly get a feel for what your viewers are thinking about what you've presented."

But does social media actually help game shows discover their audience? And does social media help an audience discover game shows? Producer Aaron Solomon doesn't think so. "I don't believe social media affects anything. A good, engaging game will always draw and maintain a viewer. But the people you answer to in this business want to see you tweeting, they want to see Facebook posts, they want to see the play-at-home games. Format is king, though. A funny moment is nice though, but if you have an uninteresting concept and a poor format, no one will sit through twenty-nine minutes of garbage just for that one big laugh that you're able to get."

May I Have Your Attention?

Game show writer Shelley Herman says, "Social media is critical. Especially in this day and age. There are so many channels, so many streaming services, so many shows. It is easier than ever to slip through the cracks, even if you're a good show. So that ability to make direct contact with your audience is critical, especially if you can provide them with a platform to play the game. That's essential, that's what a game show is."

So, when a game show fan now checks Facebook, there's a constant stream of reminders to tune in to your favorite shows. Game Show Network's *Idiotest* posts a daily puzzle for viewers to play along with. *Family Feud* asks a survey question, *Jeopardy!* posts a clue, *Wheel of Fortune* posts an unsolved puzzle. You're only looking at each of those posts for a few seconds, but if you have enough fun in those few seconds, it'll remind you of the fun you can have dedicating thirty minutes to the next episode. It's a form of advertising so simple, and so effective.

We Dare You to Watch

While new game shows have actively pursued social media, older games have had social media thrust upon them, nostalgic gems from the past that make likers and sharers feel like kids again. Arguably, the greatest beneficiary of the nostalgia kick in the Facebook age is *Double Dare*. A video montage of charmingly outdated

Obstacle Course prizes, like the Nintendo Power Pad and trips to Space Camp, went viral in 2014 . . . and then again in 2015, and in 2016. Another video of Marc Summers doing a not-particularly G-rated hosting job for a game of *Double Dare* during Philly Beer Week came to the surface too, and that was when Summers didn't have a full calendar of interviews, sharing his memories of the classic program with podcasts and websites. He's even spoken on panels at comic book conventions.

The culmination of this wave of *Double Dare* déjà vu was a thirtieth anniversary special on Nickelodeon, with clips interspersed throughout a game played by Nickelodeon stars from the past and adults who had been grown up with the original series. Marc Summers, announcer John Harvey, and assistant Robin Russo were back at their old posts, with classic physical challenges and obstacles re-built for the occasion.

Summers says that the influence of social media has been a double-edged sword for the game show business: "It's fair to say that the renewed interest in *Double Dare* couldn't have happened without social media. People watched those videos, it jogged their memories, and it made them want to see the show again, so that feels good.

"The problem is that not only do television executives pay attention to social media, if anything, they pay too much attention to social media. They prioritize it, which I think is a huge mistake. People who audition to host a game show are actually asked, 'How many Twitter followers do you have? How many times per day would you say you tweet? Do you have a YouTube channel?' None of that should matter. Your priority should be testing the show itself and making sure it's any good, and then hiring a host who has chemistry with that format and who can bring something out of it, and give something of himself or herself in the process of hosting it, and none of that has anything to do with a person's footprint on social media."

45

The Summer of the Phoenix

Play it Again!

In the summer of 2015, ABC had a smash hit in the midst of rerun season with *Celebrity Family Feud*. Steve Harvey welcomed stars and their actual families, competing on behalf of worthy charities. Naturally, it would return the following summer, but in January 2016, ABC really gave game show fans a reason to shout "Happy New Year!" The network would also breathe new life into *The $100,000 Pyramid*. A few months later, they topped even that announcement with the news that *Match Game* would also be dusted off to form a programming block called Sunday Night Fun and Games. For the first time in television history, a network's entire prime-time lineup for one night a week would be occupied exclusively by game shows.

Pyramid Power

Michael Strahan, who had replaced Regis Philbin as host of the morning talk show *Live!*, found himself again following in Philbin's footsteps as he took the helm of a prime-time game on ABC. That game would be *The $100,000 Pyramid*, arriving at ABC for a homecoming thirty-six years after *The $20,000 Pyramid* departed from the network's daytime lineup. And despite the tense background music, LED graphics, and, yes, the shiny black floor of modern prime-time game shows, the new *$100,000 Pyramid* was a wonderfully shocking throwback.

It was *Pyramid* done right, because it was done by fans. Aaron Solomon, a game show fan who had made his way up the ladder from collecting $25,000 as a thirteen-year-old on *Scrabble* Teen Week to helping run several prime-time games for ABC and GSN in recent years, would help oversee the new *Pyramid* expedition as co-executive producer. John Ricci Jr., a devoted fan who had designed home-made *Pyramid* software for his Commodore 64 as a teenager, would serve as games producer and judge. Showrunner Vin Rubino insisted on an old-school touch in the middle of the gleaming new stage. While game shows of the 2000s had been dominated by flat screens that displayed a variety of graphics on big square set pieces, Rubino, who likened the game shows sets of old to "pinball machines with people inside them," took a step backwards by using trilons, three-sided boxes that flipped back and forth as needed. Rubino reasoned it was especially important for lending some "personality" to the central set piece of the show, the pyramid at center stage. Didn't that key set piece deserve better than a big flat screen?

Yes. It deserved thirty flat screens. The main game made use of twelve monitors, two connected at the sides for each of six categories that the contestants could pick. One monitor displayed the name of category; the other waited to reveal a simple blank pyramid or the "MYSTERY 7" bonus that allowed the team to play for a bonus prize. The Winner's Circle would make use of six trilons, each assembled from three eighteen-inch flat screen TVs connected at the sides and mounted onto spinning frames; originally the trilons were going to be turned by way of a hydraulics system, but after seeing a price estimate, the show's staff decided to go even further old school. Hidden crew members behind the board turned the trilons by hand; one of them was the son of a man who had flipped the trilons for Dick Clark's *$20,000 Pyramid* forty years earlier.

Taking the throwback notion further still, Russell Emmanuel and Bleeding Fingers composed an awfully familiar sounding theme song, taking Bob Cobert's dynamic theme from the 1980s and giving it some new instrumentation and a hip-hop beat for good measure.

And the game itself was virtually unchanged. Oh sure, the material was updated—references to viral videos and smartphone apps found their way into the clues and categories—but it was still a thirty-second race to solve seven words, complete with a Mystery 7 hidden on the board that could earn the contestant a bonus prize. The winning team went to the Winner's Circle for a chance to win $50,000 or $100,000, which plenty of contestants did, with the help of stars like Martha Stewart, Snoop Dogg, Ken Jeong, Weird Al Yankovic, Fred Willard, Kevin Pollack, and, arguably the stand-outs of the show, Rosie O'Donnell and former *Pyramid* contestant Kathy Najimy.

Aaron Solomon says, "We got very lucky. When game shows from the past come back for a new run, there's always some elements that get altered, or thrown away, or replaced. And when that happens, it's a matter of somebody wanting to leave their fingerprints on the show. They want something on the new version that they can point to and say, 'I did that.' But thankfully, that didn't happen. We got to do the show exactly the way we wanted, and the way we wanted to do it was a way that we already knew would work."

Francine Bergman, who judged the Winners' Circle and coordinated the contestants for the original incarnation four decades earlier, says, "It really did my heart good when I saw the new version. It's the same music. They kept the same basic set design and made it a little fancier. But the game itself was unchanged. Bob was so proud of his creation, and all of us who worked on that show took that same pride in it. So, when I watched the new version and saw how little they changed it, I took it as a huge compliment."

The only real knock against the game was that some of the playing lacked polish. Fans so accustomed to the show's peak in the 1980s, be it through the original run of the series or over two decades of ubiquitous reruns, saw flawless game playing far more often than not from celebrities and contestants who had mastered the art of word communication right down to the tiniest nuances of *Pyramid*'s famously intricate rules for clues in the Winners' Circle. On this new version, players drew blanks, got zapped for illegal clues, or gave clues that were far too long-winded for very basic answers.

But game show expert Matt Ottinger made a compelling argument that such shortcomings were actually enhancing the game. Shortly after the second broadcast on ABC, Ottinger wrote, "This version of *Pyramid* is even more exciting a show to watch than [*The $25,000 Pyramid*] was in its heyday. Hear me out. Game play isn't as good, and that's my point. In the old days, game play was all, so much so that [creator Bob] Stewart eventually had his cadre of great game players who rotated through the final years. And if, god forbid, Teresa Ganzel only got six in one round, it meant she was probably going to lose 21–20. Today, everybody's trying hard, but nobody's perfect. Fives and sixes are just as likely as sevens, and if you stumble and waste a lot of time on one clue, you may get even less. It's still early . . . but right now I find the lack of perfection refreshing and more fun to watch. Put another way, back in the old days, seven was assumed. Now, seven happens often enough, but it's still a cause for celebration, not a sure thing."

Blank On It

The most unexpected member of ABC's triumvirate was the new *Match Game*. The format's glory days in the 1970s seemed very much to be a product of its time. Televised comedy still blushed and giggled with some sense of restraint, but as the 1970s wore on, more and more taboos were stripped away and the once-naughty *Match Game* lost its dirty luster.

The first big surprise was that a revival of *Match Game* was being attempted; new versions were mounted in 1983, 1990, and 1998; each one crashed.

The second big surprise was that it would be hosted by hot-tempered film star Alec Baldwin, who had taken a sharp turn into television comedy in the past decade as pompous network executive Jack Donaghy on NBC's surrealistic comedy *30 Rock*. Baldwin, who donated his entire salary for the summer gig to charity, had one charmingly specific stipulation for hosting the revival. As a fan of the classic '70s version, he insisted that he would only host if given a Sony ECM-51, the famously long, skinny microphone preferred by Gene Rayburn.

The third big surprise was that the show had managed to assemble some truly star-studded panels. Broadway star Sutton Foster, *Saturday Night Live*'s Leslie Jones, country singer Sheryl Crow, Ellie Kemper and Titus Burgess of *Unbreakable Kimmy Schmidt*, Debra Messing, Jason Alexander, Leah Remini, and the least expected guest of all, Sarah Palin (invited to the show by Baldwin), dropped in to fill in the blanks.

Baldwin surprised many with how well he adapted to the unexpected role of TV game show host. John Teti of AV Club wrote, "Alec Baldwin isn't Gene Rayburn, and he doesn't try to be. While Rayburn had his own moments of lunacy, he usually served as a buffer of wit and relative dignity that counterbalanced the unruly stars. Baldwin plays this moderating role, too, but as he settles into *Match Game*, he's also embracing a role as an instigator."

The ABC Sunday night lineup won its time slot again and again during the summer, and even managed to stay competitive against NBC's coverage of the Summer Olympics. The genre endured and thrived by sticking with what worked all along.

46

What's in the Future?

Where Are We Going Now?

he experts interviewed for this book were asked to give their predictions for the future of TV game shows. Here's what they said.

Thanks for Inviting Us into Your Home

For years, game show hosts have said, "Thank you for inviting us into your homes." Aaron Solomon predicts that it's going to be far more literal someday. "There have been multiple producers for years who have worked off-and-on with virtual reality, looking for some way to adapt that for game shows," he says. "Game shows are already very interactive—you shout at your TV if it's a good game—and television is generally so passive. I think that's the next big goal. Find a successful new format that involves players competing in their homes."

We're Not Going Anywhere

But one thing all the experts agree on is that game shows *do* have a future. Bob Boden says, "Game shows have been pronounced dead more than Generalissimo Francisco Franco. The genre has its problems sometimes, but it's never been worse than the occasional coma. Game shows always find a way to survive."

For Dick Block of University of Southern California School of Cinematic Arts, it's simple economics: "Game shows get good ratings, and game shows, compared to other forms of programming, are extremely inexpensive to produce. As long as those two statements remain true, game shows aren't going to go away."

Former Bob Stewart Productions staffer Francine Bergman says, "There are only so many things you can do for formats. It's a Q&A game, or a word game, and there are a few other possibilities, but there really are just so many ideas. The trick is to put it in a new package. So, creativity is important, but as long as creative people can make it into the business, game shows will endure."

Jaime Klein, Chuck Barris's former joke writer, later a vice president at FremantleMedia, says, "The future of game shows goes back to Aristotle's *Poetics*, which everything that's good is based on. Establish a character, establish that character's wants and needs, and watch how they overcome obstacles to achieve that need as their journey becomes more and more difficult, and fraught with more danger and/or elimination.

"That's what a game show offers. You establish a character—'Let's meet our contestants. Tell us a little bit about yourselves.' You establish what that character needs or wants, whether it's money, a new car, appliances, love, or a shot at fame. You give them difficult obstacles to overcome—Round 1, Round 2, the final question, the bonus round.

"Those elements will not change. They have not changed for two thousand years, and I don't care how many electronic gadgets people get. The delivery system may change, but the basic human need to feel connected will not. As long as game shows and reality shows continue to deliver that, the future of these shows is wide open."

Bibliography

"8,000 Questions in Nine Years." *Beaver Valley Times* (PA), January 29, 1955.

"ABC Radio Network to Fight Order That Would Stop 'Stop the Music.'" *Pittsburgh Press* (PA), August 7, 1948.

Ackerman, Paul, and Bob Rolontz. "Warner Tunes Swamp Goodson-Todman Shows." *The Billboard*, November 9, 1959.

Adams, Jack, "Gov't Orders Radio to End Give-Aways." *Lewiston Daily Sun* (ID), August 20, 1949.

Allsbrook, Raleigh. "The TV Scandals: 4 Years Later." *Corpus Christi Caller-Times* (TX), January 28, 1962.

Anderson, Kent. *Television Fraud: The History and Implications of the Quiz Show Scandals.* Westport, CT: Greenwood Press, 1978.

Anderson, Penny P. "Babbling Dick Enberg Man on Move." *Arizona Republic* (Phoenix), July 1973.

Arar, Yardena. "'Queen for a Day' Recalled." *Daily News* (Bowling Green, KY), June 15, 1978.

"Awards of Cash Featured in Many Quiz Broadcasts." *BroadcastingMagazine*, December 15, 1939.

"A Baby's Woes Help Win Big TV Contest." *LIFE*, May 13, 1957.

Bark, Ed. "Latest Entries Suffer Game Show Anemia." *The Journal News* (White Plains, NY), January 1983.

Barlow, Robert. "Meet Professor Quiz." *Toledo Blade* (OH), January 6, 1941.

Beck, Marilyn. "TV Closeup," *Daily Reporter* (Dover, OH), November 18, 1967.

Benke, Richard. "Ralph Edwards Marks 70 Years in Broadcasting," *Ocala Star-Banner* (FL), October 17, 1999.

Bernarde, Scott. "It's Game Show Mania!" *Palm Beach Post* (FL), June 14, 1993.

"A Big Man in the Alley." *Anniston Star* (AL), August 18, 1973.

"Big Prize Money Again Respectable on TV." *Kokomo Tribune* (IN), July 13, 1974.

"Bob Barker, TV Game Show Host, in Nielsen Top 10 Twice a Year." *Gadsden Times* (AL), June 22, 1971.

Bobbin, Jay. "Jim Perry Juggles Three Game Shows," *Ottawa Journal*, July 21, 1979.

Bowles, Jennifer. "Erasing Debt," *Salina Journal* (KS), June 14, 1997.

Boyd, Joseph G. "Time Tested Quiz Kid Successes," *Milwaukee Sentinel* (WS), March 22, 1983.

Brennan, Edwin F. "20 Questions Authors Explain Their Program," *Pittsburgh Post-Gazette*, March 12, 1952.

Brown, James. "Quiz Show Trickster Returns to TV Screen," *Asbury Park Press* (NJ), November 13, 1978.

Brunsdon, Charlotte, and Lynn Spigel (ed.). *Feminist Television Criticism: A Reader* (Second Edition). New York, NY: McGraw-Hill, 2008.

Buck, Jerry. "Comeback a Success for Barry." *Palm Beach Post* (FL), April 12, 1980.

"CBS Economy Kick: Disk Jock Show at 7 p.m. Daily." *The Billboard,* July 2, 1949.

"Celebrity Bowling Emcee Too Good at His Trade?" *Post-Crescent* (Appleton, WI), August 13, 1972.

Chase, Sam. "Radio Gifts $4 Million in '48," *The Billboard,* January 29, 1949.

Christy, Marian. "Games Host Edwards is Reaching for Pinnacle," *Salina Journal* (KS), October 2, 1974.

"Clown Stunt Aids Raymond." *The Billboard,* April 30, 1955.

Coggins, Amos. "They De-Glamorize the Stars," *Reading Eagle* (PA), March 20, 1955.

Collyer, Bud. "An Old-Time Superman Recalls Radio's Thrills," *Tuscaloosa News* (IA), July 5, 1966.

———. "Stand-Ins for Mayhem," *Boys Life,* February 1953.

Conway, Mike. *The Origins of Television News in America: The Visualizers of CBS in the 1940s.* New York, NY: Peter Lang Publishing, 2009.

Crawford, Bill. "Host of Celebrities to Visit Fort Still," *Lawton Constitution* (OK), May 28, 1968.

Crosby, John. "He Does Not Choose to Answer," *St. Petersburg Times* (FL), August 19, 1952.

Daley, Frank. "All Amateur Films Welcome at Festival," *Ottawa Journal,* April 27, 1978.

Darrow, Chuck. "Trump Card Good Deal for Casino," *Asbury Park Press* (NJ), August 9, 1990.

Davis, Rebecca L. *More Perfect Unions: The American Search for Marital Bliss.* Cambridge, MA: Harvard University Press, 2010.

Dawidziak, Mark. "Back Scenes at Jeopardy! Tryouts." *Akron Beacon Journal* (OH), October 1, 1984.

"Day and Night are Different." *The Republic* (Columbus, IN), March 15, 1975.

Deeb, Gary, "'Jeopardy' Revived by NBC," *Arizona Republic* (Phoenix), September 25, 1978.

"Dick Schippy's Mailbag." *Akron Beacon Journal* (OH), August 29, 1976.

"Don Morrow, Emcee of Camouflage." *Gettysburg Times* (PA), August 18, 1962.

"Dotto Moves Up Nielsen List to 14.1 Mark." *Austin Daily Herald* (MN), March 15, 1958.

Duffy, Mike. "ABC to Juggle Start of Once and Again," *Detroit Free Press* (MI), July 29, 1999.

Dunlop, Orrin E., Jr. "Baffling the Board." *New York Times,* November 2, 1939.

Dunning, John. *On the Air: The Encyclopedia of Old-Time Radio.* New York, NY: Oxford University Press, 1998.

Earl, Dr. Craig, a/k/a Professor Quiz. "Walter Winchell on Broadway" (Guest Columnist), *St. Petersburg Times* (FL), July 21, 1938.

Emerson, Faye. "'Winky Dink and You' is Just the Thing for Kids." *El Paso Herald-Post* (TX), January 13, 1954.

Erickson, Hal. *From Radio to the Big Screen: Hollywood Films Featuring Broadcast Personalities and Programs.* Jefferson, NC: McFarland, 2014.

"Everybody was Asleep He Thought—Then He Said 'Elvis.'" *The Tennessean*, November 4, 1956.

Ewald, William. "'Masquerade Party' Pops Back on Television Screens," *Bend Bulletin* (OR), August 5, 1958.

———. "Pantomime Quiz Heralds Summer," *Beaver Valley Times* (PA), May 12, 1959.

Ferretti, Fred. "Quiz Kids: Where Are They Now?" *Pittsburgh Post-Gazette* (PA), December 28, 1982.

"Film Rights Sold." *Pasadena Independent* (CA), March 29, 1966.

Foster, R. Daniel. "God Save the Queens," *Los Angeles Magazine*, January 1997.

"Fred Allen vs. Radio Give-Aways Continues." *Sarasota Herald-Tribune* (FL), October 14, 1948.

Freeman, William M. "Golenpaul of 'Information Please' Dies," *New York Times*, February 14, 1974.

"'Gambit' Host Martindale From Tin-Can to TV." *The Robesonian* (Lumberton, NC), November 5, 1972.

Gardner, Hy. "Legal Beaglets," *St. Louis Post-Dispatch* (MO), October 14, 1951.

Gaver, Jack. "Landing Talent for Panel Show, 'The Name's the Same,' Brings on Its Share of Headaches, Claim," *Times-News* (Hendersonville, NC), February 18, 1954.

———. "Lots of Off-Stage Work Involved in Game Shows," *Arizona Republic* (Phoenix), November 1, 1966.

"Gil Fates, 86, a TV Producer of Shows Like 'What's My Line?'" *New York Times*, May 16, 2000.

Gould, Jack. "Soldier, Mother Meet at TV Show," *New York Times*, September 22, 1950.

Graham, Jefferson. *"Come on Down!!!" The TV Game Show Book*. New York, NY: Abbeville Press, 1988.

———. "The Game Show Cable Network Makes Its Debut," *Courier-Post* (Camden, NJ), December 7, 1994.

Griffin, Merv, with David Bender. *Merv: Making the Good Life Last*. New York, NY: Pocket Books, 2003.

Gunther, Marc. "'Scrabble' Glitzed Up for TV Game Show," *Des Moines Register* (IA), July 1, 1984.

Hayden, Bill. "The King of the Joker," *The News-Journal* (Wilmington, DE), September 19, 1982.

Hill, Michael. "Being a Good Game Show Host Can Ensure Job Security for Life," *Indianapolis Star* (IN), September 13, 1987.

Hinman, Catherine. "Nickelodeon's New Arcade Puts Kids Inside Video Games," *Pittsburgh Press* (PA), December 31, 1991.

Hyatt, Wesley. *Emmy Award Winning Nighttime Television Shows, 1948–2004*. Jefferson, NC: McFarland, 2006.

"Inflation Hits Games People Play." *The Courier-Journal* (Louisville, KY), February 17, 1976.

"'Information Please' Returns; With Fadiman, Proper English." *Sarasota Herald-Tribune* (FL), February 25, 1977.

Inman, Julia. "Game Show Hosts Select Group," *Indianapolis Star* (IN), January 14, 1979.

"Is 'Headline Chasers' the Next 'Wheel of Fortune'?" *The Republic* (Columbus, IN), September 1, 1985.

"It's Child's Play." *Progress Bulletin* (Pomona, CA), July 13, 1969.

"Jack Barry Finds Games Exciting." *Mexia Daily News* (TX), October 8, 1972.

"Jack Narz Wonders About Future." *Detroit Free Press* (MI), August 31, 1958.

Kaiser, Charles. "Does Anyone Have Anything Bad to Say About Tom Brokaw?" *New York Magazine*, January 6, 1997.

Kern, Janet. "'Down You Go' Returns to TV," *Milwaukee Sentinel* (WS), May 12, 1961.

———. "It's Corn vs. Caviar," *Milwaukee Sentinel*, June 7, 1960.

———. "Summer Quiz Shows Misfire," *Milwaukee Sentinel* (WS), August 21, 1958.

Kerr, Adelaide. "Jack Barry's Radio Show Based on Age," *Corpus Christi Caller-Times* (TX), April 12, 1953.

King, Susan. "What's His Line? Those TV Game Shows." *Los Angeles Times* (CA), June 28, 1990.

Kleiner, Dick. "Jack Barry Enjoys Life on Game Show Treadmill," *Poughkeepsie Journal* (NY), March 25, 1975.

Ladd, Bill. "Canceled TV Show's Emcee in Good Shape," *Courier-Journal* (Louisville, KY), August 23, 1958.

Langley, Frank. "Success—'and We Got Teeth Fixed.'" *Abilene Reporter-News* (TX), August 25, 1968.

Lev, Michael. "Game Shows Try to Return as Prime-time Contestants," *San Bernardino County Sun* (CA), August 2, 1990.

Lewis, Dan. "Risqué Material on Daytime TV," *Lakeland Ledger* (FL), April 12, 1976.

Linkletter, Art. "Art Linkletter Proves That People are Funny," *Ottawa Citizen*, August 2, 1950.

Lowry, Cynthia. "'Beat the Clock' is going Back to Its Old-time Stunts," *Ocala Star-Banner* (FL), September 22, 1960.

———. "Bill Leyden New Champ of Commuters." *Free Lance-Star* (Fredericksburg, VA), May 14, 1965.

———. "Jack Barry Talks of His Career," *Santa Cruz Sentinel* (CA), April 5, 1971.

———. "No Brain Games for Chuck Barris," *Danville Register* (IL), May 21, 1967.

———. "TV." *The Childress Index* (TX), June 13, 1972.

———. "Where are the Quizmasters Now?" *Sunday Gazette-Mail* (Charleston, WV), December 27, 1959.

Mackay, Scott. "How to be a Good Sport," *Milwaukee Sentinel* (WS), June 28, 1953.

"Main Street." *Radio Daily*, June 3, 1949.

Maksian, George. "Game Show List Grows," *Charleston Daily Mail* (Charleston, WV), April 16, 1976.

"Mark, Bill on Top of Heap." *Herald Family Magazine*, January 13, 1952.

Martin, Bob. "Alex Trebek is Good Bet to Score as Odds Host." *Independent Press-Telegram* (Long Beach, CA), July 15, 1973.

McArdle, Mary. "Game Show Lets Kids Be Kids," *Morning News* (Wilmington, DE), October 21, 1986.

McManus, Margaret. "Gloomy Spell for Jack Barry is Over," *Des Moines Register* (IA), October 7, 1956.

Mendoza, N. F., "TV Game Shows Not in Jeopardy," *Akron-Beacon Journal* (OH), January 18, 1993.

Miller, Ron. "Duke's Son Stepping into Game Show Role," *Asbury Park Press* (NJ), December 3, 1990.

Minoff, Phillip. "Big Name Guests Get Biggest Kick from Pantomime Quiz," *Toledo Blade* (OH), January 10, 1954.

"Mistakes Can be Beautiful When They're on Television." *Herald Family Magazine*, August 24, 1952.

Morgan, James C. "'Queen for a Day' Potent Lure; Wins for Self, Fairs in P.A.'s." *The Billboard*, January 10, 1948.

Nachman, Gerald. *Raised on Radio.* New York, NY: Pantheon Books, 2004.

"Narz Boys Barely Make It to Wedding." *Louisville Courier* (KY), July 15, 1956.

"NBC Daytime Sets Gigantic Daytime Gala." *Danville Register* (IL), November 3, 1975.

"NBC's 'Jeopardy' has No Stud of Kumquats." *Southern Illinoisan* (Carbondale, IL), October 16, 1978.

"NBC Tightens Reins on Quiz Programs." *Broadcasting Magazine*, November 5, 1968.

"Networks Battle for TV Daytime Audiences with 'New Style' Game Shows." *Pottstown Mercury* (PA), February 7, 1975.

Newcomb, Horace (ed.). "Goodson, Mark (1915–1992), and Bill Todman (1918–1979)." *Encyclopedia of Television, 2nd Edition.* New York, NY: Routledge, 2004.

"New Game Show Prize is Worrisome $100,000." *Post Crescent* (Appleton, WI), August 19, 1976.

Oblander, Terry. "TV May Call It 'Scrabble,' but Show Smells Like Liver," *Akron-Beacon Journal* (OH), July 5, 1984.

Oliver, Wayne. "ABC Raps Allen Slap at Advance Calls on Radio Give-Away Shows," *Evening Independent* (St. Petersburg, FL), October 12, 1948.

"On 'Information Please.'" *Lewiston Evening Journal* (ME), February 18, 1939.

"On the Air." *Courier-Post* (Camden, NJ), October 16, 1985.

"Our Respects to Mark Goodson and William Seldon Todman." *Broadcasting Magazine*, February 10, 1958.

Ovington, Reg. "TV's Toughest Job," *Milwaukee Sentinel* (WS), July 4, 1954.

"People are Funny, but Not Backward." *Milwaukee Sentinel* (WS), May 12, 1957.

"People: Ralph Edwards." *Lodi News-Sentinel* (CA), May 4, 1996.

Peterson, Bettelou. "TV In-Laws Hold Rivalry in Check," *Detroit Free Press* (MN), August 10, 1958.

"Professor Quiz Admits Helpmate." *Kentucky New Era* (Hopkinsville, KY), January 12, 1938.

"Professor Quiz Has His Answers to Life's Questions." *St. Petersburg Times* (FL), June 30, 1977.

"Professor Quiz is Nicked for Alimony." *St. Petersburg Times* (FL), October 31, 1941.

"Professor Quiz Laments Growth of Jackpots." *St. Petersburg Times* (FL), March 6, 1949.

"Queen Abdicates—for $300." *The Billboard*, July 20, 1946.

"Quick Takes." *Los Angeles Times* (CA), June 9, 1999.

"The Quiz Kids: 50 Years Ago, A Bunch of Educated Upstarts Became Radio's Smash Hit." *Chicago Tribune* (IL), December 2, 1990.

"Quiz Scandals Station May Lose License." *Anderson Herald* (IN), June 9, 1963.

Ramaker, Artimis. "Garry Moore, That Wonderful Guy," *Lakeland Ledger* (FL), June 26, 1960.

Rhein, Dave. "The Games People Play are on TV," *Des Moines Register* (IA), February 3, 1985.

Richmond, Ray. "Dialing for Your Dollars," *Courier-Journal* (Louisville, KY), June 14, 1993.

"Rigging Charges Denied by Quiz Show Twenty One." *Herald and News* (Klamath Falls, OR), August 29, 1958.

Scott, Vernon. "Art Linkletter is Matchmaker," *Wilmington News* (DE), January 15, 1958.

———. "Betty White is Just Right for 'Just Men.'" *Salina Journal* (KS), March 14, 1983.

———. "Tom Kennedy, One of the Charm Boys," *Redlands Daily Facts* (CA), September 19, 1975.

———. "Treasure Hunt Based on Luck, Not Brains," *Times-Recorder* (Zanesville, OH), October 1973.

Shelley, Peter. *Neil Simon on Screen: Adaptations and Original Scripts for Film and Television.* Jefferson, NC: McFarland, 2015.

"Singer Now Game Host." *High Point Enterprise* (High Point, NC), May 31, 1975.

"Singer Wins $100,000; Largest Prize in Video." *Victoria Advocate* (TX), December 5, 1955.

"Some Secrets About 'I've Got a Secret.'" *Florence Times* (AL), August 25, 1955.

"Stars on Quiz Program." *New York Times,* January 30, 1947.

"Stars Reveal Strange Secrets on Secrets." *Kokomo Tribune* (IN), June 23, 1979.

Stern, Harold. "Jack Barry Plans New TV Fixproof Quiz," *Decatur Daily Review* (IL), March 5, 1961.

Stewart, R. W. "Taking the Air," *New York Times,* August 17, 1941.

"'Stop the Music' is Worth $16,000." *Sunday Herald* (Bridgeport, CT), October 2, 1949.

"'Stop the Music' Mystery is Solved." *Evening Independent* (St. Petersburg, FL), October 4, 1948.

Strom, Stephanie. "Robert Breen, 80, Arts Executive and Theater Producer, is Dead," *New York Times,* April 2, 1990.

Suchcicki, Mike. "Finn Has Fun on 'Joker's Wild,'" *Florida Today* (Cocoa, FL), September 30, 1990.

Swift, Corrine. "Bud Collyer, Man with an Open Mind," *Radio-TV Mirror,* June 1953.

"They Make Faces to Order—for TV." *St. Petersburg Times* (FL), December 12, 1954.

Thompson, Edgar A. "Riding the Airwaves," *Milwaukee Journal* (WS), November 4, 1938.

Thompson, Ruth. "TV Host Geoff Edwards Revives Fashion for Tuxedos," *Kane Republican* (Kane, PA), September 29, 1973.

"TV Awards Reported by Sylvania." *Broadcasting Magazine,* November 12, 1951.

"TV Gossip." *St. Louis Post-Dispatch* (MO), October 22, 1950.

Van Dyke, Dick. *My Lucky Life in and Out of Show Business: A Memoir.* New York, NY: Three Rivers Press, 2011.

Watts, Amber Eliza. "Laughing at the World: Schadenfreude, Social Identity, and American Media Culture." Dissertation. Northwestern University, 2008.

Weber, Bruce. "Frances Buss, Pioneer of Early Television, Dies at 92," *New York Times*, February 3, 2010.

Whittington, Dee. "Susan B. Goes After $64,000," *Palm Beach Post* (FL), December 22, 1976.

Williams, Scott. "'Newlywed Game' Back; Eubanks Still in Charge," *The Pantagraph* (Bloomington, IL), November 13, 1997.

"Willkie Cheered at Movie Debut." *New York Times*, July 5, 1940.

Witbeck, Charles. "Beauty Contests on TV, *Asbury Park Press* (NJ), December 27, 1966.

———. "TV's Dead Serious Game Shows," *Daily Reporter* (Dover, OH), May 23, 1975.

"Wonderful and Selfless Bud Collyer." *Sunday Herald* (Bridgeport, CT), May 5, 1963.

Websites

http://www.wnyc.org/history/

http://50.56.218.160/archive/category.php?category_id=23andid=43153

http://50.56.218.160/categories/category.php?category_id=27andid=43026

http://www.tvobscurities.com/articles/tv_programs_1941/

http://martingrams.blogspot.com/2014/03/clara-bow-on-truth-or-consequences.html

http://otrbuffet.blogspot.com/2011/04/sad-case-of-gerard-darrow.html

http://emceesteve.tripod.com/column_9_4_99.htm

http://historymatters.gmu.edu/d/6566/

http://emceesteve.tripod.com/column_9_4_00.htm

http://www.telegraph.co.uk/news/uknews/1535797/Who-Wants-To-Be-A-Multi-Millionaire.html

https://www.newspapers.com/image/114345757/?terms=%22deal%2Bor%2Bno%2Bdeal%22%2B%22howie%2Bmandel%22

http://web.archive.org/web/20150608070644/http://www.tvmediainsights.com/tv-ratings/gsn-the-chase-delivers-its-most-viewed-telecast-in-nearly-a-year/

https://www.newspapers.com/image/202718317/?terms=CBS%2BSurvivor

https://www.newspapers.com/image/160112859/?terms=%22big%2Bbrother%22%2Bcbs

https://www.newspapers.com/image/107994909/?terms=amazing%2Brace

Index

ABC Family, 254
ABC Radio, 22–24
ABC-TV, 24, 26, 31–34, 49–50, 55,
    108, 115–16, 120–21, 129, 131,
    134, 137–38, 140–41, 143, 153,
    156–58, 162, 165, 177, 182, 186,
    204, 213, 216, 219, 222, 227,
    230–35, *233*, 239, 242, 248–50,
    252, 254–55, 264–65, 270, 276,
    292, 296, 301–6, 309, 312, 316,
    324, 332, 334–35
ABC World News Tonight, 247–48
Academy of Television Arts and
    Sciences, 157, 318
Access Hollywood, 315
Accidental Family, 149
Act It Out, 26
Adams, Don, 158
Adams, Franklin P., *12*, 13
Adams, Nick, 147
Adelman, Barry, *307*
Adventures of Michael Shayne, The, 214
Afternoon, 244
AFTRA, 139
Alda, Robert, 27
Aldin, Ken, 172
Alexander, Jason, 334
Alexander, Joan, *35*, *40*
Algonquin Roundtable, 13
Alisi, Art, 101–2, 215
All About the Opposite Sex, 291
Allan, Jed, 158–59, 161
Allen, Bob, 191
Allen, Fred, 22–23
Allen, Marty, 144, 147
Allen, Steve, 31, 36, 127
Allen, Woody, 216
All for One, 306
Alliaume, Curt, 167
All in the Family, 193, 222

Allison, Fran, 32
All-New Dating Game, The, 254
All-New Let's Make a Deal, The, 130, 249
All-Star Beat the Clock, 229
All Star Blitz, 250, 252
All-Star Gong Show, The, 208
All-Star Secrets, 225–26, *226*
Almost Anything Goes, 301
Altman, Jeff, 229
Amateur's Guide to Love, The, 160–61
Amazing Jonathan, 260
Amazing Race, The, 318
American Bandstand, 137, 140, 171, 177
American Heart Association, 21
American Idol, 203, 213
America's Funniest Home Videos, 265
America's Got Talent, 203, 213
Amsterdam, Morery, 147, *147*
Anderson, Kent, 64, 88
Anderson, Loni, *233*, *263*
Anderson, Louie, 300, 328
Andrews, Ralph, 102–4, 188
Answer Yes or No, 31
Anthony, Susan B. (contestant), 202
Anything for Money, 249
Apprentice, The, 319
Arcaro, Eddie, 158
Are You Smarter Than a 5th Grader?, *325*,
    325–6
Armstrong, Bill, 188
Armstrong, Louis, 144
Arnall, Ellis, 13
Arnaz, Desi, 71
Arquette, Cliff ("Charley Weaver"), 147,
    147
Ash, Mary Kay, 86
Ask a Silly Question, 215
Ask-It Basket, 7
As the World Turns, 182
Attis, Jeff, 201

Aubrey, Jim, 154
Auction-Aire, 87
Auctioneer, The, 125
Auerbach, Red, 158
Austin, Bud, 43, 228
Autry, Gene, 216
Avila, Daniel, 306

Bacall, Lauren, 118
Bach, Bob, 29, 41, 153–54
Bacharach, Burt, 104
Backstage with the Original Hollywood Square (Marshall, P.), 226
Bailey, Jack, 57–58, 61–62, 65, 95
Bailey, John Ringling, 57–58
Bailey, Pearl, 118
Baird, Arthur Earl. *See* Earl, Craig
Baker, Art, 58
Baker, Phil, 18
Baldwin, Alec, 334
Baldwin, Faith, 214
Ball, Lucille, 67, 71, 116–17, *224*
Bancroft, Ann, 116
Banderas, Antonio, 300
Bank on the Stars, 48–49
Barasch, Jack. *See* Barry, Jack
Barbeau, Adrienne, 204
Barbour, John, 205, 207
Barker, Byron and Tilly, 93
Barker, Robert ("Bob") William, 93–99, *97*, 143–44, 157, 166–67, *167*, 173–74, 182–83, *183*, 186, 197–98, 210, 242, 250, 277, 313
"Barker's Follies," 96–97
Baron, Sandy, 145
Barris, Charles ("Chuck") Hirsch, *137*, 137–44, 174–75, 194–97, 203–6, 208–12, *211*, 297, 336. *See also* Chuck Barris Productions
Barris, Harry, 137
Barron, Elise, 75–76
Barry, Jack (Jack Barasch), 68, 70–71, 77–79, *80*, 109, 119, 125, 162–65, *164*, 168, 173, 175, 177, 191, 214–21, *217*, 242, 254–55, 266, 309
Barry and Enright Productions, 109, 111, 191, 215–19, 221, 255, 266, 303
Barrymore, John, Jr., 27
Bartholomew, Summer, 240, *240*, 262

Battle of the Boroughs, 38
Battle of the Sexes, 7
Battlestars, 252, 262
Baudoin (king), 34
Bean, Orson, 155, 188
Bearde, Chris, 204
Beat the Clock, 39, *52*, 52–55, 60, 69, 82, 85, 155–57, 168, 229, 326
Belcher, Jerry, *2*, 2–3
Bellamy, Ralph, 85
Bench, Johnny, *159*
Benirschke, Rolf, 263, 266
Bennett, Bern, 55, 86
Bennett, Tony, 294
Benny, Jack, 14, 20–21, 96
Benson, George, 57–58
Bergen, Edgar, 49–50
Bergeron, Tom, 299
Bergman, Francine, 170–71, 173, 176–77, 236, 272, 292, 333, 336
Berle, Milton, 184, 208
Bernstein, Shirley, 77–78
Best, Pete, 36
Best of Groucho, The, 51
Bethea, James, 283–85
Better Sex, The, 39
Beverly, Steve, 185
Beverly Hillbillies, The, 160
Beverly Hills Writers and Artists Building, 138
Bewitched, 116, 148
Big Bad Voodoo Daddy, 130
Big Brother, 316–18
Big Deal, 130
Big Game, 119
Big Payoff, The, 65
Big Surprise, The, 68, 70, 78, 215
Bill Cullen Show, The, 48
Bingo at Home, 125, 224
Bixby, Bill, 147, 149, *156*
Blake, Howard, 62
Blank Check, 216–17, 219
Blatty, William, 46, 86
Bleeding Fingers, 323
Block, Dick, 134, *290*, 290–91, 336
Block, Hal, 30
Block, Richard, 86
Blockbusters, 42, 230, 254–55
Blumenthal, Howard, 260–61, 279–83
Blumenthal, Norm, 108–13, 172

Blyden, Larry, 91
Bob Barker Show, The, 94–95
Bob's Full House, 268
Bob Stewart Productions, 90–91, 227, 272, 292, 336
Boden, Bob, 268, 274, 306–8, *307*, 312, 320, 329–30, 336
Body Language, 249–50
Boggle, 289
Bolen, Lin, 172–80, 222, 226, 244, 257
Bolger, Ray, *116*
Bolles, Susan, 260
Bonaduce, Danny, 260
Boone, Pat, 225
Borgnine, Ernest, 147, 158, 184
Bow, Clara, 20
Bowes, Edward, 203
Bowles, Jerry, 207
Boyd, Joseph G., 15
Bracken, Eddie, 33
Brady, Wayne, 130
Brady Bunch kids, 159
Breakfast in Hollywood, 94
Break the $250,000 Bank, 69
Break the Bank, 69, 191, 218, 250–51
Breen, Robert, 32
Brennan, Edwin F., 16
Brennan, Tom, 94
Bridges, Lloyd, 148, 159
Briggs, David, 303
Broadcasting Magazine, 7
Brock, Alice, 86
Broderbund Software, 279
Brokaw, Tom, 47
Brooklyn Daily Eagle, 1–2
Brooklyn Dodgers, 158
Brooklyn Eagle Quiz on Current Events, 1–2, 4
Brooks, Mel, 148
Brothers, Joyce, 68, 75
Brown, Gerry, 158
Brown, James, 118
Bruner, Wally, 153, *154*
Bryant, Anita, 144
Buena Vista, 267–68
Buena Vista Television, 294
Buggy, Richard, 154–55
Bulifant, Joyce, 207
Bullseye, 166, 218
Bumper Stumpers, 255

Burger, Michael, 298–99
Burgess, Titus, 334
Burnett, Carol, 27, 116, 157
Burnett, Mark, 315, 325
Burns, Brooke, 327
Burr, Raymond, 116
Burton, Al, 295–96
Bush, Billy, 130
Bush, George H. W., 130
Buss, Frances, 10
Buxton, Frank, 121
Bye Bye, Birdie, 148
Byrnes, Edd, 180

CableACE Award, 294
Cabot, Sebastian, 27
Caesar, Sid, 224
Caesar's Challenge, 275, *275*
Caesar's Palace, 275, *275*
Calderwood, Dana, 257, 259–61, 280–81, 288
Calhoun, Haystacks, *46*
California Angels, 158
Call My Bluff, 39, 122
Calloway, Cab, 155
Camel (cigarettes), 48
Camouflage, 106–7
Canada, 65, 124–25, 156–57, 174, 224, 243, 254–55
Canada's Global Television Network, 254–55
Canadian Broadcasting Corporation (CBC), 243–45
Candid Camera, 161
Cannell, Stephen J. *See* Stephen J. Cannell Productions
Cannon, Freddy, 137
Can You Top This?, 161
Capitol Theatre (New York), 203
Card Sharks, 39, 224–25, *225*, 230, 233, 239, 254–56, 263, 265, 272
Carey, Drew, 301
Carlin, Steve, 67, 215
Carlisle, Kitty, 86, 155, *269*
Carlston family, 279
Carpenter, John, 303–4
Carrey, Jim, 317
Carson, Johnny, 36, *50*, 50–51, 105–6, 113, 134, 149, 175
Carter, Jack, 159, 203

Carter, Nell, 299
Cartoon Network, 290
Carvey, Dana, 257
Cash and Carry, *25*, 25–26
Cash Mountain, 303
Cash on the Line, 169
Cass, Peggy, 155
Catch Me If You Can, 21–22
Catch Phrase, 251
Cates, Gil, 106
Cates, Joe, 68
CBC. *See* Canadian Broadcasting
    Corporation
CBN. *See* Christian Broadcasting
    Network
CBS Evening News, 248
CBS Morning News, 317
CBS Radio, 4–5, 7, 11, 18–19, *19*, 27–28,
    39, 44–45, 52
CBS Television Quiz, 10
CBS-TV, 10, 27–32, 34, 36, 41, 47, 49,
    53, 63, 66–68, 70–74, 77, 82, 85,
    87, 90–91, 102–3, 106, 115–17,
    126, 130, 134, 141, 145–46, 149,
    152–54, 160–66, 168–70, 172,
    174, 176, 181–82, 184, 186–87,
    189, 192, 197, 201, 215–16,
    218–19, 222–23, 226–30, 234–36,
    235, 248–50, 254–56, 263, 271,
    274–76, 308, 314–18
Cedric the Entertainer, 313
Celador, 303
Celebrity Blackjack, 161
Celebrity Bowling, 158, 161
Celebrity Doubletalk, 169
Celebrity Family Feud, 332
Celebrity Game, The, 145
Celebrity Match Mates, 189
Celebrity Sweepstakes, 176–77
Celebrity Whew!, 229
Cent Francs La Seconde, 59
Cerf, Bennett, 10, *30*, 31, 153
Chain Letter, 124
Chain Reaction, 227, 254–55
Challengers, The, 267–68
Chambers, Laura, 291, *291*
Charade Quiz, 26
Charles, Ray, 144, 148, 208
Chase, Ilka, 33
Chase, The, 326

Cheers, 271
Chen, Julie, 317
Cher, 148
Chester, Giraud "Jerry," 43, 157
Chicago, 32, 272
Child's Play, 234–35, *235*
Choose Up Sides, 39
Christian Broadcasting Network (CBN),
    254
Chuck Barris Productions, 141–43, 213,
    297
Chuck Barris Rah Rah Show, The, 208, 212
CIA, 213
Clampett, Bob, 86
Clark, Dane, 36
Clark, Dick, 120, 140, 155, 161, 169, *171*,
    171–72, 177, 235–36, *236*, 267,
    270, 273, 306, *307*, 308, 333
Clark, Roy, 144
Classic Concentration, 255–56, 269,
    272–73
Classic Concentration II, 273
Clayton, Bob, 113, 172
Club AM, 291
Cobert, Bob, 333
Coca-Cola Television, 254
Cohn, Arthur, Jr., 78
Colbert Television Sales, 241–42
Colgate, 72–73
College Bowl. *See G. E. College Bowl*
College Quiz Bowl, 102
Collins, Joan, *188*
Collins, Judy, 183
Collyer, Bud, 28, 33, *52*, 52–55, *85*,
    85–87, 152, 154–55, 269
Combs, Ray, 256, 274–76
Comedy Central, 295–96
Concentration, 79, 106, 108–13, *110*,
    167–68, 172, 251, 255–57, 262,
    269, 272–73, 279
Concentration (home game), 110, 112
Connors, Chuck, 116
Connors, Mike, 158, 184
Convy, Bert, 153, 189–190, 192, 227,
    262–63, *263*, 270
Cook, Alton, *12*, 13
Cooper, Alice, 148, 208
Cooper, Frank, 73
Copeland, Joanne, 106
Cosby Show, The, 265, 271

Cotton Bowl, 61
Coughlin, Francis, 32
Courtship of Eddie's Father, The, 149
Cowan, Louis G., 14, 22, 64, 66, 68
Cowboy Theater, 125
Cox, Wally, 147, *147*, 150, 240
Craven, Thomas, 13
Crawford, Joan, 116
Crews, Terry, 313
Cronkite, Betsy, 207
Cronkite, Walter, 35, 47, 207, 282
Cross Examination, 84–85
Cross-Wits, 191, 254
Crow, Sheryl, 334
Crystal, Billy, 300
Cullen, Bill, 22, 24, 26–28, 35, 39, 48,
    52, 64, *87*, 90, *90*, 131, *136*, 152,
    155, 165, 173, 177, 221, 225, 227,
    234–35, *235*, 242, 266, 269
Cuomo, Mario, 234
Curtis, Dick, 65
Curtis, Tony, 36

Daddy-O, *211*
Dagmar, 33
Dalton, Abby, 147, *147*
Daly, John Charles, 29–31, *30*, 34,
    152–53
Dan En, 191
Dangerfield, Rodney, 148
Darby, Geoffrey, 257
Dark Shadows, 156
Darnell, Mike, 305–6
Darren, James, 160
Darrow, Mike, 202, 255
Dating Game, The, 138–42, *140*, 156, 194,
    211, 254, 297–98
David, Madeline, 205
David Letterman Show, The, 226–27, 230
Davidson, Doug, 277
Davies, Michael, 296, 302–3
Davis, Nelson, 224
Davis, Sammy, Jr., 116, 148
Davola, Joe, 260
Daw, Hilary, 303
Dawidziak, Mark, 247
Dawson, Richard, 140, *188*, 192, *198*,
    204–5, 210, 229, *231*, 231–32,
    233, 242, 276–77, 291, 298
Day, Steve, 238, 291

Days of Our Lives, 239
Deal or No Deal, *321*, 321–24
Dean, James, 57, 144
Dean, Jimmy, 144
DeBartolo, Dick, 118, 187, 192
Debt, 294–95
DeCarlo, Mark, 130
Decisions, Decisions, 218
Deeb, Gary, 223
Definition, 224
Deliverance, 149
DeLugg, Milton, 46, 208, 212
DeLuise, Dom, 141
Dempsey, Jack, 19
Denberg, Lori Beth, 235
De Rijk, Dick, 321, 324
Dern, Richard, 63
Deutsch, Patti, 153, *188*
Dick Clark Productions, 267, 306–7
Diff'rent Strokes, 234
Diller, Phyllis, 46, 207, 225
Dillon, Frank, 219
DiMaggio, Joe, 158
Discovery, 121
Disney, 267
Disney Channel, 263
Disney-MGM Studios, 285
Dobkowitz, Roger, 167, 183
Dr. I.Q., 7, 119
Dr. Seuss (Theodore Geisel), 86
Doctors, The, 237
Dollar a Second, 59–60, *60*
Donahue, Phil, 273, 306
Donald, Peter, 33
Dotto, 71–74, *73*, 76, 106
Double Cross, 218
Double Dare, 39, 245, 257–59, *258*, 261,
    280, 284, 286, 330–31
Double Prices, 167
Double Talk, 254
Dough-Re-Mi, 71, 79, 217
Douglas, Buster, 324
Douglas, Michael, 159
Douglas, Paul, 36
Downs, Hugh, *110*, 110–13, 317
Down You Go, 31–32, 75
Do You Trust Your Wife?, 49–50
Dream Girl of '67, 143, 161
Dream House, 108
Dru, Joanne, 184

Drysdale, Don, 291
DuBois, Al, 255
Duer, Alice, *12*
Duff, Howard, 36
Duke, Patty, 79
DuMont TV network, *25*, 25–26, 31–32, 59–60
Duskin, Ruthie. *See* Feldman, Ruth Duskin

Earl, Craig (Professor Quiz), 5–6, 21
Ed Sullivan Theater, 170
Edwards, Douglas, 33
Edwards, Geoff, 174–75, *175*, *195*, 195–97, 255
Edwards, Ralph, 19–20, *20*, 22, 38, 55–57, 60, 64, 94–95, 97–98, 152, 177, 202, 222, 240. *See also* Ralph Edwards Productions
Ehrenreich, Dan. *See* Enright, Dan
Eisenhower, Dwight, 32–33, 136
El Capitan Theatre, 95
Elliott, Gordon, 268–69, *269*
Emerson, Faye, 35–36
Emmanuel, Russell, 333
Emmy Awards, 61, 104, 157, 236, 296, 317–18
Enberg, Dick, 158
Endemol, 323–24
Enright, Dan (Dan Ehrenreich), 70–71, 77–79, *80*, 109, 191, 214–21, 255, 265–66, 272. *See also* Barry and Enright Productions
Entertainment Productions, Inc., 68, 215
Eubanks, Bob, 140–41, 143, 192–93, *193*, 225–26, *226*, 232, 265, 274, 291, 298, *299*
Evans, Bergen, 32, 75, 77
Everybody's Talking, 162, 216
Every Second Counts, 251
Exorcist, The (Blatty), 46, 86
Expedition Robinson, 315–16
Exposure Unlimited, 251
Exxon-Valdez oil spill, 262
Eye Guess, *90*, 90–91

Fabe, Maxine, 135
Facebook, 330–31
Face is Familiar, The, 91

Face the Music, 254
Fadiman, Clifton, 11–13, *12*
Fairbanks, Douglas, Jr., 116
Family Affair, 160
Family Channel, 254, 289–290, 329
Family Double Dare, 259
Family Feud, 39, 41, 210, 218, 227, 229, *231*, 231–33, *233*, 239, 242, 249, 256, 261, 272, 274–78, 291, 300, 328–30
Family Feud Challenge, 274–76
Family Game, The, 143
Family Secrets, 274
Family Ties, 265
Farentino, James, 159
Farr, Jamie, 207, 225
"Fascinating Woman" movement, 155
Fates, Gil, 10, 29, 36, 41, 152–53
Fawcett, Farrah, 140
FCC. *See* Federal Communications Commission
FCC vs. American Broadcasting Co., 24
Federal Communications Commission (FCC), 8, 10, 23–24, 72–73, 150–51, 157, 162, 216, 233
Feldman, Ruth Duskin, 15, *15*
Felsher, Howard, 224, 275–76
Fenneman, George, 51
Fiala, George, 33
Fields, Nat, 75
Fields, W. C., 5, 14
Fieri, Guy, 326
$50,000 Pyramid, The, 235
Figure It Out, 288
Filmways, 252
Finn, Pat, 266, *267*, 293, *294*
Fleischman, Flippity, 183
Fleming, Art, 133, *133*, 135–36, 173, 177, 222, 246–47, 264
Fleming, Peggy, 86
Flesh, Ed, 180
Flowers, Wayland, 227
Fogg, Kirk, 287, *287*
Fogg, Phileas, 318
Fonda, Henry, 157
Ford, Whitey, 158
Foss, Joe, 47
Foster, Preston, 27
Foster, Sutton, 334
Fox, 305–8

Fox, Sonny, 68
Foxworthy, Jeff, *325*, 325–26
Foxx, Redd, 148, 184, 190
Fractured Phrases, 122, 224
Framer, Walt, 63–65
Francis, Arlene, *30*, 30–31, 153, *154*
Frank Cooper Productions, 73
Franklin, Aretha, 148
Franklin, Benjamin, 109
Fred Allen Show, The, 22–23
Fredericks, Dirk, 54
Freed, Alan, 86
FremantleMedia, 336
Friendly, Ed, 215
Frost, David, 112
Fun House, 287
FX, 299

Gabel, Martin, 153
Gabel, Peter, 153
Gabor, Eva, 32, 147, 184
Gabor, Magda, 32
Gabor, Zsa Zsa, 32
Gaines, William M., 86
Gallup, George, 86
Gambit, 161–62, *163*, 166–68, 172–74,
    181, 186, 230
Game, The, 26
Game Channel, The, 289
Game Game, The, 144, 175, 194
Game Show Biz, The, 256
Game Show Network (GSN), 193,
    290–292, 297, 314, 324, 326–27,
    329–30, 332
Ganzel, Teresa, 334
Garagiola, Joe, *136*, 155, 189, 239
Gargiulo, Mike, 87, 116
Garland, Beverly, *120*
Garrett, Leif, 239
Gautier, Dick, 192
G. E. College Bowl, 102–4, *103*, 115,
    132–33, 243
Geisel, Theodore. *See* Dr. Seuss
Gene Gene the Dancing Machine, 210
General Electric, 102
General Hospital, 182
Generation Gap, The, 162, 216
Generations, 264
George Foster Peabody Award, 104
Get the Message, 39, 121, 238

Get the Picture, 286
Giant Step, 68
Gibson, Hunter "Red," 135
Gibson, Mel, 135
Gifford, Frank, 158
Gifford, Kathie Lee, 200, 282
Gilbert, Eddie, 67
Gillam, Stu, 156
Gilman, Toni, 32
Gimbel, Norman, 104
Gleason, Jackie, 55, 291
Glenn, John, 69
Go, 262
Gobel, George, 150
Godfrey, Arthur, 33, 242
Goen, Bob, 263, *271*
Goldberg, Whoopi, 300
Goldenberg, Moe, 110
Golden Girls, The, 264, 261
Golden Medley Marathon, 69
Golder, Andrew, 295
Golenpaul, Dan, 11
Gomer Pyle USMC, 160
Gong Show, The, 204–13, *207*, *209*,
    211–12, 254
Gong Show Movie, The (film), 211
Gonzalez-Gonzalez, Pedro, 46
Goodman, Dody, *189*
Goodson, Jonathan, 270, 276–77
Goodson, Mark, 21–23, 27–29, 31, 33,
    36, 38–43, *40*, 46–47, 52–54,
    68–70, 81–82, 84–85, 87–89,
    91, 101, 114–15, 118, 127, 131,
    151–52, 154, 156–57, 166–67,
    169, 172, 232, 240, 242, 245–46,
    250, 255–56, 265, 269–70, 272,
    274–76. *See also* Mark Goodson
    Productions
Goodson-Todman Productions, 28,
    30–31, 33–43, *40*, 52–53, 69,
    81–83, 85, *85*, 85–91, 104–5, 114–
    15, 117–23, 131, 152–57, 162–63,
    166, 172, 187, 189, 197–99, 216,
    224, 228–33, 236, 239, 245, 254,
    257, 303, 326
Gordon, Ruth, 13
Gordy, Berry, 86
Gossip, 296
Gould, Chester, 86
Gould, Jack, 56

Goulet, Robert, 116
Grable, Betty, 148
Grandy, Fred, *233*
Granger, Gawn, 153, *154*
Grant, B. Donald "Bud," 160–61, 165
Grauman's Chinese Theatre, 98
Graves, Peter, 184, 282
Gray, Cat, 130
Gray, George, 312–13
Grayson, Katheryn, 33
Great American Marriage Round-Up, 59
Great Britain, 334
Great Depression, 3, 83, 184
Greatest Man on Earth, The, 65
Greed: The Multimillion Dollar Challenge,
    194–95, 306–7, *307*
Greenberg, Ron, 106, 217, 219–20,
    267–68
Greenwich Village, 134
Grier, Harry, 2–3
Griffin, Merv, 104–5, *105*, 108, 131–34,
    177–81, 241, 245–47, 253–54,
    263–64, 291
Griffith, Melanie, 300
Grocery Game, 166–67
Gross, Mason, 47
GSN. *See* Game Show Network
Guedel, John, 44, 58
Guinness Book of World Records, 98
Gunther, John, 13
Gurin, Phil, 308

Hadden, Briton, 2
Hall, Monty (Monte Halparin), 65, 84,
    106, 114, 117–18, 124, 124–30,
    128, 158, 185, *186*, 229, 242,
    270–72, 285. *See also* Stefan
    Hatos–Monty Hall Productions
Halstrom, Holly, 250
Hamilton, George, 299
Harbert, Ted, 265
Harlan, John, 157
Harmon, Mark, 139
Harris, Mel, 291
Harrison, Chris, 313
Harrison, Dick, *31*
Hart, Dorothy, 27
Hart, Moss, 13
Hartman, Phil, 212
Harvey, John, 257

Harvey, Steve, 328–29, 331–32
Hasselhoff, David, 239
Hatch, Richard, 311–13, 316, 319
Hatos, Stefan, 122, 125–30. *See also*
    Stefan Hatos–Monty Hall
    Productions
Have I Got News for You, 301
Havilland, Olivia de, 116
Hawk, Bob, 18, *19*
Hayes, Helen, 148
Haystacks Calhoun, *46*
Headline Chasers, 251, 253, 255
Headline Hunters, 224
Heatter, Merrill, 101–2, 106, 145–51,
    163, 240, 252
Heatter-Quigley Productions, 148,
    150–51, 161, 174, 177, 222–23,
    230, 252
Hecht, Ben, 13
Herb Wolf Associates, 191
Herman, Bill, 33
Herman, Shelley, 139, 142, 189, 208,
    210–11, 292–93, 305, 316,
    320–21, 330
He Said She Said, 39, 189
Hex (home game), 230
High Finance, 73, *74*, 166
High Rollers, 174, 177, 218, 223–24, 227,
    230, 245, 247–48, 255, *256*
Hilgemeier, Edward, 72–73
Hi Lo, 71
Hilton, Bob, 270–71
Hines, Connie, 72
Hit Man, 237–38, *238*
Hit the Jackpot, 22
Hoffman, Dustin, 118
Hogan's Heroes, 188
Holbrook, Hal, 118
Hollywood Connection, 218
Hollywood Game Night, 283
Hollywood on Television, 238
Hollywood Squares, The, 145–51, *146–47*,
    157–58, 161–62, 173, 176, 181,
    184–85, 190–92, 218, 222,
    226–29, 238, 252, 254–55, 275,
    299–300
Hollywood's Talking, 216, 238
Honeymooners, The, 55–56
Honeymoon Game, The, 163, 175
Hope, Bob, 44, 104

Horne, Lena, 116
Hot Potato, 268
Houdini, Harry, 5
Houston, Whitney, 300
Hovis, Larry, 188–89, *189*
Howard, Al, 292
Howard, Bob, 41, 53, 55
Howard, Ron, 140
Howard, Tom, 16–17
Howe, Quincy, 13
How's Your Mother-in-Law?, 144, 161, 194
Hubbard, Florence, 20–21
Hughes, Howard, 141
Hull, Warren, 39, 64
Hyatt, Wesley, 122
Hyman, Dick, 155

Iacono, Sal, 296
Identity, 324, 326
Idiotest, 330
I'll Buy That, 31
"I Lost on *Jeopardy!*" (song), 246–47
I Love Lucy, 56, 71
Indiana Jones (film), 287
Indianapolis Star, 318
Information Please, 7, 11–13, *12*, 16–17, 23, 31
Ireland, Kathy, 280
It Could Be You!, 64–65, 95
It Pays to be Ignorant, 16–17, 31
It's News to Me, 34–35, 39
It's Your Chance of a Lifetime, 307
I've Got a Secret, 35–37, 39, 81–82, 115, 152–53, 155, 288, 291

Jackie Gleason Show, The, 47
Jackpot, 174–75, 255
Jackson, Michael, 140
Jackson, Stoney, 77
Jaffe, Author Bernard, 12
James, Art, 126, *136*, 217, 256
James, Dennis, 21, *25*, 25–26, *35*, *40*, 69, *70*, 145, 166–67, 173, 177, 190, *197*, 197–98
Jennings, Ken, 323
Jeong, Ken, 333
Jeopardy!, 132–36, *134*, *136*, 173–74, 176, 178, 222–23, 237, 245–50, *248*, 253–55, 257, 264, 266–67, 269, 295, 299, 301–2, 323, 328, 330

Jeopardy! (home game), 245
Jerome Schnur Productions, 216
Jillette, Penn, 324
Jimmy Kimmel Live!, 296
Joelson-Baer Productions, 122
Johnson, Arte, 150, 204, 222, 225–26
Johnson, Don, 139
Johnson, Parks, 3
Johnston, Johnnie, 33
Joker's Wild, The, 163–68, *164*, 172, 182, 216, *217*, 218–19, 221, 242, 249, 254, 266–67, *267*
Jones, Carolyn, 150
Jones, Leslie, 334
Judge for Yourself, 39
Juian, Sally, 240
Jumble, 289
Just Men!, 239, 262, 275
Juvenile Jury, 162, 214, 216

Kaltenborn, H. V., 1
Kane, Joseph Nathan, 21
Kardell, Bob, 59
Karloff, Boris, 32, 104
Karn, Richard, 328
Katz, Oscar, 169
Kaufman, Andy, 139
Kaufman, George S., 13
Kaye, Milton, 110
Kay Kyser's Kollege of Musical Knowledge, 7
Keaton, Buster, 36
Keep Talking!, 131
Keep Talking (improvisational comedy show), 125
Kelly, Joe, 14
Kemper, Ellie, 334
Kennedy, Tom, 119–20, *120*, 155, 159, 191, *200*, 201, 222, *228*, 228–29, 250
Keoghan, Phil, 318
Kern, Janet, 73–74
Kidding Around, 216
Kiernan, John, *12*, 13
Kihn, Greg, 246
Kilgallen, Dorothy, *30*, 30–31, 35
Kimmel, Jimmy, 296
Kiner, Ralph, 16
King, Billie Jean, 158
King, Charles, 241
King, Michael, 264–65

King World, 241–42, 246–47, 253, 264,
    299
Kinnear, Greg, 280
Kisseloff, Jeff, 75
Kitt, Eartha, 148
Klein, Jaime, 141, 206, 208, 210–11, 213,
    336–37
Kleiner, Dick, 217
Kline, Richard, 218, 266, 268–69
Kline and Friends, 266
Klinghoffer, Michael, 257
Klinker, Effie, 49
Knight, Steve, 303
Knockout, 222
Koch, Ed, 234
Koppel, Ted, 104
Korean War, 34, 56
Krantz, Steve, 125
Kroeger, Gary, 297–98, *298*
KTLA, 162–63, 216
Kupperman, Joel, 14

Labbett, Mark "The Beast," 327
La Duke, Dee, 258–59
Lady, or The Tiger, The? (Stockton), 124
Lamour, Dorothy, 118, 148
Landau, Martin, 147
Landon, Michael, 147, 184
Lane, Nathan, 300
Lange, Jim, 138–39, *140*, 253, *253*
Langston, Murray, 208
Lansbury, Angela, 27
La Rosa, Julius, 33–34, 242
Larsen, Milt, 98
Larsen, Roy E., 2
Lassie, 158
Las Vegas, 65, 116, 129, 230, 275, *275*
Las Vegas Gambit, 230
Laugh-In. See Rowan and Martin's Laugh-In
Lawford, Peter, 116, 157
Lawrence, Vicki, 263, 299
Lawrence Welk Show, The, 233
Lawson, Jennifer, 279
Lee, Greg, 280, *282*, 282–83
Lee, Gypsy Rose, 140
Lee, Michele, 159
Lee, Ruta, 223
Lee, Spike, 281
Legends of the Hidden Temple, 287, 287–88

Legler, David, 310
Leiber, Jerry, 104
Lennon Sisters, 159
Lenya, Lotte, 207
Lester, Jerry, 27
Let's Make a Deal, 126–30, *128*, 156, 158,
    165, 168, 172, 174, 185, *186*,
    194–95, 249, 254, 271, 285, 321
Letter Machine, The, 253
Letterman, David, 188, *189*, 225–26,
    229–30. *See also David Letterman
    Show, The*
Levant, Oscar, 13
Levenson, Sam, 47–48, *48*
Lewis, Jerry, 291
Lewis, Robert Q., 33, 121
Lewis, Shari, 153
Leyden, Bill, 64–65, 122
Liars Club, 188–89, *189*, 254
Libby Foods, 25–26
Liberace, 36
License 2 Steal, 255
Life Begins at 80, 214
Lifetime, 292
Ligerman, Nat, 114, 126
Lingo, 326
Linkletter, Art, 58–60, 95
Little, Rich, 149
Live with Regis and Kathie Lee, 309
Lockhart, June, *116*, 170
Logan, Joshua, 207
Longdon, John, 158
Look Ma I'm Acting, 26
Lorimar Telepictures, 253
Los Angeles Rams, 158
Louis, Joe, 69
Love Boat, The, 233
Love Connection, 298
Love Experts, The, 227
Love is a Many Splendored Thing, 160
Love Me, Love Me Not, 254–55, 270
Lowry, Cynthia, 142, 161, 221
Lucky Pair, 174
Lucy Show, The, 160
Ludden, Allen, 102, 104, 115–16, *116*,
    120–21, *156*, 157, 163, 177,
    188–89, *189*, 223, *224*, 262
Lupino, Ida, 36

Lynde, Paul, *146*, 147–48, *148*, 151, 190, 192

MacDonald, Norm, 301
MacGuire, Bobby, 16
MacRae, Meredith, *156*
MAD (magazine), 86, 118, 187
MADtv, 300
Major Bowes' Amateur Hour, 203–4
Make the Connection, 39, 238
Mancini, Henry, 175, *176*, 265
Mandel, Howie, *321*, 321–22
Mangum, Jonathan, 130
Man Show, The, 296
Mantle, Mickey, 34, 118, 148
March, Hal, 67, *74*
March of Dimes, 20
Marie, Rose, 147, *147*, 190
Maris, Roger, 118
Mark Goodson Productions, 43, 234, 255–56, 269, 273, 300
Maronna, Michael, 235
Marshall, Garry, 239
Marshall, Peter, *136*, 145–48, *146–47*, *150*, 150–51, 159, 161, 181, 184, 190, 192, 226–27
Marsha Warfield Show, The, 264
Martin, Barney, 79
Martin, Billy, 158
Martin, Dick, 159, *224*
Martin, Jesse, 121
Martin, Ross, 226
Martin, Steve, 140, 148
Martindale, Wink ("Win"), 117, *121*, 122, 143–44, 159, 161–62, 173, 219, *220*, 230, 242, 252–53, 255, *256*, 265, 289, 294–95, 329
Marvin, Lee, *120*
Marx, Groucho, 44–48, *46*, 51, *51*, 69, 245
Mary Hartman, Mary Hartman, 193
Maryland, 63
M*A*S*H, 207, 222, 225, 242
Mason, Pamela, 147
Masquerade Party, 32–33
Massey, Marisol, 260–61
Match Game, The, 39, 41, 117–18, *118*, 121, 151, 187–88, *188*, 192–93, 198–99, 207, 210, 218, 227–28, 231–32, 256, 270, 291, 298–300, 329, 332, 334
Match Game PM, *198*, 198–99, 233
Matthau, Walter, 147
Maude, 193
Maxwell-Smith, Mark, 98–100, 163–64, 191–92, 208, 221, 268, 272, 319, 322
MBS, 7
McCain, John, 135
McCarthy, Charlie, 49
McConnell, Lulu, 16–17
McCutcheon, Richard, 74
McGavin, Darren, 61
McKee, Thom, 219–20
McKrell, Jim, 144, 159, 175–76, *176*
McMahon, Ed, 48, 50, *50*, 113, 122, 152
McNamara, Robert S., 141
McNaughton, Harry, 16–17
McWilliams, Jim, 7
Meadows, Jayne, 35–36
Meaney, Kevin, 260
Melody Marathon, 7
Menning, Lee, 240
Merkin, Jeff, *307*
Merman, Ethel, 118
Merv Griffin Show, The, 179
Messing, Debra, 334
Messmore and Damon, 109
Mike and Maty, 298
Mikkelson, David, 325–26
Million Dollar Talent Show, 213
Mills Brothers, 144
Milton Bradley (company), 110, 112, 117, 156, 245
Mindreaders, 39
Mineo, Sal, 118
Miner, Worthington, 10
Minute to Win It, 326
Miss Canada pageant, 224
Missing Links, 39
Mister Ed, 72
"Mr. & Mrs. Hush," 19–20, *20*
Mr. T, 239
Miteff, Karim, 283–85
Moffit-Lee Productions, 299
Monaco, 265
Monitor, 113, 125, 165
Monopoly, 264–65

Monte Carlo Show, The, 265
Montgomery, Elizabeth, 116
Montreal, Quebec, 156–57
Moog, Robert, 90
Moonves, Les, 315, 317
Moore, Garry, 18–19, 36, 66–67, 76, 81, 154
Moore, Phil, 285
Morehead, Agnes, 147
Moreno, Rita, 116
Morgan, Henry, 35–36, 115
Morgan, Jaye P., 207, 210, 212
Morris, Greg, 158, 225
Morrow, Don, 106–7
MTV, 270–71, 280, 294, 319
Muir, E. Roger, 140
Mulford, Lou, 240
Muppet Show, The, 233
Murray, Jan, 59–60, *60*, 69, 79, 122, 191, 195
Murray, Ken, 61
Murrow, Edward R., 35
Music Hop, 243
Mutual Network, 121
Mutual Radio, 23
Myerson, Bess, *35*, 36, *40*
My Favorite Martian, 149
My Three Sons, 161

Nadler, Teddy, 78
Najimy, Kathy, 333
Namath, Joe, 256
Name's the Same, The, 33–34, *35*, 39, 166
Name That Tune, 69, 76, 177, 199–200, 254. *See also $100,000 Name That Tune, The*
Name Three, 7
Narz, Jack, 71–73, 106, 125, 155–56, 173, 229, 291
Nash, Ogden, 33
National Association of Broadcasters, 23
National Barn Dance, 14
NATPE, 220
"Naturally Stoned" (song), 179
Naud, Tom, 146
NBC Blue Network, 6
NBC Nightly News, 247
NBC Radio, 2, *2*, 7, 11, 13–14, 23, 45–46, 48, 84, 102, 112–13, 125, 165

NBC-TV/Entertainment, 25–122, 125–26, 129–32, 134, 136, 137, 141, 145–46, 149–51, 164–66, 169, 172–73, 175–76, 181, 184, 187, 198, 201, 205, 208, 210, 214–215, 217, 219, 222–24, 226–27, 229–30, 235, 237–41, 244–52, 254–57, 262–64, 267–71, 273–75, 283, 306–11, 321–24, 326, 335
Nearing, Vivian, 71
Neighbors, The, 301
New $25,000 Pyramid, The, 235
New $100,000 Name That Tune, The, 249
New Battlestars, The, 262
New Chain Reaction, The, 255
New Family Feud, The, 274–76
Newhart, Bob, 149, 159
New High Rollers, The, 223–24
New Hollywood Squares, The, 254, 275
Newlywed Game, The, 140–42, 189, 192–94, *193*, 213, 280, 297–98. *See also New Newlywed Game, The*
Newman, Paul, 36
New Mexico, 55–56, 100
New Newlywed Game, The, 250, 254–55
New Price is Right, The, 165–67, *167*
New Tic Tac Dough, The, 219
New Treasure Hunt, The, 174, 194–97, *195*
Nicholson, Robert "Nick," 140
Nick Arcade, 283–86
Nick at Nite, 260
Nickelodeon, 257–61, 280, 283–88, 331
Nickelodeon GUTS, 286
Nielsen, Leslie, 155, 159
Nielsen ratings, 88–89, 316
Night Court, 271
Nightline, 105
Nimmo, Bill, 50
Nimoy, Leonard, 61
Nintendo Entertainment System, 249
Nixon, Cynthia, 154
Nixon, Richard, 33, 136
Noah, Robert, 251
Now You See It, 39, 174, 263
NPR, 269
Number Please, 39

Ober, Ken, 260–61
Oberholtzer, Rahim, 309–10
Object Is, The, 120

O'Brian, Hugh, 155, 158
Occupation Unknown, 41
Odd Couple, The, 121, 157
O'Donnell, Rosie, 333
O'Hurley, John, 328
Olbermann, Keith, 306
Olson, Johnny, 86, 166–67, 183, 250
Olympics, Summer, 288, 335
O'Malley, Mike, 286
Omarosa, 319
Omni Entertainment System, 245
$1.98 Beauty Show, The, 212, *213*
$100,000 Name That Tune, The, 200,
        200–1, 233, 249
$100,000 Pyramid, The, 237, 254–55, 332
$128,000 Question, The, 202, 245
$1,000,000 Chance of a Lifetime, The, 253,
        253
1 vs. 100. Full House, 323–24
Ontario, 243
Operation: Entertainment, 144
Oprah Winfrey Show, The, 272, 299
Orlando, Florida, 283–85
Ottawa, 243
Ottinger, Matt, 334
Our Gang, 241
Owens, Gary, 158, 204–6, *207*
Owens, Jesse, 158

Paar, Jack, 48–49, 51, 113, 117
Page, LaWanda, 225
Palillo, Ron, 280
Palin, Sarah, 334
"Palisades Park" (song), 137
Palmer, Betsy, 36
Pantomime Quiz, 26–27
Papp, Joe, 36
Pardo, Don, 246–47
Parent Game, The, 144
Parkinson, Dian, 250
Parks, Bert, *21*, 21–22, 24, 33, 68, 145
Part, Jack, 124–25
Parton, Dolly, 148
Pasetta, Marty, 180
Password, 39, 42, 115–23, *116*, 131, 152,
        156, 156–57, 165, 173, 223–24,
        236–37, 254, 291. *See also Super
        Password*
Password (home game), 117, 156
Password Plus, 39, 223–24, *224*, 230

Pat Sajak Show, The, 263
Patton, Gene, 208
Paul Wing's Spelling Bee, 7
PBS. *See* Public Broadcasting Service
PDQ, 166
Peabody Award. *See* George Foster
        Peabody Award
Pearson Television, 300
Peck, Jim, 212–13
"Pee Wee Herman." *See* Reubens, Paul
Pekkanen, Sarah, 315
Pennington, Janice, 197–98, 250
Pennsylvania, 137, 257
People are Funny, 58–60
People Will Talk, 145, 166
Perez, Olga, 192–93
Perfect Match, The, 291
Perry, Jim, 224, *225*, 239–40, *241*, 262
Personality, 91
Person to Person, 35
Peters, Bernadette, 300
Petersen, Paul, 143
Pharmaceuticals Inc., 70
Phelps, Stu, 121–22
Phelps, William Lyon, 13
Philadelphia, Pennsylvania, 137, 257
Philbin, Regis, 230, 237, 301–2, *302*,
        305, 309, 332
Philip Morris (company), 56
Pigmeat Markham, 203
Pimenthal, Nancy, 296
Pinchon, Rae, 118
Place the Face, 95
Planet Hollywood Squares, 299–300
Play for Keeps!, 69
Play It Straight, 84
Playmates, the, 183
Play the Game, 26
Play Your Hunch, 39, 104–5, *105*, 108, 131
Pollack, Kevin, 333
Polosie, Herb, 16, *31*
Poor Richard's Almanac (Franklin, B.), 109
Pope, Carmelita, 32
Pop Question, The, 2
Pop the Question, 38
Poston, Tom, 27
Pot O' Gold, 7
Povich, Maury, 273, 309–10, *310*
Poznick, Barry, 325
Prato, Gino, 68, *74*, 74–75

Press Your Luck, 240–41, 249–50, 291
Price, Marc, 263
Price, Roger, *40*
Price, Vincent, 27, 147
Price is Right, The, 39, 81–82, *87*, 87–89,
    89, 101, 130–31, 152, 165–68,
    167, 172, 182–86, *197*, 197–98,
    227–28, 230, 240, 249–50, 254–
    56, 265, 272, *277*, 277–78, 328
Price is Right Special, The, 265
Prince, Jonathan, 268
Probst, Jeff, 315, *315*
Professor Quiz, 4–7, 21
Professor Quiz (person), 4–6, 21, 61
Pryor, Richard, 144
Public Broadcasting Service (PBS), 51,
    220, 279–83
Puzzlers, 240

QED, 31
Queen for a Day, 61–63, 65, 206
Queen for a Day (film), 61
Queen for a Day (musical), 65
Queen for a Day Club, 65
Quicksilver, 7
Quigley, Bob, 102, 106, 145–46, 148,
    150–51, 252. *See also* Heatter-
    Quigley Productions
Quincy, 247
Quinn, Colin, 260–61
Quirk, Moira, 286
Quixie-Doodle Contest, 7
Quiz Kids, 13–16, *15*, 21, 23, 31, 68
Quiz Kids Challenge, 268
Quiz Show (film), 221, 308

Radio City Music Hall, 132
Radio Daily, 21
Ralph Andrews–Bill Yagemann
    Productions, 118–19
Ralph Edwards Productions, 191, 200,
    202
Ralston-Purina, *35*
Randall, Tony, 208
Raphael, Sally Jesse, 273
Rashad, Ahmad, 275, *275*
Rate Your Mate, 39
Rathbone, Basil, 13
Ratray, Devin, 235
Ray, Aldo, *31*

Rayburn, Gene, *35*, *40*, 43, 84–84, 113,
    115, 117–18, *118*, 125, 152, 161,
    187–89, *188*, 192, *198*, 210, 239,
    270, *270*, 291, 298, 334
Rayburn, Gene (wife of), 190
Raye, Martha, 144
Reach for the Top, 243–44
Reagan, Maureen, 236
Reagan, Ronald, 234, 236
Real World, The, 319
Redford, Robert, 105, 308
Redondo Beach, California, 216
Reed, Rex, 207
Reel Game, The, 162, 216
Reeves, Jack, 121
Reg Grundy Productions, 251, 273
Regis Philbin Show, The, 237
Reid, Don, 102
Reid, Tara, 234
Reid, Tim, 239
Reilly, Charles Nelson, 187, *188*, *198*,
    270, 298
Reilly, Mike, 264
Reiner, Carl, 145
Reiner, Rob, 159, 170
Remini, Leah, 344
Remote Control, 260–61, 280, 285
Reubens, Paul ("Pee Wee Herman"),
    140, 209
Revlon cosmetics, 66–68, *67*
Revson, Charles, 68–69, 74
Rey, Alejandro, 153
Reynolds, Burt, 118, 140, 149, 157, 263
Rhea, Carolyn, 299
Rhyme and Reason, 231–32
Ricci, John, Jr., 332
Richardson, Burton, 277
Richardson, Ethel Park, 68, 78
Richman, Adam, 234
Rickles, Don, 140, 144, 149
Riggs, Bobby, 226
Rinard, Florence, 16, *31*
Ringley, Jennifer, 317
Ritter, John, 140
Rivera, Geraldo, 273
Robinson, Anne, 311–12
Robinson, Jackie, 158
Robinson, Smokey, 236
Rock and Roll Jeopardy!, 315
Rockapella, 281, *282*

Rocky and Bullwinkle, 260
Roddy, Rod, 228, 277
Rodgers, Richard, 10
Rogers, Ginger, 116
Rogers, Roy, 159
Roker, Al, 280
Romero, Cesar, 158
Roosevelt, Eleanor, 14
Rose, Pete, *159*
Rosner, Rick, 238–39, 275
Rossi, Steve, 144, 147
Rowan, Dan, 146
Rowan and Martin's Laugh-In, 150, 204
Rowe, Red, 106
Rubino, Vin, 332–33
Ruckus, 291
Ruprecht, David, *293*
Russell, Bill, 158
Russo, Alexander, 326
Russo, Robin, 331
Ryan, Jim, 171–72
Ryan, Nolan, 158
Ryan, Steve, 42

Saget, Bob, 140
St. Fleur, Stad, 283
Sajak, Pat, 239–42, *241*, 263, 266, 328
Sale of the Century, 108, 239–40, *240*, 249–51, 254–56, 262, 264
Salter, Harry, 69, 76, 199, 224
Sanders, Summer, 288
Sanford and Son, 235
San Francisco, 38, 203–05
Saturday Night Live, 190, 193, 297, 334
Saunders, Shirley, 59
Sax, Steve, 239
Say It with Acting, 26
Say When!!, 39
Scared Straight (film), 317
Scattergories, 273–74
Schimmel, Robert, 209
Schreiber, Avery, *188*, 207
Schwarzenegger, Arnold, 140
Scott, George C., 148–49
Scrabble, 249–52, 254–56, 263–64, 273–74, 332
Scrabble (home game), 110, 245
Scramby Amby, 84
Seinfeld, 307
Selchow and Righter, 251

Serling, Rod, 118, 188
Severinsen, Doc, 150
Sex and the City, 154
Shafer, Ross, 254–55, 270
Shales, Tom, 171
Shapiro, Arnold, 317
Shark Tank, 225
Shatner, William, 150, 155, 324
Shelton, George, 16–17
Sherman, Allan, 35–36
Sherman, Robert, 224, 299
Sherwood, Brad, 297, *298*
Shoemaker, Willie, 158
Shopper's Bazaar, 179–80, *181*
Shop 'til You Drop, 293, *294*
Shore, Dinah, 164
Show Me the Money, 324
Showoffs, 39
Shriner, Herb, 46–47, *48*
Shuffle, 289
Shut the Box, 223
Sills, Beverly, 203
Silverman, Fred, 90–91, 145, 222, 226–27, 230, 257, 296
Simmons, Richard, 236
Simon, Neil, 54
Simon, Paul, 183
Simpson, O. J., 277–78
Sinatra, Frank, 203
60 Minutes, 196
$64,000 Challenge, 68, 77–80
$64,000 Question, The, 14, 66–71, *67*, *74*, 74–75, 77, 103, 201–2, 215
Skirboll, Melissa, 306
Skutch, Ira, 42–43, 105, 157, 187, 198
Sky's the Limit, The, 84, 125
Slater, Bill, 7, 16
Smart Alecks, 225
Smith, Paul, 303
Snap Judgment, 39, 122–23, 152
Snerd, Mortimer, 49
Snodgrass, James, 78
Snoop Dogg, 333
Solomon, Aaron, 236–37, 308–10, 320, 323, 330, 332–33, 336
Somers, Brett, *188*, 198, 270, 298
Somers, Suzanne, 140
Songs for Sale, 84
Sonny and Cher, 148
Sony, 297

Soupy Sales, 150, 153, 257
Southern California Edison, 94
Spaeth, Sigmund, 13
Spencer, Larry, 208
Spike Lee Presents Do It A-Capella, 281
Spillane, Mickey, 32
Spin to Win, 39
Split Second, 254
Sports Challenge, 158–59, *159*
Springer, Jerry, 273, 299
Springer, Wilton, 78
Stack, Robert, 27
Stafford, Susan, 180, 241
Standards and Practices, 107–08, 137, 164
Stang, Arnold, *35, 40*
Stark, Wilbur, 120
Star Search, 213, 257
Stefan Hatos–Monty Hall Productions, 116, 119–24
Stein, Ben, *295*, 295–96
Steinberg, Isidore. *See* Stewart, Bob
Stempel, Herbert, 70–71, 75–80
Stephen J. Cannell Productions, 275
Stern, Harold, 216
Stevens, John, 325
Stevenson, Adlai, 32–33
Stewart, Bob (Isidore Steinberg), 43, 83–92, *87, 90*, 114–15, 169–75, 177, 227, 229, 235–36, 272, 291, 333–34. *See also* Bob Stewart Productions
Stewart, Dick, 143
Stewart, Elaine, *163*
Stewart, Jay, 127
Stewart, Jimmy, 116–17
Stewart, Martha, 343
Stewart, Sande, 170, 174–75, 197, 255, 320
Stockton, Frank R., 124
Stokey, Mike, 26–27
Stone, Joseph, 74–75, 77, 79, 220
Stone, Sharon, 300
Stone-Stanley Productions, 287
Stop the Camera, 41
Stop the Music, 22–24, 29, 66
Storch, Larry, 158
Storey, Ralph, 68
Storybook Squares, 150, *150*
Strike It Rich, 63, 65

Stritch, Elaine, 27
Struthers, Sally, 184
Stuart, Barbara, 192
Studs, 238–39
Stumpers!, 177
Stump the Stars, 27
Sullivan, Ed, 206
Summers, Marc, 96, 221, 257–59, *258*, 264, 312, 331
Super Jeopardy!, 264
Supermarket Sweep, 292–93, *293*, 295
Super Nintendo, 285
Super Password, 249–50, 254–56, 262, 264, 272
Survivor, 314–18, *315*
Susskind, David, *30*, 118
Swann, Lynn, 269
Swanson, Gloria, 32, 118
Swayze, Patrick, 300
Sylvania Television Award for Excellence, 29

Take It or Leave It, 18–19, *19*, 66
Talent in High, 95
Tarrant, Chris, 303
Tartikoff, Brandon, 238
Tattletales, 39, 189–190, 192, 227–28, 230
Tauber, Jake, 314
Taylor, Josh, 239
Taylor, Rip, 207, 212, *212*
Television City, 168, 271
Tell It to Groucho, 51
$10,000 Pyramid, The, 170–73, *171*, 176–77
Tenuta, Judy, 299
Teti, John, 334
Texas, 2, 175
Texas, 237
Thicke, Alan, 65, 174, 244–45
Thigpen, Lynn, 280, *282*
30 Rock, 334
This is Your Life, 57, 64, 95
3's a Crowd, 212–13
Three on a Match, 165
Three's Company, 193, 268
Three Stooges, The, 104
Tic Tac Dough, 70–71, 75–76, 79, 215, 219–21, *220*, 242, 249–50, 252–53, 255, 265–67, 291

Time's A Wastin', 52
Tinker, Grant, 102, 132–35, 239
Tittle, Y. A., 158
Today, 75, 117, 312
Today Show, The, 291
Todman, Bill, 21–22, 27–28, 31, 33, 38–43, *40*, 46–47, 52–54, 131, 152, 166. *See also* Goodson-Todman Productions
Tolan, Bobby, *159*
Tomarken, Peter, 237, *238*, 239, 264, 291, *291*
Tomlin, Lily, 148
Tonight Show, The, 49, 51, 105, 113, 149
Torme, Mel, 116
To Say the Least, 222
Total Panic, 283
To Tell the Truth, 39, *85*, 85–87, 101, 104, 152, 154–55, 157, 165, 268–69, *269*, 291
Toutant, Ed, 305
Town Hall, 7
Treasure Hunt, 69, 79, 174, 194–97, *195*, 213, 254, 321
Trebek, George Alexander (Alex), 159, 173–74, *174*, 202, 223, 227, 243–48, *244*, *248*, 264, 267, 269, 291, 323, 328
Trivial Pursuit, 289
Trivial Pursuit (board game), 245–46
Trivia Trap, 246, 249
Tropicana Hotel and Casino, 230
True or False, 7
Truman, Harry, 34
Truman Show, The (film), 317
Trump, Donald, 268, 322
Trump Card, 268
Trump Castle Casino Resort by the Bay, 268
Truth or Consequences, 19–20, *20*, 22, 55–61, 64, 94–100, *97*, 152, 157, 257
Truth or Consequences, New Mexico, 54–56, 100
Tucker, Ted, 94
Turner, Ted, 290
TV Guide (magazine), 85–86, 242
20 Questions, 16, 29, 31, *31*, 35
20th Century-Fox, 18

$25,000 Pyramid, The, 177, 227, 235–37, *236*, 249–50, 254–56, 292, 333–34
Twenty One, 70–71, *71*, 75–78, 80, 109, 125, 306, 308–10, *311*
$20,000 Pyramid, The, 177, 227, 333
Twilight Zone, The, 188
Two for the Money, 39, 46–48, *48*

Unbreakable Kimmy Schmidt, 334
Uncle Jim's Question Bee, 6–7
Uncle Walter's Dog House, 7
United Video, 290
Universal Studios Florida, 284, 286
Universal Television, 326
Untamed World, 150
Untermeyer, Louis, 30
USA Network, 254–55

Van Deventer, Fred, 15–16, *31*, 35
Van Deventer, Nancy, 16
Van Deventer and the News, 15–16
Van Devere, Trish, 148–49
Van Doren, Charles, 70–71, *71*, 77, 79–80, 308
Van Dyke, Dick, 27, 87–88
Van Nardoff, Elfreda, 78
Vanna Speaks (White, V.), 250
Van Nuys, Larry, 265
Van Patten, Dick, 239
VH-1, 315
Viacom, 198, 201–2
Video Village, 106, 117, 125, 161
Video Village Jr., 106
Vieria, Meredith, 312
Vietnam War, 141
Vilanch, Bruce, 299
Villachaize, Herve, 239
Vox Pop, 2, 2–3

Wahlberg, Mark L., 293
Walk a Mile, 48
Walker, Jimmie, 159
"Walking Man, The," 20
Wallace, Marcia, 192
Wallace, Mike (Myron), 13, 72, 85, 317
Walt Disney World, 270, 274
Walters, Barbara, 207
Ward, G. Pearson, 94

Warner Bros., 82
Warren, Curtis, 306
Wayne, Frank, 41, 53–55, 117
Wayne, John, 265
Wayne, Patrick, 265–66
Weakest Link, The, 310–13
Weaver, Charley. *See* Arquette, Cliff
"Weird Al" Yankovic. *See* Yankovic, "Weird Al"
Welles, Orson, 13
Werner, Mort, 132–33
West, Adam, 159
West, Randy, 43
Western Cable Show, 291
Westinghouse, 95
We the Wives, 7
We've Got Your Number, 218
Whatever Happened to the Quiz Kids? (Feldman), 15
What's Going On, 34, 39
What's My Line?, 29–30, *30*, 32–33, 35–37, 39, 41, 52, 69, 82, 115, 152–54, *154*, 157, 256, 291, 326
What's My Name, 7
What's the Question?, 132
What's This Song?, *121*, 121–22, 161
Wheel of Fortune, *180*, 180–81, *181*, 184–86, 218, 222, 227, 230, 234, 237, 240–42, *241*, 249–56, 262–64, 266, 271, *271*, 285, 290–291, 295, 299, 302, 328–30
Wheel of Fortune (Good Samaritan show), 64
Wheel of Fortune (video game), 249
Where in the World is Carmen Sandiego?, 281–83, *282*
Where in the World is Carmen Sandiego? (computer game), 279, 281
"Where in the World is Carmen Sandiego?" (song), 281
Where the Action Is, 138
Where the Heart Is, 160
Whew!, *228*, 228–29, 237
White, Betty, 81, 116–17, 120–21, 157, 188, 238–39, 262
White, Larry, 106, 146
White, Vanna, 241, 249–50, 266, 291
Whitehill, Mike, 303

Who, What or Where Game, The, 267
Who Do You Trust?, 50–51
Wholey, Dennis, 216
Whose Line is It Anyway?, 301
Who's the Boss?, 31
Who's Whose, 31
Who Wants to Be a Millionaire?, 301–07, *302*, 309–13, 316, 320, 322, 324
Wilkie, Wendell, 13
Willard, Fred, 333
Williams, Kenny, 22, 106, 150
Williams, Robin, 300
Williams, Vanessa, 300
Wilson, Earl, 113
Win, Lose or Draw, 255–56, *263*, 263–64
Win, Lose or Draw (home game), 263
Win Ben Stein's Money, 295–96
Winfrey, Oprah, 272–73
Winky Dink and You, 111, 214–15
Winn, Marie, 72
Winner Take All, 27–28, 38–39
Winning Lines, 308
Winslow, Michael, 209
Winters, Jonathan, 104
Winters, Shelley, 116
Win with the Stars, 122
Wisdom of the Ages, 214
Witbeck, Charles, 141–43
With This Ring, 31
Witkowski, Rick, 286
Wizard of Odds, The, 174, 244–45
WKRP in Cincinnati, 233
Wolf Productions, 32–33
Wolpert, Jay, 135, 228, 237
Wood, Gene, 156, 291
Woodbury, Woody, 51
Woolery, Chuck, 179–81, *181*, 227, 240, 251–52, *252*, 274, 298, *299*, 306, *307*
Word, Rob, 129
Word for Word, 131
Words and Music, 161
World's Fair (1939), 83
World War II, 18–19, 21, 93
Worley, Jo Anne, 204
Wostbrock, Fred, 294
Wuhl, Robert, 140
Wyant, Scott, 265

Yagemann, Bill, 118–20
Yankovic, "Weird Al," 246–47, 333
You Bet Your Life, 44–47, *46*, 51, 61, 69
You Can Lose Your Shirt, 84
You Don't Say!, 118–20, *120*, 162, 216, 254
Young and the Restless, The, 277
Your Big Moment, 95
You're On Your Own, 71

Your First Impression, 125
Your Number's Up, 250
Your Show of Shows, 47
Youth vs. Age, 7

Zoom, 121
Zorbaugh, Harvey, 26
Zucker, Jeff, 321

THE FAQ SERIES

AC/DC FAQ
by Susan Masino
Backbeat Books
9781480394506...$24.99

Armageddon Films FAQ
by Dale Sherman
Applause Books
9781617131196.........$24.99

The Band FAQ
by Peter Aaron
Backbeat Books
9781617136139 ....$19.99

Baseball FAQ
by Tom DeMichael
Backbeat Books
9781617136061........$24.99

The Beach Boys FAQ
by Jon Stebbins
Backbeat Books
9780879309879..$22.99

The Beat Generation FAQ
by Rich Weidman
Backbeat Books
9781617136016 ....$19.99

Beer FAQ
by Jeff Cioletti
Backbeat Books
9781617136115 ....$24.99

Black Sabbath FAQ
by Martin Popoff
Backbeat Books
9780879309572....$19.99

Bob Dylan FAQ
by Bruce Pollock
Backbeat Books
9781617136078 ......$19.99

Britcoms FAQ
by Dave Thompson
Applause Books
9781495018992 ....$19.99

Bruce Springsteen FAQ
by John D. Luerssen
Backbeat Books
9781617130939.......$22.99

Buffy the Vampire Slayer FAQ
by David Bushman and Arthur Smith
Applause Books
9781495064722.....$19.99

Cabaret FAQ
by June Sawyers
Applause Books
9781495051449......$19.99

A Chorus Line FAQ
by Tom Rowan
Applause Books
9781480367548 ...$19.99

The Clash FAQ
by Gary J. Jucha
Backbeat Books
9781480364509 ..$19.99

Doctor Who Faq
by Dave Thompson
Applause Books
9781557838544 ....$22.99

The Doors FAQ
by Rich Weidman
Backbeat Books
9781617130175 ....$24.99

Dracula FAQ
by Bruce Scivally
Backbeat Books
9781617136009 .....$19.99

The Eagles FAQ
by Andrew Vaughan
Backbeat Books
9781480385412.....$24.99

Elvis Films FAQ
by Paul Simpson
Applause Books
9781557838582.....$24.99

Elvis Music FAQ
by Mike Eder
Backbeat Books
9781617130496 ......$22.99

Eric Clapton FAQ
by David Bowling
Backbeat Books
9781617134548 ......$22.99

Fab Four FAQ
by Stuart Shea and Robert Rodriguez
Hal Leonard Books
9781423421382.......$19.99

Fab Four FAQ 2.0
by Robert Rodriguez
Backbeat Books
9780879309688...$19.99

Film Noir FAQ
by David J. Hogan
Applause Books
9781557838551......$22.99

Football FAQ
by Dave Thompson
Backbeat Books
9781495007484 ...$24.99

Frank Zappa FAQ
by John Corcelli
Backbeat Books
9781617136030 ....$19.99

Godzilla FAQ
by Brian Solomon
Applause Books
9781495045684 $19.99

The Grateful Dead FAQ
by Tony Sclafani
Backbeat Books
9781617130861........$24.99

Guns N' Roses FAQ
by Rich Weidman
Backbeat Books
9781495025884 ..$19.99

Haunted America FAQ
by Dave Thompson
Backbeat Books
9781480392625.....$19.99

Horror Films FAQ
by John Kenneth Muir
Applause Books
9781557839503 ....$22.99

Jack the Ripper FAQ
by Dave Thompson
Applause Books
9781495063084....$19.99

James Bond FAQ
by Tom DeMichael
Backbeat Books
9781557838568.....$22.99

Jimi Hendrix FAQ
by Gary J. Jucha
Backbeat Books
9781617130953.......$22.99

Johnny Cash FAQ
by C. Eric Banister
Backbeat Books
9781480385405..$24.99

KISS FAQ
by Dale Sherman
Backbeat Books
9781617130915........$24.99

Led Zeppelin FAQ
by George Case
Backbeat Books
9781617130250 ......$22.99

Lucille Ball FAQ
by James Sheridan and Barry Monush
Applause Books
9781617740824.......$19.99

MASH FAQ
by Dale Sherman
Applause Books
9781480355897.....$19.99

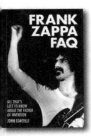

Michael Jackson FAQ
by Kit O'Toole
Backbeat Books
9781480371064 ..... $19.99

Modern Sci-Fi Films FAQ
by Tom DeMichael
Applause Books
9781480350618 .... $24.99

Monty Python FAQ
by Chris Barsanti, Brian Cogan, and Jeff Massey
Applause Books
9781495049439 .. $19.99

Morrissey FAQ
by D. McKinney
Backbeat Books
9781480394483 ... $24.99

Neil Young FAQ
by Glen Boyd
Backbeat Books
9781617130373 .... $19.99

Nirvana FAQ
by John D. Luerssen
Backbeat Books
9781617134500 ...... $24.99

Pearl Jam FAQ
by Bernard M. Corbett and Thomas Edward Harkins
Backbeat Books
9781617136122 .... $19.99

Pink Floyd FAQ
by Stuart Shea
Backbeat Books
9780879309503 ... $19.99

Pro Wrestling FAQ
by Brian Solomon
Backbeat Books
9781617135996 .... $29.99

Prog Rock FAQ
by Will Romano
Backbeat Books
9781617135873 .... $24.99

Quentin Tarantino FAQ
by Dale Sherman
Applause Books
9781480355880 ... $24.99

Rent FAQ
by Tom Rowan
Applause Books
9781495051456 ...... $19.99

Robin Hood FAQ
by Dave Thompson
Applause Books
9781495048227 ... $19.99

The Rocky Horror Picture Show FAQ
by Dave Thompson
Applause Books
9781495007477 ..... $19.99

Rush FAQ
by Max Mobley
Backbeat Books
9781617134517 .... $19.99

Saturday Night Live FAQ
by Stephen Tropiano
Applause Books
9781557839510 ...... $24.99

Seinfeld FAQ
by Nicholas Nigro
Applause Books
9781557838575 ..... $24.99

Sherlock Holmes FAQ
by Dave Thompson
Applause Books
9781480331495 ..... $24.99

The Smiths FAQ
by John D. Luerssen
Backbeat Books
9781480394490 ... $24.99

Soccer FAQ
by Dave Thompson
Backbeat Books
9781617135989 .... $24.99

The Sound of Music FAQ
by Barry Monush
Applause Books
9781480360433 .... $27.99

South Park FAQ
by Dave Thompson
Applause Books
9781480350649 ... $24.99

Star Trek FAQ (Unofficial and Unauthorized)
by Mark Clark
Applause Books
9781557837929 ..... $22.99

Star Trek FAQ 2.0 (Unofficial and Unauthorized)
by Mark Clark
Applause Books
9781557837936 ..... $22.99

Star Wars FAQ
by Mark Clark
Applause Books
9781480360181 ...... $24.99

Steely Dan FAQ
by Anthony Robustelli
Backbeat Books
9781495025129 .... $19.99

Stephen King Films FAQ
by Scott Von Doviak
Applause Books
9781480355514 ..... $24.99

Three Stooges FAQ
by David J. Hogan
Applause Books
9781557837882 ..... $22.99

TV Finales FAQ
by Stephen Tropiano and Holly Van Buren
Applause Books
9781480391444 .... $19.99

The Twilight Zone FAQ
by Dave Thompson
Applause Books
9781480396180 ..... $19.99

Twin Peaks FAQ
by David Bushman and Arthur Smith
Applause Books
9781495015861 .... $19.99

U2 FAQ
by John D. Luerssen
Backbeat Books
9780879309978 ... $19.99

UFO FAQ
by David J. Hogan
Backbeat Books
9781480393851 .... $19.99

Video Games FAQ
by Mark J.P. Wolf
Backbeat Books
9781617136306 ..... $19.99

The X-Files FAQ
by John Kenneth Muir
Applause Books
9781480369740 .... $24.99

The Who FAQ
by Mike Segretto
Backbeat Books
9781480361034 .... $24.99

The Wizard of Oz FAQ
by Dave Hogan
Applause Books
9781480350625 ... $24.99

HAL•LEONARD®
PERFORMING ARTS
PUBLISHING GROUP

FAQ.halleonardbooks.com

0218